Research Methods and Statistics in Criminal Justice

An Introduction

Third Edition

Jack D. Fitzgerald
Knox College

Steven M. Cox
Western Illinois University

WADSWORTH

TM

THOMSON LEARNING

Australia • Canada • Mexico • Singapore • Spain • United Kingdom • United States

WADSWORTH

™

THOMSON LEARNING

Executive Editor, Criminal Justice: Sabra Horne
Criminal Justice Editor: Shelley Murphy
Development Editor: Terri Edwards
Assistant Editor: Dawn Mesa
Editorial Assistant: Lee McCracken
Marketing Manager: Jennifer Somerville
Marketing Assistant: Neena Chandra
Project Manager, Editorial
    Production: Jennie Redwitz
Print/Media Buyer: Tandra Jorgensen
Permissions Editor: Stephanie Keough-
    Hedges

Production Service: Heidi Marschner
Text Designer: Andrew Ogus
Copy Editor: Jennifer Gordon
Illustrator: Heidi Marschner
Cover Designer: Yvo Riezebos
Cover Image: © Eyewire
Cover Printer: Webcom Limited
Compositor: Buuji, Inc.
Printer: Webcom Limited

For permission to use material from this text,
contact us by
Web: http://www.thomsonrights.com
Fax: 1-800-730-2215 **Phone:** 1-800-730-2214

Wadsworth Thomson Learning
10 Davis Drive
Belmont, CA 94002-3098
USA

For more information about our products,
contact us:
Thomson Learning Academic Resource Center
1-800-423-0563
http://www.wadsworth.com

International Headquarters
Thomson Learning
International Division
290 Harbor Drive, 2nd Floor
Stamford, CT 06902-7477
USA

UK/Europe/Middle East/South Africa
Thomson Learning
Berkshire House
168-173 High Holborn
London WC1V 7AA
United Kingdom

Asia
Thomson Learning
60 Albert Street, #15-01
Albert Complex
Singapore 189969

Canada
Nelson Thomson Learning
1120 Birchmount Road
Toronto, Ontario M1K 5G4
Canada

Library of Congress Cataloging-in-Publication Data
Fitzgerald, Jack D.
    Research methods and statistics in criminal justice / Jack D. Fitzgerald, Steven
M. Cox. —3rd ed.
        p.   cm.
    Rev. ed. of: Research methods in criminal justice. 2nd ed. 1994.
    Includes bibliographical references and index.
    ISBN 0-534-53437-6 (pbk.)
        1. Criminology—Research. 2. Criminal justice, Administration of—Research.
3. Corrections—Research. 4. Criminal statistics. I. Cox, Steven M. II. Fitzgerald,
Jack D. Research methods in criminal justice. III. Title.

HV6024.5.F58 2001
364—dc21   2001026106

Contents

CHAPTER 2   Perspectives and Research   30

CHAPTER 3   An Introduction to Research Methodology and Design   62

CHAPTER 4 **Sampling   93**

CHAPTER 5 **Research Tools and Techniques:
Survey Research Through Questionnaires
and Interviews   108**

CHAPTER 6 Research Tools and Techniques:
Document Research, Physical Evidence,
Observation, and Experimentation 126

CHAPTER 7 An Introduction to Descriptive
Statistics 144

CHAPTER 8	**Descriptive Statistics: Examining Relationships Between Two or More Variables Through Cross-Tabulation 177**

CHAPTER 9	**Descriptive Statistics: Measuring Relationships Between Two or More Variables Through Regression and Correlation Analysis 199**

CHAPTER 13 Preparing and Reading Research Reports 272

CHAPTER 14 Computers in Criminal Justice Research 293

Preface

The Third Edition of our text brings a number of changes in content and a new publisher. We are pleased with the latter; we hope you'll be pleased with the former.

NEW TO THIS EDITION

As for what's new in this edition, we'll mention just a few items. There are new descriptions of contemporary criminal justice research and new excerpted articles. Qualitative research is given more attention; a comparison of qualitative and quantitative approaches is offered. The postmodernist, deconstructionist, feminist, and critical theorist critiques of science are reviewed and assessed. New material on language types, internal and external validity, telephone and Internet surveys, and predictive research have been added. The chapter on computers discusses the uses of the Web as a research resource; Web exercises have been added to most of the chapters. The treatment of research ethics has expanded, and excerpts from the ACJS code of ethics replaces those from the ASA code. For teachers, there is an instructor's manual, with chapter outlines, lists of terms, review/discussion questions, Web exercises, alternative testing suggestions and a true/false, multiple-choice test bank with answer key.

ACKNOWLEDGMENTS

The folks associated with Wadsworth have been a pleasure to work with. The reviewers made a number of useful suggestions. We would like to thank Tory Caeti, University of North Texas; Mark Lanier, University of Central Florida; J. Mitchell Miller, University of South Carolina; Beverly Rivera, University of Illinois at Springfield; Robert Sigler, University of Alabama; William Stone, Southwest Texas State University; and Mary Ann Zager, Florida Gulf Coast University. We are very grateful to Dan Alpert, Sabra Horne, and Shelley Murphy for finding sufficient merit in our efforts to justify a Third Edition under the Wadsworth publishing umbrella. Our debt of gratitude is especially great to Jennie Redwitz, Heidi Marschner, Jennifer Gordon, and Dawn Mesa, as well as the compositors, designers, artists, and marketers responsible for bringing the project to fruition.

Finally, thanks to those instructors and students who buy and use our text. As always, we welcome your ideas (well, at least some of your ideas) about how to make experiences with the text better.

J.D.F. & S.M.C.

1

Research and Criminal Justice

This book is about the research process, which may be defined as disciplined inquiry. More particularly, it is about a kind of disciplined inquiry called scientific research. Doing scientific research involves seeking the most trustworthy answers possible to certain kinds of interesting or important questions. As we shall see, the trustworthiness of answers depends, in no small part, on the procedures used in obtaining them. Conclusions based only on anecdotes, haphazard trial-and-error processes, hearsay, or common sense, for example, shouldn't be regarded as very believable. To qualify as scientific, research must be guided by generally accepted principles (empiricism and objectivity, for example) and a preestablished plan (called a research design). We shall have more to say about these principles and plans later; for now, it may simply be emphasized that abiding by the principles and following the plan provide the discipline that, in turn, enhances the credibility of the results produced by the research process.

Because answers obtained through scientific methods are regarded by many as more trustworthy than those derived in other ways, scientific research exerts a powerful influence in virtually all domains of modern society. It shapes the ideas and decisions of policymakers and impacts, both directly and indirectly, on our lives in countless ways. Criminal justice is no exception. Consequently, it behooves us to know something about the process of scientific research. This book is intended as a first step in developing your research literacy.

As you are no doubt aware, the scientific approach has its critics. Even those who are persuaded that the scientific study of human behavior has some utility acknowledge that no human endeavor is foolproof and recognize that the various strategies included under the scientific umbrella have weaknesses as well as strengths. Achieving research literacy means, in part, being aware of some of the controversies and uncertainties that surround science as a way of generating knowledge and being able to distinguish between "better" and "worse" research procedures as well as more and less credible research results.

Students and/or practitioners of criminal justice, like yourselves, need research literacy for other reasons as well. First, in order to keep abreast of current knowledge in your field, you must be able to understand and critically assess research reports. Second, you may find yourself doing research, either individually or as a member of a research team, in order to improve the effectiveness and efficiency of your own or others' work. Third, you may wish to make use of the research of others in deciding whether, for example, a policy or a program implemented elsewhere is worth trying. Fourth, you may be asked to become a research subject by completing a questionnaire or being interviewed or observed, for example. Knowing something about good research procedures makes deciding whether to cooperate with the researchers easier. Finally, your working environment is almost certain to be influenced by research used by supervisors as they make policy, program, and personnel decisions. In such circumstances, understanding research methods and statistics may be vital as a matter of self-defense.

Consider, for example, a director of a Department of Corrections who wants to know why personnel turnover is so high, or a juvenile court judge in search of some guidelines for making adjudicatory decisions, or a police chief in need of information about citizens' perception of her department and its officers, or a parole officer deciding whether to respond to a questionnaire sent by another governmental agency, or a member of a policy review committee contemplating changes in the organizational structure and task allocations of a criminal justice agency. These practitioners could (and often do) gather information based on hearsay, word of mouth, or other accidental contacts in order to arrive at their answers. However, their chances of obtaining accurate, reliable information would be greatly enhanced if their search was guided by the principles and plans characteristic of scientific research.

To those who believe that research methods and statistics are extremely complex and technical matters that are best left to the experts, we offer the following observations. It is quite true that an in-depth study of research methods and statistical analysis would take years, but it is equally true that a student can achieve a basic understanding in a relatively short period of time. Furthermore, complicated research designs and sophisticated statistical procedures do not necessarily result in better or more useful research. Quite often, in fact, useful information can be gained through relatively simple research designs and elementary statistical analyses.

RESEARCH IN EVERYDAY LIFE

Humans have a well-developed sense of curiosity. We enjoy learning new things, figuring out how some piece of machinery operates, or assessing people's behavior. As we attempt to understand the objects, people, and events around us, we often gather information, or **data,*** by *observing* them in an informal but careful way. Above all, we watch for *patterns,* that is, recurring sequences of or relationships among events. Suppose you have just purchased a car. You might ask, What's the best way to get this car started on a cold morning? If I pump the accelerator three times before I turn on the ignition switch, does it usually start? If it doesn't, you might try not pumping at all, or if that doesn't work, you might try pumping the accelerator six times and then turning on the ignition switch. If one pattern works with reasonable regularity, you will use that pattern. In a sense, this is undisciplined inquiry, research by trial and error. You try one thing, and if that doesn't work, you try something else, until eventually you hit upon a combination that works at least most of the time. You also become especially aware of those instances where the pattern of actions and responses does *not* work. If it is colder, does it help to pump the accelerator a few more times? Does the humidity in the air make a difference? In short, you search for other characteristics or properties that may affect the outcome you desire—getting the engine started. We call these characteristics or properties **variables**—factors in the situation that change from time to time and alter the chances of getting the engine started. In this very simple and crude way, you may be said to be performing an informal **experiment**—changing something and observing the effects of having done what you did.

In the process of trying to figure out what works best, you develop hunches or guesses about what might work and then try them out in practice. This process is similar to developing a **hypothesis**—a statement about what effects or results certain causes or actions might produce. You then proceed to *test* the hypothesis by trying the things you think will get the car started and observing the results of each attempt. If the car does not start, you formulate another hypothesis and proceed to test it and to observe the results.

In the previous paragraphs, we have not strayed far from everyday experiences. Yet, by applying some new terms to an everyday situation, you are well on your way to understanding the fundamental concepts in research methods.

We do not want you to conclude, however, that everything you will encounter in this book will be that simple. To grasp some of the intricacies of the research process will take some careful reading (and rereading) and thinking (and rethinking)—in short, some hard work. We do want to suggest, though, that with patience and diligent study, getting your research engine started may not be as difficult as it first appears and keeping it running may not be so difficult, either.

---

* Boldfaced terms are defined in the Glossary at the back of the book.

CRIMINAL INVESTIGATION
AND SCIENTIFIC RESEARCH

Even if you have not studied the criminal justice field in detail, you are probably familiar with some of the basic aspects of criminal investigation. The process of investigating a criminal offense bears close resemblance to the research process, because, like all researchers, a criminal investigator gathers, documents, and evaluates facts about an event, in this case a crime. The investigator's first concern is gathering *facts,* for each investigation is initiated by assembling as many specific pieces of accurate information about the crime and the events surrounding it as possible. This information is assembled by carefully and systematically observing the particular details of the crime scene, especially the physical evidence (for example, objects and individuals present, wounds to the body, the position of objects and persons relative to each other and to the scene). For the most part, these initial steps are *descriptive* in nature, because the investigator attempts simply to describe those things and persons present without making inferences about their relationship to each other or to the crime itself.

Furthermore, the facts that are assembled must be recorded in some way; for example, the scene itself must remain untouched until appropriate photographic records can be made. Preserving physical traces (such as blood and hair samples) and producing accurate written records, which are used for reference and analysis later, are also essential to a successful investigation.

However, any good investigator knows that the simple observation and recording of facts is not enough. Some attempt must be made to link the information to the crime. To complete the investigation successfully, the investigator must eventually create hypotheses that link one fact to another and then, by linking the hypotheses, construct a *theory* that explains the crime as a whole. In part, this is a process of determining which apparent facts are real facts, which facts are or are not relevant to the crime, and how the facts are interrelated.

For example, a knife with apparent blood stains is present at the scene of a crime. This may lead the investigator to infer, or hypothesize, that the knife was used as a weapon in the commission of the crime. The mere presence of a blood-stained knife, however, does not necessarily mean that the knife caused the wound or killed the victim. The confirmation or rejection of this hypothesis depends upon establishing the validity of other facts. Laboratory work to match the blood type of the stains on the knife to the blood type of the victim is required. An examination of the wounds to determine if the knife could have produced the kinds of wounds that appear on the victim is also necessary. If the blood types do not match or if the observations of the body wounds do not confirm the hypothesis, the investigator will probably abandon that particular hypothesis and formulate another.

If the additional evidence does support or corroborate the hypothesis, it must be remembered that the hypothesis has not been completely confirmed. There are probably other possible explanations for the observed facts; however, the investigator has narrowed the possibilities and produced evidence that is consistent with one of his hypotheses. The investigator is likely to regard this link between the knife and the crime as factual or true unless further evidence assembled later in the investigation fails to conform with the hypothesis.

A good investigator also pays as much attention to what is missing as to what is present at the scene of a crime. The observation that something is absent may be important as evidence that can either support or undermine the validity of a hypothesis.

The investigator, then, has to put all the pieces together into a comprehensive pattern that links all of the facts and hypotheses to one another and contains no internal contradictions. These pieces and their linkages constitute a *theory of the crime.* The more facts that can be shown to be consistent with this theory, and the tighter its elements are linked (that is, the fewer the gaps in the evidence), the more confidence the investigator has in the theory of the crime that she has formulated.[1]

Making the links typically requires the application of reasoning, including inductive and deductive logic. **Inductive logic** moves from a number of particular and separate observations to a generalization. For example, from the blood stains and the wounds, together with the laboratory reports, the investigator *induces* that the knife was the weapon used in the crime.

Deductive logic, on the other hand, moves from the general to the particular. For example, if the researcher has shown that violent assaults on people are typically committed by a person with whom the victim has at least some social acquaintance, and that the last person the victim had been seen with was one of the victim's relatives, the investigator might *deduce* that the victim was assaulted by this particular relative. Of course, the deduced conclusion is only as good as the elements of the investigator's argument that led to it. Mistakes in reasoning or incorrect assertions of fact that make up the basic general observations invalidate the conclusion just as certainly as does inconsistent evidence.

Above all, it should be remembered that both criminal investigations and research are human endeavors and as such are subject to human weaknesses and strengths. It is vital that an investigator remain as objective as possible throughout the investigation process. Preconceptions and prejudices must be held at bay, especially during the hypothesis-testing phases, so that they do not interfere with an accurate reading of the assembled information or produce conclusions that are consistent with the data. At the same time, the appropriate use of expertise, learning from mistakes, intuition, patience, ingenuity, curiosity, and opportunism (taking advantage of fortuitous occurrences) all play a vital role in successful research as well as in criminal justice investigations.

BASIC AND APPLIED RESEARCH

Basic research addresses general and fundamental questions that are not easily answered. What is the relative importance of heredity and environment in explaining human behavior? How do people learn? How can human behavior be changed? Why do some people become mentally ill? Under what circumstances do people conform to rules, and under what circumstances are they likely to violate such rules? Because these questions are so fundamental and far-reaching in their implications, even partial answers are exciting. Social scientists may research these issues purely for the satisfaction derived from struggling with important questions and helping to fill in another piece of a basic theoretical puzzle, with little or no concern for how the research results might be used in a practical way. Basic research is often described as the pursuit of knowledge for its own sake.

Applied research, on the other hand, has a more practical aim. It addresses specific questions about how to accomplish a task better or more efficiently. It has become fashionable in recent years to divide applied research into a number of subcategories. We will discuss some of these types of research in later sections. Here it will suffice to note that applied research examines *connections* among formulated goals, actions taken, and results obtained. Is psychological counseling more or less effective than incarceration in reforming offenders? Is arresting one or more of the participants in a family dispute a more or less effective strategy for preventing further family violence than insisting on a temporary separation without invoking the law? Does the frequency of personal contacts between parole officer and parolee make any difference in the frequency of parole violations? How effective are seat belts and infant seats in preventing injuries to children? These questions arise from practical concerns and problems, and their answers have immediate implications for policy decisions and the behavior of criminal justice personnel.

Basic research may, of course, lead to solutions of practical problems, and applied research may shed light on underlying, fundamental questions. The distinction between applied and basic research is sometimes blurred. Still, it is probably safe to say that most research with which criminal justice practitioners are concerned falls more toward the applied than the basic end of the research continuum. Insofar as criminal justice practitioners make day-to-day decisions about how to deal with their clients, and insofar as applied research assists them in making the best possible decisions, doing good research or critically evaluating the research of others is an important, relevant skill. In short, competent research can enhance the quality of day-to-day decisions and help administrators manage both human and financial resources in the most efficient and effective way possible. Good research can significantly improve the formulation and implementation of policies and programs as well as increase the likelihood that intended results will, in fact, be achieved.

QUANTITATIVE AND QUALITATIVE RESEARCH

Another distinction often made in social science research is between **qualitative** and **quantitative** approaches. The relative merits of these types of research have been the subject of much interesting discussion—not to mention a good deal of name calling and other sorts of nastiness—throughout the history of the social sciences. Suffice it to say that these battles, which eventually made their way into criminal justice research circles, originated in philosophical disagreements about the nature of human knowledge and how it is best acquired, on the one hand, and political struggles both within and among academic disciplines on the other—a fairly dangerous combination, we might add, on a par with mixing religion and national politics. The philosophical differences will be taken up briefly in the following paragraphs, but the political struggles are beyond the scope of this book.[2]

Some contemporary researchers continue to have strong preferences for one style of research over the other; many of the issues that divide the two camps continue to arise. The alert reader will recognize, for example, the similarities between the issues discussed in this section and several of those taken up in the sections on feminist and postmodern critiques of science and objectivity in Chapter 2. Nevertheless, we believe the qualitative-quantitative wars have subsided considerably in recent years—and for good reasons. Methodologists have identified many essentially false and/or misleading distinctions, and they have recognized the degree to which good research often involves elements of both approaches. We shall first characterize these two types of research, briefly discuss their strengths and weaknesses, and then suggest some of the ways in which elements of the two approaches are blended in many research projects.

Quantitative methods are rooted in **positivism,** sometimes referred to as **positivistic empiricism,** a philosophy whose adherents seek general and universal truths through objective inquiry (that is, inquiry unbiased by the researcher's desires, beliefs, and values). Empiricists trust their senses—both to learn about what is going on and to be the final arbiter of what is to be believed about the way the world works. Their orientation is deterministic; they reject choice (free will) for explaining human behavior, emphasizing instead forces (variables) acting on and usually beyond the control of individuals or groups. Emile Durkheim—who, for example, studied relationships between suicide rates and various statistical indicators of social disorganization in European countries in the nineteenth century—was a pioneer in quantitative social analysis.

As the designation suggests, for quantitative studies data are gathered either directly in numerical form (for example, ages of juvenile offenders, number of sworn officers on a city's police force, percent of population that identifies itself as Hispanic) or in other kinds of measurements that can be readily converted to numbers (such as questionnaire items that ask how strongly the respondent agrees or disagrees with a particular statement on a scale of 1 to 7). Data analysis relies heavily on statistical procedures. Research reports include tables filled with numbers, graphs, equations, and probabilities associated with statistical tests of hypotheses. As a general rule, quantitative researchers tend to ally themselves more with the natural sciences (biology, chemistry, and so on).

Qualitative methodologies originate from a variety of related philosophical traditions, including phenomenology and existentialism, whose partisans emphasize the individual's subjective point of view (that is, the person's more or less unique perception and understanding of the world). Most qualitative researchers are nondeterministic; that is, they see humans as embedded in complex networks of meaning, exercising free choice and actively engaged in creating as well as changing their social worlds. One of their principal methods is *verstehen,* or interpretive understanding, introduced into social science by Max Weber; Weber sought to understand the rise of capitalism in Western societies by examining the theology and social beliefs of members of certain Protestant Christian denominations in eighteenth- and nineteenth-century Europe.

Qualitative studies rely mostly on some form of **participant observation.** That is, the researcher immerses himself or herself to greater or lesser degrees in the natural settings of a group, social scene, or culture (for instance, a citizen's neighborhood patrol group, a neighborhood bar, a special police unit), both observing and interacting with group members or those who frequent the scene—a process called **field research.** The intention is to come to know the members or participants intimately and in a variety of contexts over an extended period of time, thereby understanding them and the world as they themselves do. The researcher creates a detailed record of observations using written field notes, photographs, film, and/or audio or video recordings for later analysis. The field data are often supplemented by more or less structured individual or group (for example, focus group) interviews, participants' oral or written life stories (autobiographies), and analysis of the contents of other relevant documents. Increasingly, questionnaires are also used to expand the database and to achieve a more representative sample of those being studied. The classic example of fieldwork is that of the anthropologist who lives for several months with "natives" of another culture—learning about their behaviors, customs and beliefs and then reporting on or "translating" her findings for her own cultural audience.

Qualitative research reports are typically descriptive rather than explanatory and are presented in narrative form (frequently supplemented with photographs and many lengthy direct quotations), telling the story of the culture, group, or setting from the members' own point of view. These richly detailed accounts of people in their everyday, natural settings, where particular characters stand out, often read like a novel and convey a sense of reality or validity to the researcher's report.

Typically, too, qualitative researchers identify more with the humanities (history, literature, the arts) than with the natural sciences. They are also likely to be sympathetic with the feminist, postmodern, and deconstructionist critiques of science. In criminal justice, Erving Goffman (for example, *Asylums*) and Jerome Skolnick (*Justice Without Trial*), as well as Peter Manning and John Van Maanen (*Policing: A View from the Streets*) are well-known qualitative researchers.

Critics of qualitative research say that the detailed, intimate information and insight gained through participant observation comes at a very high cost. The very nature of participant observation limits the scope of a study to relatively small groups or severely circumscribed sociocultural scenes. It requires that the researcher invest a great deal of time in the field and commit substantial financial resources to sustaining this long-term engagement. Because it typically involves only one or two researchers in prolonged, direct contact with those being studied, the impact of the personal characteristics of the researcher may be substantial, and questions may well arise as to the validity and/or reliability of the observations. One may wonder, for example, whether a different participant observer (for example, an observer of a different sex, race, ethnicity, personality, ideology, and/or theoretical orientation) might connect with the group or the scene in a different way and emerge with quite a different cultural description.

Then, too, there is the practical problem of minimizing the impact of the researcher's presence on the behavior of those who know they are being observed, as well as the difficult ethical issues of disguised research, maintaining the subjects' anonymity and obtaining their voluntary, informed consent. In some cases (for instance, people or groups engaged in serious illegal behavior) the known researcher may be denied access entirely. And though those being observed usually get used to the observer's presence fairly quickly and resume their normal routines, even when access is permitted, entry to particular groups, scenes, or activities may be restricted. How does one inform or gain the consent of others who enter the scene in the course of the comings and goings in the natural settings of everyday life? In addition, unless one can legitimately assume great uniformity within a larger group or culture, the results obtained from studying a single small group or local scene should not be generalized. A small sample, especially if it is selected without procedures designed to enhance its representativeness, is always suspect if the ultimate purpose is to learn something about a larger population from which it was drawn. Finally, there is always some risk that a participant observer will, in the process of group or scene immersion, abandon the researcher role and "go native." Doing so may not be in any way deleterious to the former researcher, of course, but the possibility of doing so does remind us that the researcher's role is different and that maintaining some distance between researcher and those being observed is important.

Quantitative studies lend themselves to large-scale projects, involving, for example, thousands of crime victimization survey respondents, assault rates from all the counties in a state, or age distributions of municipal police departments in cities with populations over a million worldwide. Many studies use data already gathered by governments or other official or semiofficial agencies. Many also use mailed questionnaires or closed ended telephone interview schedules. Using these techniques and resources, a great deal of information can be assembled for relatively little cost in either time or money. Furthermore, large data sets permit complex analyses, which tease out subtle relationships among variables. Many quantitative research projects are examples of descriptive research (such as, Uniform Crime Report [UCR] or the National Crime Victimization Survey [NCVS]); many are explanatory (for example, studies seeking causal relationships between patrol frequency and crime rates or between family background and delinquency). In either case, reports typically contain lots of numbers and the researcher's commentary about what the numbers mean.

Many of the problems most difficult for qualitative researchers are more easily managed in quantitative research. The researcher's ethical obligations concerning anonymity and voluntary informed consent are relatively easy to fulfill. Carefully implemented sampling strategies make the findings more generalizable to larger populations. The personal characteristics of the researcher are largely irrelevant and most likely unknown to those being studied (although certain kinds of information about the research and the researchers should be made available—a topic taken up in Chapter 2). The social and physical distance between the researchers and their subjects makes it easier to maintain at least some forms of objectivity. Because the information-gathering process is standardized through printed questionnaires or interview schedules, the reliability of the process is increased (in some cases, the degree of reliability can be fairly accurately measured).

Critics of quantitative research doubt that numbers, no matter how numerous or ingenious in their derivation and manipulation, can adequately convey the richness and complexity of human behavior. They are extremely skeptical of determinism in almost any form, insisting that it ignores what is most unique about humans: their capacity for making choices and deliberately acting, not just being acted upon. Furthermore, the distance between quantitative researchers and those being studied may contribute to a kind of objectivity, but a great deal is sacrificed in the process, according to the critics. They cite the inevitable oversimplifications and distortions in the empiricists' reliance on a few categories or variables taken out of the context that gives them meaning. Quantitative approaches, the critics say, cannot possibly capture the passions, ambiguities, subtleties, and complexities of humans' everyday lives. They note the superficiality of data gathered from government reports or from simple, categorical choices ("choose A, B, or C") on a questionnaire. Furthermore, the validity of the data so gathered is suspect. Government or other agency records can be manipulated by administrators who desire to look good, for example, and people may easily lie in response to questionnaires and telephone interviews. Response rates are often quite low, raising issues about the representativeness of the respondents, which thereby threatens the generalizability of the results. In short, from the qualitative practitioners' perspective, quantification, because it has a scientific aura, is more likely to give the researcher false confidence than it is to reveal anything interesting or useful about human conduct.

Now, what can we make of all this? Clearly, important issues are at stake in the contrasts between qualitative and quantitative approaches to research. Careful thought and vigorous debate about the strengths and weaknesses of the two approaches will and should continue. No doubt, some research questions require qualitative methods whereas others require quantitative ones. No doubt, too, future researchers will continue to find themselves more or less firmly in one camp or the other.

But the heat of battle has too often produced gross exaggerations of the superiority of a researcher's own methodological preferences and the inferiority of others' preferred approaches. We think it is a mistake to characterize these two types of research as polar opposites. Most of the key criteria for identifying good research apply to both research styles. Researchers from both camps face similar procedural dilemmas and often make use of each other's approaches and insights. The practice of research is best viewed as a continuum encompassing both qualitative and quantitative methods.

We can suggest only a few of the common criteria and practical convergences here. First, most contemporary quantitative researchers recognize that for human observers complete objectivity is impossible, but they do believe it is a goal very much worth approximating, at least in some of its aspects. Many of the research procedures we will be discussing in later chapters are, in fact, designed to offset our natural tendencies as observers to see what we expect or want to see, rather than what is there. For their part, despite their criticisms of the empiricists' claims to objectivity, qualitative researchers have assumed they have what it takes (dare we say, the objectivity?) to describe reasonably accurately the reality (or realities) of the cultures or groups they are studying. Increasingly, they have come to appreciate that the researcher must maintain some distance, at least at certain stages of the research and reporting process. And the risks of relying on a single participant observer to learn about complex social phenomena have become increasingly apparent, as different qualitative researchers have emerged from similar study scenes with very different accounts of what they observed.

Second, careful formulation of the research questions is important in both approaches. In the case of qualitative research, the questions may change as the researcher's understanding evolves; in quantitative research, research questions are usually articulated before data are gathered. In any event, the researcher must focus on selected aspects of the phenomena being investigated and impose some structure both on the information obtained and on the way in which it is reported. Third, during the preliminary or exploratory phases of quantitative research, participant observation and interviews are often used to help formulate issues to be addressed, variables to be assessed, and questions to be included in questionnaires or interviews. Fourth, an adequate sampling strategy must be developed if the researcher wants to generalize the results. Quantitative researchers have dealt with representative sampling issues for a long time; more recently, qualitative researchers have become more sensitive to sampling problems. But in both styles the researcher is obliged to ensure that a reasonably representative set of observations is assembled.

Fifth, in order to achieve the representative sampling objective just mentioned and to increase standardization in the data-gathering process, qualitative researchers have increasingly turned to questionnaires and/or to more structured interviews (techniques usually associated with quantitative research) to supplement the information they obtain through participant observation. Sixth, questionnaires and interviews are often used in quantitative research to acquire information about the respondent's feelings, ideas, beliefs, and values. Open-ended questions and invitations to explain or elaborate on fixed alternative questionnaire items give respondents a chance to convey or clarify their meanings in their own words. In short, qualitative researchers have neither a unique interest in nor exclusive access to these sorts of data. Seventh, if the researcher's concern is with explaining human conduct, some attention must be given to the criteria of causal inference, regardless of the research style chosen. The causal arguments may appear in different form in the two types of research, but all of the basic elements must be there if the argument is to be persuasive. Eighth, largely as a result of the growing use of questionnaires and other more easily quantifiable data resources noted above, qualitative researchers have become less suspicious of frequency counts, cross-tabulations, and elementary statistical data analysis. Finally, research results should be accessible to the reasonably well-educated layperson. In this case, qualitative researchers have set the standard, but quantitative researchers have increasingly recognized the need to translate their work for the lay audience.

Many of the differences between qualitative and quantitative research (and researchers) are not as great as they are sometimes portrayed. Good researchers will appreciate the advantages and disadvantages of both approaches, recognize that different approaches brought to bear on the same research question enhance the credibility of the findings, and include both in their research tool kit.

EVALUATION RESEARCH

Evaluation research, an important component of policy analysis,[3] represents an attempt to determine the extent to which a given program is achieving (has achieved) intended goals, whether the program is (was) cost effective compared to alternative programs, and whether the program should be continued. This type of research is frequently utilized to evaluate the impact of social interventions.[4] It is a form of applied research used to provide scientific information that may be used to help guide public policy. "Evaluation research aims to provide feedback to policymakers in concrete, measurable, terms."[5] The feedback (product) provided consists of information collected while adhering to the principles of scientific research (process).

> Evaluation research is *not* another sort of research different from the (traditional) types of research. . . . Fad, fashion and catchwordism run wild in science. . . . And with recent demands by the holders of grant pursestrings that social science be "relevant" and "responsive to current social needs," there emerged the label "evaluation research" which seems super-relevant and responsive. . . . Every economic study of the effect of a minimum-wage law on employment and earnings of poor people is evaluation research, evaluating the effects of such legislation. Every medical and anthropological study tracing the impact of Western culture on an isolated tribe's physical and mental hygiene is evaluation research. . . . There does not exist a distinct kind of research known as evaluation research.[6]

Although Julian Simon and Paul Burstein are technically correct, the label "evaluation research" has stuck and does appear to describe an increasingly popular and common subcategory of research within the broader category of applied research. Evaluation researchers use the same types of research designs and data-collection techniques and have the same concerns as other researchers. Perhaps more directly than most other researchers, however, they are subject to political pressures and hidden agendas. That is, personnel involved in administering the program being evaluated welcome the research and the publication of findings *when they reflect well upon the program and its administrators.* They may be far less enamored, for obvious reasons, with evaluation research that indicates the program has not achieved its stated goals, or is not cost effective, or should be discontinued. In such instances, the need for ethical conduct and objectivity on the part of the researchers may be questioned by those with vested interests in keeping the program alive. An excellent example of such conflict currently revolves around research that shows that D.A.R.E. (Drug Abuse Resistance Education) programs have not, in general, achieved their goals. Still, the international D.A.R.E. organization maintains that parents, school administrators, and members of the organization know that the program is effective even if scientists evaluating the program don't.

There are two basic types of evaluation research. The first, **process** or **formative research,** is basically concerned with examining how a program is being implemented and/or whether a policy change is in fact being reflected in practice. It often relies upon qualitative research techniques (such as, participant observation) to collect information concerning ongoing programs on a continuing basis. This information is then provided to program personnel so that they can modify their program implementation strategy or the program activity itself. An example would be research conducted on an ongoing community policing initiative in which officers' adoption of the community policing philosophy and practice is assessed and citizens' satisfaction with police services is determined by surveying residents at regular intervals concerning their feelings of safety and security. Depending upon the results, the police might try new initiatives or modify old ones in an attempt to influence the officers' attitudes or behavior and/or residents' feelings about safety and security. The second type of evaluation research is **impact, outcome,** or **summative research.** An example would be a survey designed to determine whether a D.A.R.E. program in a particular community resulted in lower rates of drug abuse after three years for those who had been through the program than for those who had not. Here the concern is with whether a program that has been in place for some time, or has been completed, has accomplished what it was designed to accomplish. Outcome researchers tend to depend more upon quantitative data and experimental or quasi-experimental designs, to be discussed in greater detail later.[7] Both types of evaluation research involve the same basic considerations.

Some programs are extremely difficult to evaluate because they have no explicitly stated goals, or because the goals are so amorphous that they cannot be translated into assessable outcomes, or because no data have been collected and preserved over the course of the program. Others are difficult or impossible to evaluate because program personnel are unwilling to cooperate in the process. Still other program administrators simply have no desire to evaluate their programs. All of these factors should be considered before undertaking evaluation research in order to avoid the possibility that the researcher's time and effort will be wasted.

Once it has been determined that evaluation research is desirable and practical, the process begins with a review of the program to be evaluated. This review focuses on the stated goals or objectives of the program, activities conducted to achieve these goals, anticipated outcomes of these activities, and comparisons with other known programs designed to achieve the same goals. Program goals/objectives, activities, and outcomes must be operationalized (that is, defined in such a way that we can recognize and measure them). Suppose, for example, that the goal of the program being evaluated is to reduce reported commercial burglaries in a specific geographic area by 50 percent over a twelve-month period. And suppose we attempt to achieve this goal by painting the walls of buildings separated by alleys white up to a height of 10 feet in the belief that patrol officers will be better able to see people after dark in these alleys, making it more difficult to gain unauthorized entry into businesses. At the end of the specified time period, we would examine the alleyways to be sure they had been painted, count the number of commercial burglaries reported in the specified area, and compare the number of burglaries with the number committed in the twelve-month period prior to painting the buildings. If the number of burglaries reported in the relevant time period increased or remained the same, the program has not achieved its goal and may not be worth continuing. If the number of reported burglaries decreased by 50 percent or more, we might be tempted to say that the program is effective and should be continued. But, as is the case in all scientific research, we would need to examine other possible causes (rival hypotheses) before we arrived at this conclusion. For example, the arrest of a gang of burglars responsible for most of the commercial burglaries committed in the area in question (and the arrest not resulting from being observed in the painted spaces) might account for any differences we find. If no such significant events can be identified, and if no alternative programs that are less costly but are equally or more effective, in reducing commercial burglaries can be found, we would probably evaluate the program favorably and recommend its continued use under similar circumstances.

In the example above, we have (1) formulated a specific problem statement (will painting the alleyways white lead to reduction in commercial burglaries in the area in question over a twelve-month time period?), and (2) selected the research technique and design to be employed (which will later be discussed as a before-after design, in this case comparing relevant official burglary statistics). To complete the evaluation, we must (3) actually collect the relevant data (determine that the walls weren't painted before but are painted now and obtain the official statistics we need), (4) analyze the data (compare data from the two time periods), (5) draw our conclusions (about the relationship between painted alleyways and commercial crime in the city in question, always keeping in mind the caution about rival explanations), and (6) report our conclusions to those responsible for making program decisions in the area of crime prevention. The six steps discussed above are required in all evaluation research, although they are sometimes combined or further subdivided by other authors.[8]

Ideally, programs to be evaluated are conceived and implemented with evaluation in mind. That is, the variables and outcomes to be measured and the techniques to be employed in evaluation are designed into the program. This type of program monitoring allows the evaluators to exercise greater control over more variables by setting up what we shall later refer to as a classical experimental design, providing the best measure of program effects. In reality, however, a good deal of evaluative research is conducted using quasi-experimental designs because no evaluation component was built into the program. This forces the evaluator to rely on what we will discuss later as the after-only design with very few controls and makes accurate analysis difficult at best.

Including program evaluation as an integral part of new programs may also reduce the costs associated with the evaluation. Still, "A high quality evaluation is expensive and time-consuming. Indeed, it may be many times more expensive than the operational program it is designed to test."[9] Even so, having good evidence of a program's effectiveness may result in better use of resources in the long run.

Evaluation research can be conducted by in-house personnel, hired-hand researchers, or third-party researchers. The strengths and weaknesses of these types of research (discussed later in this chapter) apply to evaluation research as well.

PREDICTION RESEARCH

Another type of criminal justice research growing in popularity is **prediction research.** Scientific prediction is closely related to explanation, the main difference being that the former deals with what has happened whereas the latter purports to say something about what will happen. In principle, comprehensive explanations should translate directly into accurate predictions; unfortunately, given the weaknesses in our explanatory models as well as uncertainty inherent in the future itself, the principle is some distance from being realized.

The aim of prediction research in criminal justice is to use scientific methods (rather than, say, personal judgments or clinical assessments) to construct statistical (probabilistic) predictions that (1) maximize the chances of achieving desirable outcomes (such as deterring crime, rehabilitating offenders, decreasing traffic fatalities); (2) minimize the likelihood of undesirable outcomes (for example, increasing recidivism, encouraging drug use); and (3) use always limited criminal justice resources (both financial and human) in the most efficient way possible. In pursuit of these objectives, predictive researchers use **explanatory research** to construct and/or examine the accuracy of predictive instruments (sometimes called *prediction tables* or *experience tables*), often consisting of a list of relevant attributes or characteristics (that is, variables that previous research has shown to be related to the desired outcomes) on which individuals, situations, and/or environments are rated or scored. These scores are then used by criminal justice personnel to make decisions—for example, about which juveniles are most likely to become serious offenders, which offenders are processed through which criminal justice agencies, and how criminal justice resources (police officers, prison beds, diversion programs, probation or parole slots, for instance) are allocated. Among the predictive instruments that are widely used are the Salient Factor Score, used by the U.S. Parole Commission to guide parole decisions, and the Rand Seven-Factor Index, used to guide selective incapacitation sentencing decisions. The latter, one of several recent attempts to identify career criminals, consists of seven variables: Was there a prior conviction for the same charge? Had the person been incarcerated for more than half of the previous two years? Was the person convicted of an offense before age 16? Had the person served time in a juvenile facility? Had the person used drugs in the preceding two years? Had the person used drugs as a juvenile? Had the person been employed less than half of the previous two years? A person's score consists of the number of "yes" answers to the questions; the higher the score, the greater the predicted likelihood of the person becoming a frequent, serious offender, and, therefore, the greater the benefit to society of his or her incapacitation.

Whenever we make a prediction and then determine whether the prediction was accurate or not, there are four possible results. Suppose I have before me the case of Chris, and I need to predict whether Chris will be a serious offender. I then observe whether he did or did not do as I predicted. Figure 1.1 illustrates the four possible results. It's easy to get lost in the trues and falses and positives and negatives here because (among other things) of other associations we have with the terms *positive* and *negative*. We wouldn't ordinarily think of someone becoming a serious delinquent offender as positive, for example. It may help if you just think of a prediction as being positive when you assert that something *will* occur or that a person *has* an attribute and as negative when you assert that something *will not* occur or that a person *does not* have an attribute. Then think about what actually happened in relation to the prediction: A correct prediction is true; an incorrect one is false.

Two of the four possible results present no problem. If I predict that Chris will become an offender and he does, my prediction is a **true positive.** If I predict he will not become an offender and he doesn't, that's a **true negative.**

The remaining two alternative outcomes, however, can be troublesome. If I predict that Chris will be an offender and he stays clean, my prediction results in a **false positive.** If I predict he will not be an offender and he offends, I have a **false negative.** Predictions that turn out to be false can have dire consequences, especially in the criminal justice context. I may predict, for example, that a child molester will not offend again and turn out to be wrong (a false negative). Or I may predict that an inmate will succeed with intensive supervision on parole and be wrong (a false positive). In either case, the public's safety and well-being have been jeopardized by my prediction. If I predict incorrectly that a person will be a habitual offender and decide to selectively incapacitate him, I squander expensive prison space and waste other public resources.

There is also the problem of the *self-fulfilling prophecy.* Suppose we could say, on the basis of previous research, that 20 percent of a particular type of youngster had engaged in serious delinquent behavior. Should we identify

FIGURE 1.1	Predictions and Their Outcomes		
		Predictions	
		X will occur	X will not occur
	X occurred	True Positive	False Negative
Outcomes			
	X did not occur	False Positive	True Negative

youths of the same type as they enter the school system and treat them differently from their peers (for example, assign them to special classes in school or develop special programs for them or their families)? At first glance, that might seem an appropriate course of action. Prevention, after all, is in everyone's interests. But do such interventions have risks? Who (parents, school administrators, law enforcement officers, others in authority) would know who was in the high-risk category? Would their behavior change with respect to the youths so identified in ways that might alienate or stigmatize them? You can be certain that the youths themselves and their peers outside the high-risk designation will know who is in which group and why. Would singling out the high-risk youths as especially likely to get into trouble tend to initiate or reinforce their identification of themselves as troublemakers? And would they be more likely to live up to their reputation as a result? Would more than 20 percent of the high-risk youths end up in serious trouble? There are both theoretical and empirical reasons to suspect that such a preventive intervention might backfire, creating more serious offenders than had the intervention not occurred in the first place.

Finally, there is potential for serious abuse in prediction strategies. Racial profiling, for example, has captured our attention recently, primarily in the context of traffic stops. Minority citizens have complained bitterly about police department policies and practices that result, for example, in African Americans driving newer, more expensive cars in wealthy neighborhoods being pulled over and questioned—not because there is direct evidence that an offense has occurred (except perhaps for a minor traffic or equipment violation, which can almost always be used by officers as an excuse for the stop) but simply because they are who they are, driving those cars in those areas. Such stops might be justified by appealing to officers' experiences or departmental data suggesting these circumstances are suspicious and more likely to yield evidence of offenses or offenders than other kinds of stops. But the predictive criteria are too simple; the false positives are too numerous. Besides, law enforcement always takes place in a political context; researchers and research statistics seldom take such contexts into account. The decision of law enforcement officers to intervene in the lives of private citizens in a free society should be governed by criteria such as "probable cause" that extend well beyond the statistical associations generated by predictive research. In the context of societal racism and heightened racial sensitivity among minorities, this type of prediction-based practice creates far more problems than it solves.

There is great promise in prediction research. Even modestly accurate predictions *could* yield enormous benefits for criminal justice personnel, offenders, communities, and taxpayers. But there are significant problems to overcome before prediction research realizes its potential. Predictive instruments are only as good as the research on which they are based. Although some progress has been made—especially in understanding general biological, psychological, social, and environmental contributors to delinquency and crime and their deterrence—we still do not understand these matters in sufficient detail to make very accurate predictions. Many variables at different levels of analysis seem to be involved; some are beyond our control. In any event their associations with desirable outcomes are relatively weak. At this point, making more accurate predictions involves including more variables in the predictive equations, but to do so requires complex rating instruments that are often difficult to apply to individual cases. Simpler, easier to use instruments (that is, those involving relatively few items or attributes) are more prone to substantial prediction error (false positive and false negative) rates. Ongoing efforts to validate and refine the scales, especially those involving populations different from the ones used to construct the scales, are essential. Furthermore, whenever we try to predict relatively rare events (as is the case in many criminal justice contexts), numerous prediction errors, especially false positives, are likely to occur. Abuse of prediction research, as in racial profiling, is likely in such cases. Considerable current evidence suggests scientifically based prediction is as good as, and sometimes better than, a judge's or parole board's prognostication or a psychiatrist's clinical assessment. In situations where the risks or potential costs of false positives or false negatives are minimal, its use appears justifiable. In other circumstances, we need a better understanding of the causes of crime and recidivism, as well as the costs to individuals and society before relying too heavily on prediction research.[10]

IN-HOUSE, HIRED-HAND, AND THIRD-PARTY RESEARCH

Research projects can be divided into three categories according to the different relationships that exist between the researchers and those being researched. **In-house research** is conducted by the staff of the organization or agency under study. Sometimes an organization will have a separate research division or department that operates at the request of other departments, or individuals within the organization who ordinarily perform other duties can be requested to conduct an investigation from time to time. In any event, it is called in-house research because someone *within* the organization conducts research *about* the organization *for* the organization. Any criminal justice practitioner who does research about his own activities or any other aspect of the organization, office, or agency for which he works is doing in-house research.

Hired-hand research is carried on by an outside organization (typically one that specializes in research) that is independent of but paid by the organization under study. For example, independent consultants may be retained by a criminal justice agency to help agency administrators make changes in organizational structure or policy. In formulating their recommendations, these consultants often engage in information gathering and analysis.

Third-party research is conducted by an independent outsider, rather than someone who is part of the organization being studied or someone paid by the organization to conduct the research. Third-party research is paid for by the researching group itself or by a grant from some independent source (for example, a private or public foundation or a government agency such as the National Science Foundation). A sociologist, for example, might be given a grant by the Ford Foundation to study the process and effects of plea bargaining; although he might deal with a number of law firms, judges, or defendants, he has no direct organizational or financial affiliations with them. As a general rule, the third-party researcher has greater independence and freedom in the conduct of the research project than either of the other types of researchers.

Each of these types of research has its advantages and disadvantages. For example, in-house researchers have the advantage of being closer to the problem at hand. Hence, they are in a better position than an outside research group, whether hired-hand or third-party, to understand the complexities of the problems to be addressed and to design a project that will produce information useful to the organization. In addition, for some types of research— especially that which is concerned directly with the activities of criminal justice agency personnel—in-house researchers may have an easier time gaining the cooperation of the staff involved. Being studied by someone who is considered to be a member of one's own team or part of one's own group usually reduces the suspicion and mistrust that accompany being scrutinized.

However, the factors in the research situation that encourage this very sense of security may pose difficulties for in-house researchers. For example, they may have built-in biases because they are part of the organization being studied and so share the perspectives and prejudices of that particular organization. Or they may be subject to internal political pressures from peer groups or those higher in the command structure. Further, consumers of the research results may be suspicious of the research and its conclusions because they were derived by someone with a potentially vested interest in the results. It is not easy for an organization to admit that its present policies and practices may be ineffective, that some of its members have made significant errors, or that its financial resources have been used inappropriately. For example, the public is often suspicious of investigations conducted by internal investigation units in local police departments or of studies by lawyers on the ethical practices of attorneys—and with good reason. Some members of the organization may look bad as a result of the research. The reputation of both individual staff members and the organization as a whole may be harmed. In-house researchers may therefore be reluctant to ask controversial or potentially damaging questions. Even if they do, they may not report some of their findings in order to protect their own, the organization's, or the profession's interests.

Hired-hand research has the advantage of putting the control of the research process and the reporting of results into the hands of an outside organization with less of a direct stake in the results of the research. Because they are not part of the organizational structure they are studying, hired-hand researchers escape many of the potentially biasing pressures that can be brought to bear on in-house researchers. Also, organizations specializing in research can often bring greater expertise to the task. Both of these factors contribute to the credibility of research findings. Finally, no in-house personnel have to be taken from their assigned duties in order to conduct the research.

Hired-hand research does have its disadvantages, however. Outsiders may have difficulty understanding fully what they are expected to do and, as a result, fail to generate information that would be most useful to the organization. Furthermore, an outside research organization may bring its own biases to the situation. These biases may influence the research design and the reporting of results so as to diminish their usefulness. Of course, the fact that the researchers are hired usually means that the employer exercises some control over the research for which they are paying. A representative of the organization should communicate clearly to the hired researchers the goals of the research, participate in its design as much as possible, and have some knowledge of the research process and data-analysis techniques. Only then will the organization itself get the information it needs and be able to evaluate the research and its results.

Third-party research maximizes the distance between researchers and subjects because there are no organizational or financial connections between the researchers and the organization under study. Hence, the third-party researcher is typically less susceptible to pressures, preferences, and biases that are likely to impinge on in-house or hired-hand researchers.

Third-party research has its own problems, however. Because there are no built-in ties, organization personnel are less likely to cooperate with the researcher. As a result the data obtained may not be as complete, as accurate, or as useful. Furthermore, in hired-hand research, the hiring organization has the power to choose which researchers will conduct the study. To that degree, the organization exercises some control over the research. In third-party research, even this control is relinquished. This lack of control by the organization becomes very important (particularly to criminal justice agencies) when the third-party researcher has negative prejudices or biases concerning the organization being studied, especially because the researcher has a freer hand in expressing those biases. Because third-party researchers usually choose the topics to be studied and the research methods to be employed according to their own theoretical interests, research results may be of limited value to the organization.

Of course, the organization being studied is not entirely without leverage in third-party research. The organization may, and in some cases should, deny or limit cooperation with third-party researchers. The professional reputation of the researcher is crucial for inspiring confidence and cooperation. In any case, it is usually possible for the organization to bargain with reputable third-party researchers, trading access to information, endorsement of the study, and

TABLE 1.1	Relationship Between Researcher and Target Organization in Three Types of Research

	Type of Research		
Relationship	In-house	Hired-hand	Third-party
Dependence of researcher on researched:			
organizational	high	moderate	low
financial	high	high	low
Amount of researched organization's control over research process	high	moderate	low
Likelihood of cooperation from organization's personnel in research project	high	moderate	low
Public's confidence in research/credibility of results	low	moderate	high/low*

*Depends on reputation of researcher.

cooperation of personnel for some influence over the research process and the inclusion of research topics that are of special interest to the organization.

Credibility of research results also deserves brief mention, and the reputation of the third-party researcher is crucial here as well. For example, the results of research conducted by a third party known to be biased either positively or negatively toward the organization or policies being studied are likely to (and should) be regarded with skepticism by the public. In general, however, the greater degree of independence of the third-party researcher contributes to the public's confidence in the research and analysis.

Table 1.1 summarizes some of the more important aspects of in-house, hired-hand, and third-party research.

RESEARCH IN CRIMINAL JUSTICE: AN ILLUSTRATION

Reprinted below are excerpts from a National Institute of Justice *Research in Brief* report (NCJ 162358–March 1997). As you read it, see if you can identify some of the similarities between the research described in the excerpt and the investigation processes discussed in this chapter.

Evaluation of Pepper Spray
by Steven M. Edwards, John Granfield, and Jamie Onnen

Violent encounters between police officers and individuals resisting arrest have historically resulted in injury and frequently in complaints about the level of force used by police. In addition to concern over these issues, increased civil liability and court-imposed limitations on the use of deadly force have stimulated the search for safe and effective less-than-lethal (LTL) force alternatives. One widely used option is oleoresin capsicum (OC) aerosol, commonly called pepper spray.

Despite extensive applications in hundreds of police departments, few systematic studies of OC usage and effectiveness have been documented. A National Institute of Justice-sponsored assessment of pepper spray's usefulness focused on the Baltimore County Police Department's (BCoPD's) operations from July 1993 through March 1994.

A research team from the International Association of Chiefs of Police (IACP) analyzed the BCoPD data and found that the use of OC in arrest and other confrontational encounters effectively neutralized aggressive suspects and animals. Study findings also suggest that the use of OC reduced the incidence of assaults on police officers, injuries to both officers and suspects, and use-of-force or brutality complaints registered against BCoPD.

. . .

Chemical Weapon Use in Law Enforcement. For centuries, various forms of chemical agents have been used in war as offensive weapons. As early as 2300 B.C., Chinese armies dispersed enemy forces by using "stink pots"—red pepper burned in hot oil that produced irritating and suffocating smoke—in massive frontal assaults. After World War I, however, an interest in extending the use of chemicals into the realm of law enforcement emerged. It was hypothesized that these agents could control criminals and riotous crowds as effectively as they controlled enemies during warfare. . . .

. . .

OLEORESIN CAPSICUM (OC). OC, a naturally occurring substance derived from the cayenne pepper plant, is classified as an inflammatory agent. On contact with OC, the mucous membranes of the eyes, nose, and throat immediately become inflamed and swollen. The symptomatic swelling produces involuntary eye closure due to dilating capillaries; nasal and sinus drainage; constricted airway; and temporary paralysis of the larynx, causing gagging, coughing, and shortness of breath. The extract of peppers causes the blood vessels to dilate and the blood to rush to the upper body; the skin appears inflamed, resembling a burn.

. . .

Study Method. . . . Every officer discharging OC spray in a confrontational encounter was required to complete the OC spray data collection form, which contained both open-ended and specified-choice questions relating to prevailing weather conditions, suspect's behavior, OC application area, injury (if any) received, and decontamination. The OC data form was completed along with a departmental incident report as soon as practical after conclusion of the encounter. A second data collection instrument, an unstructured follow-up interview, was developed to validate information collected by the OC data form. These unstructured officer interviews were conducted by the onsite observer to allow for the addition of any comments, suggestions, or officer observations regarding the specific encounter and the effectiveness of the spray.

Prior to their use in BCoPD, the OC data collection sheet and unstructured follow-up interview format were pretested in the Anne Arundel County, Maryland, Police Department. Results indicated that measurement instruments were both suitable and easily completed.

. . .

Use of Pepper Spray. During the study period, Baltimore County officers used OC in response to 194 (174 human and 20 animal) incidents, which fell into various categories of complaints that beat police officers often handle. These types of complaints usually involved aggressive, excitable behavior on the part of both the complainant and victim. Moreover, they tended to escalate quickly, resulting in confrontational outcomes.

Thirty-nine percent of the incidents occurred inside some structure (e.g., house, car), while the remaining incidents occurred "out-of-doors."

Weather conditions did not seem to influence either an officer's decision to use OC or the spray's effect on suspects. Eighty-four percent of the human subjects sprayed were male and 16 percent were female. Generally, sprayed individuals were intoxicated (drugs or alcohol), belligerent, and/or combative. The majority (89 percent) of incidents involved suspects who physically threatened the police officer; very few incidents involved the use of firearms or knives. The arrest/intervention incidents necessitating the use of the spray were primarily battery, assault, and disorderly conduct. . . .

Effectiveness of OC Use. Overall, OC was very effective in the 194 incidents where it was used (see "Officers' Comments on OC". . . . A total of 156 (90 percent) of the 174 individuals sprayed were incapacitated enough to be effectively arrested.

. . .

In 144 incidents, only one spray was required to incapacitate a subject; officers used the full contents of an issued container of OC to control suspects in four separate incidents. No data indicated that spraying more than one short burst produced better effects, if the subject were given a "good" spray the first time. . . .

. . .

One hundred forty-four (83 percent) of the 174 subjects were sufficiently neutralized to yield to officer orders. Thirty individuals (17 percent) struggled or otherwise failed to follow officer instructions.

Eighteen of these 30 struggling subjects were classified by officers as not fully incapacitated by the OC spray. According to officer reports, the OC had no effect on seven suspects. These seven individuals exhibited drugged behavior or seemed to have emotional problems. These data indicate that individuals who are heavily intoxicated, drugged, or mentally unstable may be resistant or immune to OC's effects or that OC may actually exacerbate the difficulty associated with controlling such persons. Additionally, these types of encounters may cause the officer to be cross-contaminated if the incident escalates to a physical confrontation. BCoPD's experience indicates that training officers may want to stress

OFFICERS' COMMENTS ON OC

The following comments were extracted from the OC data collection sheets completed by the BCoPD officers or from follow-up interviews:

- Wish we had had it a while ago.
- I think it's a great . . . alternative to initial use of force.
- Definitely better than using a nightstick.
- The word is out (on the street). . . all people have to do is hear the Velcro© and they comply pretty quickly. (The officer who made this comment had actually pulled the OC from his holster at least 10 times, but had sprayed it only once.)
- Some subjects actually apologize after being sprayed.

the importance of accurately assessing the likely impact of pepper spray in such an encounter and of being prepared to select another control alternative.

ANIMAL CONTROL. Interest in OC's effectiveness in animal encounters was high because, prior to project implementation, BCoPD had experienced a number of incidents where officers were forced to shoot threatening or attacking dogs. During the OC field study, dogs were sprayed with OC in 20 incidents where the animals posed a danger to officers. Ten of the dogs sprayed weighed between 25 and 50 pounds, and 6 weighed more than 50 pounds.

. . .

. . . OC was effective nearly 100 percent of the time in dog encounters (one officer was bitten but required no medical treatment).

Other Results of OC Use. ASSAULTS ON OFFICERS. Three years of prior assault data (pre-OC data) were collected for comparison with data from the period after which OC was adopted by the department (post-OC data). The pre-OC data were examined to identify any possible trends regarding assaults. Overall, these data showed that officer assaults were decreasing prior to OC use. The post-OC data indicated that assaults continued to decline. In fact, the total number of officers assaulted in the post-OC period was substantially lower than in any pre-OC data period. While it is likely that the introduction of OC spray contributed to this significant decline, the finding must be considered preliminary, since the pre- and post-data for this study were not strictly comparable in all cases.

INJURIES TO OFFICERS. Data from the spray collection form showed that few officers were injured when they used OC to control a confrontational encounter. Only 21 officers (11 percent) reported receiving any injury. . . . Most of these were minor and resulted in no lost work time. Although data from the pre-OC use period were not comparable and did not permit a complete before-and-after analysis, the relatively low level of injuries sustained by officers in the post-OC period suggests that OC use has the potential to reduce officer injuries in confrontational situations.

INJURIES TO SUSPECTS. Very few suspect injuries occurred during the post-OC project period. Of the 174 spray incidents, only 14 suspects (8 percent) received any injuries, and all of these were minor, requiring no hospital treatment. . . .

. . .

USE-OF-FORCE COMPLAINTS. Departmental policy states that a use-of-force report must be completed if the subject complains of injury as a result of arrest and goes to the hospital for medical treatment. However, as is true for other less-than-lethal weapons, a use-of-force report is not required for OC, absent a complaint or hospital treatment. BCoPD officials concluded that treating OC differently could inappropriately hinder its use.

Data suggest that despite an increase in calls for service and fewer patrol officers working their beats, use-of-force complaints declined by 53 percent during the second pre-OC period (July 1991 through March 1992) and the post-OC period. Similarly, a reduction of 40 percent occurred between the third pre-OC period (July 1992 through March 1993) and the post-OC period. . . . Since no other major policy changes regarding use of force took place during pre- and post-data collection, it is likely that the use of pepper spray accounted for the decrease in complaints. Interviews with Internal Affairs officers add weight to this finding. These officers noted that, unlike those of impact weapons, the effects of OC are short-lived and nontraumatic; pepper spray thus reduces the likelihood that brutality or excessive force complaints would be lodged. In addition, sprayed individuals received aftercare from the officers who sprayed them, which may have obviated the need to complain.

During the time of data collection (July 1993 through March 1994) and over the span of 174 sprayings, five complaints of brutality and one use-of-force case were received by BCoPD. These complaints centered on the officer's purportedly inappropriate behavior and did not address the spray itself. To date, BCoPD has not had any complaints or suits filed that relate to the issue of OC spray.

Summary. Most police departments in the United States are concerned about officer and suspect safety. In recent years, this concern has focused on injuries to police officers and citizens during arrest confrontations. To meet this problem, departments have sought answers in technology involving less-than-lethal weapons. Aerosol pepper spray is one weapon from the LTL arsenal that effectively addresses the issue of officer/citizen injury.

. . .

The research report you just read provides important information about a police department's experiences with pepper spray, information that academic experts as well as criminal justice practitioners can use. Yet the chances are you had relatively little difficulty understanding the theoretical issues discussed, the general nature of the research conducted, the data that were presented, and the conclusions that were reached. The chances are, too, that you could, without a great deal of difficulty, imagine yourself doing a research project like the one described and writing a report like the one you read.

The researchers begin their discussion by noting that citizens resisting arrest present significant problems and dangers for arresting officers as well as arrestees; pepper spray has been adopted widely by law enforcement agencies as a mean of alleviating some of those problems and dangers. Yet, there have been few attempts to study *systematically* its uses and effects. So, they decide to collect relevant *data*. To do so, the researchers first had to formulate the issues or *research questions,* or in this case, implicit *hypotheses,* they wished to examine and how they were going to gather the *facts* then needed to answer their questions. They settled on questionnaires, interviews, and examination of police department and other official records. To design the questionnaires, interviews, and other data-gathering strategies, they needed to identify which aspects of pepper spray use and its effects—that is, which *variables* (for example, sex of arrestee, type of offense, weather conditions, type of threat to officer, whether the arrestee became compliant after being sprayed, brutality complaints)—they considered important in understanding the use of pepper spray and its effects.

After the data had been assembled, the researchers looked for *patterns* in the uses and effects of pepper spray. They then reported these patterns to us and discussed their implications for departmental policy and police practice.

This research report exemplifies applied and evaluation research. Both qualitative and quantitative methods were employed. You can decide for yourself if the study was in-house, hired-hand or third-party research.

There may have been parts of the research report you did not understand completely; concepts like before-and-after analysis, for example, will be discussed later in the text. You will learn that the research described here is only one of several kinds, and that this particular type of research, like all of the others, has its advantages and disadvantages. You will discover too that the data analysis might have been done in several different ways. Our purpose here is simply to convince you that significant research projects and reports are not beyond your understanding. In the following chapters, some of the complexities of research concepts and activities will be introduced so that your knowledge of the research process can be expanded and refined. You will be able to better understand the research process, to analyze data, to raise significant questions about research projects, to evaluate the contributions of research projects to the criminal justice field, and to prepare research reports.

REVIEW QUESTIONS

1. Can any investigative processes, including scientific ones, produce absolutely certain results or conclusions? Why or why not?

2. What is research? What provides discipline in the research process? Why is this discipline important?

3. What are the similarities and differences between basic and applied research?

4. What are the similarities and differences between qualitative and quantitative research?

5. What are the advantages and disadvantages of in-house, hired-hand, and third-party research?

6. What are the basic types of evaluation research, and why is each important in criminal justice?

7. What is prediction research? What are false positives and false negatives, and why are they important?

8. What distinguishes scientific research from research or problem solving in everyday life?

9. What are the similarities and differences between scientific research and criminal investigation?

10. What are the similarities and differences between inductive and deductive logic?

11. Why should someone know about research methods?

12. What type(s) of research does the pepper spray article fit? What variables did the researchers use in their study? What were their findings?

EXERCISES

1. Write three basic and three applied research questions and discuss the similarities and differences between the two types of research questions.

2. Give two examples each of qualitative and quantitative research strategies. Briefly describe a research project where qualitative approaches would be most appropriate. Then, describe one where quantitative approaches would be best. Finally, describe a research project where the two approaches could be combined to enhance the meaningfulness of the findings. Discuss the strengths and weaknesses of each of the three projects.

3. Give an example of a process evaluation research project and an impact evaluation research project. Discuss the similarities and differences between the two. Could the two be combined in a single project? How? Give an example.

4. Briefly describe a predictive research project you would like to undertake. Could you avoid false positives and false negatives? What impact might false positives have?

5. Give two examples each of inductive and deductive logic.

6. Discuss your answers to review question 12 above. Why does the project fit the type(s) you identified? Make a list of the variables the researchers used. Can you think of other variables that might be important? What research questions and hypotheses guided the research? Can you identify any cause and effect relationships among the variables in their findings?

7. Do you find the results of the pepper spray credible? Why or why not? Who conducted the study? Which aspects of the study make the results believable? Which undermine its credibility? Would the results be more credible if the research had been conducted by a team from the Baltimore County Police Department? A local university?

8. Discuss the similarities and differences between prediction and evaluation research. Should they ever be combined? Why or why not?

9. Go to *http://www.la.utexas.edu/research/cccjr/research.htm*. Read that page and follow the links near the bottom of the page to the "Research in Brief" reports and "Policy Papers" and read these as well. Then go to *http://www.la.utexas.edu/research/cccjr/research/* and read *bwribback.htm* as well as *intakerib.htm*. What kinds of research are represented? Read the description of the CCCJR at the main site. What kind of research organization is CCCJR? Would their research be best characterized as hired-hand or third-party? Answer the same questions about the commercial sites *http://www.cjresearch.com, www.gottfredson.com,* and *www.cjri.com*. Would you have more confidence in the university studies than those by the for-profit companies? Why or why not?

NOTES

1. Note the difference between what we have described here, which is a theory of a particular crime, and a general theory of crime, which might, for example, attempt to explain different rates in different cities or why one type of person is more prone than other types to commit assault.

2. For a variety of perspectives on issues related to qualitative and quantitatives research, see David Silverman, *Doing Qualitative Research: A Practical Handbook* (Thousand Oaks, CA: Sage, 2000); Normal K. Denzin and Yvonna S. Lincoln (eds.), *Handbook of Qualitative Research* (Thousand Oaks, CA: Sage 1994); George J. McCall, *Observing the Law: Field Methods in the Study of Crime and the Criminal Justice System* (New York: Free Press, 1978); Matthew B. Miles and A. Michael Huberman, *Qualitative Data Analysis,* 2nd ed. (Thousand Oaks, CA: Sage, 1994); and Jeff Ferrell, "Criminological *Verstehen:* Inside the Immediacy of Crime." *Justice Quarterly* 14 (1997): 3–23.

3. Harry Hatry, Louis Blair, Donald Fisk, and Wayne Kimmel. *Program Analysis for State and Local Governments* (Washington, DC: The Urban Institute, 1976). See also "Advising Criminal Justice Policy Through Experimental Evaluations." *Crime and Delinquency* (special issue) 46 (2000).

4. Earl Babbie, *The Practice of Social Research,* 5th ed. (Belmont, CA: Wadsworth, 1989).

5. Frank E. Hagan, *Research Methods in Criminal Justice and Criminology,* 2nd ed. (New York: Macmillan, 1989), p. 377.

6. Julian L. Simon and Paul Burstein, *Basic Research Methods in Social Science,* 3rd ed. (New York: Random House, 1985), p. 48.

7. Louise H. Kidder and Charles M. Judd, *Research Methods in Social Relations,* 5th ed. (New York: Holt, Rinehart and Winston, 1986).

8. Hagan; Hatry et al.; Michael G. Maxfield and Earl Babbie, *Research Methods for Criminal Justice and Criminology,* 2nd ed. (Belmont, CA: West/Wadsworth 1998), pp. 321–332; Jeffrey D. Senese, *Applied Research Methods in Criminal Justice* (Chicago: Nelson Hall, 1997), pp. 70–72; Mark L. Dantzker and Ronald D. Hunter, *Research Methods for Criminology and Criminal Justice: A Primer* (Boston: Butterworth Heinemann, 2000).

9. National Advisory Committee on Criminal Justice Standards and Goals, *Criminal Justice Research and Development: Report of the Task Force on Criminal Justice Research and Development* (Washington, DC: LEAA, 1976), p. 52. For an excellent brief review and summary of evaluation research focused on crime prevention, see Lawrence W. Sherman, Denise C. Gottfredson, Doris L. MacKenzie, John Eck, Peter Reuter, and Shawn D. Bushway, "Preventing Crime: What Works, What Doesn't, What's Promising," *Research in Brief* (Washington, DC: NIJ, 1998).

10. For more information on prediction research, see Thomas Gabor, *Prediction of Criminal Behavior* (Toronto: University of Toronto Press, 1986) and Glen D. Walters, *Foundations of Criminal Sciences. Volume II: The Uses of Knowledge* (New York: Praeger, 1992).

2

Perspectives and Research

To appreciate both the power and the limitations of scientific research methods, we need to understand our dependence on perspectives. In this chapter, we discuss the nature and functions of perspectives in general, and of social-science perspectives in particular.

WHAT IS A PERSPECTIVE?

In responding to their environments, humans typically assume that the world *is* as they *perceive* it. Of course, in a general sense, our actions must be guided by our sensory perceptions because, presumably, we have no other way of knowing about the environment in which we live. Yet, we all have had experiences that make us wary of trusting completely in our perceptions. Becoming acquainted with people of a different culture or having difficulty communicating with people in our own culture can reveal the limitations of our perceptions. Have you ever greeted one of your friends as you passed on the street, only to discover that you had mistaken a stranger for that friend? Experiences of this kind demonstrate that, although we depend on our senses to guide our interpretations of reality, the information they convey and the interpretations we make are sometimes inaccurate. Furthermore, even when they are accurate they reflect only some aspects of the world around us. A

perspective shapes, selects, and organizes our sensory experiences. The selective and organizational aspects of perspectives are rooted in both our bio-physiology and our language.

Suppose we could transform ourselves into newborn infants whose only knowledge consisted of a jumble of fleeting sensations of varying duration and intensity. It would be difficult for us to tell where we stopped and the rest of the world began. None of our experiences would have meaning. The philosopher-psychologist William James described the world experienced in this way as a "blooming, buzzing confusion."[1]

As we mature, we learn to make sense of the world. Patterns in sensations that tend to occur together are recognized, distinguished from each other, and responded to in different ways. As the process of selecting and organizing sensory information becomes more sophisticated, we learn that some sensations seem to come from within us whereas others come from our environment. We learn, in effect, that we are a part of, but distinguishable from, our environment.

Our senses connect us with the outside world, but imperfectly. Our physiologically limited senses transmit only some of the stimuli that impinge on us. For example, we cannot directly observe the ultraviolet zone of the light spectrum, hear high-pitched whistles that dogs can, or detect odors that many animals can smell. Furthermore, as a species, some of our senses are more important than others. We depend a great deal more on visual and auditory stimuli than on our other senses, for example. As a result, the information acquired through our senses is at best incomplete. Still, whatever their physiological limitations or built-in predispositions, our senses are the only means initially available to us for relating to the world. For each of us, the world becomes the patterns of sensations we learn to recognize.

Among the environmental events that make an impression on our senses is the spoken **language** of our fellow humans. As infants, we learn to recognize and repeat sounds and eventually to associate these sounds with other patterns of sensation. We are taught that things have names, that certain sounds stand for particular objects and events in our experience. As we learn to organize these sounds into larger and larger units, we rely more and more on language as our primary means of communicating. Eventually, we take language for granted. Precisely because we do, we are apt to miss the significant role language plays in our perceptions. We are inclined to believe that the language we use completely and accurately reflects the world as it really is. However, this impression is dangerously misleading, especially for the researcher.

Why is it misleading? A language system comes to each of us prepackaged. We do not invent it ourselves; we learn it from others. Because words learned from others stand for objects and events in *their* experience, the world, in a very important sense, also comes to us prepackaged. When we acquire a language, we acquire a culture as well, and with them comes a framework for perceiving and interpreting reality. Put another way, what we observe is a function *both* of what is actually "out there" in the real world and of how our language (and the associated cultural expectations) as well as the varying acuity of our different senses predispose us to perceived what is "out there." We are not just passive recipients of information about the real world delivered via our senses; rather, we are active observers, selecting and at least partly transforming what we perceive. Language directs our attention, sensitizes us to different aspects of our experience, and shapes our thoughts. The philosopher George Herbert Mead expressed these ideas by saying that language *mediates* (indicating influence traveling in both directions) almost all of our relationships with, including our perceptions of, the world.[2]

Although we are not accustomed to thinking about it in this way, the English language is a perspective. English grammar makes a basic distinction between nouns (words for persons, places, and things) and verbs (action words). Sentences are constructed by linking a noun with a verb. To write or speak English, we are forced to make this distinction. As difficult as it is to understand for those of us who only speak English, linguists tell us that some languages do not have this noun-verb structure. Furthermore, even among languages that do, there are many differences in vocabulary. Swahili, Mandarin, Hopi, and all other languages are perspectives that reflect the cultures and histories within which they developed. Through its grammatical structure and its vocabulary, a language represents one particular way of conceiving the world. As users of a particular language, we *perceive* the world largely in accordance with how, through that language, we *conceive* it.

The general characteristics of a perspective are familiar to us in everyday life. We say, for example, that two photographs, one taken from a point above an object and the other from below it, provide two different perspectives on the same object. Likewise, a conservative and a liberal columnist may have different points of view about the same social issue.

Thomas Kuhn, in his now-classic work, *The Structure of Scientific Revolutions*, referred to the major perspectives used in the sciences as "paradigms."[3] His study of the history of science showed how a particular perspective would dominate the theorizing and research in a particular discipline for a time, and then (often not because the accumulating evidence required it but as one generation of scientists replaced another), a "paradigm shift" would occur, with the new paradigm emphasizing different theoretical issues and variables as well as alternative modes of research. In recent years, for example, the evolutionary and bio-genetic paradigm for explaining human behavior has gained ground at the expense of other paradigms (for instance, economic and sociocultural learning theories) in many areas of study, including criminology.

On a more mundane level, consider how a variety of individuals, each having a particular perspective, might analyze events occurring as a group of people frolic in and around a swimming pool. A physicist might focus on the mechanics of the waves in the pool, the pressure the water exerts on the side of the pool, the relative density of objects in the water (including the bodies of the swimmers), the elastic properties of the diving board, the force with which it propels the swimmer into the air, the diver's mass, center of gravity, and momentum, the height reached in the dive, the acceleration achieved on descent, and the friction of the air and water on the swimmer's body.

A Christian minister might concentrate on the morality of the behavior of the people at the pool, the vocabulary used, the swimming apparel worn (or not worn, as the case may be), the extent to which sin, love, and charity are manifested, and the importance of these behaviors for the person's soul, salvation, and redemption.

The perspective of the sociologist could lead to inquiries about the social class of the persons at the pool, the status and roles assumed and enacted, the social selves projected, the strategies employed to protect self-images, the social pressures exerted on particular members of cliques, and the norms guiding behavior.

A lifeguard on duty at the pool will focus on activities that might cause injury to those using the pool: pushing or jostling, especially near the edge of the pool. Only one person at a time will be allowed on a diving board. Special attention will be paid to any signs of a swimmer in distress. In short, the lifeguard's perspective will be shaped by his or her responsibilities as rule enforcer and life saver.

A police officer might watch who hangs around with whom in order to identify networks of juveniles who the officer suspects may be involved in delinquent activities. The pool and its surroundings might also be a place where criminal activities, such as drug sales, take place. The officer will be alert for evidence that such activities are occurring. The officer's perspective, like that of the lifeguard, is shaped by his or her role as a rule enforcer, but the officer's perspective focuses on different activities and different rules.

Similarly, in a courtroom, the accused, the victim, the prosecuting attorney, the counsel for the defense, the judge, and each jury member may have very different perspectives on the same set of events. The chief administrator, the supervisor, the secretary, and the janitor of a criminal justice agency may perceive the agency in very different ways. Researchers may see the same courtroom or criminal justice agency in still other ways.

Note that each of these observers, making use of a different perspective, observes different aspects of the same events, making certain aspects salient while deemphasizing others. Thus, a social scientist attempting to explain a given set of events from a social-science perspective would likely ignore the observations and explanations that a physicist, lifeguard, minister, or police officer might regard as crucial. We know it is not possible for any of us as observers to pay attention to everything at once, but we may easily become so captivated by our own perspective that we forget that it selects *out* as well as in. Any perspective represents only one of many possible worldviews.

Perhaps you feel that the existence of several different worldviews is not in itself problematic—and you are probably right, for different perspectives can be compatible. The swimmer's social class presumably has nothing to do with the rate of acceleration achieved in a dive. The fact that the sociological perspective includes social class and excludes the rate of acceleration as relevant variables does not mean that the sociologist's observations are inaccurate. It simply means that the sociologist's perspective may lead him to select different aspects of events for observation and analysis than would a physicist. The observations and explanations of the physicist can, in most instances, exist side by side with those of the sociologist without obliging us to choose one or the other as the best or most accurate. Which perspective is best or most accurate depends in large part upon the interests or purposes of a particular observer at a particular time.

But suppose two perspectives on the same phenomena lead to significantly different conclusions. Under these circumstances, it becomes very important to ask which perspective is better. Whether it is the perspective of the defense or the prosecuting attorney that prevails in a courtroom will surely make a great deal of difference to those involved, especially the defendant. The biologist who believes that criminal behavior is genetically determined and the sociologist who believes that criminal behavior is a product of the social structure and environment would ask different research questions, investigate different aspects of the problem, and probably find different answers to the question of what causes criminal behavior. Research undertaken from one perspective may suggest that severe punishment has a greater deterrent effect on crime, whereas research done from another perspective might suggest that the severity of punishment is unrelated to deterrence. Whether we are laypersons, criminal justice practitioners, or researchers, both the questions we ask and the answers we get are, to a very great extent, shaped by the particular perspective we employ.

DIFFERENT KINDS OF LANGUAGE

Because language shapes the perspectives we use in everyday life and in science as well, it will be useful to distinguish among some different kinds of language.[4] Statements may be separated into two general categories: consensual and nonconsensual. **Consensual statements** are indicative of some person, object, or event in the world external to the speaker or writer and, therefore, are capable of consensual validation, that is, agreement among observers. The meaning of consensual statements is easily shared among those who speak the same language and readily taught to new speakers. If disagreements about the meaning arise, they can usually be resolved quickly by pointing to referents, for example, that all parties to the dispute can observe. Examples of consensual statements include:

There were forty-nine arrests for OMVI in March of 1997.

The suspect was 25 years old at the time of arrest.

The Chief of Police resides in the city limits.

Twenty-three percent of the juveniles tested positive for marijuana use.

Lighting a parking lot at night reduces theft from vehicles.

The hypotheses scientists test should be formulated so as to be as consensual as possible. Empiricism in science depends on having such statements with which to work. Note, however, that a consensual statement may or may not be true. Determining whether evidence supports the accuracy of consensual statements is the heart of scientific research.

Nonconsensual statements refer to phenomena that are not directly observable and about which it is, therefore, necessary to make inferences or interpretations. For example, we cannot see another person's internal psychological state, but we often attribute such states to a person on the basis of what we can observe about his verbal or nonverbal behavior, the context, and so on. Nonconsensual statements may be divided into two categories: interpretive/inferential and evaluative.

Interpretive/inferential statements refer to motivations, intentions, moods, and emotions. Examples include:

He was very angry.

She was hallucinating.

Her curiosity was aroused.

He clearly intended to kill his brother.

Fear of punishment deters crime.

Note that we might ask, How do you know he was very angry? The response might be cast in more consensual language: He was red in the face, he yelled loudly, and he hit the table with his clenched fist. But we cannot be very sure that the person was really angry; he may have been pretending, or he may have been uncontrollably grief stricken, and so on. Because the internal state is not accessible to the outside observer, inference is required and consensual validation is difficult.

Many scientific theorists and researchers, especially those inclined toward qualitative methods, use interpretive/inferential language often in their work. One way of managing the inevitable ambiguity in such statements is using what we will later call **operational definitions**—that is, definitions that are cast in as much consensual language as possible. As with consensual statements, the accuracy of interpretative statements is a separate question, one that may be addressed through research.

Evaluative statements convey value-based assessments or judgments about some phenomena. Assertions about behavioral morality (should/should not or must/must not statements) as well as style or taste in art or fashion are examples of evaluative language. These statements typically require a great deal of elaboration or additional explanation in order to clarify and convey the meaning intended by the speaker or writer; consensual validation is very difficult. Examples of evaluative statements include:

Thou shalt not kill.

The law of private property is immoral.

Jane is an excellent law enforcement officer.

Marxist theory is better than most other theories in accounting for crime.

Criminal justice students are cool.

Once again, we might ask, Why do you think Jane is an excellent officer? The answer might come back, at least partially, in consensual language, specifying objective criteria for earning the excellent evaluation. Sometimes, though, evaluations rest, in part, on irreducible value choices or preferences.

Researchers use evaluative language, too. They often have value-based preferences for certain perspectives or theories. They may render professional assessments of programs or policies through evaluation research. Although good research provides the basis for such assessments, observations or numbers never "speak for themselves." Research results must be interpreted and evaluated to complete the assessment.

A statement may contain words or phrases of all the types. Critical readers/listeners will try to sort them out and substitute more consensual terminology for the more interpretive or evaluative elements, especially if the statement is a research hypothesis. The divisions among language types are ones of degree, and words or sentences sometimes straddle the category boundaries. Nevertheless, we should be alert for some of the different language types used, both inside and outside science, and become more self-conscious about the kind of language we use in designing, executing, and reporting on our own research projects.

PRINCIPLES OF A SCIENTIFIC PERSPECTIVE

Robert Bierstedt has observed that "as a method of approach to the investigation of any phenomenon whatever, science implies primarily an attitude of mind, an attitude distinguished by adherence to several principles."[5] These principles are empiricism, objectivity, tentativeness, skepticism, ethical neutrality, parsimony, determinism, publication, and replication. Although science can be seen either as a method of acquiring knowledge (process) or as a compendium of acquired knowledge (product), in this book we are primarily concerned with it as a process. With this definition of science in mind, let us examine some of the principles characteristic of a scientific perspective.

Empiricism

The first principle, **empiricism,** emphasizes the role of the senses (sight, hearing, touch, and so on) in scientific research. In the comfort of her office chair, a scientist might create many interesting, plausible ideas about what influences an officer's decision to arrest rather than warn a traffic violator. Empiricism, however, requires that she actually observe officer-driver encounters in order to test the adequacy of her ideas. The more direct the observation, the better. Witnessing the encounters as they occur, for example, would be preferable to interviewing the officers about what influences them; combining these two approaches may be even better. Although the formative and selective aspects of a particular perspective cannot be eliminated (the scientist still selects what will be studied and how it will be studied), scientists must constantly verify their theories and conclusions through careful direct observations. Insisting upon empirical verification provides a powerful—though as we will see in the next section, decidedly *not* infallible—check on theories that are exciting and make sense but do not reflect what can be observed.

Objectivity

The nature of **objectivity** and the legitimacy of scientists' claims to be objective are hotly debated both within the scientific community and outside it. The major issues involved are not new, nor have they been entirely resolved. We have already touched on some of them in Chapter 1 and earlier in this chapter as well; we will, of necessity, return to them in later sections of this chapter and from time to time throughout the book. Here we will only suggest what we think are a few of the more crucial issues in this debate and our positions on them. More elaborate discussions may be found elsewhere.[6]

Objectivity is usually defined in contrast with subjectivity. Unfortunately, this word, too, has many different meanings. In general though, **subjectivity** denotes bias or distortion—some interference operating between the external world and our conscious apprehension of it. Defined in this way, it seems to us there are four kinds of subjectivity that merit discrimination.

One type of subjectivity—we'll call it **species-based subjectivity**—arises from our very nature as human beings and has three aspects. First, each of us is the center of our own experiences. I am not connected to your central nervous system, nor are you to mine. I cannot directly experience what you experience. Scientists' work, like that of every other human being, is inevitably subjective in this sense of the word.

As we noted earlier in this chapter, though, through our collective creation of language we can create communities and communicate with one another about our experiences. In this admittedly limited but essential way, our experiences and observations are sharable.

Another aspect of species subjectivity is a function of the bio-physiological limitations of our senses (our senses are capable of transmitting to our consciousness only certain ranges of the sound and light spectra, for example) and of the unequal distribution of our central nervous system's resources to different kinds of sensory information (for example, we are primarily a visual species; our olfactory senses are very limited). Although we have invented instruments that extend the range of some of our sensory capabilities, this too is a kind of subjectivity none of us can entirely escape.

Still another aspect of species subjectivity arises from the partly built-in and partly acquired propensity of our minds to more readily recognize certain patterns of sensations, to organize our sensory input in certain ways, and to "make" us perceive/believe that complete patterns are there "in reality" when they are not. Gestalt psychologists use intriguing examples to demonstrate these phenomena (for example, the vase that turns into two faces, the apparently parallel lines that are not, the incomplete circle that we perceive as complete). Cross-cultural research suggests that many of these patterns of perception and misperception are human universals—just part of the way the human senses and brain/mind work. But we also know that we can learn to *expect* to perceive something and then think we have in fact perceived it when it is not there or things did not happen as we saw them. You may have read about the classroom exercise where someone enters the room, shouts some angry words, fires a gun, and exits quickly. Class members' descriptions of the shooter and their accounts of what happened differ, sometimes quite dramatically, partly because they were paying attention to different aspects of the scene and partly because each was filling in gaps according to what she expected to occur in such a situation. For many of the same reasons, we should have much less faith in the accuracy of eye witness accounts of crime than we do. In any event, scientists are no different from other humans in being subject to this kind of subjectivity. Still, the very fact that we have recognized our susceptibility to these tricks our senses and minds play on us means that we can take steps to compensate for them—for example, by making permanent records (pictures, films, audio or video recordings) to which we can return for close inspection or invite others to view and offer second opinions.

In the second type of subjectivity—we'll call it *verstehen* **subjectivity**—being subjective means exercising empathy (that is, practicing the qualitative researchers' strategy of interpretive understanding), getting inside the consciousness of the other person, experiencing the world as he does and understanding his motives, feelings, and thoughts. We all use interpretive understanding when we interact with others; nevertheless, it is at best a tricky business. Unless one assumes telepathic powers, our interpretive understanding must be inferred in large part from observable phenomena—what the person says and does. If we are honest, we must admit that we sometimes infer incorrectly. And how do we know we have been mistaken? Usually, we observe that the person's subsequent behavior doesn't conform with our *verstehen*-derived expectations. Here, too, something observable (the behavior) is the key to confirming or negating our interpretive understanding.

A third meaning of subjectivity, **perspectival subjectivity,** also derives from an inevitable aspect of the human condition that we noted in our discussion earlier in this chapter. Our observations are almost always made through the mediation of a language-based perspective that shapes, selects, and organizes. In this sense, direct observation is not possible for any of us: neither is the kind of objectivity that requires such observations.

But consider this: If I know and can use only one perspective for examining a particular phenomenon, then I am, in effect, a prisoner of that perspective. I have no other way of selecting and organizing my perceptions, and I am quite likely to think that my perspective is the only one possible, the "natural" and "correct" one. However, from the point of view of another with a different perspective, I would appear narrow-minded and hopelessly subjective. If she will teach me her perspective, though, I may be able to think in different ways and see new aspects. Thus, although I may not be able to escape working from a perspective, I am surely not limited to using just one. I can switch perspectives or combine them (if they are not entirely incompatible) or use one perspective to critique research guided by another. When I use multiple perspectives in any or all of these ways, I escape at least some of the limitations of any one perspective.

The final kind of subjectivity, which we'll call **volitional subjectivity,** is rooted in the capacity of humans to choose and to articulate the bases on which their choices have been made. Choice implies values—that is, judgments about what is better or worse, good or evil, uplifting or degrading, justice serving or injustice serving among the options available to us. In the context of the social sciences in general and criminal justice studies in particular, the role of values can be illuminated by examining the impact of ideologies on theory and research. Questions such as the one raised by Howard Becker, "Whose side are we on?" suggest some of the issues raised by this kind of subjectivity.[7] Political conservatives, for instance, are likely to emphasize different aspects of criminal activity and different sorts of solutions to crime problems than are liberals or radicals.

As researchers, can we escape ideologically rooted values and the subjective biases inherent in them? Must we be on one side or the other? Can science, in this sense, be value free? Even if it could, would we want it to be? We probably cannot escape some value-based preferences and would not want to if we could. After all, each of us must decide what is important enough to study and how best to study it. Ideology often plays a large and legitimate role in these decisions. But just as we can choose a favorite ideological orientation, we can also choose to be reflexive about our choice—that is, to be aware of ourselves as choice makers and as capable of choosing differently; to remind ourselves constantly of the underlying assumptions on which our preferred ideology and research methodology rest; to acknowledge their limitations as well as their strengths. In case our love for a particular perspective or method blinds us to some of its shortcomings (as it almost certainly will), we can take others' criticisms of our work seriously. In short, in our view the principle of objectivity in science does not—and cannot—mean completely undistorted or unbiased observations. Furthermore, objectivity is not an either-or affair; it is rather a matter of degrees. To enhance our objectivity, we can rely heavily on empirical observation, use multiple perspectives, use consensually validated language, and be both aware and critical of our own values, points of view, and strategic preferences. We can specify what evidence would contradict our hypotheses and actively search for that evidence. And we can join with others in the scientific community in mutual debate about the strengths and limitations of our theories and research. In these ways we partially legitimate our claims to some degree of scientific objectivity.

Science, it is often said, concerns itself with "hard facts." If some kinds of subjectivity (and probably others of which we are unaware) are indeed unavoidable, the hard facts of science are a little less firm than we often suppose. But that should come as no surprise; scientific knowledge claims should always be regarded as tentative. As scientists, we should be acutely aware of our shortcomings as seekers of knowledge, making a concerted effort to overcome them when possible through the application of well-established procedures and safeguards. That is what the disciplined inquiry we call science is all about!

Tentativeness

For reasons we have just cited in our discussion of objectivity, the principle of **tentativeness** encourages scientists not to consider their conclusions as permanent, universal, absolute truths. Instead, they assume that their conclusions are subject to change as more evidence is available and/or new theories are developed. Careful scientists not only attempt to specify the precise set of conditions under which their findings may be expected to hold, but also they look for cases that do not support their conclusions. If they discover such cases, they either reject their previous conclusions or modify their statements to account for these discrepancies.

Skepticism

The search for disconfirming evidence and the scientist's unwillingness to believe he knows the final, absolute truth are closely related to the fourth principle characteristic of the scientific perspective, **skepticism.** As skeptics, scientists are willing to question almost everything, especially common sense and common knowledge, accepting little at face value and looking beneath the surface in an attempt to determine for themselves the validity of an argument or conclusion.

Ethical Neutrality

By applying the principle of **ethical neutrality,** scientists try not to permit their moral or ethical beliefs to influence their data gathering or their analysis. As researchers, scientists are concerned only with what is true or false, not what is right or wrong, good or bad. Maintaining ethical neutrality during the research process does not prevent the scientist from using his moral sensibilities to identify research questions worth pursuing or from using his moral perspective to assess the implications of his findings. Furthermore, as we note later in this chapter, the researcher must be concerned with the ethics of the research process itself. However, when the researcher makes moral judgments about phenomena during the investigation, other principles of the scientific perspective, such as objectivity, tentativeness, and skepticism, are threatened.[8]

Parsimony

Upholding the principle of **parsimony** means getting the most for the least. Presented with two theories that explain some phenomenon equally well (that is, their degree of empirical support is equally strong) but one is more complex (for example, more variables, more complex relationships among them) than the other, the simpler one is preferred.

Determinism

Determinism, which is closely related to the concepts of cause and effect, means that every event is preceded by one or more other events that cause it to occur.

Actually, we have some reservations about including strict determinism as a principle of science. To be sure, science assumes that connections of some kind exist among events in a real world. Whether those connections are best described as deterministic, however, is a matter of considerable controversy in the contemporary philosophy of science. We agree with some philosophers of science who suspect that a probabilistic rather than a deterministic principle is more appropriate. The probabilistic principle holds that the best we can hope for in the physical or social sciences is a statement that there is some probability that event x is connected to event y. Perhaps the necessity of relying on probabilistic statements is attributable to the inadequacies of our research methods or to the limitations of our current state of knowledge. But it is also possible that this uncertainty is due to the very nature of the empirical world itself. At least for the moment, there seems no way of resolving the dilemma, and there is no need to settle it. For our purposes here, we can treat reality as if it were deterministic and settle for probabilistic approximations, bearing in mind that if we insist on an underlying determinism, we may ultimately be frustrated.

Publication

Research reports typically contain a detailed account of the research project—including theory, research design, research questions or hypotheses, subject selection, data-gathering instruments and/or strategies, data analysis, findings, and the researchers' interpretations of those results. **Publication** of research reports serves several functions in science.

One function (which includes written reports, oral presentations at professional gatherings, and distribution on the Internet) is the dissemination of what the authors claim is new knowledge. In this context, the report may be viewed as an *argument;* authors give colleagues their conclusions and try to persuade them to accept those conclusions by describing how and why they (the authors) came to accept them. Others who accept the researchers' argument may apply the findings in their own work settings or add the findings to their own theory-building efforts. Whether we accept the authors' conclusions depends on the strength of the argument offered and on whether the results can be confirmed by other researchers.

Two additional functions of publication are to provide sufficient detail so that others can critique all aspects of the research process (the argument) and/or do their own study to see if their results are the same. The latter is called replication and will be addressed in the next section. The former involves the important community aspect of science. There is no such thing in science as the perfect experiment or study. Sources of bias and distortion are too ubiquitous and too easily missed in any human endeavor. The hope is that by subjecting the research to the critical appraisal of colleagues and other interested parties, at least some of the possible biases can be identified and their impacts explored in subsequent research. In fact, many of the most prestigious journals and book publishers insist on peer or colleague reviews for help in selecting research reports for publication and, if selected, for suggesting (sometimes requiring) changes in the data analysis and/or discussion of results to ameliorate the criticisms of peer reviewers. Scientific knowledge is, in this important sense, developed in and fostered by a community of scholars. As in any community, the scholarly one is full of large egos, deep prejudices, vested interests, and power struggles that interfere with the scientific enterprise.

But it can also be the site of carefully informed, self-reflective, ethically ground-ed, and enormously creative, collaborative scientific work.

Replication

The principle of **replication** is another way of acknowledging that peculiar things can happen in any research project. Other researchers are encouraged to repeat a particular research project to determine if different researchers in different settings with different samples or populations get similar or different results. If the findings of the original research project are confirmed, confi-dence in the results is strengthened. No single study should be regarded as definitive. When major decisions are at stake and time permits, it is best to wait for the accumulation of evidence provided by multiple replications and, where possible, some triangulation (that is, examining the same issue or hypothesis using different research strategies and procedures) as well.

Science as a process, then, may be defined as a systematic search for the most accurate and complete description and/or explanation of events, relying on the principles of empiricism, objectivity, tentativeness, skepticism, ethical neutrality, parsimony, a modified version of determinism, publication, and replication as guides.

SOCIAL SCIENCE AS SCIENCE

Most criminal justice research involves social science research, which is based upon adherence to the principles of the scientific perspective we have just out-lined and the methods discussed in the following chapters. Although the nature of the subject matter and the research techniques social scientists use may differ from those used by natural scientists, both are based on scientific principles.

A sociologist, for example, can imagine herself in the place of the per-sons she is studying in order to better understand their behavior and formu-late research questions. She recognizes that both she and her subjects are unique and can influence and be influenced by each other. On the other hand, a chemist cannot imagine herself to be an atom, nor can the atom imagine being her; she does not have to be concerned about the atom's influ-ence on her, or hers on it, as a problem of human interaction. (She clearly does, of course, have to be concerned about the possible influences of the machinery and techniques she uses to study it, but that is not an interactive process in which mutual influence can determine the nature of the relation-ship.) When a criminologist asks respondents questions, she must be con-cerned about whether they understand the questions and whether their responses are honest. The chemist knows that the atom cannot deliberately deceive her. Nonetheless, if both the criminologist and the chemist are attempting to be objective, ethically neutral, skeptical, and parsimonious, if both regard their conclusions as tentative and search for disconfirming empirical evidence, and if they publish their findings and encourage replica-tion, both are employing a scientific perspective.

Any given perspective is composed of a set of words (concepts) that guide observation and thought. In the case of the sciences, some of these words are common to all of the perspectives, whereas others are unique to certain categories of science. For example, the word *theory* is common to all scientific enterprise (and to other types of enterprise as well). Most scientists would agree that a theory is a set of logically interrelated propositions (hypotheses) that describes and explains some phenomenon, and that these propositions consist of asserted relationships between concepts or variables. Most scientists would also agree that *concepts* and variables represent selected characteristics of persons, events, objects, or ideas, and that the term *scientific method* refers to the application of scientific principles to a set of procedures for gathering and analyzing information.

Although many of the terms used by natural scientists are recognized by laypersons as technical and specialized, social scientists often use words that are part of almost everyone's vocabulary. Words such as *role, culture, society, norm, bureaucracy, gang,* and *delinquent* are often found in social science research reports; because they are familiar, laypersons often think that social scientists are simply repeating common knowledge. We all "know" that an actor plays a role while on stage, that a person who attends symphony concerts is cultured, that we live in a society, and that norms are rules that normal people follow. Misunderstandings arise, however, because social scientists attach different, specialized meanings to these same words. When sociologists use the term *role,* they may be referring to a set of expectations attached to a particular position in a particular social system; when they speak of culture, they may well be identifying the totality of knowledge, objects, and behavior patterns acquired by a group of people and passed on from generation to generation by means other than genetic inheritance. When they speak of society, they may be examining two or more people and the physical and symbolic interactions among them; and when they speak of norms, they are probably alluding to at least three types of regulations governing human behavior—folkways, mores, and laws. In comparison, *symbiosis, oxide, ionization,* and *photosynthesis,* which are used in the physical sciences, are immediately recognizable as technical terms with special scientific meanings.

The claim that information provided by the social scientist is little more than common sense is also deceiving in another way. It is true that most of us have learned a great deal about human behavior. But, the fact that social science often tells us things we already know is not as important as the fact that the information was obtained by scientific methods. How much confidence we have in knowledge depends a great deal on the method by which we obtained it. Scientific study has often demonstrated that common knowledge is not true. Until the days of Columbus, almost everyone believed that the world was flat. Not long ago, most people believed that mental illness was caused by demons.

Consider the following assertion: "During World War II, southern Black enlisted men preferred northern White officers to southern White officers." This assertion seems to make sense. We may reason that northern Whites were more likely to be sympathetic to the idea of equality of treatment than southern Whites and, therefore, Black enlisted men could expect less discrimination from northern than from southern White officers. Obvious! However, consider this assertion: "During World War II, southern Black enlisted men preferred southern White officers to northern White officers." This assertion, too, makes sense, because southern Blacks were more accustomed to interacting with southern Whites than with northern Whites, knew how to conduct such interaction, and were more comfortable interacting because they could predict the officers' expectations. Obvious! Although a study by Samuel Stouffer found the former to be the case,[9] either conclusion would be easy to explain in terms of common sense.

Similarly, many laypersons believe that police officers are attracted to police work because they like to order people around. They also believe that officers spend most of their time solving crimes and pursuing criminals. However, studies indicate that most candidates for law enforcement jobs choose police work as an opportunity to help others and that most patrol officers spend well over three-fourths of their time simply riding or walking their beats and responding to requests for assistance that have nothing at all to do with criminal activities.[10]

The point is, information provided by the social scientist often seems obvious to us *after* it is made available. If the information agrees with our predispositions, we think it obvious; if it runs counter to them, it seems unscientific. For this reason, many are inclined to be less impressed by the conclusions reached in social science research (or more inclined to disregard them if we disagree with them) than by the conclusions reached by research in the physical or natural sciences. To understand social science as a *science*, then, we must understand the special nature of its subjects, the technical meanings it assigns to ordinary words, and the credibility of findings obtained through scientific research.

AN EXAMPLE OF A SOCIAL SCIENCE PERSPECTIVE: SYMBOLIC INTERACTIONISM

Symbolic interactionism, one of several schools of thought in the social sciences, is a set of related concepts purporting to describe and explain certain aspects of human behavior. Researchers using this perspective often use qualitative methods. The basic assumptions of the symbolic interactionist perspective can be stated as follows. Humans are unique animals; they display enormous behavioral variability and they depend on learning rather than biological instincts as the primary mechanism for adjusting to their environment. The most significant difference between humans and other animals is the means by which they communicate—language. Language is a symbolic system. Linguistic symbols are arbitrary sounds or physical gestures to which people, by mutual agreement, attach significance or meaning. When a person uses a symbol to communicate with another person, the symbol means approximately the same thing to the speaker as it does to the hearer. People constantly invent new symbols to refer to new or different aspects of their environment. In that sense, human language is an open system. The communication systems of most other animals are very limited in scope and closed in the sense that, whether or not learning is an important factor in their development, the systems are composed of a small, fixed number of gestures, noises, and so on that show little if any change over time.

Almost all human experience is mediated by symbols. Put somewhat differently, we live in a world composed not of real but of symbolic objects. When we use language, we create symbolic objects for ourselves and then respond to the symbolic objects we have created as if they were real. That is, we categorize and attach names to objects and respond to the name we assign to the object instead of to the object itself.

A symbolic interactionist's analysis of the conversation of two people might proceed as follows. When two people (symbolic interactionists call them *actors*) are in the same place at the same time, they usually *interact*. That is, each recognizes the presence of the *other* and adjusts his or her behavior accordingly. This mutual adjustment of behaviors involves each of the actors formulating a *self-concept,* presenting the self to the other, *taking the role of the other,* and attributing a self to the other. An actor's self-concept and the self he attributes to the other actor are symbolic. That is, an actor defines himself and the other by placing each in particular categories according to sex, occupation, personality characteristics (for example, friendly, suspicious), or moods (happy, sad). Having attributed a self to himself and the other, the actor imagines himself to be that other in order to anticipate the other's behavior, and hence plan his own *line of action* during the interaction. Through his line of action, the actor presents his self to the other. The other is, of course, also an actor and is engaging in the same processes with respect to *his* other (our original actor). Each continually revises the symbolic self he claims through his line of action and the symbolic self he attributes to the other. Hence, by a process of negotiation, the interactants almost always arrive at a consensual *definition of the situation* that includes the roles and selves appropriate in this situation.

According to symbolic interactionists, it is possible to analyze any human interaction in these terms. The meeting between an officer and a juvenile on a street corner, the interrogation of a suspect, a conference between a parole officer and a parolee, and the questioning of a witness by an attorney in a court of law might each be observed, described, and analyzed using this perspective.

An example of the symbolic interactionist approach to research is Erving Goffman's book *Asylums*.[11] Goffman was interested in studying life in what he refers to as *total institutions,* places of "residence and work where a large number of like-situated individuals, cut off from the larger society for an appreciable period of time, together lead an enclosed, formally administered round of life."[12] Total institutions include mental hospitals, prisons, monasteries, and juvenile homes. In his research carried out at St. Elizabeth's, a mental hospital in Washington, DC, his objective was to learn about the social world of the institution as subjectively experienced by its inmates. He began with the assumptions that any group of inmates in a total institution

> develop a life of their own that becomes meaningful, reasonable, and
> normal once you get close to it; and that a good way to learn about any

of these worlds is to submit oneself in the company of members to the daily round of petty contingencies to which they are subject.[13]

Thus, Goffman assumed the role of an assistant at the hospital and passed the day with patients while trying to avoid being identified with staff. Combining his observations with those made by researchers studying other total institutions, Goffman was able to say a great deal about the characteristics of total institutions and what he calls the "underlife" that exists among inmates. For example, he found that inmates have what he refers to as a "moral career" in the institution, during which a number of changes routinely occur. Their self-concepts change dramatically when they realize that decisions about personal hygiene, sleeping, eating, and working are now being made by others. Inmates are stripped of their previous identities (their hair is cut, they wear uniforms) and are treated in much the same way we treat a child. Inmates learn an institutional lingo (the vocabulary by which their selves are defined) and a line of action that allow them to maintain some sense of personal dignity while still apparently adhering to institutional rules and enacting the roles the institution prescribes.

As a result of Goffman's research, we learned a great deal about inmate life not only in mental hospitals but in other total institutions as well. Many of his conclusions confirmed the results of prior research, while his somewhat unique approach gave us greater insight into both the symbolic and physical processing and life of inmates.

Like all perspectives, the concepts and assumptions of the symbolic interactionist perspective are selective, emphasizing certain aspects of the situation being studied and organizing the observations for the investigator. A given perspective generates answers to some of the questions one might ask about a phenomenon, but is, by definition, limited in scope, though some are more limited than others. Science, for example, is a fairly comprehensive perspective composed of several more limited perspectives (*social* sciences, *natural* sciences, and so on). Each of these contains yet more limited perspectives. Thus, symbolic interactionism is one perspective within the sociological perspective within the social-science perspective within the scientific perspective. In principle, at least, more limited perspectives must meet the same general requirements as the broader perspectives of which they are a part. Thus, social science must meet all the requirements of the scientific perspective.

OTHER PERSPECTIVES IN CRIMINAL JUSTICE STUDIES

As you have no doubt discovered in your previous work, criminal justice studies is characterized by many different points of view. An examination of any introduction to criminal justice or criminology textbook will reveal several contemporary perspectives besides symbolic interactionism. Included among them might be behaviorist, biogenetic, psychoanalytic, psychological, social control, social learning, social constructionist, labeling, conflict (Marxist and others), and urban ecology perspectives, as well as structural-functional, rational choice, routine activities, feminist, and critical theories. Of course, as we noted earlier, any one person can use several different perspectives, a variety of perspectives can be applied to a single issue, and perspectives may or may not conflict with each other.

THEORY

One way of viewing a perspective such as symbolic interactionism is to see it as a kind of theory. A **theory** may be defined as a set of two or more related, empirically testable assertions (statements of alleged facts or relationships among facts) about a particular phenomenon. A theory serves as a symbolic guide to the observation, interpretation, and explanation of phenomena in the empirical world.

Note that our definition of theory leaves considerable room for variation. Theories may differ in scope, degree of integration, and amount of empirical verification.

Scope

One theory may refer to a narrow range of phenomena whereas another is broader in scope. For example, a theory on the nature and consequences of plea bargaining has a smaller scope than a theory on the connection between the criminal justice system and the political system in American society.

Integration

Some theories consist of a relatively loose collection of concepts and assertions. The propositions of another theory may be tightly linked with one another, so that each proposition follows logically from the others. To construct a tightly knit theory is the goal toward which scientists strive. Some theories in the natural sciences have achieved such coherence and integration that they can be expressed in a series of closely related mathematical formulas. Although great progress has been made in the last fifty years, there are few theories in the social sciences that approach this level of development.

Verification

A theory consists of assertions or statements that are *symbolic* in nature. That is, they are humanly generated verbal or mathematical assertions of fact, and not fact themselves. Anyone can say anything; a mere verbalization does not make something true. A theoretical assertion is only a *claim* that something is true. Whether scientists accept a theoretical statement as true depends on how much empirical verification (evidence) supports the statement. Remember that scientists must always regard their research findings as tentative rather than absolute truths. But, research conducted according to scientific principles produces very persuasive evidence concerning the truth of an assertion.

Relationships Among Theory, Research, and Methodology

Although some theories have not been tested through research, others have had some empirical verification, and still others have been subjected to extensive empirical testing. Both theory and research are essential elements in the scientific pursuit of knowledge. Meaningful research cannot be conducted unless it is guided by a theory. A theory without empirical support is simply one person's claim or speculation, no better and no worse than any other person's claim or speculation.

Viewed in the context of science as process, the relationship between theory and research is dynamic. When research evidence fails to support a proposition in a theory, the theory must change to incorporate the evidence. The revised theory then must be tested and, in turn, either be confirmed or disconfirmed. If disconfirmed, the theory must be revised again. Research improves a theory, which leads to new research, which ideally tends to confirm the improvement in the theory. As a result, our confidence in the theory grows and scientific knowledge progresses.

The support or nonsupport of a particular proposition in a theory has implications for the other propositions in that theory. If evidence supports a proposition, confidence in the other proposition(s) of the theory is strengthened. This is more true for a tightly integrated theory than for a loosely connected one, and is a principal reason why scientists regard tightly integrated and parsimonious theories as better than loosely integrated ones. A more cohesive theory is easier to confirm or reject as a whole and permits a more dynamic relationship between theory and research.

Finally, note that our definition of theory specifies that propositions be *empirically testable*, implying that a particular methodology for testing the propositions is required. Although different methodologies exist, empirical tests demand scientific methodology, which follows the principles of empiricism, objectivity, tentativeness, skepticism, ethical neutrality, parsimony, determinism, publication, and replication.

Hence, we may say that there is an integral relationship among theory, research, and methodology. Only if research is performed according to the guidelines and principles of science can it be called scientific research. Only if research is scientific can it confirm or disconfirm an empirically testable proposition. Moreover, the application of scientific methodology gives the researcher confidence in the results of the research and in its implications for the theory that guided the research.

RESEARCH ETHICS

The scientist should maintain ethical neutrality toward the phenomena being investigated during research. In research about drug use, prostitution, organized crime, plea bargaining, sentencing practices, or the use of force by police, for instance, a researcher's personal moral judgments may cloud his observations, bias his conclusions, and otherwise interfere with achieving objectivity.

Therefore, the researcher should attempt to identify whatever moral preconceptions he holds and endeavor to set them aside during the research process.

There are, however, some ethical principles that should be very much
involved in the design and execution of a research project. These pertain not
to the subject matter but to the research process itself, including the human
relationships between researchers and the persons they study.

In selecting the scientific perspective as a way of viewing the world, and scientific methodology as a way of studying it, we make ethical commitments. We
have obligations to our subjects and to science. We must be concerned about
the right of our subjects to anonymity and confidentiality, to voluntary
informed consent, and to freedom from risk of harm.

Anonymity and Confidentiality

In almost all research, subjects have the right to remain anonymous. Protecting
anonymity can take different forms in different research projects. Sometimes
it means no one but the subject himself knows he participated. Usually,
though, at least someone else must know, either by virtue of the way the data
are gathered (for example, other respondents on a group-administered questionnaire or members of a group being studied by a field researcher) or
because the research design requires it (such as follow-up calls or questionnaires to first-round survey nonresponders). In some of these cases, protecting anonymity means not revealing the names of participants to anyone
beyond those research staffers who must know in order to execute the
research design (whose number should be kept to an absolute minimum,
with careful provisions for guarding any written, computer, or other records
where names and/or other codes associated with the names are stored). In
other instances, it means referring to participants by code number or letter
or pseudonyms (for example, false names—certainly for participants and usually for any other groups, institutions, locales, and so forth that might lead to
the identification of participants—made up by field researchers for use in
their research reports).

Maintaining **confidentiality** generally means preventing anyone from connecting the research participants' names with the information they provide to
the researcher, that is, their individual responses, statements, or actions. As
with anonymity, protecting confidentiality can take different forms. If a questionnaire or interview record does not include the respondent's name or any
other identifying information, confidentiality and anonymity are relatively easily maintained. Sometimes it is necessary for researchers to maintain some
traceable link, in which case numerical codes may be assigned to records, with
a master list carefully guarded by a designated staffer linking the record codes
with the corresponding respondents' names. In other cases, pseudonyms help
protect confidentiality as well as anonymity.

Ethical researchers carefully protect their subjects' identities and responses
because in most circumstances doing so encourages honest answers and/or
more genuine behavior and because failing to do so may bring harm to their
subjects. Suppose we ask a group of patrol officers to evaluate their immediate

supervisors. To encourage honest responses, we guarantee our respondents anonymity. Suppose further that, in reporting our results, we fail to disguise the identities of patrol officers sufficiently, and the supervisors, reading the research report, are able to identify them. The supervisors may subject those respondents who gave us honest but negative opinions to punitive treatment or refuse to recommend them for a promotion or a salary increase.

In addition to being injurious to respondents, failure to protect anonymity can have damaging consequences for the research enterprise as a whole. For example, other potential subjects may refuse to participate in future research projects if they find out that researchers have failed to protect confidentiality and anonymity of their participants.

Risk and Voluntary Informed Consent

We must also be concerned about other sorts of harm that may come to subjects as a result of the research procedures themselves. If there is the slightest risk to the psychological or physical health or safety of subjects in an investigation, the researcher has a moral obligation to inform subjects about all known risks and to obtain subjects' voluntary agreement to participate in the study.

It is ethically preferable to inform subjects that they are being observed. There are occasions, however, when it is scientifically advantageous to gather information without the knowledge or permission of the subjects. The researcher must be certain in those cases that the interests of the subjects are not compromised. Secret observations should be made only if there is no physical, mental, or social risk to those observed.

To further complicate the issue of **informed consent,** suppose we ask: Are all potential subjects equally capable of giving voluntary informed consent? The answer would seem to be no. Recently enacted regulations, for example, prohibit the use of prisoners in some research projects. The rationale for these regulations is that, because of their status as prisoners, inmates cannot be regarded as voluntary participants in a study. They may believe that their participation will increase the likelihood of early parole, or they may fear personal repercussions from prison authorities if they refuse to participate, for example. Furthermore, some prisoners as well as other potential subjects may be insufficiently educated or experienced to understand either the nature of research, the vocabulary used by the researcher to describe the research project, or any risks that may be associated with participation in it. It is difficult to argue, in such circumstances, that a person can give voluntary, informed consent.

There is also the issue of the seriousness of risks posed by the research process. In a medical study not too long ago, black prisoners serving life sentences were deliberately denied treatment for venereal diseases so that doctors could study the progression and long-term effects of the diseases and the effectiveness of available treatments. The prisoners were clearly subjected to significant risk in this study.[14] They were not informed that they were subjects in an experiment, nor were they apprised of the risks associated with the withholding of treatment. Their informed, voluntary consent to participate was not sought. Although this project may have seemed appropriate and even ethically acceptable to the researchers at the time, these procedures would be considered morally reprehensible by contemporary ethical standards.

Deception in Research

Stanley Milgram, a research psychologist, wished to understand the effects of various circumstances on the tendency of humans to obey authority figures.[15] To study these phenomena, he created an experimental situation in which subjects who volunteered to participate were asked to teach another person, located in an adjacent room, a simple word association task. To encourage learning, the experimenter instructed the subject-teacher to deliver electrical shocks to the learner when the learner made mistakes. The shocks progressed in intensity with each mistake the learner made, to the point where they were potentially lethal and the learners no longer responded at all to the teacher's efforts.

There were many forms of deception involved in this experiment. For example, the subjects were told that they were participating in an experiment on learning, not obedience to authority. Also, the learners were part of the research team and did not actually receive any electrical shocks. But the subjects (the "teachers") did not know this and were led to believe that the shocks were real. The behavior of the teachers, as they delivered more and more intense shocks to the "learners," confirmed that they did, in fact, believe that the shocks were real. Many of the teachers manifested extremely emotional reactions to the situation, some laughing hysterically, some apparently going into a trancelike state, and others shaking and sobbing uncontrollably as they delivered what they believed to be severe shocks to the learner.

Milgram debriefed his subjects after their participation, telling them the true nature of the experiment and informing them that the learner had not received any shocks. He also contacted the participants several months after their participation in the experiment and reported that there were no long-term negative psychological effects on his subjects. Nevertheless, Milgram agreed to suspend his experiments when ethical issues were raised about them by a committee of the American Psychological Association.

Most contemporary standards of ethical research conduct allow some benign deception of subjects in research. The general rationale for permitting benign deception is that subjects who know what the researcher is really studying may deliberately alter their responses or behavior in a way that distorts the research findings. We agree that benign deception of subjects is ethically permissible, but we cannot leave the topic without asking you to think about this: How valid is the researcher's assumption that data gathered when subjects are deceived are better than data gathered when subjects have been informed of the true purpose of the study?

Sharing Results and Benefits with Research Participants

Finally, scientists increasingly recognize that they are ethically obliged to share the results of their research with participants. Some ethicists argue that—in almost all circumstances but especially those where participant observation has been the primary data-gathering strategy and the groups being studied have low social status and are relatively powerless—researchers have an obligation to seek critiques of the research report from their subjects before publication, to make those critiques a part of the published report, and when substantial financial benefits accrue, to share those with participants as well. Accomplishing any of these can take many forms, depending on the nature of the research. Perhaps a summary of the results and/or an invitation for comment and criticism might be sent to each participant and/or published in media easily accessible to participants (in newspapers, an intranet, or the Internet). Or, in cases where it is feasible to do so, researchers may meet with interested participants in person to discuss the results and invite comments and questions. (This can be a tricky situation, of course; anonymity and confidentiality may be breached, and sometimes participants don't like the picture of themselves or their group or organization that emerges from research.) In the relatively rare cases where the research report produces substantial revenue to the researchers (such as through book sales or movie rights), researchers should find ways to share the proceeds with participants, perhaps through donations to a community project or a citizens' benefit fund.

Research Ethics and Other Standards of Fairness

When research is focused on evaluating the effectiveness of some policy, program, or treatment, as is often the case in criminal justice studies, special ethical issues may emerge, sometimes involving conflicts among standards for good research and other standards pertaining to fairness or justice. Suppose you want to know whether a warning is as effective as an arrest in a certain kind of situation (for example, spouse abuse). Is it fair, for research purposes, to choose at random one alleged abuser for arrest and another for a warning, when the immediate consequences for the two individuals are quite different and when having (or not having) an arrest record may shape subsequent law enforcement decisions with respect to the persons included in the study? Or suppose the research question is: Is probation as effective as a week in jail? Is it ethical for the purposes of research to violate the judicial standard of fairness that emphasizes equal punishment for equal offenses? Suppose you were the person randomly chosen to spend the time in jail. You can spell out your own illustrations relating to the death penalty.

To put the same sort of question in a slightly different context, is it fair to deny someone access to a program or treatment that one believes is very effective in order to apply rigorously the principles of scientific inquiry? This sort of question arises most dramatically in medicine, and the controversy over testing procedures for AIDS drugs represents a recent example. But such situations can emerge in criminal justice studies as well. Suppose a new drug shows great promise in reducing violent impulses or a new drug abuse prevention program seems to be especially effective. Is it just to deny someone access to this drug or program for the purpose of comparing those who did with those who did not receive this treatment? Or, for that matter, how would you feel about the justice of the situation if you were a victim of the person denied access to the drug?

There are no easy answers to these questions. Often, the potential negative effects of being included in a study can be minimized by limiting the study to carefully predefined cases. In other cases, if the study suggests clearly that the drug or treatment is effective, the study can be halted earlier than planned or those denied access during the study can be given access after the study is finished. But it is seldom possible to eliminate completely the risks of research. As in most areas of life, the potential benefits of research procedures must be weighed against the potential costs. The basic issue is: How much is it worth to have more trustworthy answers to the particular questions we are asking? In some cases, it will be concluded that the risks outweigh the benefits, and the research project should be scuttled. Remember, though, that *failing* to subject our questions and proposed solutions to rigorous scientific investigation can harm individuals and squander financial resources as well. At a minimum, it seems reasonable to insist that a few people other than the researchers and directly interested parties (in hired-hand or in-house research situations, for example) be involved in considering the many difficult ethical issues involved in research projects. Such is the function of professional associations and institutional review boards

Responsibility to Scientific Community

Finally, science itself imposes ethical demands on the researchers. As scientists, we must present the research process and the findings in an honest fashion, even when they do not support our hypotheses. It would be ethically irresponsible deliberately to omit, alter, or misrepresent data in a research report so that they appear to support a favored proposition or belief.

Although most researchers do not deliberately violate this principle, some ask us to ignore or discount the fact that some of their findings do not support their contentions. Or they may fail to note weaknesses in the design or execution of the research, which would affect the confidence one has in the results obtained. Omitted or altered data may mislead us into believing that something has been demonstrated when it has not. We may then fail to propose alternative hypotheses that might better explain what has been observed, and the development of scientific knowledge is impeded.

Researchers are also ethically bound to acknowledge the contributions of others to their work. Acknowledging co-workers by name or including them as co-authors, as appropriate, in published research reports, as well as citing the authors and sources of key ideas, direct quotations, and paraphrases, are among the ways of fulfilling this obligation. Failing to provide these acknowledgments is in effect to claim others' work as one's own, an important ethics violation called **plagiarism.**

Applying ethics and enforcing ethical standards in research, as in other realms of life, often pose dilemmas for which there are no clear and absolute resolutions. Nevertheless, for ethical reasons, as well as for practical and professional ones, protecting subjects' rights, presenting data honestly, and giving back to participants should be overriding concerns in all research activities.

Who enforces researchers' ethical standards? First, a professional is supposed to monitor his own conduct. Second, professional associations such as the Academy of Criminal Justice Sciences (ACJS) and the American Society of Criminology establish codes of conduct, adjudication procedures, and sanctions for violations, which are generally limited, at the maximum, to dismissal from association membership. Excerpts from the ethics code adopted by the ACJS are included in Appendix F.

Third, the federal government has mandated that colleges and universities (and other institutions) receiving federal grants establish **institutional review boards** (IRBs) to protect research subjects' rights. Typically, institutional staff members not involved in the research project being reviewed, as well as outsiders who represent the community at large, serve on IRBs. They review the provisions made in research proposals to protect subjects' rights, sometimes demanding changes; project funding is contingent on the IRB's approval. They also monitor ongoing studies for research ethics compliance and investigate allegations of ethics violations.

CURRENT CRITIQUES OF THE SCIENTIFIC PERSPECTIVE

The most significant contemporary critiques of science come from critical theory, feminism, and postmodernism. There are many different versions of each of these perspectives. We'll focus here on what we think are the core ideas in each, devoting most of our attention to postmodernism because it includes many of the critiques offered by the other two.

Critical theory derives largely from the Marxist theoretical tradition.[16] It focuses primarily on how social hierarchies are created and maintained by the dominant classes. Mainstream science is seen as the product of a powerful elite and/or as a tool used by the dominant classes to justify and sustain social inequalities. Critical theorists view the scientific perspective as an ideology that bolsters scientists' high social status and provides intellectual support for the policies and practices of the ruling classes. They point out the connections among science (and scientists), major corporations, and the government. They also critique the power inequalities within the institutions of science (academic departments, professional associations, and so on) and among scientists as well, analyzing how the scientific elite maintains its control of the scientific establishment.

The **feminist perspective,** which is espoused by both men and women, invites us to consider the role of sex and gender in shaping the perspectives as well as the politics of science.[17] Feminists note that historically women have been considered unsuited for any serious, rational work, including scientific theorizing and research. Opportunities for women in science have been and continue to be restricted in many disciplines. Although their numbers have grown in recent years, women remain significantly underrepresented in the judicial system and law enforcement as well as in criminology and criminal justice.

Feminists contend that science might be quite different if women's perspectives were respected as much as men's. Scientific work might be more often conducted by sexually and culturally diverse teams, where collaboration rather than individual initiative was rewarded. The descriptive and explanatory metaphors and theories scientists use might more regularly feature cooperation instead of competition. More scientific interest might be devoted to exploring ways in which women's modes of aggression differ from men's or to looking for contexts in which men prefer cooperation to competition. Patterns of female criminality and crimes in which females are often the victim might be studied more often. Whether the community policing philosophy might take root more easily among female officers might be examined. Alternatives to the currently popular "get tough" methods of crime prevention and deterrence might be taken more seriously. Qualitative research might have greater prominence among the methodological approaches considered acceptable in science.

According to **postmodernists,** the entire philosophical foundation of the modern era (essentially the time from the Enlightenment to the mid-1950s) has collapsed, and new ways of thinking are necessary.[18] The defining features of the modern era identified by postmodernists fall into two categories: sociopolitical (that is, how power is attained and sustained) and epistemological (that is, how we know that we know). In the sociopolitical realm, the modern era was characterized by beliefs in natural sociocultural inequalities (and the accompanying racism, sexism, classism, oppression, and exploitation—both globally and domestically); individualism (that weakened community ties and increased alienation); and centralized, hierarchical, patriarchal authority structures (for example, bureaucratic governments and male-dominated families). Epistemologically, modernism entailed beliefs that our senses give us direct, reliable access to the real world; universal, absolute truth exists; and this truth can be discovered through rational, objective, empirical inquiry. In other words, science was the means of acquiring certain knowledge about the natural world.

Postmodernists note that these two sets of ideas are closely related. For example, science in the early modern era "proved" that Caucasians were more evolutionarily advanced (hence, superior) to other races and that social inequality was "natural" within races, and between the sexes as well, and that progress in human development and controlling the forces of nature could be achieved using scientific knowledge. So, say the postmodernist critics, science was not an objective means of establishing absolute truth but rather a thoroughly value-laden ideological tool used by Caucasian males of Western culture to attain and maintain their dominance at home and abroad.

A crucial breach of the modern era's philosophical armor came, according to the postmodernists, with the deconstructionists' assault on the *correspondence theory of meaning,* which holds that there is a one-to-one correspondence between words and their referents and that words derive their meanings from their accurate representation of those objects or events in the real world. Hence, we can observe the world and describe or explain it linguistically as it really is, that is, objectively. **Deconstructionists** argue, on the other hand, that words do not exactly correspond in this way with anything in the world and, therefore, that objective observation is impossible. Why? Because what we observe is inevitably shaped by the limitations of our senses, the way our brains and minds process sensory signals, the language we use to talk about our experiences, the culture in which we were raised, the social positions and statuses we occupy, our unique autobiographies, our values, and our unconscious. In short, what we perceive cannot be separated from us as perceivers; our observations are always fundamentally subjective. Meaning, then, cannot come from the exact correspondence between words and things. Hence, the basic goal of science, which is to discover the truth about the real world through objective observation, is by definition unachievable.

If the correspondence theory of meaning is rejected, say the critics, then words and their meanings must be regarded as sociocultural constructions with referents decipherable only within the context of the language system itself and the particular sociocultural communities within which it is created and used. Rather than a knowable real world waiting "out there" to be discovered, there are instead multiple realities created by a multitude of different human communities. All of these realities are value laden, that is, inevitably shaped by human choices (values) that determine not just what is important but also ultimately what is conceived of as real.

If scientists must abandon their illusion that they are studying the real world, what can they study? They can study what they have always studied, except now those phenomena are considered "texts" scientists create or construct rather than "facts" they discover. Just as texts are constructed, they can be deconstructed, by examining, for example, how they were created, by whom, for what purposes and audiences, and under what circumstances. The creators' unstated values and hidden political agendas can be ferreted out, value conflicts or tensions within the texts can be uncovered, and illegitimate claims to power or knowledge can be revealed. Texts are stories we tell ourselves and each other about the worlds in which we live. Science has no legitimate claim to a superior means of acquiring knowledge. Scientists are simply one group of storytellers among many, each with its own assumptions about what is real, its own methodology and criteria for establishing its own truth, its own rhetoric, and its own ways of organizing and narrating its stories. A story cannot be verified or falsified outside the story itself or other stories sharing the same context. Truths are always multiple, contextual, and contestable; certainty is nowhere to be found.

Critical theorists, feminist, and postmodernist critics offer many valuable insights into the pursuit of knowledge. Among other points, we share the critics' view that early philosophers of science were too optimistic (though not nearly so naïve as some critics portray them) about the human capacity for objective observation. We think, too, that scientists are too often arrogant in their pronouncements about reality, overconfident in their favorite theories and research results, and too willing to apply scientific approaches to areas beyond the reach of science. They are also often too eager to claim—in the heat of intellectual debate, or in the struggle for prestige or money or power, or in the perceived necessity for immediate action—that they know the ultimate truth. Furthermore, we agree that phenomena can and should be thought about and researched from different perspectives (*triangulation*) as we try to determine the more viable among them for particular purposes. Especially important here is to take seriously the perspectives of those whose voices have been silenced by sexist, racist, and classist political and social structures. The deconstructionists' search for unacknowledged values and hidden political agenda in scientific texts should be welcomed by scientists.

But we also think the critics are wrong about several important matters and have pushed their arguments too far in still others. First, in their depiction of science, they miss the longstanding emphasis within the scientific perspective on the tentative nature of scientific knowledge. In fact, philosophers of science—and scientists themselves—were pioneers in the analysis of the foibles of human observers. Many of the basic scientific research strategies (such as, control groups, double-blind procedures, publication, and replication) are specifically designed to help overcome some of our shortcomings as knowledge seekers. Second, although science was and can still be used to justify horrendous social injustice, it does not follow that science itself is an illegitimate undertaking or that science is without substance, that it is nothing but an ideological tool of the oppressors. Third, although many perspectives on important matters do exist and many other potentially useful ones have been (and continue to be) ignored or suppressed, it does not follow that every perspective is equally valuable for every purpose or that we cannot tentatively distinguish better from worse perspectives for a particular purpose. Although there may indeed be many different and important kinds of truth, we nevertheless maintain that, compared to other ways of seeking knowledge, the scientific perspective does offer significant advantages when pursuing questions for which the scientific approach is appropriate.

Fourth, although significant difficulties have been identified in the correspondence theory of meaning, we are not convinced that it is beyond repair. We may acknowledge that our observations of the world are inevitably subjective in some ways without denying either the existence of that world or the possibility of learning something useful about it. Furthermore, we have some profound doubts about the adequacy of the critics' alternative theory of meaning. When words or other symbols (texts) have only other words or symbols as referents, we are left in a solipsistic circle of meaning, with no connections to anything outside the circle. This theory seems at least as flawed as the correspondence theory.

In the final analysis, though, we think adopting a pragmatic approach is the best way of managing most of these issues. Science lives or dies on whether it works—that is, whether it provides reasonably reliable answers to particular kinds of questions. Are the patterns in the way the world behaves revealed through scientific research laws inherent in some external reality; that is, are they "out there" to be discovered? Or are they creations or inventions of the human mind; that is, are they more or less enduring habits of thought or behavior that people have created and that may change as people make different choices, develop different values, and therefore come to see and behave in different ways? We suspect there are patterns of both kinds; perhaps most laws are a combination of the two. In any event, if the net effect of the critique of science is to make researchers more self-critical, more open to alternative interpretations and perspectives, more humble in our claims to knowledge, so much the better. But we remain convinced that many of the fruits of the Enlightenment—including the scientific perspective, flawed though it may be—still have very important and useful applications for us as seekers of both knowledge and justice.

REVIEW QUESTIONS

1. What are some of the physiological limitations of our senses of hearing, sight, touch, taste, and smell? Can we overcome these limitations?

2. How does the language we learn influence what our senses tell us? Why is it potentially misleading for a researcher to think that language merely reflects the world? Do people who speak different languages perceive the same object or event in different ways?

3. What does it mean when we say that language mediates our perceptions?

4. What is a perspective? What is the relationship between language and perspective?

5. What is the difference between consensual and nonconsensual language? Why is consensual language important in research?

6. What are the nine principles of the scientific perspective?

7. Why are scientists' claims to be objective controversial? Compare and contrast subjectivity and objectivity.

8. What parts do publication and replication play in scientific research?

9. Why should researchers share their results with their subjects?

10. What is a theory? How do theories differ?

11. Can we have a theory without a language?

12. What is the relationship among theory, research, and methodology?

13. Why are research ethics important?

14. What ethical principles should guide research?

15. What are the basic ideas of critical theorists, feminists, and postmodernists? What critiques do they offer of science?

EXERCISES

1. How does an aerial photograph of a city building differ from one taken at ground level? Can we tell it is the same building? Why or why not? How would an article about a police department written from a liberal perspective differ from one about the same department written from a conservative perspective? Could we tell that it is the same department? Why or why not?

2. Pick some local social scene (for example, a bar, a fraternity or sorority house, a church service, a pool hall, a courtroom, a street corner hang-out, a university cafeteria) and describe the scene from the perspective of people playing different roles in the scene (such as a police officer, a minister, an attorney, a criminal justice researcher, a janitor, a hustler, a biologist, a bouncer). To what extent are the different perspectives compatible with one another? Is it possible or necessary to resolve all the differences in perspective?

3. Find at least two examples each of consensual, interpretive/inferential, and evaluative and mixed statements in this chapter. Discuss why you regard them as examples of each type. Share your examples and rationale with a classmate. Do you agree on the categorizations? Why or why not?

4. If one language (say, English) can be translated into another (say, Spanish), what implications does this have for the role of language in our perceptions? For perspectives? For consensual statements? For objectivity and subjectivity?

5. What do you think are the main perspectives in criminal justice studies and research? Are they compatible with one another? Why or why not?

6. Do you think achieving objectivity is easier in the natural sciences (physics, chemistry, biology) than in the social sciences? Why or why not?

7. Discuss the application of the principles of the scientific perspective to the pepper spray research described in Chapter 1.

8. Formulate at least two different theories about one or more of the following: police-juvenile encounters, the causes of crime, the effects of imprisonment, the training of police officers, the courtroom behavior of prosecuting attorneys, a researcher's relationship with police officers.

9. For two of the theories you developed in question 8, briefly describe at least two research projects that would produce evidence concerning the theory.

10. What ethical problems might have confronted the pepper spray researchers as they did the research described in Chapter 1?

 11. Go to *www.asc41.com* and read the code of ethics of the American Society of Criminology. Compare and contrast it with the excerpts in Appendix F. The complete code of the Academy of Criminal Justice Sciences should be available at *www.acjs.org*.

 12. Enter "critical theory," "feminism," "deconstructionism," and "postmodernism" in any of the major search engines and follow links that interest you.

NOTES

1. Of course, this discussion is speculative, because we cannot get testimony from an infant. For James's analysis, see his *Psychology: Briefer Course* (New York: Collier, 1962).

2. For a more thorough discussion of the influence of language on thought and perception, see Benjamin Lee Whorf, *Language, Thought and Reality: Selected Writings,* ed. John G. Carroll (New York: Technology Press and Wiley, 1959) and George Herbert Mead, *Mind, Self and Society* (Chicago: University of Chicago Press, 1934).

3. See Thomas S. Kuhn, *The Structure of Scientific Revolutions,* 2nd ed. (Chicago: University of Chicago Press, 1970).

4. This discussion of language types is derived from the unpublished "Coding Manual" (no date) for scoring responses to the Twenty Statements Test, developed by the late Manford Kuhn of the University of Iowa.

5. Robert Bierstedt, *The Social Order* (New York: McGraw-Hill, 1970), p. 16.

6. For further discussion of the objectivity/subjectivity debate, see Egon G. Guba (ed.), *The Paradigm Dialog* (Newbury Park, CA: Sage, 1990); and Norman K. Denzin and Yvonne S. Lincoln, *Handbook of Qualitative Research* (Thousand Oaks, CA: Sage, 1994).

7. Howard S. Becker, "Whose Side Are We On?" *Social Problems* 14(1967): 239–248.

8. Bierstedt, p. 19. Actually, this is a matter of considerable controversy in both the social and natural sciences at present. Many laypersons as well as scientists contend that scientists must recognize the ethical and moral implications of their work, both while they are engaged in research and in deciding whether, when, and in what way the results are to be published or employed. We agree with this position inasmuch as we recognize that questions of ethics and morality are relevant to all human behavior, including the behavior of the human being who happens to be a scientist. For a more detailed discussion of the issues involved, see Becker; George A. Lundberg, *Can Science Save Us?* (New York: David McKay, 1961); or Jacob Bronowski, *Science and Human Values* (New York: Harper Torchbooks, 1956).

9. See Samuel A. Stouffer, Edward A. Suchman, Leland C. DeVinney, Shirley A. Star, and Robin M. Williams, Jr., *The American Soldier: Adjustment During Army Life* (New York: Wiley, 1949), especially pp. 580–582.

10. See, for example, Steven M. Cox and Jack D. Fitzgerald, *Police in Community Relations: Critical Issues,* 3rd ed. (Dubuque, IA: Brown and Benchmark, 1996), pp. 28–29.

11. Erving Goffman, *Asylums* (Garden City, NY: Doubleday, 1961).

12. Goffman, p. xiii.

13. Goffman, p. x.

14. For example, see M. H. Pappworth, *Human Guinea Pigs* (Boston: Beacon Press, 1967).

15. Stanley Milgram, *Obedience to Authority: An Experimental View* (New York: Harper & Row, 1974).

16. For more on critical theory see, for example, Stuart Henry and Werner Einstadter (eds.), *The Criminology Theory Reader* (New York: New York University Press, 1998), especially Chapters 19–21; Guba, *The Paradigm Dialog*; and Joe L. Kincheloe and Peter L. McLaren, "Rethinking Critical Theory," Chapter 8 in Denzin and Lincoln, *Handbook of Qualitative Research.*

17. For more on feminism see, for example, Sharlene Hesse-Biber, *Feminist Approaches to Theory and Methodology: An Interdisciplinary Reader* (New York: Oxford University Press, 1999); Henry and Einstadter, especially Chapters 22–23; Anthony Elliott (ed.), *The Blackwell Reader in Contemporary Theory* (Cambridge, MA: Blackwell, 1999), especially "Part V: Feminism, Gender and Sexual Differences"; Nancy A. Wonders, "Determinant Sentencing: A Feminist and Postmodern Story." *Justice Quarterly* 13(1996): 611–648; Carol Smart, *Law, Crime and Sexuality: Essays in Feminism* (London: Sage, 1995); and Nicole Hahn Rafter and Frances Heidensohn, *International Feminist Perspectives in Criminology: Engendering a Discipline* (Buckingham, UK: Open University Press, 1996).

18. Additional information about postmoderism may be found, for example, in Martin D. Schwartz and David O. Friedrichs, "Post-Modern Thought and Criminological Discontent: New Metaphors for Understanding Violence." *Criminology* 32:2(1994): 221–246; Elliott, "Part VI: The Modernity/Postmodernity Debate"; Henry and Einstadter, especially Chapters 24–27; Guba, *The Paradigm Dialog*; Bruce Arrigo, "The Peripheral Core of Law and Criminology: On Postmodern Social Theory and Conceptual Integration." *Justice Quarterly* 12(1995): 447–472; and Dragan Milovanovic, "Postmodern Criminology: Mapping the Terrain." *Justice Quarterly* 13(1996): 567–610.

3

An Introduction to Research Methodology and Design

In the first two chapters, we have discussed some key aspects of the larger context within which research takes place. In this chapter, we begin our discussion of the research process itself.

As a point of departure, it is important to distinguish between two related aspects of the research process: methodology and methods. This distinction is analogous to the difference between strategy and tactics. Research **methodology,** like strategy, is concerned with the researcher's ultimate goals and the general plan the researcher formulates for achieving those goals. Research **methods,** like tactics, are the specific techniques the researcher uses to implement the plan and collect data. Methodology includes such things as the study of the role of concepts, variables and their definitions in research, the purposes and structures as well as the advantages and disadvantages of different types of research design, the logic of causal inferences, and sampling theory. Methods include specific data-gathering and analyzing techniques to be used (for example, direct observation, interviews or questionnaires, and making graphs and tables). An appropriate general methodology must be selected before specific methods are chosen. In fact, as we shall see, the credibility of research depends as much on the quality of the researcher's methodology as it does on the quality of her methods. In this chapter and most of the next one on sampling, methodological issues will be considered. The remainder of the book will be concerned primarily with methods.

The research process is typically divided into a number of related steps:

1. Choosing a research topic
2. Specifying units of analysis and defining concepts and variables
3. Selecting a research design
4. Selecting the particular people, objects, or events to be studied (sampling)
5. Gathering the data
6. Summarizing and analyzing the data
7. Interpreting the data
8. Writing the research report

In many qualitative research projects, especially those using participant observation, step 2 is collapsed into steps 6 and 7 because researchers do not wish to impose their own conceptual scheme, but rather to learn and report about how their subjects categorize, define, and interpret their world. Although qualitative researchers have a plan for carrying out their project (step 3), it may not be as formal and detailed as that of quantitative researchers in part because sometimes the former's objective is description rather than explanation and in part because the plan needs to be flexible so that they can adapt to changing field opportunities and conditions. Step 4 is also often different for qualitative researchers, because they are often less interested in issues of the representativeness of their observations and more interested in simply finding persons or locations where the phenomena they are interested in are likely to be found. (See the discussion of sampling in Chapter 4.) But qualitative researchers nevertheless must select a group of persons and/or a research setting and have some idea of the issues or topics they wish initially to explore. We discuss the first three steps of the research process in this chapter.

CHOOSING A RESEARCH TOPIC

A number of factors may influence the selection of a research topic. Of course, the particular social-scientific perspective (for example, symbolic interactionism, behaviorism) the researcher uses determines in part the kinds of topic areas that come to his attention. The topic a researcher chooses always reflects to some extent his judgments or feelings about what is important to study. The personal values of the researcher also clearly influence his choice of topic. Selection of a topic may also be based on theoretical or intellectual concerns or the practical desire to alleviate a specific problem. Finally, it is not uncommon for a researcher to choose a topic because funding is available for its study.

A symbolic interactionist, for example, may choose a research topic that involves the self-concepts and face-to-face interactions of judges and defendants, or correctional officials and prison inmates. A behaviorist would be more likely to focus on a topic that emphasizes the role of punishment and reward in shaping human behavior. A researcher whose primary interest is the legal profession would likely choose a different topic than one whose interests are in probation, parole, or cross-cultural analysis of crime. A researcher who is personally convinced that the plea bargaining system is in serious need of reform may select a research topic related to this personal belief.

Although research questions may originate from a variety of sources and assume a variety of forms, they must all be questions for which scientific answers are possible. Not all questions, not even all important or interesting questions, can be approached scientifically. Questions like, Does God exist? and, Is premarital sex immoral? cannot be answered scientifically because supreme beings and ultimate moral standards are not subject to direct observation or measurement. To be sure, people's beliefs concerning such matters can be subjected to empirical investigation, but the matters themselves are beyond the scope of the scientific perspective and cannot be approached through scientific methodology. Issues such as the relationship between police response time and the number of crimes cleared by arrest, or between court disposition of convicted offenders and recidivism, however, can be approached scientifically because relevant data can be obtained through systematic, controlled observation of empirical and at least potentially measurable phenomena. Every scientific research project involves observing at least one kind of person, object, or event. The particular entities selected for study are referred to as units of analysis.

IDENTIFYING UNITS OF ANALYSIS

Ordinarily, the units of analysis are explicitly or implicitly included in the statement of the research topic. For example, a study of job-related stress among police officers indicates that individual police officers will be the unit of analysis for this study. An investigation of jail capacity and overcrowding makes jails the units of analysis. An examination of the exercise of discretion by police officers during encounters with juveniles involves those encounters as units of analysis. Of course, a single study may be concerned with more than one unit of analysis.

Carefully identifying the **units of analysis** is important for good research for a number of reasons. First, these units are the core around which observations are organized and about which conclusions are drawn. Being clear about the unit of analysis helps avoid the serious error of inferring something about one unit of analysis from observations of a different unit of analysis. Studies involving more than one unit of analysis require special care in confining conclusions to the appropriate unit of analysis. Second, as we shall see in the next section, selected aspects or attributes of the unit of analysis become the concepts and variables in the study. Third, as we shall see in a later chapter, when sampling is a part of the research design, it is usually units of analysis that are sampled.

Finally, the selection of a unit of analysis typically reflects what is sometimes referred to as the **level of analysis** to be employed in the study. We might think of criminal justice research as involving three general levels of analysis: biochemical, psychological, and sociocultural. A study of the changes in blood chemistry associated with the ingestion of crack cocaine would be at the biochemical level, with blood samples as the units of analysis. A study of motivations for shoplifting among teenagers would be at the psychological level, with teen shoplifters as the units of analysis. A study of youth gangs in a city would be at the sociocultural level, with the gang as the unit of analysis. Of course, a study may involve examination of phenomena at more than one level of analysis and/or relations among phenomena at different levels of analysis. As with units of analysis, when different levels of analysis are employed in a study, special care must be taken in forming generalizations and drawing conclusions about different levels of phenomena.

DEFINING CONCEPTS AND VARIABLES

The language of science is primarily a language of concepts and variables. **Concepts** are symbolic, shorthand ways of representing some aspect of perceived reality. That is, they are words or other symbols the scientist uses to describe one or more dimensions of an object or event serving as the unit of analysis for the study. Remember that concepts, like perspectives, are selective devices; they emphasize certain aspects of an object or event and ignore others. For example, the concept of color refers to only one dimension of our experience, only one property of an object. Similarly, the concept "crime" refers to one dimension of a person's behavior, the concepts "judge" and "correctional officer" to one property of the person. Many different objects or events can have certain characteristics or properties in common; hence, we can *categorize* them according to the properties that they share. Remember, though, that although two objects or events have properties that are alike, they may have many others that are different. A group of acts categorized as crimes are similar in some respects (they all violate criminal law), but may be quite different in others. To say that murder, arson, and theft are all crimes is to emphasize what they have in common and to ignore their differences.

Using language precisely is crucial to good scientific research. Because different researchers use the same words (for example, *crime, delinquency, poverty, justice,* and *stress*) but attach different meanings to them, researchers *define* key concepts in their research reports so that they and others who read their reports will know as clearly as possible what they mean.

Types of Definitions

There are several different kinds of definitions used by researchers. Some concepts are defined in terms of other concepts. When we define crime as any act that violates the criminal law, we are using a collection of other concepts to define the concept "crime." Concepts that are defined in terms of other concepts are called *constructs.*[1]

A concept may also be defined by physically pointing to an example of it in the empirical world—definition by indication. We might define a courtroom, for example, by showing one to the person for whom we are defining it. Concepts that we can define by pointing to something in the empirical world are said to have direct empirical referents.

Closely related to definitions by indication are **operational definitions.** To operationally define a concept, such as "delinquent," the researcher specifies exactly how she will identify the objects or events that fall under that category. They are called operational definitions because they specify the operations (actions) the scientist will perform in order to recognize an instance of a category. Consider the category "delinquent." If the research is primarily a study of police records and documentation, *delinquent* may be operationally defined by specifying that "any juvenile whose name appears two or more times in the police records" will be placed in the category "delinquent." If the research includes interviews of young people, *delinquent* may be operationally defined as "any juvenile who indicates involvement in two or more acts of illegal or anti-social behavior" during the interview. If both records and interviews are used, the operational definition of delinquent may include information from both sources. Because different "operations" applied to the same group of juveniles may well produce different lists of delinquents, and because a particular operational definition may have important consequences for what is discovered about delinquents, specifying the definitions used is crucial.

Variables

A category may be divided into two or more subcategories to create a **variable.** Each subcategory is then called a value of the variable. The concept or category "sex," for example, has two subcategories (two values)—male and female. Categories may be subdivided in different ways, depending on the requirements of the research. One researcher may assign the concept "crime" the values misdemeanor and felony, whereas another might assign the values murder, robbery, breaking and entering, and theft. "Stress" may be assigned the values low stress, moderate stress, and high stress. "Size of police department" may be assigned any number of values from 1 to 30,000, for example.

By converting concepts into variables and specifying operational definitions for each value, the researcher is in a position to observe stability or change (that is, variability) in the values of the variable. The researcher can also look for relationships (related changes) between two variables.

VALIDITY, RELIABILITY, AND PRECISION IN CATEGORIZATIONS AND MEASUREMENTS

For scientists, as for all humans, there is always the possibility that the conceptual categories, subcategories, or measurements themselves don't represent reality very well or that the process of applying the categories or measuring instruments to the empirical world is to some degree faulty. In scientific methodology, the examination of these issues is concerned with the degree of validity, reliability, and precision of categorizations and measurements.

Validity

A categorization is **valid** if it reflects a characteristic or property of the real, empirical world. We are raising the issue of validity when we ask questions such as, Is what we are categorizing a crime actually a crime? Is what we are calling stress really stress, or is it something else? Is the person we are calling a criminal really a criminal, or perhaps the victim of social prejudice in the criminal justice network? Establishing or defending the validity of a concept or measurement is not always easy. A full discussion of the issues involved is beyond the scope of this text. We will simply note here that research methodologists have identified several different kinds of validity. We shall mention only three here. When a categorization or measurement seems, on general appearances, to be appropriate for its stated purpose, it is said to have **face validity.** If a concept or measurement is logically related to other concepts or measures in the same realm of inquiry, if its internal components are logically consistent, mutually exclusive, and exhaustive, it is said to have **construct validity.** If, in applying the concept or measurement, the results are what would be anticipated (or are more or less identical to the results derived from other independently validated measures), it is said to have **predictive validity.**

Sometimes the concept of validity is applied not to the quality of categorizations or measurements of particular variables but to (a) the legitimacy of applying research findings beyond the particular group or events studied, referred to as **external validity**; or to (b) the strength of the causal argument(s) made in the research, referred to as **internal validity.** A study's external validity depends on the degree of homogeneity of the phenomena in question and on the sampling techniques employed, subjects to which we return in Chapter 4. Internal validity issues arise when variables other than the ones identified by the researcher may be responsible for the observed effects. Several of the more common threats to internal validity and ways of managing them will be addressed in the section on explanatory research later in this chapter.

Reliability

Reliability refers to the extent to which the procedures we use to make our categorizations or measurements of the empirical world produce the same results upon repeated application of those same procedures to the same objects or events. A yardstick, for example, is a fairly reliable device for observing the length of an object. We can assess the reliability of a count of the number of recorded arrests in a given period of time by counting them again and comparing the two results. The degree of similarity of results from repeated application of the same measurement device or process to the same phenomenon is called the measurement's **test-retest reliability.** Of course, it is sometimes difficult to interpret the results of a test-retest reliability assessment. Suppose, for example, we ask a judge a series of questions about the factors that she weighed in arriving at a series of sentencing decisions. As soon as we are finished, we ask her the same questions. Aside from annoying the judge, what could we conclude about the reliability of our measurement if her answers were nearly identical? Perhaps such a result is evidence of reliability—but we may also simply have tested her memory. Suppose we wait for two weeks and then repeat our questions to her and she answers our questions differently. Are our questions, therefore, unreliable measures? Perhaps, but it is also possible that she has reconsidered our questions and come to a different view of the bases for her decisions. The passage of time can change the phenomenon being measured, thus obscuring the results of the test-retest procedure.

To deal with some of the problems of test-retest reliability assessments, other procedures have been developed. One, referred to as **split-half reliability**, may be used when the researcher has developed a questionnaire containing several items that are supposed to measure the same phenomenon. The split-half reliability of the questions can be arrived at by dividing the questions into two groups and comparing the two measurements. Obviously, this approach to establishing reliability is applicable in relatively limited situations.

Precision

Precision refers to the number of subcategorizations of a concept (values of a variable) that are available. Some subcategorizations divide a phenomenon into relatively few parts, whereas others produce many subdivisions. One procedure might result in categorizing objects simply as longer or shorter than some standard we have chosen, whereas another permits us to say how many inches longer or shorter one object is compared to another, and still another may permit us to determine such differences to a hundredth of an inch. Many, though not all, categorizations in criminal justice research are relatively imprecise, at least compared to those in the physical sciences. The time an officer takes to respond to a call can be quite precisely determined by using a stopwatch, for example, but the levels of stress experienced by the officer in different types of law enforcement situations may not be subject to very precise determination.

Validity, reliability, and precision are separate dimensions of categories and categorizations. That is, a category we are using may be valid, but our process of categorization may be unreliable, or the process may be reliable but imprecise, or it may be precise but neither valid nor reliable. Furthermore, we are always dealing with *degrees* of validity, reliability, and precision. We shall have more to say about these concepts when we discuss statistics and measurement later in the book.

CHOOSING A RESEARCH DESIGN

A research design is the general plan for carrying out the research project and must be established well in advance of the actual data collection. It specifies who or what will be observed, sets how many times and in what time sequence observations of the variables will take place, and lays the logical foundation for drawing conclusions on the basis of the data gathered. The choice among the wide range of designs available depends first and foremost on the basic goal of the researcher, which may be either the description or the explanation of some phenomenon in terms of the variables that have been defined.

Exploratory Research

Exploratory research is a loosely structured but valuable methodological strategy. When scientists are interested in some phenomenon but feel they need to know more about it before they can put together a well-organized and thorough study, they often engage in exploratory research. Qualitative researchers and others who do their studies in the field often use exploratory research. Suppose you were interested in the significance of adolescent groups to the lives of adolescents in inner-city neighborhoods. Unless you had grown up in the inner city or had had contacts with such adolescents and their groups, you would probably not know what to look for or what might be important in understanding the relationship between these individuals and their groups. Under these circumstances, you need to familiarize yourself with the general nature and functioning of such groups. You might contact an inner-city neighborhood center and volunteer to work in its youth program. Or you might ask to talk with some of the adolescents who frequent the center. In either case, your purpose would be to observe the lives and activities of the adolescents in a general way, with an eye toward forming some preliminary ideas about important aspects of the relationships between the individuals and the groups to which they belong.

Most researchers undertake exploratory research (1) to familiarize themselves with the selected research territory, and (2) to determine the desirability and feasibility of conducting a more rigorous investigation in the future. The exploratory researcher typically begins with some general questions but few specific ideas or topics to investigate. When he emerges from this type of research, the researcher has simply become better acquainted with the subject; he has not developed definitive descriptions or explanations. However, the researcher has been able to identify specific aspects of his subject that may be significant, and this information can be useful in preparing a more rigorous study of the phenomenon at a later date. Another potential benefit is the insight that can be gained concerning an appropriate strategy for conducting a subsequent investigation. Often the exploratory researcher is able to identify which research techniques would be feasible and which would not. Occasionally, researchers discover that they are not as interested in the phenomenon as they initially thought, or that there seems to be no feasible means of studying the phenomenon further at the present time. Any of these outcomes of exploratory research would make the effort worthwhile.

Descriptive Research

Many studies in criminal justice, both qualitative and quantitative, are **descriptive.** The researcher's goal is to identify and communicate important properties or characteristics of a particular group or category of objects or events. The census of the population of the United States and the Uniform Crime Reports are good examples of very large-scale descriptive studies. A survey on the nature and types of unreported delinquent behavior or a study on the extent of drug use in a community or open-ended interviews to identify the social service needs of the elderly residents of a neighborhood are also examples of descriptive research. The aim in all these cases is to describe some phenomenon as it exists. No attempt is made to determine why the phenomenon is as it is.

Although descriptive research is generally less complicated than explanatory research, it is not easy to conduct. The researcher must formulate and define useful concepts, contend with the issues of reliability, validity, and precision of the observations, and select an appropriate research design.

Suppose we were interested in the incidence of crime in a particular population. We must decide if we are interested in crime as a single category or as a variable with several subcategories. If we choose the latter, how many subcategories shall we include? How shall we operationally define crime or its subcategories? We might decide to look at police records of crime, but would this provide us with a valid measure of the actual incidence of crime? A survey of the population could be conducted, but how could the validity and reliability of self-reports about criminal activities be determined? Should we compare the information obtained from a survey with crime statistics maintained by the police? The answers to these questions depend at least to some extent upon what we want to do with the data we collect. Each of the possible answers has merit, depending upon the goals of the researcher.

In the case of a delinquency survey, how should we define *delinquency?* What behaviors should count as delinquent? Whom shall we survey about this behavior—teenagers or adults? How reliable are self-reports of delinquent behavior? If we ask the same juveniles to report their delinquent behaviors on two different occasions, will the same delinquent behaviors be reported by each juvenile? Again, these are only some of the questions that the investigator must consciously and deliberately attempt to resolve if he is to have any confidence in the description provided by the data. The investigator who conducts descriptive research, then, must be methodologically aware, skillful, and attentive to detail if he hopes to obtain credible results.

Then, too, there are issues related to the overall design of the research that must be resolved. Many descriptive studies are like the ones described above—single snapshots of a particular phenomenon at a given point in time. Others, however, are designed to describe changes in some phenomenon over time. Research designs of this nature are either **longitudinal,** including panel designs and multiple group trend designs, or **cross-sectional.**

Panel or Cohort Designs

Suppose that we wanted to study changes in drug use among teenagers over time. In a **panel** or **cohort design,** one group of teenagers might be selected for study. (We shall have more to say about selection procedures—called sampling—in Chapter 4.) The same group of individuals would be asked about their current drug use at as many different points in time as we felt appropriate or necessary. We might diagram a panel design like this:

Time ⟶ T_1 T_2 T_3 T_4

Panel measurements M_1 M_2 M_3 M_4

This diagram indicates that each member of the panel would be observed (that is, the variable "current drug use" would be measured [M_1, M_2, and so on]) at four different points in time (T_1, T_2, and so forth). Panels can be large or small and observations can be continued for shorter or longer periods of time.

A minor variation on the panel is the **cohort.** Although panel members are usually selected individually from some larger group by the researcher, cohort members are chosen on the basis of some shared characteristic, such as being born in the same year, convicted of the same offense in a particular court, and so on. Cohorts are usually much larger than panels, and observations are extended over a relatively long time period—often years, even decades. Marvin Wolfgang and his associates, for example, followed a birth cohort—all the males born in Philadelphia in 1945—through their eighteenth birthdays. Using a variety of official records, including school and police records, he found that a small percentage of juveniles was responsible for a large percentage of offenses, including the most serious offenses. He replicated the study with another Philadelphia cohort—this time all the males and females born in 1958—that basically confirmed the earlier study's results. Others have replicated it too. Lyle Shannon studied youth cohorts in Racine, Wisconsin, and David Farrington studied a cohort in London: All tended to show the same general pattern of delinquency participation.[2]

The most difficult problem encountered by researchers using the panel design is dealing with the almost inevitable loss of some panel members (called **subject mortality**) from one observation time to the next, especially if the time between observations is relatively long. Members of the panel may die, refuse to participate in the study again, change address, or otherwise be unavailable for subsequent observations. When panel members are lost, any observed changes in the values of the variables (such as in the proportion of drug users in the panel) may reflect changes in panel membership rather than actual changes over time in variable values. In addition, being repeatedly asked questions (about drug use, for example) may make panel members more self-conscious about their opinions or activities, and they may change their behavior as a result. This possibility is a general problem with which researchers must contend whenever people are aware of being observed: If we know someone is watching us, sometimes we change our behavior. (We shall have more to say about this phenomenon, called the *Hawthorne effect,* in Chapter 6.)

Multiple Group Trend Designs

In **multiple group trend designs,** different groups are selected at different points in time from the same larger group. This design can be diagrammed as follows:

Time $\longrightarrow$	T_1	T_2	T_3	T_4
Group 1	M_1			
Group 2		M_2		
Group 3			M_3	
Group 4				M_4

In our drug use study, for example, we might have selected four different groups at different points in time from students attending a particular high school and asked each group about their current drug use.

Each census might be considered a single observation of the entire population of the United States; each Uniform Crime Report is a single observation of all the crimes reported to police in a particular year. By comparing several of these descriptive reports, changes over time in various aspects of the phenomenon being described can be observed and analyzed. In this design, the problem of repeated exposure to observation is solved because each group is observed only once. Furthermore, because different groups are chosen each time an observation is made, we don't have to worry about loss of subjects from one observation time to the next, as we did in the panel design. Unfortunately, though, in solving some problems, we have created others. The most serious problem in interpreting data from this design is the possibility that differences among the groups selected for observation, rather than changes in the phenomenon, may be responsible for variations in the values of the variables we have chosen to observe. Random sampling (see Chapter 4) would help.

Cross-Sectional Designs

In **cross-sectional designs**, a larger group is divided into subgroups and each of the subgroups is observed at a given point in time. The subgroups are chosen so that differences in their memberships may reflect changes over time. That is, rather than observing a given phenomenon at different points in time, we observe at a single point in time persons whom we believe are at different stages in a process of change. Returning to our study of drug use, we might divide students from a particular high school into four age groups (14 and younger, 15, 16, and 17 and older) and then compare drug usage among the different groups. We might diagram our cross-sectional design like this:

Time ⟶ T_1

Subgroup 1
(14 and younger)   M

Subgroup 2
(15 years old)   M

Subgroup 3
(16 years old)   M

Subgroup 4
(17 and older)   M

Differences in drug use among age groups might be interpreted as reflecting changes that have occurred through time as those being observed have grown older. Of course, this interpretation may be questioned because, as with multiple group trend studies, there may be differences other than the passage of time among the subgroups. For example, to interpret any observed differences among the subgroups as real changes in drug use patterns we have to assume that the "17 and older" group had the same patterns of drug use when they were "14 and younger" that the "14 and younger" group we actually observed has. Nevertheless, this design is often used because it requires less time and is less expensive to complete than the longitudinal design.

Descriptive research has a basic structure, in the sense that it is executed according to a carefully devised plan designed to produce valid, reliable information about a particular phenomenon at a given point in time or changes in a phenomenon over time. The quality and usefulness of a description depend on the appropriateness of the concepts, constructs, or variables the researcher chooses, the validity and reliability of the categorizations, and the effectiveness of the research design. Repeated testing of the adequacy and usefulness of the descriptions by comparing them with the reality to which they refer improves their quality.

Explanatory Research

Describing phenomena is an essential part of all scientific activity, but many researchers, whether they use qualitative or quantitative methods, also attempt to determine *why* some phenomenon has occurred—to go beyond description to explanation. Scientific explanation is accomplished when statements about the causal relationships among variables have both empirical and logical support. The degree of empirical support for an explanatory statement is determined by gathering and analyzing data. Logical support is provided by reasoning guided by the rules of logic. The investigator who does explanatory research must be concerned with the logical structure of the research design as well as the empirical evidence—the data—collected. In order to understand explanatory research, we need to be familiar with some elementary principles of logic.

Logic and Causality

Logic is a system of rules for making arguments and drawing conclusions. It is primarily concerned with the *form* of those arguments rather than their content. Most causal arguments in the social sciences proceed from statements in the conditional form. A **conditional proposition** takes the general form "if *x*, then *y*." This statement is called conditional because it states the condition(s) (*x*) that must be present if another condition (*y*) is to be present as well. Arguments involving conditional statements proceed as follows:

Major premise	If *x*, then *y*
Minor premise	*x* is present
Conclusion	Therefore, *y* is present

In this case, *x* is often referred to as an *antecedent* or *independent* condition, and *y* as the *consequent* or *dependent* condition. The independent condition (or, in methodological language, the **independent variable**) is defined as a *cause,* and the dependent condition (or **dependent variable**) is defined as its *effect.* The presence of *y* is said to be explained by the major and minor premises through deduction.

Research hypotheses often take the form of conditional statements. Suppose we believe that larger cities have higher rates of crime. We can convert this statement into conditional form as follows: If city J is larger than city R, then city J has a higher crime rate than city R. This is, as you will note, simply another way of hypothesizing that city size is causally related to crime rate.

Conditional statements may appear in both logically valid and logically invalid forms of argument. (Note that the term *validity* in this context has a different meaning than those assigned to it earlier.) The argument given above is an instance of *affirming the antecedent;* that is, given the truth of the major premise, if we can affirm that the antecedent x is present, we may then validly conclude that the consequent y is present as well. We may also argue validly by *denying the consequent;* that is, if we can show that y is not present, we can validly conclude that x is not present either. According to the rules of logic, however, given the statement "if x, then y," we cannot make a logically valid argument either by denying the antecedent or affirming the consequent. In the former case, if x is not present, y may nonetheless be present, because x may not be the only antecedent to y. Similarly, in the latter case, the fact that y is present does not permit us to conclude validly that x is present, because y may be present without x.

Causes can be related to resultant conditions in a variety of ways. The independent variable may be a *necessary* cause of the dependent variable. If x is a necessary cause of y, then y never occurs without x. The independent variable may also be a *sufficient* cause of the dependent variable. In this case, the occurrence of just x is sufficient for the occurrence of y, although there may be other sufficient causes of y as well. Or the independent variable may be both a necessary and a sufficient cause (y occurs if, and only if, x occurs).

It is easy to assert that one event or condition causes another; justifying the assertion is another matter. Some philosophers of science have even argued that we would be better off if we did not use the concept of cause at all. Although it is beyond the scope of this text to go into the details of this debate, we can make four observations. First, as we noted above, saying that one event (the independent condition) is causally related to another event (the dependent condition) does not necessarily mean that there is a one-to-one correspondence between the two. Several conditions may be causally related to a single other condition, with each condition contributing separately or in combination to the determination of another condition. We refer to this as **multiple causation.** Multiple causation is likely in criminal justice research.

Second, both students and scholars often think of cause as a unidirectional concept. We can easily imagine a chain of causes in which x causes y, y causes z, and z causes a. But if we consider a *system* of conditions where each condition is connected directly or indirectly to every other condition in the system, a change in condition x will produce changes in some or all of the others. These changes may, in turn, eventually cause another change in x. This kind of relationship among conditions is called a **feedback relationship** or a *feedback loop.* For example, the uncivil behavior of a defendant in court may change the judge's behavior from civil to threatening, which may change the defendant's behavior to civil. A researcher bound in his thinking to a unidirectional concept of causality may be unable to recognize this type of relationship.

One other type of variable is often used in explanatory research: the **intervening variable.** An intervening variable is one that comes between the independent and dependent variables in time, so that a causal chain or sequence of variables is created.

Finally, we must always remember that in science a cause can never be established with absolute certainty: "We are always in a position of *inferring* from observed data that the hypothesis that x is a condition for the occurrence of y is or is not tenable with some specified degree of confidence."[3] Furthermore, as we noted in Chapter 1, causality is perhaps best regarded as probabilistic rather than deterministic. Cause, then, is a complex concept, and its application is always subject to question. In spite of the difficulties associated with its use, however, we continue to talk about cause because no better alternative has been found. So long as we bear in mind when using the concept of cause that we are making *inferences* from data, the risks associated with speaking of causal relationships are minimized.

Logic gives researchers rules for making arguments that are valid in form. But scientists must be concerned with an argument's empirical content—the data—as well. Scientists rely on observation to determine the empirical support for statements about the world. The major and minor premises in a scientific argument are assertions about some empirical phenomenon. If these statements are supported through observation and the form of the argument is logically valid, the conclusion arrived at has both empirical and logical support.

In the methodology of explanatory research, both logic and data are combined in reaching conclusions about causal relationships. It is, in fact, this linkage of logical and empirical support that makes science such a powerful tool for acquiring knowledge. Explanatory research designs must be structured so that they permit the assessment of the degree of empirical support for the statements that comprise the major and minor premises in a logically valid argument.

Before we discuss specific types of explanatory research designs, then, we must examine in greater detail the concept of causality, including the conditions logically and empirically necessary for a causal inference.

Requirements for Causality. Generally, there are three criteria that must be satisfied to infer a causal relationship between conditions. Qualitative and quantitative researchers may structure their projects differently and gather their data in different ways, but both must satisfy these criteria if they wish to make a causal argument. The first requirement is that of **concomitant variation**; that is, when a change occurs in x, a change also occurs in y. When this situation occurs, we say that x is *correlated* or associated with y. The conditions must vary systematically with each other. If we contend that greater alienation causes more frequent participation in radical political activities, then the data must show that those people who are more alienated participate in radical political activities more frequently than those who are not. If the data reveal a systematic variation among the conditions, the concomitant variation requirement for making a causal inference has been met.

The second requirement is one of **appropriate sequence in time**: if x causes y, then x must occur before y. An event that takes place *after* another event cannot be the cause of that event. To return to our example, if more frequent participation in radical activities precedes increasing feelings of alienation, the feelings of alienation cannot be a cause of the participation. The investigator demonstrates that he has satisfied this requirement by observing that the appropriate temporal sequence of conditions has occurred.

The third requirement is to eliminate from consideration as possible causes all other conditions *in a particular research situation* that satisfy the first two requirements. (We emphasize "in a particular research situation" here because we do not wish to deny the possibility of multiple causation. Rather, this requirement pertains only to other possible causal variables that may be involved in a specific research project.) In practice, this requirement, unlike the two preceding ones, is very difficult to satisfy. At best, we can only satisfy this requirement approximately, by eliminating as many alternative, potentially explanatory conditions as we can when we do our research.

We can summarize our discussion with the statement of a major premise in conditional form: If and only if condition x varies concomitantly with condition y, and condition x (the independent condition) has preceded condition y (the dependent condition) in time, and all other possible independent conditions have been eliminated, then condition x is a cause of condition y.

As we shall see, with varying degrees of precision, the structures of explanatory research designs permit us to establish the concomitant variation of conditions and the time sequence within which the conditions exist or occur. They also take us some, though never the entire, distance toward eliminating other possible independent conditions.

Hypotheses and Theories

In scientific methodology, explanation is accomplished by establishing a strong logical and empirical argument that a causal relationship exists between two variables, that is, demonstrating that changes in the values of one variable are caused, and therefore explained, by changes in values of a second variable. Some theorists contend that poverty is causally related to crime. In this formulation, poverty is the independent variable (x) and crime the dependent variable (y). Such assertions about causal relationships between two variables are called hypotheses. We might represent this hypothesis as follows:

Time ⟶

Independent Variable   ⟶   Dependent Variable
          Poverty   Causes   Crime

In criminal justice research, we are seldom able to explain a complex phenomenon like crime by referring to a single causal variable. Because several variables taken together are more likely to account for crime, we might hypothesize that poverty, ethnic or racial discrimination, and age cause crime. This is an example of multiple causation, and it can be represented as follows:

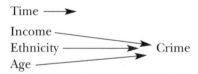

Time ⟶

Income
Ethnicity ⟶ Crime
Age

Finally, we may hypothesize that persons who are poor and then begin to associate with others who commit crimes are likely to commit a crime. That is, criminal association is an intervening variable between poverty and crime.

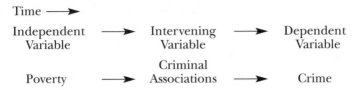

All these formulations are hypotheses generated by the researcher. The researcher creates and imposes a tentative, hypothetical structure on the phenomenon he is studying. The same researcher, or another one, seeing the phenomenon from a different perspective, might propose a different hypothetical structure for the same phenomenon. For instance, in a given research project, crime might be considered a hypothetical cause of poverty; in another project, crime might be seen as leading to criminal associations. In any event, it is the researcher who decides how to formulate hypotheses, and he may change his formulation if he desires. In the end, it will be the structure of the research design together with the data collected by the researcher that determine whether or not a particular explanatory hypothesis should be tentatively accepted or rejected.

Two or more related, empirically testable hypotheses constitute a theory. If they can be linked together according to the rules of logic, two principal advantages ensue. The first advantage is that new hypotheses can often be logically derived from the set of original ones. Consider, for example, the following three hypotheses:

If x, then y
If y, then z
If z, then a

Applying certain rules of logic (the details of which are beyond the scope of this text) to these three hypotheses, we could derive three new ones:

If x, then z
If x, then a
If y, then a

These new hypotheses are then incorporated into the logical net that comprises the theory.

The second advantage of logically integrated theories over single hypotheses is that empirical support for any *one* of the hypotheses in the theory lends some empirical support to *all* of the other hypotheses that make up the theory.

With these preliminary considerations of logic and causal analysis in mind, we turn to a discussion of explanatory research designs.

Preexperimental Designs

Explanatory research, as we have noted, involves the search for causal relationships among two or more conditions or variables through the use of a number of different types of research designs. These research designs are differentiated from each other by their forms and by the strength of the arguments they permit the researcher to make concerning the existence of cause-and-effect relationships. The least persuasive of these designs are called **preexperimental designs,** of which there are two kinds: after-only and before-after.

Suppose we let y_{M1} represent our observation of the value of the dependent variable y at a given point in time (T_1). We let y_{M2} represent a second observation of the same variable at a later point in time (T_2). Finally, we let x represent our observation of the independent variable, the one that we think explains y. We could then represent a sequence of observations of these two variables in the following way:

Time $\longrightarrow$ $\quad$ T_1 $\qquad\quad$ T_2

$\qquad\qquad\qquad$ y_{M1} $\quad x \quad$ y_{M2}

This indicates that we observed x at some time between our first and second observations of y. Now, suppose we compare our two observations of y—that is, we compare y_{M1} and y_{M2}. There are two possibilities: either y changed or did not change in value. If no change in y is observed, there is presumably nothing to explain, because x has nothing to do with y. If y did change, then there is something to explain and it is at least possible that x caused the change.

After-Only Design. The after-only design is a strategy for attempting to assess the effect of a particular event after the event has occurred. It is called after-*only* because no observation of the dependent variable (y) took place before the presumed cause (x). The **after-only design** may be represented as follows:

Time $\longrightarrow$ $\quad$ T_1 $\qquad\quad$ T_2

$\qquad\qquad\qquad$ $\boxed{y_{M1}}$ $\quad x \quad$ y_{M2}

The box around y_{M1} indicates that the researcher had not observed y at that time, and therefore has to guess or estimate what would have been observed. In general, this is the only type of design that can be used to study the effects of unexpected events. Studies of the impact of civil disorders or cataclysmic natural events, such as earthquakes and tornadoes, often use an after-only design.

An investigator may use an after-only design when he has no alternative, but its form provides the least persuasive basis for causal inference. Using it for any purpose other than to describe the state of affairs following a significant event and to speculate about its effects is fraught with methodological hazards. Because the investigator has been unable to observe the dependent variable (y) prior to the hypothesized causal event (x), he cannot be very confident either that y actually changed or that the causal factors he hypothesized are really causal. The only requirement of a causal inference that has been met is that of time sequence. Concomitant variation is not established by this design, and nothing has been accomplished in the way of eliminating other possible causal factors.

One strategy a researcher can use to strengthen the inferences drawn from after-only research is to study a similar population that has not been exposed to the *presumed* causal condition (that is, the earthquake, storm, riot, or revolution). If observations of both of these populations show the same presumed effect, we can be reasonably sure that the presumed cause was not a real cause. If the exposed population shows the effect and the unexposed population does not, we have not proven that the independent variable caused the effect because some other unmeasured or unknown variable may be responsible. However, we have at least increased the likelihood that the presumed independent variable was responsible for the effect, and in doing so, we make the argument for causal inference more persuasive.

Before-After Design. If the researcher is able to anticipate the independent variable, or to create it in a research situation, she can use a **before-after design**. Here, the investigator actually observes *y* before *x* occurs (a preobservation of the dependent variable). Then, the event (*x*) occurs or is introduced by the investigator, and *y* is observed again (postobservation of the dependent variable). This design can be diagrammed as follows:

$$\text{Time} \longrightarrow \quad T_1 \qquad T_2$$
$$y_{M1} \quad x \quad y_{M2}$$

Finally, the pre- and postobservations of the dependent variable are compared to determine if any change has taken place, and an appropriate inference is drawn about the relationship between the independent and dependent variables. If a change is observed, the independent variable can be viewed as responsible for the change because the before-after design provides reasonably clear evidence of both concomitant variation and appropriate time sequence between the variables.

Internal and External Threats to the Validity of Research Results

Although the before-after design has significant advantages over the after-only design, it has serious shortcomings. The inference that the dependent and independent variables are causally related is justified only if the event (the independent variable) was the only thing that changed between the pre- and postobservations. If any other changes took place, then any of these changes might have generated the observed effects, or several in combination may have done so. Therefore, the before-after design also fails to provide strong justification for causal inference, because the intervention of unforeseen and/or unobserved events in the research situation is *always* a possibility.

Methodologists have identified several types of changes (besides the occurrence or introduction of the independent variable) that may occur in the time between the pre- and postobservations of the dependent variable. Some of the more common changes, often referred to as threats to **internal validity**, will be described here; others will be discussed later.

Maturation refers to changes that occur within individuals as they age—such as physical growth, expanding experiences, and lessons drawn from those experiences. Generally speaking, the longer the time period between the first and second observations of the dependent variable, the greater the chances that maturation effects will occur—that is, maturational changes, rather than our independent variable, may be responsible for observed changes in the dependent variable. For example, a longitudinal study following a group of juveniles from age 11 to 18 and testing the hypothesis that drug use leads to other types of criminal offenses, would run a very high risk of maturational effects.

History refers to changes not in the individuals under observation but in the general social environment in which they live. For example, changes in the crime rate may be related, not to the imposition of stiffer penalties (our independent variable), but to changes in the economic environment (such as increasing employment or aging of the population). Here, too, a longer time period between pre- and postmeasurement of the dependent variable increases the likelihood of history effects as an alternative explanation for our observed results.

Another threat to internal validity is **regression toward the mean.** This phenomenon is most often encountered when researchers select only those at one extreme or the other of a distribution for study. It is a well-established observation that the measurements used to identify these low or high scorers (for example, on an intelligence test or a test for job stress) will, if applied to the same individuals on a subsequent occasion, tend on average to go up (if they were low scorers) or go down (if they were high scorers); that is, they would tend to move toward the mean of the scores for the group from which they were selected for study. This tendency of the scores to regress toward the mean may be responsible for observed changes in our dependent variable, rather than our hypothesized independent variable.

Subject mortality refers to the loss of subjects or respondents between the pre- and the postmeasurement of the dependent variable. Actual deaths may occur, of course, but more commonly subjects simply drop out or are removed from the study for one reason or another. For example, some may refuse to cooperate further with the research; the researcher may be unable to locate others. Here too the longer the time frame of the research design, the larger this problem is likely to be. Of course, when subject mortality occurs, observed changes in the dependent variable may be the result of these changes in the membership of the study group, rather than of our proposed independent variable.

Selection bias threatens both internal and external validity. Externally, it comes into play when an atypical, extreme, or peculiar (that is, nonrepresentative) sample of subjects is chosen for a before-after study, making generalization of any findings to larger populations inaccurate or misleading. Good sampling procedures, to be discussed in the next chapter, alleviate the threat to external validity of this form of selection bias. Internally, even when a control group is included in the design, selection bias can result in initial (pretest) differences between the experimental and control groups that substantially weaken the researcher's causal argument if posttest differences are observed. Selection bias is an especially serious danger whenever people select themselves or are selected by someone other than the researchers into the experimental and/or control groups. Matching or randomizing differences between control and experimental groups alleviates selection bias's threat to internal validity.

If we change the method by which we have operationally defined and observed or measured the dependent variable, we are changing how or what we are observing and, in effect, introducing another variable into the investigation. Any differences in our two observations of the dependent variable may be the result of observation or measurement changes and not changes of the independent variable.

Another kind of problem with the before-after design and all other designs incorporating observation is that the process of observation itself may affect the results obtained. Asking people questions (for example, about their attitudes toward the death penalty, the police, or the Supreme Court) or making them aware that they are being observed by researchers (even if they do not know specifically what the researchers are observing) may influence the pre- or postobservation results, quite apart from any effect generated by the independent variable itself. Subjects may lie in responding to questionnaires or interviews; police officers may modify their usual demeanor if they know their interactions with the public are being observed. An effect generated by the process of observation itself is known as an experimenter effect or a *Hawthorne effect*, which will be discussed more thoroughly later.

Experimental Designs

All of the explanatory research designs considered so far have substantial flaws that seriously weaken the argument that variable x causes variable y. The basic problem in each case has been satisfying the third condition for a causal inference—the elimination of other possible causes for changes in the dependent variable in the particular research situation. A causal inference is significantly strengthened if the research design includes a control group. This is the advantage of **experimental designs.**

Before-After-with-Control Design. When an investigator recognizes that variables other than the independent variable—such as maturation, history, measurement methods, or the Hawthorne effect—are present and potentially influential, and wants to assess or neutralize their effects, he can use a **before-after-with-control** research design:

Time $\longrightarrow$	T_1		T_2
Experimental Group (E)	y_{EM1}	x	y_{EM2}
Control Group (C)	y_{CM1}		y_{CM2}

Two separate groups of subjects are included in this design: an **experimental group** (E) and a **control group** (C). In the experimental group, the independent variable occurs or is introduced by the investigator, just as in the before-after design. In this design, however, there is also a control group, for which the independent variable does not occur or is not introduced.

The inclusion of the control group in the design permits the researcher to argue quite strongly that the combined effects of several alternative causal variables can be measured and then eliminated from consideration. The difference between the values of the dependent variable observed at T_1 and T_2 in the control group is a measure of the changes that may have occurred because of maturation, history, initial exposure to the measuring device, the Hawthorne effect, or any other changes that occurred between T_1 and T_2, *without the*

RESEARCHERS IN ACTION—EXPERIMENTS

The purpose of this experiment was to explore the ability of subjects to detect deception. The study applied the Behavioral Analysis Interview (BAI) developed by John Reid and Associates, Inc. The subjects consisted of 52 student volunteers who were enrolled in law enforcement classes at a Midwestern university. Twenty-seven students were in the experimental group and twenty-five participated in the control group. The control group was randomly selected by flipping a coin and selecting odd and even numbers of students from the sign-in sheet.

In order to examine the student's ability to classify subjects as truthful or deceptive, ten videotapes previously used in a similar study were select-ed. The ten videotapes were selected from tapes correctly classified by all evaluators in the previous experiment. The subjects portrayed in the ten tapes were suspected of committing a theft. The tapes were classified as truthful or deceptive based on a confession and additional factual evi-dence that supported the suspect's statement.

The research was conducted using a classical experimental design. The experimental group and control group were pretested at the same time. The experimental group received six hours of Behavioral Analysis Interview Training from John E. Reid and Associates, Inc. The control group was posttested the day after the pretest. The six hours of training was conducted one week later. Immediately after the training, the experi-mental group was posttested.

A fixed alternative survey was constructed, consisting of a single global assessment question and confidence assessment for each of the ten BAI subjects viewed on the tapes. The alternatives for the global assessment

---

additional effects, if any, of our independent variable. Therefore, we can subtract out from the total differences between y_{EM1} and y_{EM2} in the experimental group dif-ferences associated with maturation, history, and so on, in the control group and we are left with the difference in our dependent variable that can be attrib-uted to the effects of our hypothesized independent variable.[4] We might rep-resent the subtraction as follows:

Experimental Group   Control Group

$$(y_{EM1} - y_{EM2}) \quad - \quad (y_{CM1} - y_{CM2}) \quad = \quad \text{Effect of } x \text{ on } y$$

If the data indicate that some change in y remains after this subtraction is per-formed, this design gives us strong evidence of concomitant variation and appropriate time sequence as well as good reason to believe that the change was caused by x, because we have measured and then eliminated many of the possible extraneous causal factors. As a result, we can argue persuasively that a causal relationship exists between the independent and dependent variables.[5]

question were "truthful" or "deceptive." The confidence assessment asked the students to rate their confidence in their global assessment of each BAI subject on the tape. The choices were presented on a Likert scale and varied from 1 to 5, with a 1 indicating no confidence and a 5 indicating complete confidence. Survey sheets were issued to the students for the pretest and the posttest. The definitions of "truthful" and "deceptive" were read aloud. "Truthful" was defined as being completely honest with the interviewer (not withholding any relevant information). "Deceptive" was defined as being less than completely honest with the interviewer (withholding any relevant information). The students were instructed to watch each tape and then score the BAI subjects on the survey sheet.

The results of this study support the belief that truthful and deceptive suspects have discernable differences in behavior and suggest that the Behavioral Analysis Training (BAI) developed by John E. Reid and Associates, Inc., is an effective tool to differentiate behaviors associated with truth and deception. Furthermore, the BAI training increased the confidence of the subjects to correctly classify the theft suspects. Participants who received the BAI training correctly classified (with higher levels of confidence) more theft suspects than those who had not received the BAI training.

This study cannot be generalized beyond the sample selected for the experiment. Ideally, an experimental design should be utilized to control for the effects of pretesting the subjects. The pretesting process may have affected the ability to correctly classify subjects on the posttest. Additional research is needed to confirm and expand the findings of this study.

Source: J. P. Blair, *Detecting Deception: The Effects of Reid Behavioral Analysis Interview Training.* Unpublished master's thesis. (Macomb, IL: Western Illinois University, 1999).

Solomon Four-Group Design. The **Solomon four-group design** is an extension of the basic experimental design and can be represented as follows:

Time $\longrightarrow$	T_1		T_2
Experimental Group 1 (E1)	y_{E1M1}	x	y_{E1M2}
Control Group 1 (C1)	y_{C1M1}		y_{C1M2}
Experimental Group 2 (E2)		x	y_{E2M}
Control Group 2 (C2)			y_{C2M}

In this design, another experimental and another control group are added to the basic experimental design. These additions permit us to assess the effects, if any, of some of the potential causal variables in the experimental situation by comparing observations from the four groups in various combinations. Consider, for example, a comparison of the two experimental groups (E1 and E2). The difference between these two is the absence of the preobservation of the dependent variable (y) in E2. Suppose that we wanted a measure of the effects of the preobservation. Note that while in C1 the dependent variable was assessed initially, in C2 it was not. Now, $y_{C1M1} - y_{C1M2}$ is a difference that includes the effects of the preobservation *as well as* the effects of any other variables (except the independent variable) that changed between T_1 and T_2. A measure of the effects of these other variables is provided by $y_{C1M1} - y_{C1M2}$. Hence:

$$y_{C1M1} - y_{C1M2} - y_{C1M1} - y_{C2M2} = \text{The Effect of the Preobservation}$$

The Solomon four-group design does not provide any stronger support for an inference that there is a causal relationship between the independent and dependent variables than does the before-after-with-control design. However, it does permit the researcher to measure separately the effects of some of the other variables in the research situation, such as the effects of the preobservation.

Matching and Random Assignment. Although using a control group helped us solve some of the problems associated with justifying a causal inference, unfortunately we have introduced some new ones that demand attention. The most significant new difficulty is the possibility that the experimental and control groups are initially different from each other in some important way. If they are, the benefits we have derived from this design are negated, because any such difference is also a variable that may account for observed changes in our dependent variable. However, two strategies can be used to ensure that the experimental and control groups are as similar as possible: matching and random assignment.

One way of ensuring that the two groups are as similar as possible is by finding pairs of subjects that closely resemble each other and then assigning one to the experimental and one to the control group. This strategy and others similar to it are called **matching.** Matching "controls" (that is, makes the two groups "identical" on) whatever variables the subjects are matched on so that any observed differences in the independent variable cannot be attributed to them. Ordinarily, the two groups are matched on what the researcher considers possible causal (independent) variables other than the one(s) in which she is interested. This frees her to look for and explore the effects of her hypothesized independent variables without having to worry about the influence of the matched variables. This strategy requires, of course, that the investigator be able to identify the important variables and to assign individuals to the two groups accordingly. She may select pairs of subjects who are alike on selected variables, thereby assuring similar experimental and control groups (pair matching). She may also select groups so that the proportions or percentages of certain characteristics are equal in the two groups (sample matching); that is, both groups are 50 percent male, 25 percent middle class, 35 percent under age 19, 50 percent felons, and so on. The groups can be matched on as many different variables as the research situation permits, but obviously, the more variables involved, the more difficult the matching process becomes.

Matching does not completely solve the problem of similarity between the experimental and control groups, however. There is always the possibility that the two groups differ on one or more important variables that the researcher did not recognize and therefore did not consider in the matching process. These differences may account for observed changes in the dependent variable.

Random assignment involves placing individuals in the two groups according to the laws of probability, a form of sampling about which we shall have more to say in the next chapter. This strategy begins with establishing the total pool or collection of persons or events to be studied, and then making assignments so that each individual person or event has an equal chance of being placed in either the experimental or control group. This is a way of randomly distributing differences among the people or events between the two groups, thereby minimizing the likelihood of any systematic (nonrandom) differences between the two groups. When the data are analyzed, differences larger than those that can be attributed to random variation indicate a relationship between x and y. Random assignment does not guarantee, however, that systematic differences have been eliminated.

Matching and random assignment help ensure that the experimental and control groups are as similar as possible. Nevertheless, as we have seen, there remains some uncertainty concerning this similarity regardless of the strategy chosen. As a result, causal inference based on an experimental research design remains to some degree uncertain as well.

Longitudinal Explanatory Designs. Some kinds of research situations call for modifications of the basic types of research designs we have discussed. Perhaps the most common adaptations involve using the panel and multiple group trend designs discussed in the earlier section on descriptive research. Evaluation research often follows this kind of research design. Suppose, for example, that we wanted to assess the effects of a police department's public relations campaign (the independent variable) on attitudes toward the police (the dependent variable) in a particular urban neighborhood. A study might be designed that involved a measurement of the dependent variable before the campaign was launched and three measurements after the campaign was completed. We could choose either a panel or a multiple group trend design. The explanatory panel design (sometimes called an *interrupted time series design*) might be diagrammed like this:

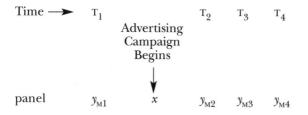

Where the research situation permits, a control group should be added to this design, consisting, for example, of a neighborhood very similar to the one where the campaign is being conducted, thereby increasing substantially the persuasiveness of an inference that the campaign, rather than some other possible causal variable, is the cause of any observed before-after differences in citizens' attitudes.

A multiple group trend study of the same research question might be diagrammed like this:

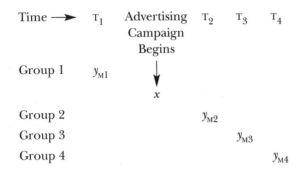

Here, too, control groups should be included in the design whenever possible. Pollsters hired by political candidates often use one of these two designs to gauge the effectiveness of TV, newspaper, or radio advertising campaigns. They are useful, in fact, for assessing the effects of almost any kind of information or persuasion program. Multiple observations following the occurrence of x provide evidence concerning both the duration and the changes in the intensity of its effects.

Longitudinal explanatory designs have the advantages and disadvantages of their descriptive design counterparts. When used without control groups (as they often are), causal inferences derived from them are no better than those based on preexperimental before-after designs. With control groups, though, they offer strong evidence for causal inference.

Quasi-Experimental Procedures

Research that conforms to all of the aspects of the experimental research design typically takes place in a laboratory setting, because it is imperative that a researcher have control over the assignment of subjects to experimental and control groups and the occurrence of the independent variable. However, exercising these controls is often difficult in criminal justice research. It is virtually impossible, for example, for a researcher to persuade a judge to assign different sentences for the same offense in order to test the effects of sentencing policy on recidivism. It would also be difficult to request public defenders (on a random basis) to act as if they adhered to two different legal strategies in defending their clients to examine the effects of these strategies on conviction rates. Even if subjects could be controlled in such ways, some very difficult ethical issues are raised by these practices.

For ethical, practical, and methodological reasons, then, researchers must often resort to **quasi-experimental procedures** in some phases of the research process. These procedures diminish some of the persuasive power of experimental design but still provide some logical and empirical support for causal inferences. Perhaps the two aspects of the research process most often compromised through quasi-experimental techniques involve assigning subjects to experimental and control groups and separating the time of measurement from the time of occurrence of the variables.

Experimental design requires that membership in the experimental and control groups be determined before the experiment begins so that differences between the two groups can be controlled through matching or random assignment. When the researcher is unable to do this, he may attempt to find two groups in the real world who are similar in most ways but who differ in their values on the independent variable. Their values on the dependent variable could then be compared, and any differences observed might be attributed to the differences in the independent variable values. Although this procedure has merit, it is considerably less persuasive than experimental procedure. Finding adequately matched groups in the real world is extremely difficult, and the researcher is usually forced to use groups that have larger differences than are desirable, undermining support for a causal inference.

The logic of causal inference also requires that changes in the independent variable occur *before* changes in the dependent variable. The best empirical evidence for this time sequence is provided by the experimental design, where the researcher controls the time at which the independent variable occurs. For many research projects, however, exercising this control is neither possible nor practical. In these cases, it is possible to approximate the strict time sequence requirements of the experimental design by gathering data at one point in time (the *time of measurement*) about variables whose values have changed at some previous time (the *time of occurrence*). Interviews and questionnaires often seek information of this nature.

Suppose we hypothesize that family instability (x) is related to juvenile delinquency (y). For obvious reasons, it is not possible to test this hypothesis using an experimental design. However, we could give a large group of older juveniles a questionnaire asking them to tell us (1) if they had ever been convicted of a juvenile offense and, if they had, when the first offense occurred, and (2) if their parents were divorced and, if they were, when the divorce occurred. We could then use the responses to the questions about time of occurrence of x and y as evidence concerning their actual time sequence. Of course, when time of occurrence does not coincide with time of measurement, support for the time sequence condition in a causal argument is weakened because the validity of the measurements can be questioned. Are the reports about times of occurrence accurate? Still, sometimes evidence of this kind is the best we can get.

Whatever the choice of research design, it must be made explicit before the research begins, especially in quantitative explanatory research. It is less crucial in descriptive qualitative research. In the former, though, the quality of the results and the degree of confidence that the researcher can place in the causal inferences that result depend upon the structure of the design within the context of which the data were collected. The researcher's knowledge of the characteristics, the strengths, and the limitations of these designs is vital to understanding and doing effective research.

TRIANGULATION

Triangulation means collecting different types of data from different sources using different types of research methods with respect to a single research question. With *observation,* the researcher records the activities and events she has seen. Our confidence in interpretations based on observation alone, however, is limited by the possibility that the observations may not be accurately recorded or interpreted. If, however, we *interview* the people involved about their behavior, and their remarks concur with the researcher's observations, we can have more confidence in the conclusions. If we are also able to use *document analysis,* that is, read others' accounts of the people and events we have witnessed, and if their observations and conclusions are similar to ours, we can say with still greater assurance that our conclusions are justified. We have, in short, used the technique of triangulation.

Triangulation is valuable not only because it allows us to have more confidence in our findings, but also because it often brings discrepancies in our data to light. People may tell us they behave in one way, but our observations might show they behave in another. We can then focus on the source of this discrepancy and its resolution and, perhaps, design an experiment to investigate the discrepancy we have discovered.

Whenever possible, the researcher should use triangulation to minimize error resulting from the use of any single method for collecting data, to maximize the possibility of discovering discrepancies, and to make full use of the principles characterizing the scientific perspective.

A FINAL NOTE
ABOUT THE RESEARCH PROCESS

Lawrence W. Sherman and his associates have developed the Maryland Scale of Scientific Methods; we can adapt it a bit and use it as a general guide to assessing the relative strengths of any particular explanatory research project by "grading" it on two scales according to the presence or absence of specific characteristics of the research design employed.[6]

In part A of Figure 3.1, each row represents a set of research design characteristics, the particular characteristics forming the columns. The more yeses in the row, the higher the level or grade, the more of the desirable design characteristics the research project has, and the stronger is the evidence provided for a causal inference. In part B, studies are ranked or graded according to whether specified threats to internal validity (which form the columns) are managed appropriately in the research project. Here too the more yeses in a row, the stronger the design. In general, then, the higher the level a particular research project reaches on both scales, the higher the quality of the methodology employed, and the more confidence we can have in the causal inference(s) claimed by the researchers.

Remember though that we have emphasized dangers inherent in accepting the results of any scientific research at face value. Our experiences teach us that things are not always as they seem, so the validity and reliability of our

FIGURE 3.1	Research Design Quality Ratings

A. Research Design Characteristic present?

	Before-after measurements	Control group used	Multiple study groups observed	Randomization
Methods Score				
Level 1 (lowest quality)	no	no	yes*	no
Level 2	yes	no	no	no
Level 3	yes	yes	no	no
Level 4	yes	yes	yes†	no
Level 5 (highest quality)	yes	yes	yes†	yes

B. Threats to Internal Validity accounted for/controlled?

	Time sequence/ causal direction	History, maturation	Subject mortality and other related internal chance factors	Selection bias
Methods Score				
Level 1 (lowest quality)	no	no	no	no
Level 2	yes	no	no	no
Level 3	yes	yes	no	no
Level 4	yes	yes	yes	no
Level 5 (highest quality)	yes	yes	yes	yes

* Multiple examples of after-only design included.
† More than one experimental and/or control group included in the design.

categorizations may be questioned. There may be discrepancies between what people say they do and what they actually do. People who say they would welcome minority group members as neighbors are often the first to leave the neighborhood when minorities arrive, and politicians' campaign promises may be regarded with suspicion. Causal inferences, even if based on experimental designs, are subject to debate.

Even the best scientific methodology provides no foolproof mechanism for removing all doubt about the validity and reliability of data collected or causal inferences drawn in its name. The best we can do as researchers is to eliminate as many sources of error as possible in our own work, make it available for the criticism of other scientists, and subject our findings to further tests.

REVIEW QUESTIONS

1. What is the difference between research methodology and research methods?
2. From what sources might research topics emerge?
3. How do constructs differ from operational definitions?
4. What is the difference between a category and a variable?
5. What distinguishes validity, reliability, and precision in categorizations?
6. Discuss the different types of validity and reliability, including external and internal validity.
7. What is a research design?
8. How do descriptive and explanatory research designs differ?
9. What are the advantages and disadvantages of panel, multiple group trend, and cross-sectional designs in descriptive research?
10. What are the valid forms of argument from conditional statements?
11. What is the difference between the form and the content of arguments?
12. What is the difference between necessary and sufficient causes?
13. What are the logical conditions necessary for making a causal inference?
14. How do independent, dependent, and intervening variables differ?
15. How do preexperimental designs differ from experimental designs? Why are preexperimental designs less persuasive as foundations for causal inference than experimental designs?
16. What are the Hawthorne effect, history, maturation, subject mortality, regression toward the mean, and selection bias?
17. Compare and contrast experimental and quasi-experimental designs.
18. What is triangulation and why is it an effective research tool?

EXERCISES

1. Collect at least three physical objects of the same general type (for example, three writing instruments, or three cups, or three books) and place them in front of you. Identify ways in which the objects are different. Identify the categories (variables) you are using and the subcategories corresponding to each category. (For example, you may say one object is blue and another is red. The concept you are using is color, and the sub-categories—the values of the color variables—are red and blue.) Construct at least four such variables and their associated values. Then, consider three persons and perform the same comparative activities,

identifying variables and corresponding values of each variable. Next, consider three events of the same general type and do the same things.

2. Identify values for each of the following variables and describe at least two different operational definitions for each variable.

   - police officer
   - crimes
   - citizens' evaluation of the performance of the state's attorney
   - laws
   - punishments
   - judges
   - verdicts
   - penal institutions
   - criminals

   Compare your results with those of another member of the class and discuss any similarities and differences you discover. How would you establish the validity and reliability of the operationalizations you chose?

3. Identify three different research designs for a research project describing drug use patterns among students at a particular university over time.

4. Identify at least three possible causal variable chains in criminal justice involving independent, intervening, and dependent variables.

5. Suppose you are interested in studying the effects of a human relations or sensitivity training program on White officers working in Black neighborhoods. Describe and discuss the logical supports for causal inference provided by each of the following types of design for studying this research question.

   - after-only design
   - before-after design
   - before-after-with-control design
   - Solomon four-group design

6. Return to the research reports you visited online in exercise 9 of Chapter 1. What research designs did the researchers use? Discuss what aspects of each research project lead you to identify its design type as you have.

NOTES

1. See F. S. C. Northrop, *The Logic of the Sciences and the Humanities* (New York: World, 1959), especially pp. 102–107, for a thorough discussion of concepts and constructs.

2. A summary of these and other longitudinal studies may be found in David P. Farrington, Lloyd E. Ohlin, and James Q. Wilson, *Understanding and Controlling Crime: Toward a New Research Strategy* (New York: Springer-Verlag, 1986).

3. Claire Selltiz, et al., *Research Methods in Social Relations* (New York: Holt, Rinehart & Winston, 1965), p. 83.

4. This inference, of course, depends upon the assumption that no other influences have acted on the control group between measurements that have not also acted on the experimental group. If this assumption is correct—and we may have no way to tell whether it is—then we may justifiably infer that the difference between experimental and control groups represents the effect of the independent variable.

5. The use of experimental design in criminal justice research has grown a great deal in recent years. For some examples of studies using experimental and quasi-experimental designs, see two "special issues" of *Crime and Delinquency* published in 2000: 46(2) and 46(3).

6. Adapted from Exhibit 1 in Lawrence W. Sherman, et al. *Preventing Crime: What Works, What Doesn't, What's Promising.* Research in Brief (Washington, DC: NIJ, 1998).

CHAPTER

4

Sampling

After stating a research question and developing an appropriate research design, we must select one or more persons, objects, or events (that is, units of analysis) on whose properties or characteristics our research will focus. Any of the procedures discussed here can be used by researchers using quantitative or qualitative methods, though the latter, especially if they are participant observers, are not concerned with the statistical representativeness of a sample per se, but rather with identifying people who will exemplify what they are studying.

Sometimes, we can take a *census* of a population by studying every element involved. For example, to determine whether the 400 registered voters in Hitsville would support a tax referendum to provide funds for a new police station, we might interview every voter. This group of persons is called the research **population,** and each individual person is referred to as an *element* of the population. Populations may be *finite* and consist of a specifiable number of elements, or *infinite* and include an unspecifiable number of elements. The population of registered voters in Hitsville is a finite one, whereas the population of all possible flips of a coin is infinite.

If we were interested in citizens' opinions on a tax referendum not just in Hitsville but statewide or nationally, census taking would not be feasible for a typical researcher because of the expense involved. Even the federal government undertakes a national census only once every ten years because of the tremendous cost. In such cases, we obtain information from some but not all of the elements in our population; that is, from a **sample** of that population. A sample consists of selected elements from a population that will be observed in order to learn something about the entire population.

Because the sample will represent the population for our research purposes, we need to be concerned about the *quality* of that representation. Our goal is to select a "good" sample—one whose characteristics accurately represent the characteristics of the population. To the extent that the sample is representative, inferences can be drawn about the population.

But sampling is inevitably a risky business. Some samples are good representatives of their populations, whereas others are not. Furthermore, even a good sample may not mirror *exactly* the population from which it is drawn. Any differences between the characteristics of the sample and those of the population are said to be the result of **sampling error.** We can expect any sampling procedure to produce some sampling error. To make matters worse, the researcher cannot determine the extent of the sampling error because the whole population has not been observed, and therefore the characteristics of the sample cannot be directly compared to those of the population.

Given this situation, the procedures researchers use to select the sample become critical. Some sampling techniques are more likely than others to produce "good" samples. Furthermore, some sampling procedures permit us to estimate the amount of the sampling error statistically, and these sampling procedures are clearly preferable to those that do not permit such estimates. Inferential statistics (Chapter 11) allow us to say precisely how much risk we are taking when we make an inference about the population on the basis of the sample data. For now, we will discuss the more powerful sampling techniques first and then consider the less powerful ones.

PROBABILITY SAMPLING

Although there are many kinds of sampling techniques, they can be divided broadly into two types: probability and nonprobability sampling. **Probability sampling** allows us to specify the probability that any given element in our population will be included in our sample. **Nonprobability sampling** does not permit us to determine the likelihood that an element in our population will be selected. Probability sampling has very significant advantages over nonprobability sampling, especially because it allows us to use statistical inference. Statistical inference, in turn, permits us to estimate the extent of sampling error.

Suppose we are interested in theories of crime causation, and we have identified five theorists as our population, namely Edwin, Cesare, George, Jeremy, and Robert. This list of all the elements in our population is called a **sampling frame.** Because we cannot afford to visit all five, we decide to select two for our sample. After writing each of the names on a small piece of paper and putting those slips of paper into a hat, we then, without looking, draw one from the hat. Because each theorist is one-fifth or .20 of the total group of five, each man's **probability** (p) of being selected is 1 in 5, or $p = .20$, at the outset.

The name on the slip of paper we pick initially is the first element in our sample. After our first draw, we have a decision to make before we make our second draw. We may either put the drawn slip back in the hat or leave it out. If we leave it out, there are only four names remaining in the hat, so the probability of drawing one of those four is 1 in 4 or .25. Hence, the probability of drawing any single name has changed from .20 on the first draw to .25 on the second. To keep the probability of drawing any one name from the hat the same from one draw to the next, we would have to place each name drawn back into the hat before we made the next draw. That creates the possibility that we will draw the same name again, and that possibility will be discussed later. For now, we can simply note that when we put an element back into the population before we select another element for our sample, we are *sampling with replacement*. Not returning the drawn element is called *sampling without replacement*. When we are drawing relatively small samples from relatively large populations, the changes in probability associated with sampling without replacement are very small, and sampling without replacement is quite common.

We can also determine the probability of drawing any two particular names from our population of five names. The first step would be to list all of the potential combinations of two names, and for our purposes we will use the first letters in each of the five names. The ten possible combinations for this population would include the following: EC, EG, EJ, ER, CG, CJ, CR, GJ, GR, JR. The probability of getting any one of the ten combinations is 1 in 10 or .10. Obviously, if we had a much larger population, the task of determining the probability of getting any one of the combinations would be tedious indeed if we used this rather simple method. Fortunately, statisticians have worked out a formula for determining the number of possible combinations (c) of elements drawn (r; in our example, 2) at a time from a population of size n (in our example, 5). That is:

Formula 4.1

$$_nC_r = \frac{n!}{r!(n-r)!}$$

The ! is a mathematical notation for "factorial," and n factorial is given by $n(n-1)(n-2)(n-3)\ldots(1)$. In our example, $(n-4)$ would be the last factor needed because $(5-4)=(1)$. The formula can be computed as follows:

1. $$_nC_r = \frac{n!}{r!(n-r)!}$$

2. $$_nC_r = \frac{5!}{2!(5-2)!}$$

3. $$_nC_r = \frac{5(n-1)(n-2)(n-3)(n-4)}{2(r-1)\times(3)(3-1)(3-2)}$$

4. $$_nC_r = \frac{5\times4\times3\times2\times1}{(2\times1)(3\times2\times1)} = \frac{120}{12} = \frac{10}{1}$$

This tells us that there are ten possible combinations of five things taken two at a time. The probability of getting any one of the combinations, then, is 1 in 10 or .10.

If we take a census, that is, if we contact all persons in our population and ask them appropriate questions, we will have relatively complete information concerning their thoughts on the causes of crime. But if we select only two individuals (elements) and learn their views, we will almost certainly not have represented the views of all five exactly. Hence, we take a risk when we generalize from the responses of any sample to the population, but that risk decreases as we increase the size of our sample. When we use probability sampling, the larger the number of elements we sample from our population, the more assurance we have that our sample is representative of the population from which it was drawn.[1]

Random Sampling

The most basic type of probability sample is a simple **random sample,** which gives each individual element in the population an *equal* chance of being selected, and makes all combinations of a specified number of elements equally probable as well. (In our previous example, the probability of drawing any specific name on the first draw was .20, and the probability of any particular combination of two being selected on the first draw was 1 in 10, or $p =.10$.)

Theoretically, in order to select a simple random sample, *all* of the elements in a population must be listed only once; however, a complete list of population elements may be very difficult to obtain, and creating our sampling frame may present a number of problems. Even an accurate and complete list of voting residents of Hitsville collected today might contain inaccuracies tomorrow, because some voting residents may die or move away, and newly qualified residents may register. Often, no list (for example, a list of rape victims in Hitsville) enumerating a population will exist. When lists do exist, they may be biased and inaccurate, for they may systematically exclude or underrepresent some categories of events or people and overrepresent others. Clearly, our initial list of elements must be carefully constructed and evaluated for accuracy, and corrected where possible. Unavoidable inadequacies should be noted and reported. Although it is unlikely that any enumeration of elements in a large population will remain accurate for any length of time, checking for these sources of error may improve the quality of the list considerably.

After we have drawn up our list, we can use any of a number of techniques to select a sample of the size we need. Suppose we wish to select a sample of a hundred respondents (elements) from a population of 500 by using a table of random numbers. First, our 500 respondents would have to be numbered consecutively, beginning with 001 and ending with 500. Then, we would turn to the table of **random numbers** (see Appendix A), close our eyes, and place a pencil somewhere on the table. Starting from the nearest number, we could move either horizontally or vertically, selecting a respondent for our sample each time we come to a number between 1 and 500, until we have selected a hundred subjects. Assuming that we are sampling without replacement, if we encounter the same number a second time or if the number in the table is greater than 500, we simply skip that number and go on to the next number until we find one that does correspond and has not already been chosen.

A simple random sample is less costly both in time and in labor than taking a census, but it can still be relatively expensive if we have to put a lot of effort into constructing and "purifying" our list of elements. However, when we know little or nothing about our population and can get a reasonably accurate list of its elements, a simple random sample is usually the best choice.

Stratified Random Sampling and Proportionate Sampling

If we want to be sure that our sample is representative of our population in certain specifiable ways (for example, proportion of males), or if we believe that a certain variable may affect our subjects' responses (for example, ethnicity), we can use a **stratified random sample,** assuming that relevant information about each element is available. To draw a sample of this type, we divide our population into categories, or *strata,* ensuring that each population element falls into one and only one of the established categories or stratum. Simple random samples could then be selected from each of the subpopulations. Usually, the size of the simple random sample drawn from each strata is adjusted so that the proportion of elements is equal to the proportion of the whole population contained within that stratum. This procedure is referred to as **proportionate sampling.** If we stratified a population of 1,000 subjects by sex and discovered that there were 600 females and 400 males, we could draw a sample of one hundred from the whole population consisting of sixty females and forty males. Our sample would then be exactly representative of the population, at least as far as the sex variable is concerned. Furthermore, each element in the whole population had an equal chance of being selected for the sample. By using a stratified sample, we can often reduce the number of cases we need in order to maximize our chances of representativeness by making certain that members of each of the categories we believe to be important are included. For instance, if we hypothesize that ethnicity is related to the frequency of rape victimization, and we enumerate the population of Hitsville, we could select a simple random sample large enough to ensure that all ethnic groups in the city would be included. If, however, the percentage of ethnic minorities is very small, our sample size would have to be extremely large to include enough minority group members to conduct a meaningful analysis. If we could obtain or construct lists for each of the ethnic minority groups in the population, we could stratify it according to ethnicity and select simple random samples of Whites, Blacks, Hispanics, and so forth, thus ensuring that all minorities would be represented in our sample in the appropriate proportions.

Disproportionate Sampling

So far we have discussed only one type of probability sample, a simple random sample, in which each element in the population has an equal chance of being selected. However, the probabilities associated with an element's selection do not have to be equal. We can use a **disproportionate sampling** strategy and draw a sample so that some elements have, for example, twice the probability of being chosen. The crucial feature of any probability sample is being able to specify the probability that any given element will be included.

Consider again our example of a population with a small percentage of minority persons, stratified by ethnic group. Suppose we would like to examine our data on Blacks in some detail, and to do that, we need a relatively large number of Blacks in our sample. We would simply decide that we wanted each Black person in our population to have 1 chance in 10 (or 5 or 2, and so on) of being included in the sample, while leaving the probability that a White would be selected at 1 in 100 (or 200 or 1,000, and so on). The result, of course, is that we end up with a greater number and proportion of Blacks in our sample, and that our total sample is no longer representative of the ethnic distribution within the population. Therefore, when we analyze our data, we should not place all of the selected people into a single pool and use the data from this pool to generalize to the population as a whole.

Suppose that we are studying whether people are in favor of capital punishment in a city whose population is 90 percent White and 10 percent Black. We stratify our population by ethnic group and sample disproportionately, selecting 2 percent of the Whites and 20 percent of the Blacks. In comparison to their respective proportions in the whole population, Blacks will be overrepresented and Whites will be underrepresented in our sample. If Blacks and Whites differ in their views on capital punishment, combining these two groups into a single pool to estimate the proportion of people (regardless of ethnic group) in the city who favored capital punishment would be misleading. Our estimate would be distorted by the differences in the proportion of Blacks in our sample compared to their proportion in the population as a whole.

We *could* legitimately use the proportion of Blacks in our sample to estimate the proportion of Blacks in the population who favor capital punishment, and the proportion of Whites who favor capital punishment in this sample to estimate the proportion of Whites in the population who favor it. We could also legitimately compare the proportion of Blacks with the proportion of Whites who favor capital punishment because our stratified sampling procedure has produced two separate random samples, one of Blacks and one of Whites. The differences between the two samples in the proportion that each represents of the population as a whole is, for all practical purposes, irrelevant to a comparison of the proportions in the two separate groups.

There is a relatively simple solution to the problem of making statements about a population as a whole on the basis of sample data when disproportionate sampling is desirable. It consists of drawing a second sample of one or more of the separate strata so that the sample contains proportionate representation of a particular subpopulation (for example, ethnic groups). These proportionate samples from the various strata can then be combined to make estimates of the percent of people in the population as a whole who support capital punishment.

Systematic Sampling

Sometimes, an acceptable approximation of a random sample can be achieved through a technique called **systematic sampling.** To use systematic sampling, instead of using a table of random numbers to select each element in our sample, we randomly select only our first element, and then choose every 10th, 15th, or kth element in the sampling frame. The size of k is determined by the number of elements on our population list and the size of the sample we desire. If there are 500 names on a list and we want a sample of fifty, we would select every 10th name ($500 \div 50 = 10$) on the list.

If an adequate list of elements in a particular population is available to the researcher, systematic sampling may save considerable time, but it also entails a potential hazard. This hazard involves lists that are ordered in some way—for example, by rank or cycle. Suppose we have a list of military personnel in which every 5th subject holds a supervisory rank (such as sergeant). If we intend to sample every 5th subject, a systematic sample starting with the randomly selected number two clearly could provide us with considerably different responses to questions about authority than a sample starting with the number five. In the first case, we would include only nonsupervisory personnel in our sample; in the second, only supervisory personnel.

Cluster Sampling

Another type of probability sampling, known as **cluster sampling,** involves dividing our population into a number of groups, called clusters, on the basis of some criterion (such as geographic area). Each cluster is assigned a unique number, and, using a random numbers table, we select a random sample of clusters. Data may then be gathered about each element in each of the selected clusters in order to complete the research project.

At first glance, cluster sampling may seem like another version of stratified sampling, but there are four important differences between the two. First, remember that in stratified sampling we used one or more potential independent variables such as age and sex to create the strata. We wanted to be sure that our sample accurately reflected the population on these variables because we thought they were important for our analysis. We create clusters using a criterion that we think is unimportant for our analysis and that merely permits us to divide up the original population into clusters. Cluster sampling is a strategy most often used as a relatively quick, convenient, and inexpensive method of approximating a random sample of individual elements in a population.

Second, the strata created in stratified sampling typically contain unequal numbers of individual elements, whereas clusters are specified so that they contain approximately equal numbers of individual elements.

Third, a researcher must have information about each element in the population to create the strata from which the samples will be drawn. Cluster sampling requires only that the researcher have a means of dividing the population into a number of subgroups of equal size, so that in sampling clusters, we can argue that each element of the population has about an equal chance of being selected as a part of one of the clusters we draw. No other information about the individual elements in the population is needed to select a cluster sample.

Fourth, in stratified sampling, we first define the strata (groups) and then sample individual elements within each stratum. In cluster sampling, we are sampling not individual elements but groups of elements (see Figure 4.1, B).

Cluster sampling is often used to study public opinion or voter preference in a large and geographically dispersed population. In such studies a small compromise is made with the requirement of equally sized clusters, because an existing territorial basis may be used to define the clusters. Suppose we wish to determine the amount of public support for a bond issue in a city. Rather than attempting to construct a sample frame for a simple random sample of the city's residents, we might define the city as composed of a collection of city blocks as indicated on a city map, and each residential block might be further defined as a cluster of citizens of the city. A researcher might then take a random sample of the city blocks and include the residents on the blocks selected for the cluster sample of the city's population. Congressional districts might also be treated as population clusters; however, not all blocks or congressional districts will have exactly the same number of residents, and, therefore, the rule of equally sized clusters is not strictly met. In many cases, though, the differences in size are relatively small, and the sample that results from such a procedure is regarded as close enough to a random sample of the residents for most research purposes. You might try to identify some circumstances in which such approximations of a cluster sample might lead to distortions in the sample.

Multistage Sampling

It is possible to draw a sample by applying the cluster sampling technique in successive stages (**multistage sampling**) or to combine random cluster sampling with individual element random sampling in a variety of ways. Suppose we wish to sample the opinion of registered voters on the national level. As a first step, we would randomly select ten districts from a list of all U.S. congressional districts. In stage 2, we would obtain lists of census districts from each of the ten congressional districts we selected, and randomly select ten census districts from each of the ten congressional districts. In the final stage, for each of the census districts we selected we would obtain a list of registered voters, and from that list we would randomly select one hundred voters to be interviewed. The three stages can be summarized as follows:

Sampling Stage	*Sampling Technique*
Stage 1	Random cluster sample of congressional districts
Stage 2	Random cluster sample of census districts
Stage 3	Random sample of individual voters in each census district

This process generates a sample of 10,000 voters to be interviewed, but unlike a simple random sample of the registered voter population in the United States, our voters are all located in one hundred census districts in ten congressional districts. It would be much less expensive to send interviewers to these people than to all of the congressional districts and to thousands of census districts. In addition, we are not faced with stratifying our population and then interviewing subjects from each stratum, a task of considerable difficulty if we were to hypothesize that ethnicity, religious affiliation, education, and occupation, for example, affect voting behavior.

Though cluster sampling may save us much time, money, and personnel, it also increases the risk of making errors when generalizing from our sample to the population from which it was selected. Congressional and census districts may vary substantially in population, and at each stage in the sampling process after the first one, some clusters and some elements (individual voters) have no chance of being included in the final sample. Generalizations about a population based on that kind of procedure have some obvious shortcomings. In the foregoing example, we have excluded all voters residing outside the ten congressional districts and the hundred census districts chosen. In using cluster sampling plans, whether single or multiple stage, we must always be concerned with balancing the cost of our operation with the amount of sampling error we are willing to accept.

Figure 4.1 summarizes the various types of probability sampling we have discussed.

NONPROBABILITY SAMPLING

The major advantages of nonprobability sampling, the second basic type of sampling, are economy and convenience. However, its major disadvantage is that sampling error cannot be accurately estimated, for biases introduced in nonprobability sampling cannot be evaluated. Because we cannot determine the probability that any given element will be included in our sample, we cannot legitimately use inferential statistics in the analysis of our data. Therefore, making statements about the population on the basis of data obtained from such samples is very risky.

Four different types of nonprobability samples—accidental, quota, typical-case or purposive, and snowball—will be considered briefly. An **accidental sample** is composed of respondents who "accidentally" happen to come into contact with the researcher and become part of his sample. Person-in-the-street interviews, which are typical of accidental samples, are not likely to accurately represent their populations. Too many biasing factors, such as the time of day or the place, influence the type of respondents that the researcher accidentally encounters.

A **quota sample** offers some improvements over the accidental sample because the sampling procedure ensures that various elements of a population will be included in the sample. Here a researcher selects a sample that replicates the population by establishing an appropriate quota for each subgroup in the sample. Thus, a quota sample for the United States might include 12 percent Blacks, 4 percent Jews, 25 percent Catholics, and 25 percent poor, assuming that these are the correct population proportions for these particular groups.

FIGURE 4.1 Probability Sampling Techniques

A. Simple Random Sampling

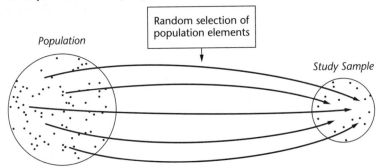

Population

Random selection of population elements

Study Sample

B. Stratified Sampling

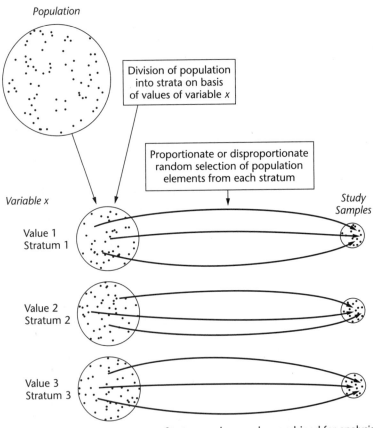

Population

Division of population into strata on basis of values of variable *x*

Proportionate or disproportionate random selection of population elements from each stratum

Variable *x*

Study Samples

Value 1 Stratum 1

Value 2 Stratum 2

Value 3 Stratum 3

Strata samples may be combined for analysis only if sampling has been proportionate

FIGURE 4.1 Continued

C. Cluster Sampling

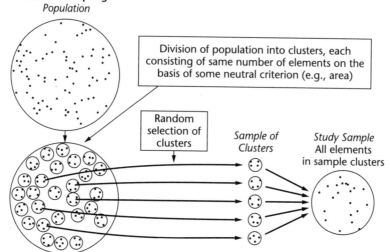

Population

Division of population into clusters, each consisting of same number of elements on the basis of some neutral criterion (e.g., area)

Random selection of clusters

Sample of Clusters

Study Sample All elements in sample clusters

D. Multistage Sampling

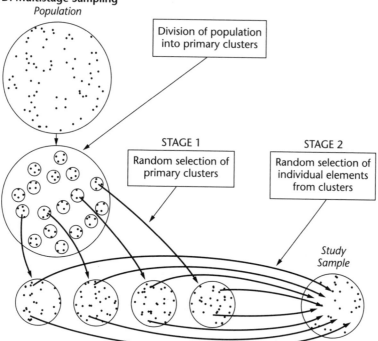

Population

Division of population into primary clusters

STAGE 1

Random selection of primary clusters

STAGE 2

Random selection of individual elements from clusters

Study Sample

The underlying assumption of a **typical-case** or **purposive sample** is that the researcher has enough skill to select subjects who ought to be included in the sample. He hopes to select cases that are "typical" of the population in question, and assumes that errors in his judgment will cancel out one another.[2] The problem with the typical-case method is that one cannot know whether the cases chosen really are typical. Nonetheless, purposive sampling is still used, for example, to predict election outcomes by interviewing voters in counties or states that have typically or always voted for the winner.

In contrast to the other processes of sampling we have discussed, where one goes from a large group to a small one, **snowball sampling** begins with an individual or small group and ends with a larger one. Snowball sampling, which may be thought of as a kind of purposive sampling, is most often used by qualitative researchers who ask initial-study participants to recommend others like themselves; these contacts are in turn asked for referrals and so on, usually resulting quickly in a large number of at least potential study participants. A sample generated in this way is not likely to be statistically representative of a larger group (that is, as a random sample of a group would likely be), but qualitative researchers using this sampling procedure aren't concerned with this sort of representativeness anyway; instead, they are trying to identify people who will likely manifest the phenomena they are studying. Often snowball sampling is used for studies of those engaged in illegal or illicit activities or of participants in informal groups for which no membership lists are available (for instance, drug users and/or sellers, street prostitutes, card players, and pool sharks, as well as police officers engaged in semi-organized graft or shakedowns).

In addition to sampling people, the researcher may also take samples of places, times, and events. Although it is clearly possible to conduct such samples *randomly* and to observe subjects at the places, times, and dates so selected, this usually is a waste of time for the researcher whose investigation is concerned with particular types of events. It is more sensible to observe at those times when and in those areas where specified, relevant events are likely to occur. The researcher may spend long periods of time with her subjects and record information about the events as they happen to occur (a type of accidental sampling), or she may determine in advance where and when such events will occur and then observe during these periods of time (a type of purposive sampling). For example, interaction among police officers, patients, and staff in a hospital emergency room could be observed in one or two emergency rooms, around the clock for several weeks, thus including in our sample *all* time periods and interactions during that specified period. This procedure would clearly be costly, because we would need at least four researchers (one for each 8-hour shift and an alternate in case of an observer's personal emergency or illness), and we would be paying salaries on a continuous basis (24 hours per day). However, a review of emergency room records might show that most cases are seen between the hours of 3 P.M. and 2 A.M. If we were willing to allow a small percentage of cases (events) to go unobserved, our research staff and salary outlay could be reduced considerably.

SAMPLE SIZE

In assessing a research project, we should begin with an evaluation of the sampling techniques employed. Three important questions to ask are (1) Is the sample a probability or nonprobability sample? (2) Is the specific type of sampling procedure used (simple random, multistage, snowball, and so on) appropriate to the hypotheses and the data? and (3) What is the size of the sample?

The relevance of the third question will become clearer in our discussion of statistics, but a brief example here will illustrate its importance. Not long ago, an auto parts manufacturer claimed that taxis using its products in a large American city had not experienced a breakdown for "450,000 taxi-tough miles." Apparently, the company hoped to convince readers of the ad that their parts last mile after mile after mile. Unfortunately, the advertisement failed to mention how many taxis were included in the study. If the number of taxis using these parts was, for example, four, the manufacturer's claim would appear to have some substance, because, on the average, each taxi could have driven over 100,000 miles on the parts. The reader can estimate the substance of the claim if the number of taxis sampled was not four, but 4,000!

The objective of any sampling plan is to obtain a sample of the relevant population that is large enough to permit data analysis and can be studied within the researcher's time and budgetary limits. Although small samples can be used, they do not permit very sophisticated analysis because there are too few cases to sort into the various categories of our variables for quantitative research or to get a well-rounded picture of the group and its activities in qualitative research. As a rule of thumb, for quantitative research the sample size should not be less than thirty, and most researchers would prefer a sample size nearer a hundred. For samples drawn from extremely large populations, a sample size of up to 1,500 may be desirable.[3] With probability sampling there are ways to determine the size of sample required to meet specified limits of sampling error, and these techniques are discussed in detail in most statistics texts.[4] We shall consider some elementary principles of determining sample size for quantitative analysis in the chapter on inferential statistics.

DETERMINING THE POPULATION TO BE SAMPLED

Many research questions can be answered by selecting samples from a number of different populations. The selection of the actual population to be sampled depends largely upon the objectives of the researcher. If, for example, we wanted to determine citizens' attitudes toward the police in a particular community, we might select our sample from the phone book, the city directory, or voter registration lists. However, each of these populations contains some inherent biases because some people, for example, do not own phones and others have unlisted numbers. The city directory is compiled on the basis of volunteered information and not everyone chooses to be included; moreover, not all citizens register to vote. Which of these populations we select, then, depends upon our research goals. If we want to investigate citizen attitudes toward the police to determine if they will support a bond issue to finance a new police building, we might sample the list of registered voters. If our goals were different, one of the other populations might be more appropriate.

Whatever population we identify, it is important for a researcher to remember the basic requisite of any sample: It must represent as well as possible the population from which it was drawn. Furthermore, generalizations made on the basis of the sample data refer at best only to the population sampled. It is tempting to overgeneralize, giving the impression that the results of a study of police officers in Chicago, for example, apply to police officers elsewhere. If Chicago police officers were sampled, then it is to that population that one can generalize. Any implications for police officers in other cities that might be drawn cannot be justified by the Chicago data. To talk about police officers elsewhere, we must sample and study them too.

REVIEW QUESTIONS

1. Why do researchers sample?
2. What is the essential difference between probability and nonprobability sampling procedures?
3. How can we maximize our chances that a sample represents the population from which it was drawn?
4. What is sampling error?
5. What are some of the principal sources of sampling error?
6. What is the difference between a population and a corresponding sampling frame?
7. How does a simple random sample differ from a stratified random sample?
8. How do random sampling and systematic sampling differ?
9. Why would a researcher use disproportionate sampling?
10. How does cluster sampling differ from simple random sampling and stratified random sampling?
11. Compare and contrast accidental, quota, purposive, and snowball sampling.
12. Populations of people are often sampled. What are some other types of populations that might be sampled?

EXERCISES

Use the directory of students for your college or university or a phone directory for exercises 1 through 7:

1. Pick two adjacent pages and consider the persons named on these two pages as a sampling frame. Using the random numbers table, draw a random sample of twenty names, writing down each step you went through

in drawing the sample. Then, using the same pages, draw a systematic sample of the same size, writing down each step you went through.

2. Discuss the possible differences between the sampling frame you used in exercise 1 and the corresponding population. Then discuss what you might do to improve the sampling frame.

3. Consider each page of the directory as a cluster and draw a two-stage sample, randomly selecting twenty clusters and then a simple 5 percent random sample of each of the clusters, writing down the steps you went through at each step in the sampling process.

4. Using data available in the directory about a variable (such as, dormitory or home state or year in school) draw a proportionate stratified random sample of students at the school. Then draw a disproportionate stratified random sample.

5. Is the proportionate stratified random sample you drew in exercise 4 a better sample than a simple random sample of the same population?

6. Draw a purposive, an accidental, and a quota sample of size twenty from the two adjacent pages of the directory you used in exercise 1. Then discuss the similarities and differences in sampling techniques used.

7. Why should we consider the sample you drew in exercise 1 better than the ones you drew in exercise 6?

8. Consider each 15-minute period in a day an element of the population of 15-minute periods in a two-day period. Draw a simple random sample of twenty elements, writing down each step in the process.

9. Specify some population of events occurring in your immediate environment and draw a simple random sample of them, writing down each step in the process.

10. Try snowball sampling people who makes bets on local sporting events.

 11. Go to *www.randomizer.org* and take the tutorial. Then read "About Research Randomizer" and follow the link to "HotBits."

NOTES

1. For a more complete discussion of probability sampling, see Hubert M. Blalock, Jr., *Social Statistics,* 2nd ed. (New York: McGraw-Hill, 1972), pp. 392–409.

2. Clair Selltiz, Marie Jahoda, Morton Deutsch, and Stuart W. Cook, *Research Methods in Social Relations* (New York: Holt, Rinehart & Winston, 1965), p. 520.

3. Edwin S. Johnson, *Research Methods in Criminology and Criminal Justice* (Englewood Cliffs, NJ: Prentice-Hall, 1981), p. 156.

4. Blalock, *Social Statistics,* for example.

5

Research Tools and Techniques: Survey Research Through Questionnaires and Interviews

In our daily attempts to understand the world around us, we rely on three basic techniques for gathering information: we observe directly, we communicate with others about what they have observed, and we learn from sources such as books, newspapers, films, television, and the Internet. The scientific approach to understanding relies on the same techniques for gathering information but uses them more systematically with respect to specific problem situations. We will consider direct observation and use of recorded sources of information (such as document research) in the next chapter. Here we shall be concerned with information gathering through communication with others, that is, through surveys.

Surveys can be conducted either by *interview,* with an interviewer asking the questions and recording the subjects' responses, or by *questionnaire,* with the respondents reading the questions and recording their own responses.

QUESTIONNAIRES

Researchers often use questionnaires rather than interviews to collect information about a large number of subjects because they require less time and fewer trained staff members to administer. Questionnaires can also provide anonymity to respondents, which is a desirable feature in many criminal justice research projects. They are frequently distributed by mail, because that is an inexpensive, easy way to reach a large number of subjects in many types of groups for which a mailing list can be obtained (such as residents of a city ward, students, magazine subscribers, or association members).

Unlike other information-gathering techniques (such as interview and direct observation), questionnaires can be used successfully only when the respondents are literate and both willing and able to report the desired information. A further limitation of questionnaire surveys is that respondents may misinterpret some of the questions asked, and, similarly, the researcher may misinterpret the meaning of some of the responses. This is especially true for mailed questionnaires and for questionnaires administered by persons other than the researcher because both the physical and the social distance between the researcher and the respondent is great. Under these circumstances, the researcher cannot resolve problems in the wording of questions or responses as they arise, and in many cases cannot resolve them at all. For this reason, great skill and care in the design of the research instrument, before it goes out to respondents, are critical.

Another potential disadvantage of questionnaire surveys is poor **response rates.** Part of the budgetary advantage of using written questionnaires may be offset if a relatively small proportion of the questionnaires are returned, which often happens when questionnaires are distributed through the mail or respondents are given several days to complete and return the survey instrument. Over the last few years, in our own research, we have seldom achieved a response rate of better than 50 percent for mailed questionnaires, and as many as 15 percent of respondents who have taken questionnaires home with them have failed to return them. When questionnaires are administered to an assembled group and collected immediately, higher return rates may be expected. Because the researcher anticipates low response rates, the questionnaire must be distributed to a large number of potential respondents in order to provide an adequate number of returned questionnaires. Low response rates also present data analysis and interpretation problems for the researcher because there may be important differences between those who did respond and those who did not. Often it is impossible to determine what those differencies might be; even when it is possible it is often time-consuming. Both of these adjustments, larger sample size and response-difference analysis, add to research costs.

Types of Questions

Questions included in questionnaires range from highly structured, fixed-alternative items to open-ended ones. **Fixed-alternative questions** require the respondent to choose an answer from a printed list of choices. Such questions may include a simple yes/no or true/false response, a multiple-choice list, or a series of degrees of agreement or disagreement in relation to a variety of assertions. Fixed-alternative questions are simple to administer, easy for the respondent to complete, and relatively easy to analyze. One major weakness often cited by qualitative researchers is that respondents feel compelled to select one of the alternatives provided by the researcher even when none really fits their position. **Open-ended questions** allow respondents to answer in their own words. This can mean greater detail and a broader range of responses.

However, it can also mean lower response rates because the respondent must think and write more than he would with a fixed-alternative item. Furthermore, the information the researcher does obtain may be very difficult to analyze and summarize. For example, a questionnaire concerned with the incidence of property crimes might contain questions like this:

- Has your home ever been burglarized? _____
- If yes, how often has your home been burglarized in the last six years?

_____

Responses from different respondents might be "once in a while," "frequently," or "twice in the last year." Such responses are difficult to interpret and to compare. A fixed-alternative question might look like this:

- Has your home ever been burglarized? _____ Yes _____ No
- If yes, how often has your home been burglarized in the last six years?

  _____ Once _____ 2–3 times _____ 4–5 times

  _____ More than 5 times _____ Not in the last six years

The responses given with this format will be much easier to manage when it comes time to analyze and summarize the data from the many questionnaires received.

When the researcher is seeking data, not about easily quantifiable phenomena, such as "how many times," but about opinions and feelings, open-ended questions can be much more effective. They are also very useful when all the possible answers to a question are either not known or very numerous.

Many researchers use both fixed-alternative and open-ended questions in their questionnaires. This approach is often advantageous, but it does not eliminate the weaknesses of either type of question, and it may greatly complicate analysis.

Constructing Questionnaires

Once a researcher has decided that the questionnaire is the appropriate research instrument in a particular research project, he begins to construct the questionnaire. If other questionnaires on the same topic are available in the literature or from a colleague, they may be used (with the permission of the original developer) in whole or in part. If not, a researcher may begin by listing the various topics to be covered in the questionnaire. Once the topics are listed, their best order must be determined. For example, questions of a personal nature (such as concerning income or sexual behavior) should usually be placed toward the end of the questionnaire, for two reasons. First, if the respondent has already cooperated with the researcher in answering earlier questions, she is more likely to answer sensitive questions that come later. Second, should posing a personal question cause a respondent to discontinue the questionnaire, the researcher will at least have some useful information in the respondent's answers to earlier questions.

Next, the researcher must decide upon appropriate response forms. Is the questionnaire to be basically a fixed-alternative instrument, an open-ended instrument, or some combination of the two? If the researcher is examining a subject about which he knows a good deal, and if comparisons across respondents are to be made, fixed-alternative questions might be most appropriate. If the researcher is doing exploratory research on a subject about which he knows very little, and if comparisons across respondents are not critical, open-ended questions may well be employed. In many instances, both types of questions are used to provide respondents the opportunity to address in open-ended questions issues that the researcher failed to address in fixed-alternative questions.

After these issues are resolved, the researcher begins writing questions. Each question is reconsidered and rewritten until the researcher is satisfied that it will not be misunderstood and that it will provide the information sought. Appropriate alternatives must be listed for each fixed-alternative question, and space must be provided for answers to open-ended questions.

When fixed alternatives are used, they must be mutually exclusive and exhaustive. A list of response categories is **mutually exclusive** if there is one and only one response category appropriate for each respondent. To illustrate, the categories in Figure 5.1 are not mutually exclusive because a respondent who earns $15,000 could check either (a) or (b). A set of responses is **exhaustive** if it includes all possible answers to the question posed. The categories in Figure 5.1 are not exhaustive because there is no category for annual incomes under $10,000 per year or for incomes of more than $20,000 and less than $25,000. Because the categories provided are neither mutually exclusive nor exhaustive, they constitute a very poor device for measuring income and make meaningful comparisons and analysis almost impossible. Figure 5.2 illustrates mutually exclusive and exhaustive response categories for the same question.

How many categories of response should there be? Essentially, response categories should generate as much detail as needed to shed light on the research question. If there was reason to believe, for example, that there may be important differences between individuals whose incomes differ by $2,500, response categories with that range should be created.

Suppose we were interested in the effect of marital status on certain attitudes of the study population. We could ask:

FIGURE 5.1	FIGURE 5.2
What is your annual income? *(check one)*	*What is your annual income?* *(check one)*
_____ (a) $10,000–$15,000	_____ (a) $10,000 or less
_____ (b) $15,000–$20,000	_____ (b) $10,001–$15,000
_____ (c) $25,000–$30,000	_____ (c) $15,001–$20,000
_____ (d) over $30,000	_____ (d) $20,001–$25,000
	_____ (e) more than $25,000

What is your current marital status? (check one)

_____ (a) married

_____ (b) not married

These two response categories will give us information—perhaps enough for our research purposes. But compare the information they produce with that generated by the following:

What is your current marital status? (check one)

_____ (a) single, never married

_____ (b) single, divorced

_____ (c) single, widowed

_____ (d) married for the first time

_____ (e) remarried

These five response categories generate much more detailed information about the respondent group.

One other point needs to be made about the advantages of fixed-alternative questions. The income question, for example, could be asked with an open-ended format:

What is your annual income, rounded to the nearest $1,000? $_____

If respondents are willing to answer this question, the raw data generated by the question can be used to create whatever categories of income are useful during the analysis phase of the research. However, income is a sensitive matter for many respondents. Researchers have found that respondents are often more willing to identify a general range for their income than to state the exact amount. Hence, the likelihood of gaining at least some information about respondents' incomes may be increased by asking a fixed-alternative question with fairly broad income categories rather than an open-ended one. Pretesting the questions with different response categories, a technique discussed later in this chapter, is one way of choosing which question format is best for a given set of respondents.

Both the wording of questions and the response categories provided have an effect on the quality of the information collected in a survey. If the researcher wants to know the gender of the respondent, for example, it is generally best to present the question in a fixed-alternative form, such as:

gender: _____ male _____ female

Experience shows that asking respondents the open-ended question:

Sex? _____

sometimes results in answers such as "sometimes," "yes!," and so forth. Skilled researchers take into account not only their research topic but also the characteristics of the respondents in designing questions and response categories. We shall return to these and related matters when measurement of variables is discussed in Chapter 7.

As a questionnaire is developed, a researcher also must decide what instructions to provide respondents to assist them in completing it. Are they to fill in blanks, circle appropriate responses, check appropriate spaces, or use some special code to indicate their response? Are respondents to select only one or more than one of the alternatives provided? How often should instructions be repeated? When the format of the questions changes, are new instructions required? Again, the researcher has to consider the best form for the data to be collected and must provide clear-cut instructions to obtain the data in that form.

In addition, the proper length of the questionnaire is an important consideration for two reasons. First, all the information needed for the research project at hand must be collected, and if important questions are omitted, there may be little or no chance of asking them of the same respondents later. Second, although all relevant information must be included, the length of the questionnaire is an important factor because researchers are asking respondents for a valuable commodity—their time. The longer the questionnaire, the more time will be involved, and, as a result, the more likely it is that the response rate will be low. On the other hand, if a questionnaire is too short, valuable information may not be collected. Therefore, a compromise is often required to construct a survey instrument that allows a researcher to collect the necessary information while asking a minimum number of questions.

Two other considerations are essential to the construction of a good questionnaire. The first concerns the overall appearance of the instrument, for the more professional the questionnaire looks, the more likely respondents are to complete it. If you have ever received a mailed questionnaire that was mimeographed, difficult to read, crowded on the page, and printed on poor-quality paper, you can understand the importance of this consideration. Easy-to-read print, proper spacing between questions, adequate margins, and enough space to answer open-ended questions are essential in the development of a good questionnaire.

Second, it is necessary to prepare a cover letter or an introductory statement emphasizing the importance of completing the questionnaire. Typically, this is done by briefly explaining the purpose and importance of the survey and the significance of the information the respondent will provide. To encourage participants to respond honestly, the cover letter or introductory statement may indicate, if appropriate, that there are no right or wrong answers, that the respondents will remain anonymous, and that the results will be presented only in grouped, summary form and only to designated audiences and will be used only for specifically stated purposes. The researcher is, of course, ethically bound to abide by these statements. Instructions for returning a mailed questionnaire are also included in the letter or statement, and these generally state that the questionnaire is to be returned in an enclosed, self-addressed, stamped envelope or that the group-administered questionnaire should be placed in a plain envelope or in a sealed box at a specified location. In most cases, a time frame for returning mailed questionnaires is also established. Researchers should identify themselves clearly by using letterhead stationery and a complete signature block. A statement indicating the institutional affiliation of the researcher and who is sponsoring and paying for the research should also be included. Finally, the researcher should always thank respondents for their time and cooperation.

Pretesting Questionnaires

Questionnaires should always be pretested before they are distributed to the respondents. A *pretest* is conducted by asking a small number of respondents similar in background characteristics to the target population to read the cover letter, listen to or read the introductory statement, and complete the questionnaire. As they complete the questionnaire, they should note any problem areas they encounter—unclear instructions, words that are unfamiliar or not clearly defined, embarrassing questions, spelling errors, and so forth. At the end of the pretest, the researcher can make any necessary revisions in order to eliminate problem areas before administering the questionnaire to the study group.

Precoding Questionnaires

A researcher who collects survey (questionnaire) data should, whenever possible, determine in advance how this information can be recorded or coded in a shorthand form suitable for systematic analysis with or without the aid of a computer. *Coding* is facilitated when fixed-alternative questions have been used, because these can easily be *precoded;* that is, code numbers can be assigned to each alternative response before the questionnaire is administered. When the questionnaires are returned, the preassigned code numbers, rather than the respondents' actual written responses, are recorded.

This procedure is sometimes used with open-ended questions as well. For example, the researcher might pose the question "How would you evaluate the services of the public defender?" and then devise categories and assign code numbers as follows: positive rating (1), mixed rating (2), negative rating (3), and other (4). An open-ended question of this type might yield responses such as "rotten," "very good," "so-so," "in some respects good, in others bad," and so on. In order to use these responses, the researcher must place the actual responses into the mutually exclusive and exhaustive categories he has prepared, assigning appropriate code numbers to each of the responses.

In either case, if a computer is to be used in the data analysis, the code numbers would be transferred to a computer tape or disk. Note that the question could easily have been asked in fixed-alternative form:

How would you evaluate the services of the public defender?

_____ very good _____ good _____ fair _____ poor _____ very poor

The questionnaires could then be coded easily by recording a 1 for every respondent who checked the "very good" category, a 2 for those who checked the "good" category, and so on.

A Sample Questionnaire

Figure 5.3 shows part of a precoded questionnaire from an actual research project, and as you can see, the code value for every alternative is included in parentheses next to each question.

Typically, coding merely substitutes one set of numerical symbols for another set of either verbal or numerical symbols (the raw data). Because the code numbers assigned are usually not the same as the actual responses given, a researcher must create and maintain a master code sheet that specifies what each code designation represents.

Perhaps the best way to summarize the steps involved in constructing a questionnaire (all of which are interrelated even though we have discussed them separately) is to go through the process step by step. Let us suppose that we wish to know the attitudes of residents in our community toward the municipal police. Let us also assume that we have decided that a standardized, fixed-alternative questionnaire is the most desirable means of collecting the information we desire. As a first step, we might review survey instruments previously used to obtain this type of information. That review would probably indicate a number of topics that should be addressed. We might decide, for example, to examine the attitudes of the public regarding the police in areas such as:

1. traffic enforcement
2. police/community relations
3. police/juvenile relations
4. police as investigators
5. police as crime preventers
6. the trustworthiness, competency, and manners of police officers
7. police actions with respect to minority group members
8. police patrol practices
9. fear of crime among citizens
10. police handling of liquor and other drug violations

At this point, we would have to determine the proper form for the fixed-alternative questions and write one or more questions for each of these areas. For example, we might use a **Likert scale** for some of our questions. Respondents are asked to express the degree to which they hold certain attitudes by choosing among the response categories "strongly agree," "agree," "undecided," "disagree," and "strongly disagree" to a series of statements. Each of these categories is assigned a number (1 for "strongly agree," 2 for "agree," and so on), and respondents are instructed to circle the appropriate number for each question. Sample questions might include:

The local police department puts enough emphasis on enforcing traffic laws.

1	2	3	4	5
strongly agree	*agree*	*undecided*	*disagree*	*strongly disagree*

FIGURE 5.3 Crime and the Police Questionnaire

No information = 9

Background Information—Please check the correct blank for each question.

Age (actual age in years) _____

Marital Status
(1) ___ Single   (4) ___ Divorced
(2) ___ Married   (5) ___ Separated
(3) ___ Widowed

Type of Residence
(1) ___ Own Home   (4) ___ Sr. Citizens Housing
(2) ___ Apartment   (5) ___ Nursing Home
(3) ___ Relative's Home   (6) ___ Other

Education
(1) ___ 8 years or less   (5) ___ College graduate
(2) ___ Some high school   (6) ___ Some graduate work
(3) ___ High school graduate (7) ___ Graduate or professional degree
(4) ___ Some college

Approximate Annual Income for Your Household
(1) ___ Less than $10,000
(2) ___ $10,000–$20,000
(3) ___ More than $20,000

Police Contacts—Please check the correct blank for each question.

1. Have you ever contacted the Burlington Police   (1) ___ Yes   (2) ___ No
   Department for assistance? (If no, check the correct
   blank, and go on to question 2.)

1a. If yes, were you satisfied with the services provided? (1) ___ Yes   (2) ___ No

2. Have you ever contacted a Burlington Police Officer on (1) ___ Yes   (2) ___ No
   the streets for assistance? (If no, check the correct
   blank, and go on to question 3.)

2a. If yes, were you satisfied with the services provided? (1) ___ Yes   (2) ___ No

3. Have you ever been arrested by the Burlington Police? (1) ___ Yes   (2) ___ No

4. Have you ever been issued a traffic ticket by the   (1) ___ Yes   (2) ___ No
   Burlington Police?

5. Do you know any Burlington Police Officers personally? (1) ___ Yes   (2) ___ No

Crime Information—Please check or fill in the correct blank for each question.

6. Have you ever been the victim of a crime in Burlington? (1) ___ Yes   (2) ___ No
   (If no, check the correct blank and go on to question 7.)

6a. If yes, how many times? (actual number) _____

or,

The local police department does a satisfactory job of handling juvenile problems.

1	2	3	4	5
strongly agree	agree	undecided	disagree	strongly disagree

After the respondents circle their choices, we could prepare the data for computer analysis by entering the code number corresponding to each of the respondents' answers in a database.

In addition to the general topics listed above, we would probably also want to find out something about the background characteristics of the respondents. A person's sex, race, social class, education, occupation, place of residence, number of times arrested, marital status, income, number of traffic tickets received, and a variety of other factors *may* be related to attitudes toward the police. We would request this type of information for each of the respondents so that we could cross-tabulate the specific items concerning police performance with each of these variables either singly or in combination. (We shall discuss the details of cross-tabulation in Chapter 8.)

Finally, we might want to give respondents the opportunity to comment on other areas they feel are important even though these areas were not included on the form. The questionnaire could be concluded with a statement such as "Please feel free to make additional comments concerning the local police in the space below."

A cover letter should be attached to mailed questionnaires indicating who the researchers are and explaining why responses to the questionnaire are important and in what form and to whom they will be made available. It also might indicate that the local police are interested in improving their services and that they will have access to the results of the study in order to get a better feel for public attitudes concerning them. We should pretest the questionnaire and make appropriate modifications before distributing it to the sample we have selected.

Essentially the same steps are followed each time a survey instrument is designed. The research can often benefit by reusing sections of questionnaires previously used on the same topics, either by this researcher or by another. Because how a question is worded influences the responses obtained, an advantage of using a question or a set of questions that is identical to one in earlier research is comparability of responses. Again, if part or all of another researcher's survey instrument is to be used, permission must be secured.

Increasing Response Rates

For reasons we have already discussed, good response rates are both important to survey researchers and difficult to achieve. There are several strategies that can increase response rates during various stages of the research process. As was suggested earlier, well-designed and well-printed questionnaires with relatively few, clearly written, fixed-alternative questions are easier to complete than are longer ones with many open-ended questions, and they usually produce higher response rates. Including a self-addressed, stamped envelope with mailed questionnaires also increases response rates. Where appropriate, it is helpful to publicize the study in the local news media; this underscores the legitimacy of the researchers and of the study itself. Finally, whenever feasible, it is at least a good gesture to offer to share a summary of the study's results with the respondents, at their request.

Once the first administration of the questionnaire has been completed, follow-up techniques may be used to obtain questionnaires that have not yet been returned. Among these are sending reminder notes to nonresponders, perhaps with another copy of the questionnaire; putting notices to the same effect in local newspapers; and phoning nonresponders, either to urge them to complete and return the questionnaire on their own time or to complete it now over the phone.

Great care must be taken, however, in using follow-up techniques. Some of them add substantially to research costs. Also, if a respondent has been promised anonymity and has not been asked to provide his name and address on the questionnaire, sending him a reminder may make him feel deceived. In such circumstances, reminders should be sent to *all* persons on the original mailing list, a fact that should be clearly stated in the note itself. In general, monetary and other costs of follow-up procedures must be weighed against gains in response rates that may be achieved.

INTERVIEWS

Like questionnaires, interviews can give a researcher access to information about respondents, including their experiences, their knowledge of events, and their plans for the future as well as their opinions, attitudes, and motivations. Unlike a questionnaire, an interview is a person-to-person interaction, usually either face-to-face or over the telephone.

Like questionnaires, interviews fall into two general categories, depending on the types of questions asked. A structured, standardized, or **formal interview** has a fixed-question content and structure. Standardized interviews are generally used when the researcher has already determined what specific information she is seeking. In this type of interview, predetermined questions are asked in a prescribed order. As with the questionnaire, often a set of *fixed alternatives* or standardized responses is read by the researcher following each question, from which the respondent selects the one that most nearly describes his position. The parallel types of information obtained from all respondents enable the researcher to compare and analyze responses relatively easily.

Unstructured or **informal interviews,** although starting with planned areas of questioning, are more flexible in both the questions used and the directions taken. Informal interviews are generally used in exploratory studies, when the researcher needs more detailed or extensive information than can be given with structured interviews. In interviews of this type, the structure of the questions is often open-ended, and the order of the questions to be asked may not be as completely predetermined. Rather, the interviewer explores preselected general question areas, follows up on particular responses, and pursues additional topics suggested by the respondent.

Although informal interviews may or may not generate responses that can be compared among respondents, they often give more insightful, extensive information about the research topics as well as about the emotions and attitudes of the respondent. As a result, such interviews are often used by those criminal justice researchers who have a preference for qualitative research strategies.[1]

As with questionnaires, an interview may include both highly structured questions and open-ended ones. Basically, the same advantages and disadvantages associated with fixed-alternative and open-ended questionnaire items apply to these types of interview questions.

Whichever type of interview the researcher selects, he must be concerned with three things: (1) establishing good rapport with respondents; (2) determining the meaning and truthfulness of their responses; and (3) using the type of questioning that will elicit the required information.

Establishing rapport means creating a situation in which the respondent feels comfortable and free to give his frank opinions, without fear of being laughed at or of having his opinions inappropriately passed on to others. An interviewer can take several steps to establish rapport. First, he should produce credentials that legitimate his presence (normally, a letter of introduction and/or a simple identification badge stating who he is and who he works for will suffice). Second, the interviewer should answer reasonable questions about the research project posed by respondents. Third, he should assure respondents of confidentiality and anonymity. A thorough knowledge of the interview questions will enable the interviewer to be courteous and conversational, putting the respondent at ease.

The interviewer's personal appearance and presentation often determine his success in establishing and maintaining rapport with respondents. Sending a White, middle-class interviewer into a lower-class Black neighborhood during a period of racial disturbance to conduct interviews on Black attitudes toward Whites, for example, would probably make it impossible for either the interviewer or the respondent to feel at ease. Likewise, the interviewer's remarks and attitudes have an effect upon the respondent. The interview is an interactive situation; the interviewer's actions and words serve as cues to the respondent. If, for example, an interviewer collecting data on attitudes toward abortion expresses or implies contempt for people who participate in abortions, she may lead the respondent to conceal or misrepresent her own attitude toward abortion. In short, the interviewer should maintain a neutral attitude toward the issues in question, even though she may privately have opinions about them.

The interviewer's second major concern is the meaning and truthfulness of the responses he obtains. As in day-to-day conversation, it is seldom sensible to take every statement at face value. The respondent may be unwilling to answer honestly for a variety of reasons—embarrassment, dislike of interviewers, and so on—or he may not remember accurately, or he may misunderstand the question, or simply tell the interviewer what he believes the interviewer wants to hear. Thus, the interviewer often may have to *probe* to learn the basis for, and truthfulness of, responses. One must do this without suggesting any particular response to the interviewee; for example, the interviewer can ask the respondent to explain his answer in a little more detail, or ask him what his answer means. It would not be appropriate, however, to

RESEARCHERS IN ACTION: INTERVIEWS

In this research project, in-depth interviews were conducted with eighty-six active armed robbers recruited from the streets of St. Louis, Missouri. The robbers were recruited using a snowball sample in which one convicted armed robber put the researchers in contact with former associates and other known offenders, who then arranged for further interviews with their associates. Each referral resulted in a payment of $10 to the person doing the referring. The authors indicate that the representativeness of the sample is impossible to calculate, although they did attempt to avoid geographical bias.

The semi-structured informal interviews focused on the offenders' thoughts prior to, during, and after robberies in an attempt to determine how and why robbers move from an unmotivated state to one in which they are determined to commit robbery. The interviews were left open-ended in order to gain as much information as possible, were taped, and lasted between 1 and 2 hours. The tapes were then transcribed verbatim for analysis. According to the authors, many of the interviewees were skeptical at first but eventually opened up and discussed their thought processes as related to robbery. Some even produced newspaper accounts, parole reports, and other evidence to support their stories. The authors further indicate that although the interviews may have been susceptible to "exaggerations, distortions, self-serving rationalizations, or drug-induced forgetfulness," different interviewees mentioned many of the same factors in their thought processes related to robberies. Thus the researchers conclude that the interviews are probably "less susceptible to inaccuracy than some might think" (p. 153).

The findings of this interview-based research indicate that although the need for cash is certainly a motivator for robbery, the decision to rob is "activated, mediated, and shaped by participation in street culture" (p. 149). Participation in the street culture allows robbers to assess risk factors and may present robbery as the only viable alternative to obtain money quickly.

Source: B.A. Jacobs and R. Wright. 1999. "Stick-Up, Street Culture, and Offender Motivation." *Criminology* 37(1): 149–173.

---

probe by saying "I can't believe you really mean . . ." or "Did you mean. . . ." To determine the truthfulness of responses, the interviewer can ask the same question twice, but in different ways ("Have you ever voted for a Democrat for office?" and later, "How many Democrats would you say you have voted for?"). He can then compare the respondent's answers to see if there are discrepancies.

Attempts to determine the meaning and truthfulness of responses are of little value unless the interviewer accurately records the responses. The interviewer must always separate, insofar as possible, his interpretations of responses from the responses themselves. In some cases this may require tape recording the interview; in other cases, it may require note taking; and in others, simply marking an "x" in the appropriate column on the interview sheet. The latter, of course, may require the interviewer to make additional written comments about the respondent's answer, which can lead to problems of interpretation; this should be kept in mind when training interviewers and analyzing the data they collect.

In considering what type of questioning will most likely yield the desired information, a researcher—regardless of whether he uses a formal or an unstructured interview—must phrase and order the questions carefully. The wording of the questions should be clear and concise, and should not suggest any particular response. Usually, a respondent must feel comfortable before she will answer personal questions. Because even a skilled interviewer needs some time to achieve rapport with his subject, personal questions should generally follow less sensitive ones.

Interviews can be used with virtually any kind of respondent (including those who are illiterate), and when probing is used intelligently, they can yield detailed information. Their disadvantage is their high cost if the interviewee group is large or the interview is long. When a researcher must gather information from a large, literate group, he may be able to collect the data less expensively with a questionnaire.

Telephone Surveys

Telephone surveys are popular among contemporary researchers because they are quick, easy to complete, and enable the researcher to contact large numbers of people quickly. Such surveys frequently employ random or systematic samples of telephone directories or depend on random digit dialing (RDD) to sample a specific population (all of those individuals with a particular area code and prefix). When RDD is employed, a computer is programmed to select the numbers to be called, based on randomly constructed combinations of the last four digits of the phone number remaining after an area code and prefix have been selected. RDD eliminates the problem of unlisted phone numbers, a major problem when telephone directories are used as the population base (some suggest that as much as 40 percent of the population in a given area may have unlisted numbers).[2]

Telephone surveys are best suited to the administration of fixed-alternative, standardized surveys that allow the researcher to input the data directly into a computer as is it is being collected. Such computer–assisted telephone interviewing skips questions that are not relevant as the result of answers to previous questions. For example, if the question "Have you ever contacted the police department by phone?" is answered negatively, the immediately following questions concerning the responses of the phone receptionist/dispatcher would be skipped, and the interviewer would be directed to the next relevant question. In fact, such telephone surveys are basically questionnaires administered by a researcher who fills in the correct answer for the interviewee. If an answer is unclear, the researcher has the opportunity to ask for clarification, keeping in mind the cautions we have discussed for interviews in general.

Interviewer bias in the form of nonverbal cues is largely eliminated through the use of telephone surveys. Further, the costs of maintaining a field staff may be greatly reduced (no travel time, no mileage costs). With low-cost long distance plans, concise telephone surveys may actually cost less than mailed surveys and can be conducted for populations that are widely dispersed (one could include, for example, interviewees living in Chicago, New York, and Los Angeles). Callbacks are also easily made and relatively inexpensive. Finally, if the interviewing staff is centrally located, it is easier for the researcher to supervise interviewers and to address problems concerning the survey as they are encountered.

Disadvantages of telephone surveys include the difficulty of collecting lengthy, in-depth responses (from open-ended or unstructured surveys), the aggravation they often cause recipients who do not wish to participate (perhaps making future refusals more likely), the lack of nonverbal cues to assess interviewee responses, and the elimination of those potential subjects without telephones. The latter disadvantage affects perhaps 5 to 10 percent of the population and disproportionately impacts the homeless, transients, the institutionalized, and those lower social classes. Further, there may be language problems with those selected to be interviewed, although these may be mitigated if the interviewers are centrally located and include those who speak Spanish and other languages fluently. Use of call-screening devices, answering machines, the unpopularity of telemarketing, and calling at inappropriate times negatively affect the success of telephone surveys. Finally, response rates, particularly those associated with RDD, may be relatively low for phone surveys.[3]

Internet Surveys

Surveys may also be administered over the **Internet,** using email exchanges or Web sites with interactive capabilities. As with printed or face-to-face versions, Internet surveys should be carefully constructed, attractively presented, thoroughly pretested, and accompanied by the equivalent of a cover letter. They should also take advantage of the special capacities of the Internet. Questionnaire items may be read on screen by respondents, answered with mouse clicks (for fixed-alternative items) or keyboard entry (for open-ended questions), and forwarded directly to the researcher's database. They can be customized on the fly (that is, questions may be dropped, added, or altered depending on the respondent's previous answers), making questionnaire administration more efficient and less confusing to participants than printed versions (for example, instructions like, "If you answered yes to question 8, skip to question 18" are unnecessary). Furthermore, the Internet makes it possible for respondents to obtain immediate feedback of various kinds, so that they can compare their individual responses with a summary of other participants' answers to the same questions. As the "live" interactive capacities of the Internet grow, however, so will opportunities for a facsimile of face-to-face interviewing, with the attendant issues of nonverbal cues biasing results.

Getting questions to potential participants and entering data for analysis are very inexpensive on the Internet. On-the-fly customization of questionnaire versions and immediate feedback capabilities may increase potential respondents' interest as well as response rates. If necessary, follow-up contacts with respondents or nonresponders are economical as well.

Sampling may pose some special problems for Internet surveyors, however. As we noted with respect to phones, not everyone has a computer and not all who do have email accounts, Internet access, or cams. As concern about the digital divide illustrates, neither ownership of nor access to this technology is evenly distributed in society. Anonymity and confidentiality may be issues as well in some circumstances. Furthermore, in many cases it will be difficult to identify clearly the target population and to assess what kind of sample the respondents comprise. Email addresses may not be as available or reliable as postal addresses or phone numbers for locating individuals (and postal addresses and phone numbers are troublesome enough in their own right). Announcements in other media that a survey is being made available on the net may help. In general, net questionnaires and interviews have the same general strengths and weaknesses as other more traditional applications of these techniques. They are ideally suited for in-house projects and other circumstances where the target audience can be clearly specified and access to required equipment is readily available.

REVIEW QUESTIONS

1. What are the advantages and disadvantages of using interviews compared with using questionnaires as research instruments?
2. What are the advantages and disadvantages of fixed-alternative and open-ended items on surveys?
3. Why is it important that fixed-alternative answers to survey questions be mutually exclusive and exhaustive?
4. Why should a researcher pretest a survey instrument?
5. What purposes do a cover letter and instructions serve on a questionnaire?
6. How can questionnaire response rates be improved?
7. How might the personal appearance of an interviewer affect both the willingness of a respondent to answer questions and the answers given?
8. Why is recognizing that an interview is an interactive situation important?
9. What are the advantages and disadvantages of telephone surveys? Of Internet surveys?

EXERCISES

1. Write both a fixed-alternative and an open-ended question for measuring the following variables pertaining to a person:

- sex
- age
- arrest record
- income
- education
- opinion concerning equality of treatment in the courts of defendants of different ethnic groups
- opinions concerning the performance of the local police force or campus security
- reasons for coming to this college or university
- reasons for studying criminal justice research methods

2. Compare the questions you wrote for exercise 1 with those of another member of the class and discuss the strengths and weaknesses of the questions.

3. Pretest the questions you wrote on eight or ten friends or classmates. Then make any revisions in the questions you think necessary and indicate why you changed them.

4. Ask the revised questions of eight or ten other friends or classmates. Compare the responses to fixed-alternative and open-ended questions and write an essay discussing the advantages and disadvantages of the two types of questions.

5. Prepare a questionnaire, complete with cover letter, combining fixed-alternative and open-ended questions focused on determining the respondents' opinions concerning alternative ways of dealing with juvenile delinquency.

6. Prepare an interview schedule combining formal and informal interview styles focused on the issue of exercise 5.

7. Assume you were going door-to-door to interview respondents in a large city. Would you dress differently depending on which neighborhoods you were interviewing? Why or why not? Would your plans change if you were to do the survey by telephone? Why or why not?

8. Write an essay discussing what aspects of your own behavior you should be especially aware of and attempt to control during an interview if you wanted to improve the validity of your research.

9. Have someone observe you interview another person, looking for clues (nodding, smiling, frowning, and so on) you may be giving to the respondent during the interview. Discuss the results and their implications for the validity of your research.

10. Critique the questionnaire in Figure 5.3.

11. Go to *http://blackstone.ojp.usdoj.gov/bjs/pub/pdf/ncvs2.pdf* and read the Crime Incident Report Survey.

12. Go to *http://blackstone.ojp.usdoj.gov/bjs/cvict_rd.htm* and follow the links to read about the redesign of the National Crime Victimization Survey (NCVS).

 13. Go to` *http://blackstone.ojp.usdoj.gov/bjs/abstract/ntmc.htm* and read "The Nation's Two Crime Measures" for a comparison of the NCVS and the UCR as sources of crime data.

 14. For some examples of Web-based surveys, go to *http://www.surveyview.com*, *http.//www.surveycrafter.com*, and *http://www.websurveyor.com*.

NOTES

1. For another discussion of specific types of interviews see Louise H. Kidder, in Selltiz, Wrightsman, and Cook, *Research Methods in Social Relations,* 4th ed. (New York: Holt, Rinehart & Winston, 1981), pp. 178–97.

2. Jeffrey D. Senese, *Applied Research Methods in Criminal Justice* (Chicago: Nelson Hall, 1997), p. 165.

3. Ralph B. Taylor, *Research Methods in Criminal Justice* (New York: McGraw-Hill, 1994).

Research Tools and Techniques: Document Research, Physical Evidence, Observation, and Experimentation

Although surveys may be the backbone of social science research, they provide a body of information very much controlled by the researcher, in both content and structure. The data result from the interaction between researcher and respondent. In spite of all precautions, the researcher faces one source of error that she can neither eliminate nor assess accurately when using interviews and questionnaires, as well as other types of research methods: the effects that the researcher's activities will have on the people she is studying. The simple act of filling out a questionnaire, for example, may modify a respondent's view of himself and, in turn, his responses to subsequent questions. The mere presence of an observer may lead people to act in unaccustomed ways. A respondent who feels obliged to answer an interview question may hastily formulate opinions about issues he had not thought about before.

Nonreactive or unobtrusive data-collection methods remove biases introduced by the research process itself by eliminating the subjects' knowledge that they are being studied. In this chapter several nonreactive research methods are examined, along with other data-gathering methods. These methods can take the place of or complement the quantitative approach of surveys, providing alternative ways to test ideas and hypotheses against the real world. Nonreactive techniques are document research, study of physical evidence, and complete observation, whereas more interactive methods include participant observation, disguised observation, and experimentation.

DOCUMENT RESEARCH

An investigator can obtain a great deal of information by analyzing written documents, mass media reports, or data kept by institutions for administrative or governmental purposes. Institutional data include the U.S. Census, which represents an attempt to collect data from every household in the country and contains a wealth of demographic information about our population. Media reports include articles such as those appearing in *Time* and *Newsweek,* which might be used to assess the current state of public knowledge and concern about criminal justice issues. And the National Institute of Justice and other criminal justice agencies produce hundreds of written reports annually. In addition, the researcher may rely upon personal accounts such as letters, memoirs, and diaries, or reports consisting of video- or audiotapes covering events with historical significance. In short, if the researcher wants information about a past event, he can visit libraries or archives to request the use of personal and historical documents. If his concern is with ongoing events, he can often supplement his knowledge by collecting current documents prepared by or about the people he is studying. Research based upon analysis of existing sources of information is often referred to as archival or **document research.**

Let us consider the kinds of information routinely available in document form. For most individuals in our society, a great deal of biographical data can be obtained, including information about birth, schooling, marriages, divorces, military service, and death, as well as dates and causes of police arrests. Sources include official documents such as birth, death, and marriage certificates and school, military, and court records; they can be supplemented by unofficial sources such as newspapers, high school and college yearbooks, employment records, and personal documents such as letters and diaries. For well-known persons or well-publicized events, a wealth of information may be found in books, magazines, newspapers, films, and videotapes. Using these and other sources, both historical and contemporary data about the person, group, or event under study can be obtained without relying on the participants themselves for answers, as is done in survey research.

A tool particularly useful to the document researcher is **secondary analysis,** in which the researcher reexamines the method, data, and results of earlier research. The researcher may analyze the data in new ways, or look for possible sources of error or bias in the data itself, the data analysis, or conclusions drawn by the original researcher. The researcher may also use others' research to shed some light on her own research problem.

As with all research, the investigator must be aware of potential errors or biases in the documents she is using as data sources. These errors stem from the fact that the documents being examined are created by persons other than the researcher for purposes other than that of the research project. First, the person who originally reported the information is likely to have been selective in both recording events and filing documents. The researcher's reliance on available documents means that her data sources are

RESEARCHERS IN ACTION: DOCUMENT ANALYSIS/ SECONDARY DATA ANALYSIS

In this research, data from the FBI's *Uniform Crime Reports, Supplementary Homicide Reports,* and *The Comparative Homicide File,* as well as data from the Bureau of Census, were used to determine whether structural conditions (racial composition, local economic and labor opportunities, racial inequality, and racial segregation) affected four types of homicide: Black intraracial, White intraracial, Black interracial, and White interracial. Each of the structural variables was operationalized in such a way as to be able to use census data to determine the extent to which they existed. For example, local opportunity was calculated based upon census data in terms of percent not employed, job accessibility, and changes in employment between 1980–1990. Economic deprivation was determined using the percentage of population below the poverty level. Racial inequality was determined by the extent of residential segregation.

Census data from cities with populations of 100,000 or more in 1990, and with populations that were at least 2 percent Black, were used to select cities for study. This resulted in the selection of the 196 largest cities in the United States. Analysis of data for a five-year period was accomplished in order to minimize year-to-year fluctuations in homicide rates, and the years 1987–1992 were selected because of the midpoint, 1990, when census data were collected. Data on the incidence of homicide and the race of the offender and victim were obtained from analysis of FBI data for the five-year period.

The researchers found economic deprivation and local opportunity were related to rates of intraracial homicide, whereas racial inequality also contributed to Black intraracial homicide.

Source: K. F. Parker and P. McCall. 1999. "Structural Conditions and Racial Homicide Patterns: A Look at the Multiple Disadvantages in Urban Areas." *Criminology* 37(3): 447–478.

biased by the original recorder's selectivity. Second, there may be clerical or typographical errors or omissions in the documents or archives themselves. Although infrequent unsystematic mistakes such as clerical errors may have small effect on research findings, systematically incorrect or incomplete information can create a bias in research results. Third, much of the information contained in documents consists of the original recorder's reconstructions or interpretations of what the client, suspect, witnesses, or participants said or did. There is always a possibility that the original recorder misinterpreted what he heard, saw, or read. And, of course, the document researcher may compound the difficulty by misinterpreting the contents of the documents. Finally, documents may be deliberately altered for a variety of reasons (for instance, to hide errors, prevent embarrassment to others, make an administrator look good, and so on).

Perhaps an example will help clarify some of the dangers inherent in the use of preexisting sources of data. The *Uniform Crime Reports* (UCR), prepared and distributed by the Federal Bureau of Investigation (FBI), are the most commonly used official statistics on crime in the United States. However, researchers using these reports as data sources are confronted with a number of problems.

First, they are incomplete. Reporting by the various police agencies is voluntary. Although approximately 97 percent of the total population is covered by agencies that do report to the FBI, the figure for rural areas is about 93 percent and that for cities with fewer than 50,000 residents is about 95 percent. If a researcher is investigating crime in rural areas based on UCR statistics, there is a greater possibility of error in drawing conclusions than if the subject population resides in cities with over 50,000 residents (about 99 percent of these cities are covered in the UCR).

Second and potentially more serious than this bias is another dimension of incompleteness in the UCR. Independent surveys of crime victims consistently reveal that fewer than 50 percent of all serious crimes are reported to the police. Further, the extent of reporting varies by the type of offense. For example, most homicides are reported, but most burglaries, rapes, and assaults are not. Therefore, relying upon the UCR to provide an accurate picture of crime in the United States is unwise particularly when focusing on some types of offenses, because UCR data drastically underestimate the extent of many crimes.

Third, errors in categorizing crimes undoubtedly occur because state codes may differ from the categories used by the FBI. Fourth, information may be biased. Motivations other than simply contributing to our knowledge of the extent and nature of crime may be involved in some cases. For instance, estimates of future crime by law enforcement agencies may be slightly higher than actually expected in order to justify new budget requests; these possibly inflated estimates may be submitted to the FBI. The situation becomes even more complex if the researcher is interested in developing a profile of a certain type of offender based upon UCR data, because only about 20 percent of the serious crimes reported to the police lead to an arrest. As a result, our knowledge of the characteristics of rapists (based upon studies of arrested persons or convicted offenders) is incomplete, because we have studied only a small proportion of all persons who commit this offense. Some researchers suggest that such studies focus on the least successful of these offenders—those who have been apprehended. Even the most widely used criminal justice documents, such as police records and reports and the UCR, then, have serious faults. The incident-based reporting (IBR) system is gradually replacing the UCR. It will suffer from the same limitations as the UCR, and there are likely to be additional problems as well, because some of the IBR classifications are quite subjective. In the case of the UCR, it should be pointed out that the FBI recognizes the biases in the data and cautions users of the UCR as a data source.

When a researcher collects documents from subjects he is studying (with their knowledge), he must be concerned about the possibility of deceit, misinterpretation, and misunderstanding. Some subjects may deceive the researcher by presenting him with documents that may make their performance look better than it actually is. Thus, a police officer providing the researcher with information detailing her career in law enforcement might present letters of commendation from citizens and superiors but might not present the written reprimands contained in her file. Misinterpretation or misunderstanding occurs when subjects fail to understand the purpose of the research (in this case, that the researcher wants them to collect and present documents of both a positive and negative nature) and so do not provide complete or correct information. Such misinterpretation and misunderstanding can also occur when a researcher tries to interpret unfamiliar material. For example, an investigator studying police crime-solving rates might note that according to police records twenty burglaries had been "cleared by arrest" and might assume that twenty burglars had been caught. In fact, however, only one burglar may have been caught, who was then persuaded by the police or district attorney to plead guilty to all twenty burglaries in exchange for a relatively light sentence.

Content Analysis

In order to use a great many documents (such as newspaper or magazine articles and audio- or videotapes) for research purposes, the researcher must employ **content analysis.** This technique systematizes the use of documents by providing a predetermined coding scheme and categories for tabulating the contents of the documents. The number of entries tabulated in each category indicates the direction or weight of the archival evidence.

The steps involved in a typical research project using content analysis are as follows. First, the material to be analyzed must be selected. Are all narrative police reports to be studied, or only those about certain kinds of incidents? Are all newspaper headlines from certain papers over a specified period of time to be analyzed? Are randomly selected sentences or paragraphs to be analyzed? Are certain radio or television broadcasts to be included? Second, a sample of the material to be used is analyzed in order to develop a coding scheme and a set of categories. These tell the researcher how to determine what material belongs in which category. Third, a panel of judges is selected and familiarized with the rules of the coding scheme and the categories to be employed. Using a panel of judges helps guard against the bias that might occur were the researcher to do the coding of the research documents herself. These judges are asked to evaluate one or more sets of materials, and their evaluations are compared. The judges then discuss discrepancies in their evaluations and attempt to resolve them. Finally, when the judges agree on categorization of the material most of the time (such as 80 percent), they are asked to evaluate the material selected for the research project. Perhaps some examples will help illustrate the manner in which content analysis may be employed.

Suppose we were interested in whether newspaper accounts of the residents of skid row during a certain time period were negative, positive, or neutral so that we could develop an effective campaign to convince the public to support a new alcohol treatment program designed to operate on skid row streets. If we found newspaper accounts to be basically positive, we could build on this image.

If the accounts were basically neutral, we could perhaps try to convince the public that the residents of skid row were worthy of our help. If the accounts were basically negative, we would have to start a campaign to counter that image. First, we would select the newspapers and time period to be included in our sample. Then we would identify the kinds of words and their usages (in headlines, paragraph headings, the article narrative, and so on) that would be coded as positive, neutral, and negative (our three categories). Next we would impanel and train our judges and compare and discuss preliminary evaluations until the desired degree of agreement was reached. Finally, we would provide our judges with the newspapers we had included in our sample and ask them to evaluate those papers. Suppose our judges found a newspaper account referring to a skid row residence as a "house of horrors," to panhandling as "the touch of terror," and to the presence of skid row men as an "infection" or "blot on the city."[1] Other articles might include references to skid row men as animals who gather in packs, insects who swarm the city, demonic, and less than human.[2] Each of these references would be placed in the negative category and the total number counted. References that are neutral or positive would also be placed in appropriate categories and counted. The total number of references in each category could then be compared in order to enable us to answer our research question and help us make policy decisions.

If we were interested in understanding why the image of the police in the United States is what it is, we might go to the library and look at newspaper or magazine articles concerning the police to gain a historical perspective. Following the same procedure outlined above, we would evaluate statements such as the following from 1840: "It is notorious that the New York police is wretchedly inadequate to the arrest of offenders and the punishment of crime; as to *prevention* of crime, we might almost as well be without the name of a police, as we are all but without the substance." And, "Destructive rascality stalks at large in our city streets and public places, at all times of the day and night, with none to make it afraid. . . ."[3] These clearly negative references would be counted and compared to the numbers of positive and neutral references in order to help us understand the image of the police as portrayed in the articles selected over the time period under study.

Document analysis can be used rather effectively to conduct research, especially when used in conjunction with other techniques. It is often the only way to collect data about past events, it is relatively inexpensive, and, with the exception of documents given the researchers by his subjects, the presence of the researcher has no effect on the content of the materials being analyzed. There are, of course, as we have noted, a number of potential sources of error in documents of which the researcher should always be cognizant.

OBSERVATION

So far in our discussion of the three basic ways both laypersons and scientists gather information, we have considered communicating with others (through questionnaires and interviews) and examining the recorded reports of others (through document analysis). We come now to the final strategy: direct observation of the people or events by the researcher himself. As a data-collection technique, observation allows a researcher to record events as they occur, without having to rely on the introspective or retrospective powers of the subjects, or on records created by others. As we shall see, however, this strategy has its own weaknesses. Remember that the goal in research is to improve understanding while maintaining objectivity. Yet the closer researchers get to subjects in an attempt to understand them, the harder it becomes to maintain objectivity. If, on the other hand, researchers remain aloof from the subjects in the hope of remaining objective, they increase the danger of not understanding the meaning of what is observed or heard.

Three types of observational roles are employed by researchers, depending on the constraints and demands of the research purpose and setting: the complete observer, the participant observer, and the disguised observer. Each role has different implications for researcher objectivity and understanding.

The researcher who observes his subjects without their knowledge and without physically participating in their activities is called a **complete observer.** The complete observer studies his subjects from afar, so to speak. Examples are a researcher who sits, unknown to the observed, behind a one-way mirror, and the person who observes subjects through field glasses. The complete observer may be able to record the behavior he sees in great detail and may concentrate on reporting these observations objectively. His interpretations of the meaning of that behavior, however, are quite another thing. He may misinterpret the meaning of what he has observed as a result of his own subjective biases about the behavior; or he may be unable to interpret what he sees at all because his personal repertoire of behavioral categories does not include the ones observed (a danger, for example, when observing cross-culturally). In either case, the complete observer cannot ask the subjects what their behavior means, and he may be so far removed physically that he cannot hear their comments on their behavior. Thus, although the complete observer may maximize objectivity, he may fall short of the goal of understanding.

A **participant observer** is one who identifies herself as an observer, states her purpose, and physically participates in the activities of the observed. The extent of participation can vary greatly. It may be limited simply to being present among the subjects in order to observe (sometimes referred to as the role of "observer as participant") or it may extend to include complete participation in the activities of the subjects with observation a secondary concern (often referred to as the "participant as observer" role).[4] In either case, the participant observer has a much greater opportunity to understand the flow of events observed than does the complete observer, because through participation, the observer can use all her senses and can ask questions about events she does not understand.[5] At the same time, however, the participant observer finds it more difficult to be objective in reporting than does the complete observer. This is so because, in the process of participating, the observer makes friends (and possibly enemies), begins to feel more at home in the activities of the observed, and concentrates both on her role as observer and on her role as participant. Still, because the participant-observer role improves the possibility of understanding, while allowing the conscientious observer to work hard at being objective, it is an observer role frequently selected by social scientists.

Both the advantages and disadvantages of participant observation are illustrated in George Kirkham's book *Signal Zero*. Kirkham accepted a challenge from a police officer who was among his students and actually became a police officer himself in order to determine to what extent his theories of policing applied on the streets. He became a complete participant by meeting the same requirements as other rookie officers and being assigned a regular beat; the police department was aware of his research. Initially, Kirkham attempted to keep an accurate, objective log of his observations and actions, but he soon found it impossible to maintain objectivity and difficult even to write daily logs. Kirkham concludes:

> I do not pretend that what follows [in *Signal Zero*] is an objective book about either the police or crime in our society. This could never have been such a work, although in the beginning I had thought it might be. But what happened to me in those months made it impossible for me ever again to view a policeman's world from the detached perspective of a social scientist. I realize that now.[6]

In fact, Kirkham had "gone native." When the time came for him to return to the classroom, he decided to continue working as a police officer on a part-time basis, and found himself accepted only marginally by his colleagues in academia, who found some of his comments concerning theoretical criminologists offensive.[7]

The third type of observer, a **disguised** or secret **observer,** misrepresents himself to his subjects and observes them while participating as a group member. A researcher may adopt the disguised observer role if he would not otherwise be allowed to observe, as in the case of certain religious sects or criminal groups; or if he feels that being treated as one of the observed is essential to understanding them. Arguments against the use of disguised observation concern ethics and loss of objectivity. Many social scientists feel that it is unethical for a researcher to conceal his identity to gain inside information. Others feel disguised observation is ethical as long as the welfare of the subjects is protected.[8] Both groups agree that problems of objectivity are greatly compounded when the observer pretends to be a group member, because he may come to see himself as such ("going native") and be unable to report or analyze objectively the behavior he observes. A secret observer, of course, is engaged in a deception and must constantly be concerned with being discovered, a fear that compounds his difficulties.

Clearly, the problems of attaining understanding while remaining objective are inherent in the use of observation as a data-collection technique. A unique difficulty for observation is encountered when the investigator cannot predict when or where the event to be observed will happen (as with criminal activity or traffic accidents). Nevertheless, observation can be a valuable tool for the researcher who does not wish to interrupt unnecessarily the flow of events being studied by reading questions from a survey form.

Recording and Coding

As in survey research and content analysis of documents, recording techniques usually must be decided before observation, for best use of the observation period. Questions such as how structured the observations are to be (is a suitable code scheme available?) and the effects the researcher anticipates her note taking will have on subjects must be answered. If a set of categories has been prepared ahead of the observation period, the observer may need to do no more than place an "x" in the appropriate columns to indicate that a particular event occurred, initiated by a particular subject, at a particular time.[9] If no code scheme exists, she may make extensive notes on the events she considers to be important or videotape the session. If recording procedures seem to interrupt the flow of events unnecessarily, the researcher may retire from the field of observation to make notes in private. Different research settings will provide variable opportunities for record keeping. For example, a staff meeting in a police department is a setting in which everyone present is taking notes, and the observer would be conspicuous only if she failed to do so. If, however, the observer were attending a confidential meeting where no one else present was taking notes, she might retire at convenient intervals to the office or the washroom to record observations.

Observations that are to be recorded exclusively through note taking and will extend over a fairly long time should be entered in what anthropologists call a *field notebook*. There are several ways of organizing such a notebook. One particularly effective way is to allocate a section for each observation period, specifying date, time, and location of observations. The contents of each section can be divided into at least three distinct subsections. In one subsection, observations are recorded with as much concreteness, specificity, and objectivity as can be mustered. A field note entry in this subsection might be something like:

> Officer A removed her cap, placed it on the right front seat, and stepped out of the patrol car. She walked toward a group of five young people leaning against the building, saying nothing until she was within about two feet of the person nearest the doorway.

The words used to record the observations are objective (subject to consensual validation; see Chapter 1) in the sense that they refer to phenomena that are more or less visible to anyone on the scene, and other observers would probably agree with the description. The language is descriptive in the sense that the observer has not included her interpretations or inferences, for example, about the officer's feelings or intentions or her own feelings about what the officer did. If conversations are being recorded, it is important to record them accurately. If the observer must paraphrase, a note should so indicate.

A second subsection is reserved for tentative interpretations and explanations that occur to the observer and research issues or questions the researcher wishes to keep in mind during subsequent observation periods. An entry in this subsection of the field notebook for this day might be:

The officer seemed to be arrogant and faking anger as she approached the youths. The youths seemed unconcerned. I wonder if this has become a kind of ritual and what sorts of signals are used to indicate when it is really serious. Her attitude toward the youth seemed insulting and demeaning.

A third subsection might be devoted to a kind of personal diary in which the researcher records her or his feelings or reactions to being an observer or to the people and events that have been observed, sometimes including evaluations. An entry in this subsection of the diary might look like this:

My first day observing was a little rocky. I'm not sure if I was really accepted by Officer A. She seemed a little suspicious. I'll have to keep at it, I guess, and hope I can gain her confidence as time goes along. I found her attitude toward the youth very inappropriate.

However one chooses to organize a field notebook, the researcher should be able to sort through the range of experiences one has as an observer and to deliberately select language appropriate to each of those experiences. Each of the types of observation records discussed here is important in the research process, though often for different reasons. Being able to distinguish among them and keep them separate from one another is essential for good observational or field research. The portions of the records that are objective, descriptive, and specific deserve special emphasis because they are the empirical foundation on which the researcher constructs interpretations and explanations. The other types of records are, of course, also essential to the research process. It can be argued, in fact, that in selecting among the available types of vocabulary and language forms in our field notebook, we are selecting different perspectives and stances vis-à-vis what we have observed and our experiences as observers.

Accuracy of Observations

As with all research methods, observation has sources of error. Accuracy of observations often poses serious difficulties for the observer. He may have been thoroughly trained to separate what he observes happening from what he expects to see happening and may record observations in great detail. Still, the possibility exists that another observer viewing the same events might see and record them differently. One method of assessing observer accuracy is to employ more than one observer and compare their reports. Unfortunately, the presence of more than one observer may further disrupt the flow of events, especially in a small group of subjects, who may come to view themselves as outnumbered by outsiders. As described in Chapter 3, another method for attempting to improve scientific accuracy, triangulation, is especially suited for use by observers.

PHYSICAL EVIDENCE

It is well known that *physical evidence* is often the key to solving criminal cases. Physical evidence is also sometimes used in scientific research, usually in conjunction with other research techniques. For example, if we wished to know whether police officers assigned to narcotics units are involved in narcotics use themselves, we might interview selected officers or send them a questionnaire concerning drug use. We might also collect physical evidence by giving them blood tests or asking them to provide samples for urinalysis. Such physical evidence could then be compared with the information collected by interview or questionnaire to provide a more complete answer to our research question. Both blood samples and urinalysis belong to a category of physical evidence referred to as **accretion evidence,** or evidence produced by the accumulation or deposit of materials.

Erosion evidence is another category of physical evidence that includes evidence of use or wear. As a supplemental method of determining which of a series of educational tapes for inmates are more frequently used, we might examine replacement records to determine which tapes must be repaired or replaced most frequently.

Other types of physical evidence are also available to the researcher. In order to help determine the validity of self-report questionnaires, we might give our subjects polygraph tests. The polygraph measures changes in blood pressure and respiration, and sometimes the subject's electrodermal responses (changes in the activity of sweat pores in the subject's hands), or changes in muscular pressures and movements. Such physical changes can be used under certain conditions to help us determine whether an individual is telling the truth and therefore can help us assess the validity of data collected through other research techniques.

EXPERIMENTS

The words *science* and *experiment* seem almost synonymous to most of us, because when we hear or read about science or scientists, experiments frequently are mentioned. Although scientists engage in many scientific activities that are not experiments (and although many activities that are labeled "experiments" are not scientific), this link of science and experimentation is justified because an important part of scientific study is engaging in controlled observation under controlled conditions, the essence of experimentation.

A *scientific experiment,* as we use the term, has several identifying characteristics. It is bound by the perspective and rules of science discussed earlier and conducted according to a research design formulated by the experimenter before the experiment is undertaken. Moreover, it is performed in an environment that the experimenter can at least partially control, either through selection or through construction (such as the laboratory). The experimenter also has control over, and usually manipulates deliberately, at least some of the variables he regards as independent or causal.

As we noted in Chapter 3, the classic experiment conforms to the before-after-with-control type of explanatory research design and involves comparing an *experimental condition* with a *control condition*. In the **experimental condition,** the researcher measures an experimental group on the dependent variable, exposes the group to the **experimental treatment** (the presumed independent or causal variable), and then measures the group again on the dependent variable. In the **control condition,** a control group is measured once, *not* exposed to the experimental treatment, and then measured again. Although not all experimental designs conform precisely to this pattern, all do involve some form of control that permits the investigator to assess the effects of changes in the value of one variable on changes in the value of another variable under controlled conditions. We use controls because they help eliminate alternative explanations for changes we observe in the dependent variable for the experimental group, and hence strengthen causal inferences.

In a classic set of experiments called the Western Electric studies, a group of social scientists was hired by an industrial firm to study the effects of variables such as illumination and different forms of employee compensation (the independent variables) on the productivity (the dependent variable) of assembly-line workers.[10] To conduct these experiments, a special work environment was constructed and equipped so that the experimenters could control the conditions in the area. The research design called for changing these variables in an orderly fashion and observing the impact of these changes on productivity. Regular employees of the company were selected for participation in the study, and their work was performed inside the specially constructed area. The investigators then executed their research plan, systematically varying the environmental conditions in the work area while observing the number of articles the workers produced in a given time span under each variation in condition.

This type of experiment has some significant advantages. First, because the investigator controls the independent variables, it is possible to isolate and manipulate a single variable (say, illumination) while holding another variable (temperature) constant, thereby gaining information about the contribution of this single variable to changes in the dependent variable (productivity). Second, the interactive effects of the independent variables can be systematically explored. The investigator might discover, for example, that certain combinations of values of two or more of the independent variables produce greater effects than the sum of the separate effects of the two variables. In short, a scientist uses an experiment to reduce a situation that may be very complex in its natural setting to manageable proportions and to do a controlled and orderly exploration of the relationships among the variable components of these simplified units.

The characteristics that give the experimental technique its strength, however, also carry with them significant hazards. The Western Electric researchers did observe a significant increase in the productivity of the workers as the experiment progressed. However, these changes bore practically no relationship to changes in the independent variables. Productivity increased greatly and stayed at a high level, despite the relatively extreme variations in conditions introduced by the investigators.

How can we account for such findings? The investigators concluded that the special treatment of the workers itself—being selected for participation in a scientific study, being closely observed by the scientists, and so on—rather than any of the particular experimental variations, led to the workers' increased productivity. The effect produced by special treatment of experimental subjects is now known in the social sciences as the **Hawthorne effect** (after the Hawthorne, Illinois, site of the Western Electric plant studied), a phenomenon likely to occur whenever people are aware of being given special treatment, whether the research setting is inside or outside a laboratory.

Apparently, the investigators introduced a variable into their experimental procedure that they had not taken into account in their research design. The assumption that all relevant variables were accounted for in the research design turned out to be inaccurate in this case, and that possibility exists in any experimental procedure. The effects of unknown or unrecognized variables cannot, by definition, be assessed, and their presence and influence are always a possibility. Even if we do discover relationships among the variables being investigated, we have no guarantee that the variables are related in a **causal** way. That is, relationships among variables may be **spurious,** in the sense that an unknown and unaccounted-for variable may be responsible for the observed relationship.

Furthermore, the very advantages of experiments—they enable us to select and isolate a small number of variables for careful study—also increase the risks of impracticality. The relationships that we observe in a simplified and purified laboratory environment may not hold in the complex natural settings of the real world with numerous variables affecting the flow of events. Some social scientists (especially those who emphasize qualitative methods and the situational determinants of behavior) contend that all we learn about human behavior through laboratory observation is how people behave in a laboratory, and, furthermore, that there is no necessary connection between people's behavior in this situation and their behavior in other situations that humans encounter in day-to-day life.

Of course, not all experiments are plagued by the artificiality of the laboratory, and one of the most interesting experiments in criminal justice was conducted *in the field* in Kansas City in 1972–1973. The Kansas City Preventive Patrol study clearly illustrates a number of the problems we have just discussed.[11] The study was designed to determine whether routine preventive patrol, considered by most police administrators and officers to be the backbone of police work, was important in deterring crime, responding to crime, and citizen satisfaction with the police. This was to be accomplished by dividing the city into fifteen beats that were further divided into five groups of three each—computer matched on the basis of crime data, calls for service, income, racial/ethnic composition, and other selected factors. Within each group of three, one beat was designated reactive, one proactive, and one control. In the reactive beats, there was no preventive patrol—officers entered them only in response to calls for service. In the control beats, the usual level of patrol (one car per beat) was maintained. In the proactive beats, the patrol was increased by two to three times its usual level. The results of the experiment indicate that, in Kansas City at least, increasing or decreasing the level of preventive patrol has no effect on crime, citizen satisfaction with police services, or response time.

As might be expected, the Kansas City experiment generated considerable controversy. First, there was a concern among many involved with the study about the ethics of removing patrol cars from some beats and possibly endangering the lives of citizens by increasing response time or failing to detect crimes in progress. Second, many people were (and some still are) concerned about whether experimental conditions were maintained and if the data collected can be generalized to all cities and patrol policies. Last, but not least, many police administrators remain convinced that preventive patrol deters crime despite the results of this experiment and other studies conducted later. It is difficult to admit that one of the assumptions upon which police administrators have based their operations over many years may be inaccurate. It is much easier to find fault with the research conducted and to continue to adhere to traditional beliefs. This is a common response to research that challenges such beliefs, in the criminal justice field and in other fields as well.

ENTERING THE FIELD

Some research strategies (especially participant observation, but also some types of interviewing) require that the researcher go to natural settings where his subjects live or work. The sometimes difficult process of beginning research in such settings is called *entering the field*. What is the best way to enter the field? There is no simple answer to this question, but a researcher's venture into the field can be less traumatic if he considers which participant observer role to assume as well as the following issues both prior to and during field research activities:

- What questions do I want to answer?
- Who can give me the answers I need?
- How do I want subjects to view me?
- How are subjects likely to view me?
- What alternative strategies for entering the field are available?
- Should I disclose my identity as a researcher?
- What kinds of opposition might I expect and from whom?
- What strategies might be effective in coping with this opposition?

Suppose we want to learn about the interaction among judges, prosecutors, and defense attorneys. We decide that the best way to understand this interaction is to observe it and to question members of each category of professionals about it. Although we want our subjects to view us as legitimate researchers, they are likely to view us, at least initially, as intruders. Because we anticipate that some judges and attorneys may oppose our presence at their meetings, we believe that authorization from the chief judge of the circuit will give legitimacy to our presence and reduce potential opposition from other judges and attorneys. Because some of the information we collect may be of a sensitive nature, we recognize that appropriate assurances of confidentiality will have to be made and kept. Therefore, we obtain the support of the chief judge (who may write a letter indicating her approval of our research to the other judges and attorneys) and guarantee our subjects' anonymity and confidentiality at the outset.

This is, of course, only one strategy for entering the field. In some cases, identification with or support from administrators might make it extremely difficult for us to obtain the desired information, and we might need to use a different strategy. In any case, a clear, concise statement of our research problem coupled with careful consideration of the other seven issues mentioned above will usually enable us to begin translating our research plans into action.

Perhaps the most important thing for the prospective researcher to keep in mind is that he is entering an interactive setting that will be altered by his very presence, regardless of the techniques employed (with the exception of the complete observer). His entry into the field almost always disrupts the flow of events to be observed to some extent, and his personal values, techniques, and questions all affect his subjects to varying degrees. Therefore, the effects of a researcher's entrance and presence in the field and his personal values (where appropriate) should be identified, assessed, and presented as part of his research documentation.

Jerome Skolnick's classic study of the police provides considerable insight into the process of entering the field. Skolnick explored the day-to-day behavior of the police and other individuals in the criminal justice system in an attempt to "learn how those who are charged with enforcing criminal law in a constitutional democracy come to interpret rules of constraint—thereby giving these life and meaning—and to analyze the practical dilemmas they face."[12] Skolnick's first entry into the field was as a participant in the "Westville" criminal courts community. His first observations were made in the public defender's office for several months, and then, as a result of contacts made with assistant prosecutors, a recommendation from the public defender, and a long interview with the prosecutor, he proceeded to observe the workings of the prosecutor's office. Through contacts developed in the prosecutor's office, Skolnick approached the chief of police, who proved willing to allow him to observe police officers in action, and a lieutenant was assigned to introduce Skolnick to the police officers to be observed. Skolnick proceeded to observe patrol officers as they performed their duties and to question them concerning their actions. Based on his belief that additional information concerning his specific topic might be collected by observing detectives, Skolnick eventually had the opportunity to observe the vice, burglary, homicide, and robbery squads. In the long run, Skolnick had entered the field so successfully that he was sometimes taken as a detective and even performed police tasks for the detectives (see our discussion above on the dangers of "going native"). Skolnick concludes that the more time an observer spends with his subjects, the more accustomed to his presence they become; that open, sometimes enlightening discussions frequently occur when an observer has good rapport with his subjects; and that the police are often not free to alter their behavior so as to deceive the observer. Successful entry into the field may help minimize disruptions while making it possible for the researcher to exercise drop-in privileges with those previously observed.

Another example of entering the field comes from Howard S. Becker's study of marijuana users, in which he took advantage of a special skill he possessed in order to gain access to his subjects:

To develop and test my hypotheses about the genesis of marihuana use for pleasure, I conducted fifty interviews with marihuana users. I had been a professional dance musician for some years when I conducted this study, and my first interviews were with people I had met in the music business. I asked them to put me in contact with other users who would be willing to discuss their experiences with me.[13]

In addition, Becker's colleagues working with opiate users made available to him some interviews that dealt with marijuana as well as opiates: "Although in the end half of the fifty interviews were conducted with musicians, the other half covered a wide range of people, including laborers, machinists, and people in the professions."[14]

In concluding this chapter, we need to caution you that conducting research is an art as well as a science. Although we have separated the research steps here, we do not mean to imply that they constitute a recipe that, if followed faithfully, will result in successful research. As the example from Skolnick's research clearly indicates, the research process is an interactive one. Subjects and situations do not wait passively for the manipulations of the researcher. Rather, the researcher must always be ready to respond sensitively, flexibly, and creatively to the demands of the research situation.

REVIEW QUESTIONS

1. What are the advantages and disadvantages of nonreactive data-collection techniques?
2. Of what possible problems in the accuracy of the data should a researcher who uses documents be aware?
3. Of what possible errors of interpretation should an investigator using physical evidence be aware?
4. What are the advantages and disadvantages of being a participant observer as compared with being a secret observer or a complete observer?
5. What questions should a researcher ask himself or herself before entering the field as an observer?
6. What are the advantages and disadvantages of being an observer compared with using nonreactive research methods?
7. What scientific advantages are there in experimentation as a research technique? What are its limitations?

EXERCISES

1. Identify and discuss the usefulness in document analysis of at least three different sections of a daily newspaper.
2. What kinds of documents might one use to study:
   - criminal behavior
   - educational background

- political philosophy of newspersons
- citizens' views of police or court performance

3. Discuss how you might draw a simple random sample of newspaper editorials for a daily paper over a two-year period.

4. Develop a coding plan for at least one variable pertaining to newspaper editorials about the law-and-order issue.

5. Write an entering-the-field plan for doing an observational study of police encounters with juveniles.

6. Suppose you wanted to do an observational study of drug use on your campus. Discuss the advantages and disadvantages of being:

- a participant as observer
- an observer as participant
- a disguised observer
- a complete observer

Include in your discussion issues concerning recording observations, accuracy of observations, and objectivity.

 7. Go to *www.csun.edu/~hcchs006/gang.html* and read selections from an ongoing ethnography of Latino street gangs. Note the section on the interview schedule and methodological difficulties.

 8. Go to *http://www.google.com* and do a search on "qualitative research." Follow a few of the links that interest you.

 9. For further discussion and some examples of content analysis, go to *http://www.lehman.cuny.edu/courses/sociology/soc247/contentexamples.html.*

 10. For a detailed critique of a content analysis of pornography on the Web using many of the concepts discussed in this book, see *http://ecommerce. vanderbilt.edu/novak/rimm.review.html.* To check out the original publication, see Martin Rimm, "Marketing Pornography on the Information Superhighway," *Georgetown Law Journal* 83 (June 1995): 1849–1934.

NOTES

1. Howard M. Bahr, *Skid Row: An Introduction to Disaffiliation* (New York: Oxford University Press, 1973), pp. 59–61.

2. Ibid.

3. James F. Richardson, *The New York Police: Colonial Times to 1901* (New York: Oxford University Press, 1970), pp. 23–29.

4. For a comprehensive discussion of these and other observer roles, see Raymond Gold, "Roles in Sociological Field Observations," *Social Forces* 36 (March 1958): 217–223.

5. The possibility of misunderstanding is never eliminated for the participant observer, because her subjects may deliberately deceive her, or she may think she understands when, in fact, she doesn't.

6. George Kirkham, *Signal Zero* (New York: Lippincott, 1976), p. i.

7. Other good examples of participant observation as a technique for studying deviance and criminal justice include Albert J. Reiss, *The Police and the Public* (New Haven, CT: Yale University Press, 1971); Jerome H. Skolnick, *Justice Without Trial* (New York: Wiley, 1967); Laud Humphreys, *Tearoom Trade: Impersonal Sex in Public Places* (Chicago: Aldine, 1970); Ned Polsky, *Hustlers, Beats, and Others* (Chicago: Aldine, 1967); and William F. Whyte, *Streetcorner Society* (Chicago: University of Chicago Press, 1943); Peter K. Manning, *Police Work: The Social Organization of Policing*, 2nd ed. (Prospect Heights, IL: Waveland Press, 1999; Manning and John Van Maanen (eds.), *Policing: A View from the Streets* (Santa Monica, CA: Goodyear, 1978); Michael K. Brown, *Working the Street: Police Discretion and the Dilemmas of Reform* (New York: Sage, 1981); Van Maanen, *Tales of the Field: On Writing Ethnography* (Chicago: University of Chicago Press, 1988); Neil Websdale, *Rural Woman Battering and the Justice System* (Thousand Oaks, CA: Sage, 1998); and Steve Herbert, *Policing Space: Territoriality and the Los Angeles Police Department* (Minneapolis, MN: University of Minnesota Press, 1997).

8. For a discussion of both sides of this issue, see Kai T. Erikson, "A Comment on Disguised Observation in Sociology," *Social Problems* 14 (Spring 1967): 366–373; and Norman K. Denzin, "On the Ethics of Disguised Observation," *Social Problems* 15 (Spring 1968): 502–504.

9. See, for example, Edgar F. Borgatta and Betty Crowther, *A Workbook for the Study of Social Interaction Processes* (Chicago: Rand McNally, 1965).

10. F. J. Roethlesberger and W. J. Dickson, *Management and the Worker* (Cambridge, MA: Harvard University Press, 1939).

11. *The Kansas City Preventive Patrol Experiment: A Summary Report* (Washington, DC: Police Foundation, 1974).

12. Skolnick, p. vii.

13. Howard S. Becker, *Outsiders. Studies in the Sociology of Deviance* (New York: Free Press, 1963), p. 45.

14. Ibid, pp. 45–46.

CHAPTER

7

An Introduction to Descriptive Statistics

Statistics are numerical tools used by researchers to help them describe and explain phenomena. Any numerical *datum* qualifies as a statistic (though the term is often employed in a more specialized sense), and most social-science data are presented in statistical form. Statistics appear in criminal justice textbooks and research reports. Law enforcement administrators and other government officials use a variety of statistical information in making policy decisions. Advertisers trying to convince us of the desirability of their product frequently present us with statistics to bolster their case, whereas consumer information groups use statistics to assess the relative merits of products. If we are to do research or to understand and assess the research of others, we must know something about statistics.

However, there are dangers here for the unwary, for in our number-conscious culture, "statistics" have almost become synonymous with "facts." Because statistics seem to have a hardness, an immutability, a finality to them, we are inclined to think that they are unquestionable. But just as facts do not speak for themselves, neither do statistics, for statistical data can be misused or misinterpreted, and in the discussion that follows, we will note some of the errors and ambiguities that sometimes emerge. A few of the more elementary statistical concepts and procedures will be discussed in detail, while several more complex statistical techniques will be introduced to give the reader a sense of their importance. For a more complete discussion, the reader should consult more advanced statistics texts.

There are two basic types of statistics: descriptive and inferential. **Descriptive statistics** show relationships between variables or describe and summarize a particular data set. They will be the focus of this and the following two chapters. **Inferential statistics,** considered in chapters 10 and 11, help us draw conclusions (make inferences) about the characteristics of populations, based on the characteristics of samples drawn from those populations.

MEASUREMENT AND SCALES

We are all familiar with certain kinds of measurement and the procedures for obtaining them. If, for example, we wanted to find out if a piece of lumber was long enough to use for a particular purpose, we could hold a yardstick up to it and measure its length. To determine the sex distribution or age range in a given group of people, we can obtain data with a good degree of accuracy by examining birth certificates. However, measurement of variables in social-science research is seldom so straightforward, and consequently we must often devise our own yardstick for obtaining required measurements. For example, psychological attributes such as stress can be measured only indirectly, for instance, through the administration of a questionnaire designed to assess stress for each member of a group. The respondent's answers could be converted to a score representing whether, or to what extent, the respondent possessed the particular attribute.

Continuous and Discrete Variables

Scientists classify variables into two types—continuous or discrete—based upon the kinds of values the variables can, in principle, assume. Suppose we were interested in the variable "length" of a piece of lumber. A particular piece of wood can have infinitely many measurements of length because we can always, at least theoretically, make the spaces between measurement units smaller (3.2 inches, 3.217 inches, 3.21795 inches, and so on). **Continuous variables** such as length, age, and time can in principle assume infinitely many values; measurement of continuous variables are always approximations. In contrast, **discrete variables** such as sex (with values of male and female), political party affiliation (values of Democrat, Republican, Independent, and soon), number of children in a family (values of 0, 1, 2, . . . but not of 1.2, 2.36), number of crimes committed by a person (values of 0, 1, 2, . . . but not 1.6), and type of crime (the concepts "misdemeanor" and "felony") can assume only a finite number of values; measurements of discrete variables can be exact. Understanding whether the variables under investigation are continuous or discrete is important because the variable type is related to both the *level* at which we can measure the variable and the *statistical techniques* available to describe and analyze our data. For example, many statistical procedures assume continuous variables.

It should be noted, however, that in most cases, with relatively minor modifications of the mathematical formula for calculating the statistic (referred to as a **correction for continuity**), the same procedures may be used with discrete data as well.

Levels of Measurement

Norminal Level

The simplest level of measurement is called **nominal.** Data measured at the nominal level can be placed in exhaustive, mutually exclusive categories but cannot be ordered further. Examples of data measured at the nominal level include responses categorized as true or false; information about religious affiliation categorized as Protestant, Catholic, Jewish, and other; and information about ethnic affiliation such as Irish, Dutch, English, and so on. Variables measured at the nominal level are always discrete variables. In analyzing nominal data we can count the responses in each category (for example, there were six males and four females) and cross-tabulate responses (relate responses given in one category to those given in another—for example, there were three male Protestants, two female Catholics, and so on). We can also convert the raw data frequencies into fractions, percentages, or ratios.

Ordinal Level

Measurements at the **ordinal level** make it possible not only to categorize but also to rank elements in the population according to the degree to which a certain attribute is present. Although ordinal level measurements are, in theory, continuous, they are often treated as discrete. Suppose we asked people to respond to the following attitude questionnaire item:

The death penalty is an effective deterrent to crime. (Circle the appropriate letter.)

(a) strongly agree

(b) agree

(c) neutral

(d) disagree

(e) strongly disagree

We could then rank respondents according to the degree of agreement or disagreement they had expressed, an ordinal measurement. Is such a measurement discrete or continuous? Although we may imagine an infinite number of gradations in the degree of agreement, the measurement itself is discrete.

Now suppose we asked respondents to check a point on the following line (a Likert scale; see Chapter 5) corresponding to their opinion.

+3	+2	+1	0	-1	-2	-3
strongly agree			neutral			strongly disagree

In this case, the response range is, in theory, continuous in the sense that a checkmark may be placed at any point along the line. But how will the researcher record responses for the purpose of analysis? Usually the response will be recorded as a +2 or a −1, for example. But remember that these numbers are not real quantities; they are better regarded as only numerical codes for more or less discrete ordinal responses.

Several other types of scaling have been developed to create ordinal data, including sociometric scaling, which measures degrees of friendship; Guttman scaling, which ranks' respondents according to the patterns of their responses to a set of questions that measure attitudes; and social distance scaling, which measures respondents' degrees of acceptance of various categories of people.

For example, to measure the social distance between respondents and convicted felons, we might ask respondents if they would (1) marry a felon or accept one as a close relation; (2) accept one as a close friend; (3) accept one as a next-door neighbor; (4) accept one in your church, school, and so on; (5) accept one in your community., but have no contact; (6) accept one as a resident of your country, but not your community; (7) not accept one.[1]

Furthermore, if our assumption that these items form a continuum of acceptance is true, then a respondent willing to accept a felon as a spouse or close relative also would be willing to accept one as a neighbor, church member, community member, and so on. If, on the other hand, our respondent said he would accept a felon as a resident of his community but would have no contact with him, we would expect that he would reject him on items 1 through 4 on the scale. So, a respondent's answer concerning the social distance he would put between himself and a felon yields additional information about his level of acceptance. The same question could be asked about other types of nonconformists to learn if a respondent generally accepted or rejected nonconformity; or we could compare responses, for example, male and female, to determine whether one sex was more accepting of felons. Note, however, that we could not say *how much* more with this level of measurement, because the difference or distance between ranks has no quantitative meaning.

Interval Level

With **interval level measurement,** we can categorize and rank order respondents (as in ordinal measurement), *and* we can also specify the *quantity* of variation between responses. An interval scale has an arbitrarily designated zero point, but a fixed and constant unit of measurement, such that the difference between any two adjacent points on our scale is the same as the difference between any other two adjacent points on the same scale. Temperature, as measured in degrees centigrade or Fahrenheit, is an example of interval level data, and we can say that the difference (interval) between 50°C and 25°C is quantitatively the same as the difference (interval) between 40°C and 15°C. Interval data can be added and subtracted, but multiplication and division of measurements themselves are theoretically inappropriate. For example, it makes no sense to say that 50°C is twice as hot as 25°C, because the zero point on the centigrade scale is arbitrary. To understand the effects of an arbitrary zero point on mathematical operations, consider what would happen if we moved the arbitrary zero point on the centigrade thermometer up 10 units. The point on the scale that was originally 25° would now read 15°, and the point that was originally 50° would now be 40°; 40 is certainly not twice 15, but the difference between 15 and 40 is still 25. Measures of intelligence, such as IQ, are also, technically, interval scales; a person with an IQ of 60, for example, is not regarded as being half as smart as a person with an IQ of 120. We can calculate averages for interval measurements and compare differences among averages but, as we saw with two raw temperature readings, dividing or multiplying the averages themselves would be inappropriate. Variables measured at the interval level may be either discrete or continuous.

Ratio Level

Ratio level measurement has all the properties of nominal, ordinal, and interval measurement and in addition has an absolute zero point representing a complete absence of whatever is being measured. Because of the absolute zero point, we can legitimately multiply and divide ratio data. Age, time, weight, area, volume, length, the number of days in office (or jail), number of contacts between parole officer and parolee, frequency of coffee breaks, and number of court cases are all examples of ratio level data. Variables measured at the ratio level may be discrete or continuous.

Levels of Measurement—Some Additional Considerations

It should be noted that data for variables measured at the nominal level for one unit of analysis (such as, a police officer) can usually serve as the basis for data for a variable measured at the ratio level for a different unit of analysis (such as, a police department). For example, although male is a nominal value of the discrete variable sex, proportion of males is a continuous variable pertaining to a group of persons measured at the ratio level (see Table 7.1).

Furthermore, as Hubert Blalock points out, the distinction between interval and ratio scales is often academic. In most cases, a legitimate interval scale can at least theoretically be converted to and treated as a ratio scale, because once the size of a unit on the scale has been determined, an absence of units can be conceived, even though we may not be able actually to measure this condition.[2] The level at which we measure data is important because it will determine the type of mathematical and statistical procedures we can use in analyzing our data. In general, arithmetic operations (addition, subtraction, division, and multiplication) can be used only with interval and ratio data.

Finally, as noted in our discussion of ordinal level data, it is extremely important not to confuse numbers used as codes for categories of a variable (recording a "1" if the survey respondent is male and "2" if female) with numbers that are frequency counts (one male and two females were involved in the robbery) or with measured quantities (she was 21 years old and had committed fifteen offenses).

DESCRIBING THE DATA

Once variable type (discrete or continuous) has been identified, measurement level has been determined, and data have been gathered, we must choose among several options for describing the data.

TABLE 7.1	Measurements of Students in Criminal Justice Methods Class	
Sex as a Nominal Variable pertaining to Persons		*Sex as a Ratio Variable Pertaining to Group*
Males: 6		Proportion of males: 6/10 = .60
Females: 4		Proportion of females: 4/10 = .40
Total: 10		Total: 1.0

Raw Numbers

Suppose, as a project for a law enforcement class, we asked a number of people who passed by on a street corner if they regarded crime as a serious problem in their city. After collecting their answers, we might report the results of our informal survey in several ways. We could say, one hundred people said they did consider crime a serious problem in their city, and twenty-five people said they did not. In this case, the *raw numbers* that fell into each of the response categories were reported. These simple frequency counts are called raw because the numbers have not been "processed" in any way; that is, they have not been converted to ratios, percentages, and so on.

Raw numbers, which are usually designated by the letter n (in our example, $n = 125$), are the point at which any statistical description must begin, and these numbers have the advantages of being simple, straightforward, and easy to understand. Statistical descriptions should always include raw numbers, or at the very least should be presented in a way that enables a reader to derive the basic raw numbers involved. If you read a statistical report that does not include the raw numbers upon which the other statistics, such as proportions or percentages, were based, be suspicious, for statistical data presented without raw numbers can be very misleading.

Let us add a further caution here. Returning to the data from the crime survey, note that the description includes only the responses of those people who answered the question. We said nothing about the number of people who refused to answer, or who answered "don't know." Perhaps no one fit into those categories, but unless the presentation of the data indicates that, we can't be sure. Maybe n was really equal to 575, and 450 people said they did not know if crime was a serious problem. That would have a considerable impact on our interpretation of the raw numbers presented earlier. Whether the data are presented in raw numbers or in any of the other forms we will discuss, it pays to think about other response categories for which data may not have been presented. As with all descriptions, what is left out of a statistical description may be more important than what has been included.

Before we proceed to another way of presenting our data, think back to your days in junior high and high school math classes. You undoubtedly studied ratios, proportions, decimals, and percentages, and you probably recall the way in which these statistics were expressed. You will also remember that any of these expressions can be transformed into any of the other forms; thus, 1 out of 5 = 1/5 = .20 = 20 percent. Now, let us return to an alternative way of presenting the data from the crime survey: we could say 4 out of 5 (or 4/5, .80, 80 percent) of the persons said crime was a serious problem whereas 1 out of 5 (or 1/5, .20, 20 percent) said it was not. In this case, we have used ratios, proportions, decimals, and percentages to report the data and communicate the thrust of the raw number data. By examining these statistics alone, you know that considerably more people thought crime was a serious problem than did not, but you would not know *how many* people responded in a particular way. We might have talked to five people or 5,000. Consider the following statements: "Two out of three doctors recommend . . ."; "One out of four marriages ends in divorce"; "College professors are right at least 50 percent of the time." Although these expressions may appear precise and scientific at first glance, they are, in fact, almost meaningless. To make sense of them we must know, among other things, the raw numbers involved.

The raw number of responses alone is not a reliable guide to the amount of trust one should have in a given set of statistics. A well-planned study reporting on a relatively small number of cases should elicit greater confidence than a poorly planned one reporting on a larger number of cases. So, although it is important to know the raw number basis for the calculation of ratios, proportions, and so on, one cannot assess a statistic exclusively on this basis. In general, the method used to identify or select the cases is more important in the assessment of the data than is the raw number of cases studied.

Assuming that the raw numbers have been provided or can be derived and the cases for study have been carefully identified or selected, ratios, proportions, decimals, and percentages are very useful statistical expressions in certain circumstances. Because percentages are probably the most practical and widely used form of statistical expression in the social sciences, we will focus on them, though many of our observations apply to other types of statistics as well.

Percentages

Percentages are standardized fractions, in the sense that they have a common denominator of 100. Because the common denominator is understood (percent means "for each 100"), only the numerator of the fraction is given, followed by the percent sign. Thus 80/100 = 80 percent. Given the fraction $x/100$ and any other fraction connected by an equals sign, you can solve the equation for x. The solution for x is the percentage that the numerator is of the denominator in the second fraction. For example:

$$\frac{x}{100} = \frac{1}{5}$$
$$5x = 100$$
$$x = 20$$

Thus, 1 is 20 percent of 5. (In practice we can simply divide the numerator by the denominator and multiply the result by 100 to calculate the percentage:

$1 \div 5 = .20$; $.20 \times 100 = 20$ percent). Given the raw number of responses in a specific response category and the total number of responses for all response categories, we can calculate the percentage for that particular response category. The sum of all the percentages for all of the response categories should, of course, equal 100 percent, or the whole. We might say that percentages result when we treat a group of any number of cases for statistical purposes as if there were 100 cases.

Sometimes we hear an expression like "Service requests increased 200 percent this year compared to last." Percentage expressions that involve amounts greater than 100 percent can be interpreted in the same way as those involving amounts of 100 percent or less. Thus, 200 percent is twice the amount used as the base for the original calculation, and 150 percent is one-and-one-half times that base amount. Percentages of less than 1 percent are expressed as a decimal percentage; thus, 0.2 percent is two-tenths of 1 percent.

Confusion is sometimes created when percentages are used to describe increases. For example, a 100 percent increase in the jail population means that the jail population doubled; a 200 percent increase reflects a tripling of the original count; and a 50 percent increase means that the count is now one and one-half times as large as it was.

When should you go beyond the presentation of raw numbers to the calculation and presentation of percentages? Percentages can be used to deal with a large number of cases, or to compare two different sets of data about a given phenomenon when there are sizable differences in the number of cases involved. Suppose that instead of 125 people, we had asked 38,400 people whether they regarded crime as a serious problem, and 24,576 said they did. It is easier to grasp the meaning of these data by saying that 64 percent of the persons we talked to thought crime was a serious problem. Now let us further suppose that we had taken a similar survey a year. ago, obtaining responses from 12,400 people, 7,936 of whom said they regarded crime as a serious problem. Has the tendency to regard crime as a problem changed? It is difficult to tell simply by comparing the raw numbers, but if we compare the two results in terms of percentages, we discover that in both cases 64 percent of the people surveyed felt crime was a serious problem in their city. Because percentages are standardized forms of numerical expressions, they should be used when raw numbers alone would be confusing.

However, when the raw numbers involved are small, percentages may be misleading. For example, if the total number of cases is ten, converting to percentages magnifies the differences in the numbers reported by a factor of 10. If there are four cases in one category of response and six in another, the raw number difference is 2, whereas the percentage difference is 20 percent. This magnification may well distort our interpretation of the data presented, and as a rule of thumb, we suggest that percentages not be used unless one is reporting on at least thirty cases.

Just as the conversion of very small raw numbers to percentages magnifies apparent differences, the conversion of very large raw numbers diminishes apparent differences. If 1,000,000 votes were cast in an election with a 490,000-to-510,000 candidate count, a raw number difference of 20,000 yields a percentage difference of only 2 percent. The difference created by such conversions is more dramatic if we consider another example. Suppose two different surgical procedures are available for repairing a damaged valve in the heart. One group of 50,000 patients is operated on using one procedure, and another group of 50,000 patients receives the other procedure. Suppose further, that 9,500 patients in the first group and 9,000 patients in the second group die during surgery. Saying that the outcome of the two procedures differs by 1 percent may give the impression that there is very little difference between them, but stating that 500 more people survived the second procedure provides quite a different impression. Still, statistically these two presentations of the data are equally correct. Because there is no simple rule of thumb indicating the maximum number of cases for which conversion of raw numbers to percentages is appropriate, one should always know the raw numbers involved and bear in mind what the statistics are about. Finally, one must be very careful not to confuse decimals and percentages; remember that .25 = 25/100 = 25 percent and that .0025 = 25/10,000 = .25 percent.

Rates

Another statistical expression we may read or hear about often is rate—the crime rate, the rate of inflation, production rates, interest rates, and so forth. **Rates** express the frequency of an event in relation to a fixed unit or units of measurement, and time is usually one of the fixed units. A rate of speed, for example, is expressed in number of miles per hour; a crime rate is the number of crimes of a particular kind per fixed unit of population (say, 100,000) per fixed unit of time (say, one year). In the latter case, a fixed unit of population is added to the fixed unit of time.

Like percentages, rates can be very useful statistics for comparative purposes. As long as the fixed units are explicit and constant, existing differences or changes taking place can be compared and assessed. For example, crime rates for different societies or for different time periods in the same society can be compared as long as definitions of criminal acts are the same across societies or at different times.

In addition to expressing the frequency with which something occurs, rates can be used to calculate the extent to which that frequency is changing, that is, increasing or decreasing. Again, these are useful expressions, as long as you do not get tangled up in them. Consider, for example, the following statement: "The rate of increase in the nation's crime rate is decreasing." This means that although the crime rate is still going up, it is not going up as fast as it had been. The statement does make sense, but you must interpret such statements carefully to avoid being misled.

In using or interpreting rate statistics, the units must be fixed, known, and remain unchanged from one citation to another. Furthermore, because percentage expressions are frequently combined with rate expressions (for example, there was a 15 percent increase in the rate of felonies this year as compared to last), and since rates are also standardized forms of statistical expression, the cautions we raised about percentages apply here as well.

Frequency Distributions

Another way to present data is to construct a **frequency distribution.** A frequency distribution indicates how many times a particular event or value of a variable occurs in the assembled data. In addition to counting and reporting the raw number of responses falling into each response category for a given variable, the researcher may want to represent the data graphically in the form of a *bar* or *line graph* (discussed further in Chapter 12) that is derived from raw numbers.

Suppose that you are interested in the sex distribution of shoplifters. Sex is a variable with two values: male and female. You could begin your analysis by making two columns on a sheet of paper, one labeled "male shoplifters," the other labeled "female shoplifters," and listing the names of the shoplifters under the appropriate heading. Suppose your lists looked like the ones in Table 7.2. By counting the number of names in each list, you would find the frequency distribution of the sex of the shoplifters to be seven males and four females. To convert this expression into a graph, you could create a two-dimensional space defined by a horizontal and vertical axis. Along the horizontal axis, you would provide an equivalent space for each of the response categories (male and female). Along the vertical axis, you would provide space for each of the possible frequencies with which each response category might appear in the data. You would then create a rectangular space for each response category by raising a bar to the height corresponding to the frequency with which that category appears in the data. Figure 7.1 shows what a graphic representation of the data might look like. Note that the zero frequency category is located at the point where the horizontal axis intersects with the vertical axis.

The advantages of graphic presentation of frequency distributions become more apparent when the number of response categories is large. Suppose, for example, that a test has been given to a class of thirty-six police recruits and that a perfect score on the test is 20. After scoring the exams, the tester might use a frequency distribution to provide herself and the recruits with a picture of class performance. To construct the frequency distribution, the tester must count the number of people who received a particular score on the examination. Again, a range of frequencies—in this case 0 to 9—is arrayed along the

TABLE 7.2	Sex of Shoplifters

Male Shoplifters	*Female Shoplifters*
Bob	Sally
George	Matilda
Tom	Joan
Richard	Francine
Henry	
Alphonso	
Beauregard	

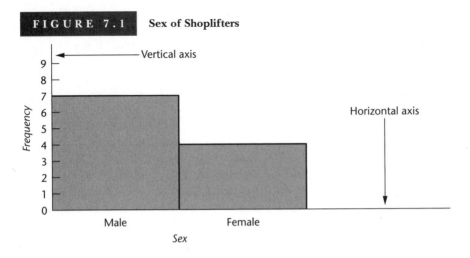

FIGURE 7.1 Sex of Shoplifters

vertical axis, and the range of possible examination scores—in this case 0 to 20—is arrayed along the horizontal axis. Remember that each bar in the graph represents the frequency with which the corresponding score occurs in the distribution. Suppose our graph looked like the one in Figure 7.2. The graph indicates that no one in the class scored lower than 8, and that one person scored 8, two scored 9, six scored 13, three scored 16, and so on.

Line graphs, sometimes called **histograms,** communicate essentially the same information as bar graphs, though perhaps less vividly. In contrast to bar graphs, a line graph is constructed by assigning each of the possible scores a point (rather than a space) on the horizontal axis and each of the frequencies a point on the vertical axis. A point is also used to represent the intersection of a score and its frequency in the line graph. To locate this point in the graph, we draw an imaginary line perpendicular to the horizontal axis at the location of the score, and another imaginary line perpendicular to the vertical axis at the location of the frequency with which that score appears in the data. The point where these two imaginary lines intersect is the point we use. We repeat this procedure for each score and its corresponding frequency. We create the line in the graph by connecting the points we have located with a series of straight lines. The line graph corresponding to the bar graph of police recruit test scores looks like the one in Figure 7.3.

In addition to graphing data, researchers often find it useful to describe or summarize a distribution of variable values using statistics such as *measures of central tendency* and *measures of dispersion.* Bear in mind that in the following discussion we are no longer just considering the measurement of variables per se; we are describing measures of the *distributions* of those variable measurements.

MEASURES OF CENTRAL TENDENCY

Measures of central tendency describe a distribution by indicating midpoints of various kinds. There are three frequently used measures of the central tendency: the mean, the median, and the mode.

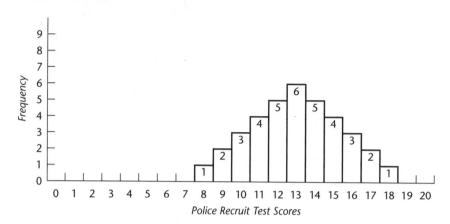

FIGURE 7.2   Bar Graph Frequency Distribution of Police Recruit Test Scores

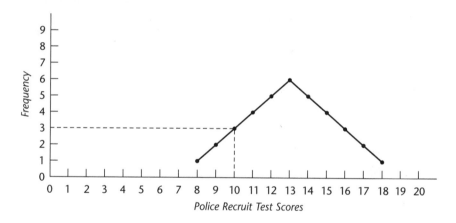

FIGURE 7.3   Line Graph Frequency Distribution of Police Recruit Test Scores

The Mean

The **mean** (referred to as $\bar{x}$) is the arithmetic average of the individual numerical scores that make up a distribution of a variable measured at the interval or ratio level. It is calculated by summing all the scores and dividing by the number of scores that went into the sum.

The general formula for the mean of a distribution is:

Formula 7.1

$$x = \frac{\sum x}{n}$$

where x is a score (such as one person's exam score), $\sum$ (the Greek letter sigma) is a summation sign and n is the number of scores summed. So, $\sum x$ tells us to add all the individual scores in the distribution. Dividing this sum by the number of scores (n) gives us the mean score.

Using the test scores from our hypothetical police recruit exam, we calculate the mean as follows. We add all the scores in the distribution and divide by 36, the total number of scores. The sum of the scores is 468.

$$\Sigma x = 8 + 9 + 9 + 10 + 10 + 10 + \ldots + 18 = 468.$$

The mean is the sum of scores divided by the number of scores.

$$\bar{x} = \frac{\Sigma x}{n} = \frac{468}{36} = 13.$$

Hence, the mean or arithmetic average score on this test is 13.

The Median

The **median** is the middle score or category of a ratio, an interval, or an ordinal variable distribution; half the recruits have made that score or less and half have made that score or more. To find the median of a distribution, we must (1) arrange all of the individual scores in numerical order, either from lowest to highest or from highest to lowest, and (2) find the score that is in the center of this array, by counting in from both ends of the array simultaneously. For example, if the police recruit test scores represented by the frequency distribution in Figure 7.2 were arrayed in ascending numerical order they would look like this: 8, 9, 9, 10, 10, 10, 11, 11, 11, 11, 12, 12, 12, 12, 12, 13, 13, 13, 13, 13, 13, 14, 14, 14, 14, 14, 15, 15, 15, 15, 16, 16, 16, 17, 17, 18. Because there are 36 scores (an even number of scores), the center of the array falls between two scores, counting 18 scores from each end. In this case, we take the, arithmetic average of these two scores: 13 + 13 = 26; 26 ÷ 2 = 13. Hence, the median of this distribution is 13. If the number of scores in the distribution were odd, a single score would occupy the point equidistant from each end of the array, and that score would be the median of the distribution.

The Mode

A distribution's **mode** is the score or category that occurs most frequently in a distribution regardless of the level of measurement. By inspecting the frequency distribution (Figure 7.2), it is easy to locate the mode. Because the score 13 appears six times, and no other score appears more than five times, the mode of the distribution is 13.

SELECTING MEASURES OF CENTRAL TENDENCY

In the example we have used, the mean, median, and mode all have the same value. This relationship among measures of central tendency will hold for some, but not for most, distributions.

To further understand the issues involved in the choice among measures of central tendency, suppose that the distribution of police recruit test scores looked like the one in Figure 7.4.

Figure 7.5 shows how a line graph of this distribution would look. Now compare Figure 7.5 with Figure 7.3, noting the differences in the shape of the distribution. Distributions similar in shape to the one in Figure 7.5 are called **skewed distributions,** which are characterized by a bunching of scores toward one end or the other of the horizontal axis.

Now suppose that we calculate the three measures of central tendency for this distribution. Again, we have 36 scores; the sum of the scores in this case is 400. The mean is 400 ÷ 36 = 11.1 (rounded to the nearest tenth); the median is 12.5; and the mode is 15. Note that in this distribution, the mean, median, and mode have different values, and the value of the median lies between the

FIGURE 7.4   **Bar Graph Frequency Distribution of Police Recruit Test Scores**

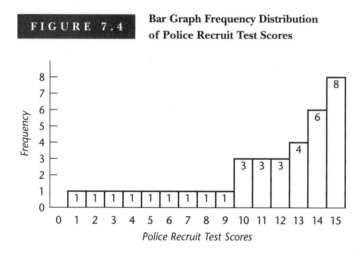

FIGURE 7.5   **Line Graph Frequency Distribution of Police Recruit Test Scores**

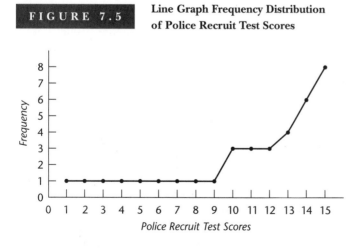

values of the mode and mean. This is typically, though not always, the case in skewed distributions.

Choosing a particular measure of central tendency for skewed distribution may seem a relatively arbitrary matter, but the measure we use may influence the interpretation of our data. If a tester wanted to demonstrate how well the class performs, he might choose to report the modal score, 15, and to play down the group's performance, he might report the mean, 11.1. In most cases the safest and most honest way to describe a distribution in terms of central tendency is to report all three measures, because there is less chance of misleading or being misled. Substantial differences among the reported mean, median, and mode are a sure sign that the distribution is highly skewed.

In some cases, not all the measures are appropriate because one or more may not be meaningful for the type of data collected. A variable such as sex measured at the nominal level has only one appropriate measure of central tendency—the mode—because it makes no sense to speak of "mean sex" or "median sex." For ordinal level data—those that permit the ranking of individual scores—both median and mode are appropriate. In the case of interval or ratio levels of measurement, any one or a combination of the measures of central tendency can be used.

The selection of an appropriate measure of central tendency also depends on whether the variable investigated is discrete or continuous. Modes and medians can be used with either discrete or continuous variables, but strictly speaking, a mean should be utilized only when the variable is continuous. In practice, demographers and other social scientists do calculate means for discrete data, telling us, for example, that the average American family has 2.3 children. A mode for discrete data cannot assume a fractional value, and a median can do so only when the distribution contains an even number of scores and the procedure for determining the median discussed previously is employed.

Finally, we must caution the reader that the three measures of central tendency are affected differently by extreme scores—that is, those scores in a distribution that are either very large or very small in comparison to the other scores in the distribution. A simple example will highlight the differential impact of extreme scores. Given the following scores: 4, 5, 5, 4, 6, 3, 4, and 1, the mean, median, and mode of this distribution have the same value: 4. If the highest score was 20 instead of 6, neither the median nor the mode is affected, but the mean is now 5.75. Because the calculation of the mean depends on summing all the scores, it is most affected by extreme scores. Extreme scores have a distorting effect on the mean; hence, when they are present, the mean is a misleading indicator of central tendency.

The three different measures of central tendency are computed to reflect somewhat different aspects of a distribution, and the meanings of their variant forms are important. Often, the terms *average* and *typical* are used imprecisely, for in some instances, they may refer to an arithmetic average (the mean), and in other instances to the value that occurs most frequently (the mode). In any case, measures of central tendency provide us with only a limited amount of knowledge about any particular distribution. To learn more about the nature of a distribution, we need to use one or more measures of dispersion.

MEASURES OF DISPERSION

In addition to knowing the central tendency of a distribution, it is helpful to know the *dispersion* of a distribution; that is, how wide a range of values the distribution includes. Figure 7.6, where several symmetrical distributions (A, B, and C) have been drawn on the same set of axes, illustrates the additional information that a measure of dispersion communicates. Although each of the distributions is bell shaped, or symmetrical, and all have the same mean, median, and mode, they represent quite different arrays, some spanning most of the potential scores (A), and some encompassing only a small part of them (C). Measures of dispersion permit us to summarize these differences.

Range

The **range** of a distribution is indicated by reporting the largest and the smallest scores that appear in the distribution. In Figure 7.2, for example, the first distribution of police recruit test scores previously discussed, the lowest score was 8 and the highest 18; therefore, the range of the distribution is from 8 through 18. Sometimes the range is indicated as a single number, arrived at by subtracting the smallest score from the largest one (in our example, 18 − 8 = 10). Note, however, that when the range is reported only as a single number, the reader has no way of knowing what the highest and lowest scores obtained were. It is best, therefore, to report both of these measures of range.

Average Deviation

The **average deviation** from the mean is the arithmetic average of the differences between the distribution's mean score and each of the individual scores in the distribution. To find the average deviation from the mean, the mean must be calculated and then subtracted from each of the scores in the distribution. The *absolute value* of the differences (that is, the value without regard

| FIGURE 7.6 | Three Different Symmetrical Distributions with the Same Mean, Median, and Mode but Different Dispersions |

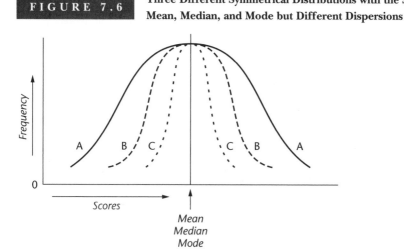

to a plus or minus sign) is used in these calculations. The absolute value differences are then added and the total is divided by the number of scores in the distribution. Again, we shall use the first set of police recruit test scores to illustrate. The mean score was 13, and subtracting 13 from each of the 36 scores gives us the absolute values shown in column 3 of table 7.3. The sum of the absolute values of the differences is 70, and because there are 36 scores, the average difference, or deviation, is given by 70 ÷ 36 = 1.9 (rounded to the nearest tenth). The greater the average deviation from the mean, the more dispersed are the scores in the distribution.

Standard Deviation

The **standard deviation** (referred to as *sd* or *s*) is probably the most frequently used and reported measure of dispersion. It is closely related to the average deviation from the mean, but differs from it in that the standard deviation of a distribution expresses differences from the mean in units of equal size for that particular distribution. The interesting and valuable uses to which we can put standardized units of deviation from the mean in certain types of distributions will be discussed later. The standard deviation of a distribution is calculated by squaring the difference or deviation from the mean of each score (multiplying the deviation times the deviation), summing these squared deviations, dividing the sum by the number of scores (the value obtained at this point is called the **variance** or s^2), and taking the square root of the result. The number thus obtained is the standard deviation of the scores from the mean. This process is given by:

Formula 7.2

$$s = \sqrt{\frac{\sum (x - \bar{x})^2}{n}}$$

where *s* is the standard deviation, *n* is the number of scores in the distribution, and $\sum (x - \bar{x})^2$ indicates the sum of the squared deviations of each individual score from the mean score. In statistical parlance, "the sum of squared deviations from the mean" is conventionally shortened to *the sum of squares*; we will follow that convention from time to time in the following chapters.

In the example from Table 7.3:

$$s = \sqrt{\frac{(8 - 13)^2 + (9 - 13)^2 + (9 - 13)^2 + \ldots + (18 - 13)^2}{36}}$$

$$s = \sqrt{\frac{210}{36}} = \sqrt{5.8} = 2.4$$

As with the average deviation from the mean, the greater the dispersion of the scores in the distribution, the larger the standard deviation and variance. Because it is easier to use, the following formula (which is algebraically equivalent to Formula 7.2) is usually preferred to calculate the standard deviation:

Formula 7.3

$$s = \sqrt{\frac{\sum x^2}{n} - \left(\frac{\sum x}{n}\right)^2}$$

TABLE 7.3   **Calculations for Police Recruit Test Scores ($n = 36$)**

Score (x)	Square of Score (x^2)	Mean ($\overline{x}$)	Difference (Absolute Values) from Mean ($x - \overline{x}$)	Squared Difference or Deviation from Mean ($x - \overline{x})^2$
8	64	13	5	25
9	81	13	4	16
9	81	13	4	16
10	100	13	3	9
10	100	13	3	9
10	100	13	3	9
11	121	13	2	4
11	121	13	2	4
11	121	13	2	4
11	121	13	2	4
12	144	13	1	1
12	144	13	1	1
12	144	13	1	1
12	144	13	1	1
12	144	13	1	1
13	169	13	0	0
13	169	13	0	0
13	169	13	0	0
13	169	13	0	0
13	169	13	0	0
13	169	13	0	0
14	196	13	1	1
14	196	13	1	1
14	196	13	1	1
14	196	13	1	1
14	196	13	1	1
15	225	13	2	4
15	225	13	2	4
15	225	13	2	4
15	225	13	2	4
16	256	13	3	9
16	256	13	3	9
16	256	13	3	9
17	289	13	4	16
17	289	13	4	16
18	324	13	5	25
Sums 468	6294	468	70	210

The term on the left side of the minus sign tells us to square each of the scores in the distribution, sum these squares, and divide the total by n; the term on the right side of the minus sign tells us to sum the scores in the distribution, divide the total by n, and square the result. The value of s is then given by taking the square root of the difference between these two terms.

Let us pause here to note a special property of the mean in relation to the standard deviation. The mean score of a distribution is the score that minimizes the sum of deviations (and, hence, of the average deviation, the standard deviation, and the variance) for a distribution. That is, if you picked any other score in a distribution, calculated the deviations between it and the other scores in the distribution, and added these deviations, the sum would be larger. In this sense, the mean score best represents the distribution of scores. Put another way, the mean score is the best estimate of the scores in a distribution, because the differences between it and the other scores is the smallest possible. We shall have occasion to make use of this special property of the mean in our discussion of inferential statistics.

Each measure of dispersion has its own strengths and limitations, and choosing the most appropriate measure depends on the particular situation. A range is seriously affected by relatively large and relatively small scores isolated at the extremities of a distribution; for example, if all the scores of a particular distribution fell between 35 and 50 except one that was 10, reporting the range as 10 to 50 does not summarize the actual dispersion of the scores in the distribution very well. The average deviation from the mean expresses how far, on the average, scores differ from the mean score, but it does not in itself tell us what the range of the scores is, and it is also greatly influenced by extreme scores, though less so than the range. The standard deviation, which is still less influenced by extreme scores, is preferable to the average deviation from the mean if a researcher is interested in more than a simple description of the dispersion of the data. However, neither the average deviation nor the standard deviation is very useful if one is dealing with a highly skewed distribution (that is, one that is not a symmetrical curve).

Finally, although a range can appropriately be used with either discrete or continuous data measured at the ordinal level or above, both the average deviation from the mean and the standard deviation assume that the data are continuous and are measured at least at the interval level. Again, as in the case of measures of central tendency, these measures of dispersion are often used with discrete data. When this is done cautiously and explicitly, little harm is done in this compromise with statistical rules.

We can use crime statistics to illustrate the application of many of the measures of central tendency and dispersion described here, and in the process we can also demonstrate how complex and tricky things can get even with these relatively simple statistical measures.

If someone tells you that the crime rate for city A was 4 per 1,000 in 1986, can any sense be made of such a report? For reasons that will become obvious, the answer is no. We need to know a great deal more about how that rate was calculated before we have any idea of what it really means.

The first thing that we need to ask is what was the population base used— per 1,000 what? The rate may have been calculated on the basis of:

- The total population in the city
- Only adults in the city (defined how?)
- Adults and juveniles (defined how?)
- Only males
- And so on

The rate means very different things depending on what "per 1,000" is involved.

When and how was the population counted? During the last census? If it was some years ago, has the population in the city changed very much? How do we know? If it has, was the population count used for the base adjusted? How and on what basis was the adjustment made? Was the count of crimes made in at least roughly the same period as the count for the population base? A rate calculated on the basis of a 1980 population census and a count of crimes in 1985 may be seriously misleading.

Furthermore, what was counted as a crime? How was crime defined? Felonies only? Misdemeanors and felonies? Consider also the following possible ways of counting crimes during a specified period of time:

- Crimes actually committed (the "real" crime rate)
- Crimes observed by others
- Crimes reported to the police
- Crimes recorded by the police (the basis for most official crime statistics)
- Crimes for which someone was arrested
- Crimes for which someone was prosecuted
- Crimes for which someone was convicted

Any of these could be used to arrive at the "4" of the 4 per 1,000, and a reasonable argument could be made that any one of them would be useful for some purpose. In any event, it should be obvious that which of them is used is quite important in making sense of the reported crime rate. Likewise, meaningful comparisons of crime rates depend on knowing that they were calculated according to the same criteria.

In addition to crime rates, we might want to consider other crime statistics that are potentially useful, always being alert for complications that might enter into making sense of them. What proportion of crimes are cleared by arrest? What are the mean, median, and mode of the distribution of the lengths of sentences handed down by courts in a given jurisdiction? What are the average deviation and standard deviation of the distribution of the number of months persons convicted of felonies in your state actually spend in confinement?

INDICATORS OF LOCATION IN A DISTRIBUTION

Suppose that you have just received a report on the results of a scholastic achievement test that you and 267,598 other students have taken. Suppose, further, you are told that your score on the test was 575. This information would not be very helpful to you, would it? In order to make sense of your score, you would want to know both the maximum score possible and how your score compared with the scores of the other students who took the test. In other words, you would want to be able to locate your score in the distribution of test scores.

If the report included a bar graph frequency distribution of the test scores, you could find the bar representing the frequency of your score in the distribution. By examining the location and height of this bar relative to the other bars in the graph, you could learn something about how you performed relative to others. Because this is a simple and straightforward procedure for communicating information, we recommend that you use bar graphs whenever feasible.

However, when the range of test scores is large, constructing and presenting a bar graph frequency distribution may be impractical. In the absence of the frequency distribution itself, it would be somewhat helpful if the measures of central tendency and dispersion for the distribution as a whole were reported. You might be told, for example, that the scores ranged from 100 to 800 and that the median for the distribution was 523. Given this information, you may conclude that your score was in the upper half of the scores in a distribution. But that is only a rough indication of the location of your score relative to the other scores in the distribution. How can we improve your ability to locate your score in the distribution?

The median, you will recall, is found by dividing the scores arrayed in ascending or descending numerical order into two groups, each of which contains the same number of scores. What if, by extending the principle used to determine the value of the median, the scores were divided into more than two groups? The greater the number of groups into which the scores are divided, the more division points analogous to the median would be available for reference in locating a particular score. In principle, we could divide the scores into any number of groups, each containing the same number of scores, as long as the number of scores is equal to or greater than the number of groups we chose to create. In practice, statisticians often use three different subdivisions of the scores in a distribution: quartiles, deciles, and percentiles. *Quartiles* (Q) are arrived at by dividing the scores into four groups, *deciles* (D) are based on a division of the scores into ten groups, and *percentiles* (P) are determined by dividing the scores into one hundred groups. As in locating the median, the scores must be arranged in numerical order before the values of these various **quantiles** (the general term used to refer to all of these measures) can be determined.

Because determining the value of the various quantiles depends on the division of the scores into more than two groups, some special procedures must be introduced. Although there is only one median for a particular distribution, there are three quartiles, nine deciles, and ninety-nine percentiles. Therefore, we need a procedure for distinguishing among the various quantiles of a particular type. The scores should be arranged in ascending numerical order and identifying numbers should be assigned to the quantiles, beginning with the first division point that occurs in the array. However, it is not always possible to find points that divide the scores into groups containing exactly the same number of scores. In such instances it is necessary to compromise with reality a bit and come as close as one can. Since the smaller the number of scores in the distribution, the greater the impact of this difficulty, it is best to restrict the use of quartiles, deciles, and percentiles to distributions that contain a relatively large number of scores.

Imagine that the horizontal string of dots at the top of Figure 7.7 represents an array of scores listed from left to right in ascending numerical order, each dot representing an individual score. The dots can be divided into various numbers of segments or groups containing the same number of dots (scores). The boundary points of these divisions correspond to the scores that are used to determine the values of the various types of quantiles (quartiles, deciles, and percentiles). To find the quartile division points we would divide the scores (the dots) into four groups of (approximately) equal size and label the first division point from the left the 1st quartile, the second division point the 2nd quartile, and so on. For deciles, the scores would be divided into ten equally sized groups; for percentiles, into one hundred equally sized groups. Note that the median, the 2nd quartile, the 5th decile, and the 50th percentile all have the same value. Similarly, the 1st quartile and the 25th percentile have the same value, and so on.

If we know both the values of the various quantiles for a given distribution and a particular individual's score, we can locate that score approximately, rel-

FIGURE 7.7   **Quantiles**

Scores in ascending order—Each dot represents an individual's score.

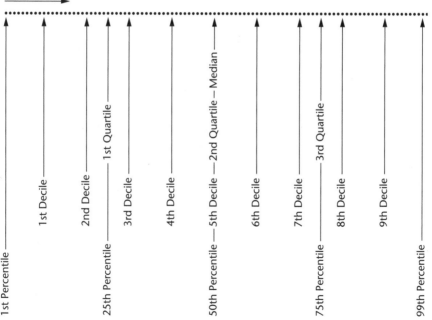

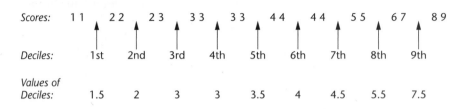

FIGURE 7.8

A Series of Scores and the Deciles of the Distribution

ative to the other scores in the distribution, by saying it is less than, equivalent to, or greater than a particular quartile, decile, or percentile. Because percentiles provide more reference points in the distribution, they permit a more precise location of a particular score than do quartiles or deciles and are, therefore, the most frequently used quantiles, especially when both the number of scores in the distribution and their range are very large.

When we speak of a percentile, we refer to the percentage of scores in the distribution that are either equal to or less than the value of the given percentile. For example, if you are told that your score on a promotional test is equivalent to the 76th percentile, your score was higher than or equal to 76 percent of the scores, but 24 percent of the scores were higher than yours.

Although quantiles are useful as indicators of location, we must be careful not to misinterpret them. First, the smaller the number of quantiles used as reference points in locating a particular score, the less apparent may be the differences in the scores reported by referring to their quantile values alone. Two scores may, for example, both be reported as "below the 1st quartile." But one may also be below the 1st decile, whereas the other is above the 2nd decile. Furthermore, one may be equivalent to the 2nd percentile, and the other may be equivalent to the 24th percentile. Obviously, the nature of the particular quantiles being used is critical when interpreting reports of scores made in terms of quantiles alone.

Other difficulties can be illustrated by examining a particular distribution of deciles, but the difficulties discussed apply to the use of quartiles and percentiles as well. Consider twenty scores ranging from 1 to 9 and the deciles for the distribution illustrated in figure 7.8. At the outset, we see that the 3rd and 4th deciles have the same value: 3. Now, suppose that your score on this test is 3. How would you report your score by reference to decile values? You must resist the temptation to identify the last 3 in the distribution as yours and contend that your score was above the 4th decile, because for the purposes of determining the decile values, it is irrelevant which of the 3s is yours. Surely, it would not be fair to a friend who also scored 3 to designate the first 3 as his and say it fell below the 3rd decile. After all, you both received the same score on the test. To be honest, you would have to say that your score (and your friend's) was equivalent to the value of the 3rd and 4th deciles.

Using the same distribution for illustrative purposes, suppose that your score is 4. What would be a conventional interpretation of a report indicating that your score is equivalent to the 6th decile? Your score would apparently be equivalent to or higher than 60 percent of the scores, but when we observe the actual distribution, your score is, in fact, equivalent to or higher than 70 percent of the scores. We hasten to note that the use of percentages here violates the aforementioned rule of thumb about having at least thirty scores before using percentages, but the general point is valid nonetheless: There is a margin of imprecision in the conventional interpretation of quantiles.

This imprecision arises because the procedures used to determine the values of the quantiles entail dividing the scores into groups that contain equal numbers of scores. Hence, it is true, for example, that 50 percent of the scores in the distribution fall below the 5th decile (and the 2nd quartile and the 50th percentile). But this procedure takes into account only the number of scores; it ignores the *values* of the scores themselves. Hence, the relationship between the values of the quantiles and the values of the scores is imperfect. A number of scores that have the same value may overlap quantile division points. When this happens, the conventional interpretation in terms of the percentage of scores equivalent to or below a particular quantile must be regarded as an approximation rather than a precise statement.

Finally, the range of values of scores encompassed between a pair of adjacent quantiles and any other adjacent pair of quantiles in a distribution can vary greatly. This is most apparent in highly skewed distributions. Quantiles, then, are most useful and least misleading as indicators of location when both the number of cases and the range of score values are large, and the scores are at least approximately symmetrically distributed.

DISTRIBUTIONS: SYMMETRICAL AND OTHERWISE

We have already become acquainted in a very general way with two types of distribution: symmetrical and skewed. Having discussed the measures of central tendency and dispersion of distributions, we can now extend our discussion of the different types of distributions. Remember that we create a line graph by connecting the points representing the frequencies of the scores in a distribution (see Figure 7.3).

Unimodal and Multimodal Distributions

First, it is useful to distinguish between unimodal and multimodal distributions. A **unimodal distribution** has only one hump, whereas a **multimodal distribution** has two or more humps (see Figure 7.9). Another way of saying this is that if we traced the curve of the distribution with a pencil from left to right, in a unimodal distribution the pencil would move always up (as in distribution d) *or* always down (as in c) *or* change directions only once, from up to down (a, b); in a multimodal distribution, the pencil would change directions more than once (e, f, g) *or* change directions only once, but from down to up (h). Thus, although a particular distribution has only one mean, median, range, average deviation from the mean, and standard deviation, it may have more than one mode.

FIGURE 7.9   Unimodal and Multimodal Distributions

Unimodal distributions

Multimodal distributions

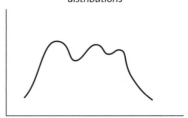

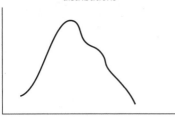

a

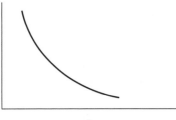

b

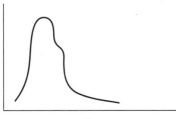

c

d

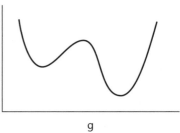

e

f

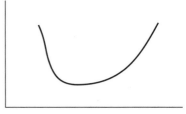

g

h

Both symmetrical and skewed distributions, as we have used these terms here, are assumed to be unimodal. They differ in that the symmetrical distribution is symmetrical with respect to the mean—that is, its shape on one side of the mean is the mirror image of its shape on the other side of the mean— whereas the skewed distribution is not, as shown by the distribution curves in Figure 7.10. Skewed distributions may vary in their direction and degree of skewedness (note Figure 7.11), but many distributions, though slightly skewed, closely approximate the symmetrical distribution and can be treated as if they were symmetrical for most purposes.

In the case of the central tendency of a unimodal, symmetrical (or approximately symmetrical) distribution, it is sufficient to state that the distribution is symmetrical (or nearly so) and report the mean, median, or mode, because all three measures of central tendency will be approximately equivalent. If the distribution is considerably skewed, however, all three measures of central tendency should be reported.

To know the mean and the standard deviation of a unimodal, symmetrical distribution is to have a fairly complete description of that distribution. Consequently, in many data reports, the actual graphic presentation of at least approximately symmetrical distributions is omitted, and these two statis-

FIGURE 7 . 1 0   **Skewed and Symmetrical Distributions**

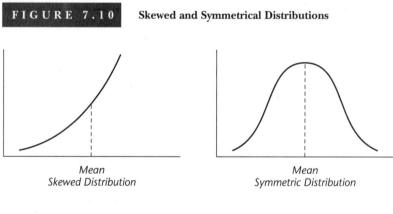

Mean
Skewed Distribution

Mean
Symmetric Distribution

FIGURE 7 . 1 1   **Skewed Distributions**

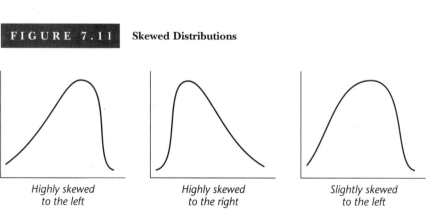

*Highly skewed
to the left*

*Highly skewed
to the right*

*Slightly skewed
to the left*

tics are reported instead. However, the less symmetrical a distribution is (for example, the more skewed is the distribution), the less reliable and useful are these statistics as descriptions of the distribution. Therefore, be suspicious of data reports that present only summary measures and not the distribution itself, unless it is clear that the distribution is unimodal and at least approximately symmetrical. If the distribution is highly skewed or multimodal, it is safest and most honest to present the distribution itself in addition to the summary statistics.

The Normal Distribution and Standard Scores

The **normal distribution** is a unimodal, symmetrical distribution with especially useful statistical characteristics.[3] To comprehend these special properties, we must understand the relationship between particular segments of the area encompassed by a bar or line graph and the proportion of times particular outcomes (such as test scores) occur in the distribution represented by the graph. Suppose that we calculated the area of each of the bars in a bar graph (such as the one in Figure 7.12) by multiplying the width of a bar by its length. We could then determine the total area encompassed by the graph by summing the areas of the bars. Assuming that the bars have the same width, we could then express the area of any .particular bar as a proportion of the total area of the graph. With a little effort you can demonstrate that the proportion of the total area of the graph included in a particular bar is equal to the proportion of times (the proportional frequency) the particular outcome represented by that bar occurs in the distribution. Suppose we superimposed a line graph over a bar graph, as we have in Figure 7.12. Remember that these two graphs represent the same data. Note that the area under the line (curve) is essentially the same as the area encompassed by the bars. We can, therefore, speak of the equivalence between proportions of area under the line (curve) and the proportions of times particular scores (outcomes) occur, just as we did when we referred to areas of the bars. Statisticians put to very effective use this rela-

FIGURE 7.12   Bar Graph with Line Graph Superimposed

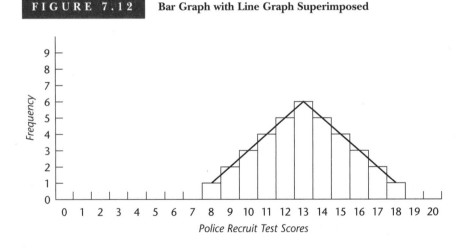

tionship between areas under the curve of a particular kind of distribution and proportional frequencies of outcomes.

Suppose we have another unimodal curve, representing the frequency distribution of a continuous variable measured at the interval or ratio level. Let us assume that the distribution is symmetrical and that it includes a very large number of cases. By using the procedures discussed earlier in this chapter, we can calculate its mean ($\bar{x}$) and standard deviation (s). Once we know the values of these two statistics for our distribution, we can use them to divide the area under the curve into segments. Consider Figure 7.13. Using the mean as the point of departure, we can locate the points on the horizontal axis corresponding to $\bar{x} + s$, $\bar{x} + 2s$, $\bar{x} - s$, and $\bar{x} - 2s$. If we draw a line perpendicular to the horizontal axis at the points we have located, we will divide the area under the normal curve into segments.

It is a special property of the normal curve that, of the total area under the curve, the proportion included between $\bar{x}$ and $\bar{x} + s$ is always .3413; the proportion between $\bar{x} + s$ and $\bar{x} + 2s$ is always .1360; and the proportion beyond $\bar{x} + 2s$ is always .0227. Note that, as we might expect, if the proportions on one or the other side of the mean are summed, the result is .5000, and if we sum the proportions on both sides of the mean, we get 1.000. Because the normal curve is symmetrical, the proportions of the area under the curve contained in corresponding segments below the mean ($\bar{x}$ to $\bar{x} - s$, $\bar{x} - s$ to $\bar{x} - 2s$, and beyond $\bar{x} - 2s$) are the same as those above the mean. Thus, 68.26 percent of the area under the curve ($.3413 + .3413 \times 100 = 68.26\%$) falls within one standard deviation of the mean, or between $\bar{x} - s$ and $\bar{x} + s$.

Using the same general principle we have been discussing, it is possible to construct a **standard normal curve** with a mean of 0 and a standard deviation of 1.0, as shown in Figure 7.14, and to express the deviation from the mean of any actual score in a normal distribution in terms of its corresponding **Standard Score** or *z-score*. Let us see how these results can be achieved.

FIGURE 7.13	**A Normal Curve Subdivided by Units of Standard Deviation, with Corresponding Proportions of Area Under the Curve**

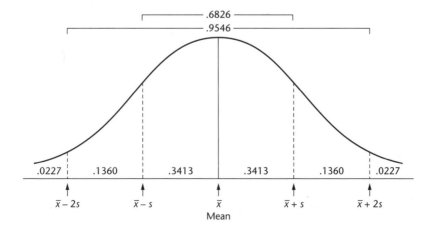

FIGURE 7.14 The Standard Normal Curve Subdivided by Units of Standard Deviation, with Corresponding Proportions of Area Under the Curve

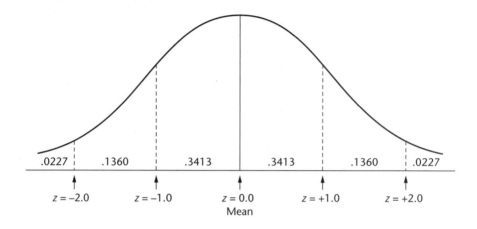

We begin by computing a z-score equivalent for each of the raw scores in the distribution using the formula:

Formula 7.4

$$z = \frac{x - \bar{x}}{s}$$

That is, to find the value of z corresponding to a particular individual score (x) we subtract the distribution's mean score ($\bar{x}$) from that score (x) and divide by the distribution's standard deviation. For example, refer to Table 7.3. The first individual score listed is 8. To find the z-score equivalent, we need to know the distribution's mean score (which we found to be $\bar{x} = 13$) and standard deviation (which we found to be $s = 2.4$). The z-score corresponding to the score of 8 is then given by:

$$z = \frac{8 - 13}{2.4} = \frac{-5}{2.4} = -2.1$$

So, for this 8 in the original, raw score distribution we substitute a z of −2.1. Repeating this calculation process for each of the original scores will yield an array of thirty-six z-scores, which has a mean of 0 and a standard deviation of 1, like the distribution in figure 7.14. (The alert reader may have noted that the one score of 8 represents $1/36 = .028$ of the scores in the exam score distribution, which is marginally greater than the .023 of area under the curve beyond $z = -2.0$ in figure 7.14. Can you explain this?)

As indicated by the proportions between the dotted perpendicular lines under the normal curve in figure 7.14, 68.26 percent ($.3413 + .3413 \times 100 = 68.26$ percent) of the area under the curve and, hence, 68.26 percent of the scores in the distribution fall within one standard deviation above and below the mean, or between points on the z axis of $z = -1.0$ and $z = +1.0$; and 95.46

percent of the area (and scores) falls between $z = -2.0$ and $z = +2.0$, and so on. To put it the other way around, slightly less than 5 percent of the area (and scores) falls outside the area of the normal curve between $z = -2.0$ and $z = +2.0$. Note that, in our example, $z = -2.1$, which tells us that the score falls on the far left side of the distribution, which is in fact where the score of 8 falls in the distribution in Figure 7.3.

Z is a continuous variable and can in principle assume infinitely many values between 0 and 1.0, 1.0 and 2.0, and so on. In practice, it seldom exceeds a value of 4.0. The table of z-scores (Appendix B) permits you to determine the proportion of area under the normal curve (and, therefore, the proportion of scores in the distribution) between the mean and z, as well as the proportion of area beyond z corresponding to any z value between 0 and 4.0. The proportions of area under the curve included between the mean and any particular z-score are constant for any normal curve, regardless of the actual value of the mean and standard deviation of the distribution. Thus, z is an expression, in terms of standard units of deviation, of the area under the normal curve between it and the mean.

Suppose that the FBI has given a written entrance test to 3,410 applicants for entry-level positions with the agency. You are charged with the responsibility of analyzing the scores. In doing so, you discover that the scores the applicants received on their tests range from 125 to 765 and are approximately normally distributed around a mean score of 445, with a standard deviation of 95. If one of the applicants writes you inquiring about her score on the test and how her performance compared to the others who took it, you could look up that person's test paper and determine that she received a score of 658. What will you tell her about the place of her score in the distribution of scores?

Actually, it will be very convenient for you to transform the raw score of 658 into a z-score, by using the following calculations:

$$z = \frac{x - \bar{x}}{s} = \frac{658 - 445}{95} = \frac{213}{95} = 2.24$$

Consulting the z-score table in Appendix B, you discover that the area under the standard normal curve beyond $z = 2.24$ (in column A) is .0125 (in column C). Hence, you can tell her that she scored in the top 2 percent of the applicants.

You might also use the z-score formula to set a passing score for the test. Suppose you were told that there were 341 actual openings in the FBI for this group of applicants. This is 10 percent of the applicant pool. You want to know what score on the test a person would have to receive in order to score in the top 10 percent of the applicants. What z-score corresponds with an area beyond z of .10? Going to the z-score table we look in column C until we find .10. Locating .1003 (which is the closest we can come) in column C, we read the corresponding z-score, $z = 1.28$ in column A. We now know the z-score that determines approximately the top 10 percent of scores. Hence,

$$1.28 = \frac{x - 445}{95}$$

Solving this equation for *x* we have:

$$95 \ (1.28) = x - 445$$
$$445 + 121.6 = x$$
$$566.6 = x$$

About 10 percent of the applicants received scores above 566, so you might set the passing grade as a score of 567. Z-scores are of considerable utility when questions about the location of one score relative to others in the distribution are the researcher's concern.

Finally, we can think of the standard normal curve as having uses analogous to those of percentages. Percentages permit us to compare proportions with different base numbers (denominators) by converting them to equivalent expressions with a base of 100. Converting normal frequency distributions to their standard normal equivalents allows meaningful comparisons when measurement ranges or scales are different. For example, one police recruit test may be marked in such a way that scores range from 20 to 150 whereas another may produce scores ranging from 400 to 800. If the raw scores received by test takers are normally distributed in both cases, converting the distributions to their standard normal equivalents makes comparing performances on the two tests as easy as comparing percentages, despite the differences in raw score ranges.

REVIEW QUESTIONS

1. What is the principal difference between descriptive and inferential statistics?

2. How do continuous and discrete variables differ?

3. What are the differences among nominal, ordinal, interval, and ratio measurements?

4. What is a frequency distribution?

5. What are the most frequently used measures of central tendency and dispersion in a distribution, how are they arrived at, and what are their principal differences?

6. Which measures of central tendency and dispersion are appropriate for distributions of nominal data? Of ordinal data? Of interval data? Of ratio data?

7. How do the various types of quantiles differ and how are they arrived at?

8. How do skewed and normal distributions differ?

9. How do unimodal and multimodal distributions differ?

10. Are all unimodal distributions normal distributions? Why or why not?

11. How does a normal distribution for data on a particular variable differ from a standard normal curve?

12. What are z-scores?

EXERCISES

Use the following hypothetical data for the exercises below.

Subject	Sex	Number of Arrests	Highest Level of Education Achieved*
1	M	2	3
2	M	4	1
3	F	5	1
4	F	3	4
5	M	1	4
6	F	3	1
7	M	2	4
8	F	0	6
9	M	3	2
10	F	4	2
11	M	5	4
12	F	3	6
13	M	2	5
14	M	1	1
15	F	4	1
16	M	6	1
17	F	3	3
18	M	4	5
19	F	2	4
20	M	3	4

*Code	Category
1	grade school or less
2	junior high school
3	high school
4	community college
5	4-year college
6	more than 4-year college

1. At what level of measurement is each of the variables measured?

2. Are the variables discrete or continuous?

3. Calculate appropriate measures of central tendency and dispersion for the distributions of each variable.

4. Construct a bar graph frequency distribution for each of the variables.

5. Are any of the distributions normal distributions?

6. Are any of the distributions skewed? Multimodal?

7. Calculate quartile values for the number-of-arrests variable.

8. Convert the number-of-arrests scores into their z-score equivalents and construct a frequency distribution of the z-scores. Compare this z distribution to the distribution of raw scores you constructed in exercise 4.

9. Find at least two examples of measures of central tendency and dispersion and bar or line graphs in newspapers, magazines, or textbooks other than this one. Are you given the information necessary to make sense of them? What else would you like to know about the data represented? (Pay especially close attention to such data presentations in advertising!)

10. Using the data in Table 7.3, confirm for yourself that Formula 7.2 and Formula 7.3 are equivalent.

 11. Go to *www.crime.org* and follow the link to the "crime statistics tutorial." Rad and critique "Where Does Crime Data Come From?" Explore links to city, county, state, and national and international data as examples of descriptive statistics.

 12. Go to *www.ojjdp.ncjrs.org/ojstatbb/index.html* and follow links that interest you.

13. Go to *http://blackstone.ojp.usdoj.gov/bjs/cvict_v.htm* and construct two bar graphs from the data presented in the first two "bullet" items on the page.

 14. Go to *http://blackstone.ojp.usdoj.gov/bjs/glance.htm#crime* and view the line graphs.

 15. Go to *www.ruf.rice.edu/~lane/hyperstat/normal_distribution.html* for another discussion of the normal distribution.

16. Go to *http://blackstone.ojp.usdoj.gov/bjs/nibrs.htm* and read about the National Incident-Based Reporting System (NIBRS). Follow the link to the Incident-Based Reporting Resource Center (IBRRC) (or go to *www.jrsa.org/ibrrc/* and follow the link to the state reports. Find the Vermont report (or go to *http://www.jrsa.org/ibrrc/reports_using_data/state_reports.html* and follow the links to Vermont.

NOTES

1. This scale was presented by Jerry L. Simmons in *Deviants* (Berkeley, CA: Glendessary Press, 1969), p. 32. For a further discussion of scales at the ordinal level, see William J. Goode and Paul K. Hatt, *Methods in Social Research* (New York: McGraw-Hill, 1952).

2. See Hubert M. Blalock, Jr., *Social Statistics,* 2nd ed. (New York: McGraw-Hill, 1972), pp. 14–15.

3. Many of the properties of the normal distribution, including the sum of squares and variance, essential in a wide variety of statistical analyses were introduced by the statistician R. A. Fisher.

8

Descriptive Statistics: Examining Relationships Between Two or More Variables Through Cross-Tabulation

As we saw in Chapter 7, frequency distributions and measures of central tendency and dispersion are useful when a researcher wishes to describe or analyze data concerning a single variable. Often, however, the researcher is interested in testing a hypothesis asserting a causal relationship between two or more variables. For example, is length of sentence related to recidivism? Is marital status related to support for police? Does changing the law produce changes in behavior addressed by the law? Answering such questions requires the researcher to consider at least two variables simultaneously. In this chapter we will consider three approaches to this problem: comparing frequency distributions, cross-tabulation, and elaboration analysis.

COMPARING FREQUENCY DISTRIBUTIONS

Suppose we are interested in whether there is a relationship between type of offense and sex of offender in a particular population of adult offenders, say the twenty-six adults convicted of petty theft, assault, or drug possession in the Horsetail Switch county court in the last six months. Clearly, a frequency distribution of the sex of these offenders alone would not give us sufficient information to answer this question. Nor would a frequency distribution of the type of offense. To find out if there is a connection between these two variables, we must find a way of considering both of the variables at once.

One strategy that could be employed is to construct two bar-graph frequency distributions of the type of offense, including only males in one and only females in the other, and compare them. Suppose the two graphs look like those in Figure 8.1. A major difference in the two distributions is immediately apparent. The modal category for males is assault, whereas the modal category for females is petty theft.

Is there a relationship between the two variables? The answer may not be obvious, but generally speaking, if there are no differences between the distributions, there is no relationship between the variables; if there are differences, there may be a relationship (although not necessarily a causal one).

Why do differences in distributions suggest a relationship between the variables? Consider what we have done in constructing the distributions. In each distribution, we have held the sex variable constant (that is, we used only one value of the sex variable) and examined the distribution of the type-of-offense variable *within* that particular value (male or female) of the sex variable. We proceeded in this way (rather than holding the type-of-offense variable constant and examining the distribution of the sex variable within each of these values) because we assumed that sex was the *independent* (causal) *variable* and type-of-offense was the *dependent* (effect) *variable.* Another way of saying this is that we constructed the distributions to answer the question: If we know what sex an offender is, what do we know about the type of offense he or she has committed? When, in comparing the two distributions, the data indicate that what we know about type of offense is different, depending upon the sex of the offender, we have some reason to believe that sex is related to type of offense. In our example, if we know the offender is male, we would be right 8 out of 13 times if we said that the person committed assault. If we know that the offender is female, we would be right 6 out of 13 times if we said that the offense committed was petty theft. This difference suggests that there is a relationship (though clearly not a perfect one) between sex and type of offense. Note, in this case, that both of the variables are measured at the nominal level and that we focused our attention on the modal type of offense category.

The basic idea of using differences between distributions as indicators of relationships between variables can be extended to include variables measured at other levels and to other summary statistics concerning distributions. With variables measured at the ordinal level, we might look for differences in the modal or median rank order of persons on the dependent variable, given particular ranks on the independent variable. For example, do persons of different social class (the independent variable) rank differently in their degree of support for the local police? For variables measured at the interval or ratio level, we could look for differences in the mean or standard deviation of two distributions. For example, is there a difference in mean age at time of first conviction for males and females? Finally, when the *n*s for the independent variable categories (values) are large and unequal, we could convert to percentages to facilitate comparison of the distributions.

FIGURE 8.1	Frequency Distributions of Type of Offense by Sex of Offender

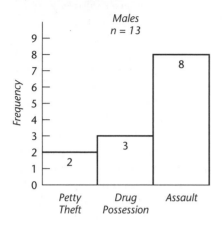
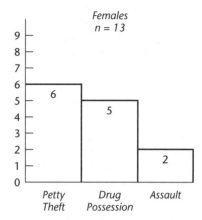

These procedures have their uses, and they do help us answer some of the questions we might have. Nevertheless, the more frequency distributions you have to eyeball in order to make a judgment about the existence of a relationship, the more difficult it becomes. If you are dealing with two variables, each of which has four or five values, this method might be highly impractical. Fortunately, cross-tabulation provides a much simpler and more comprehensible alternative for handling many of these situations.

FUNDAMENTALS OF CROSS-TABULATION

A **cross-tabulation** can be thought of as the intersection of two frequency distributions. Cross-tabulating data on two variables permits us to see relatively easily whether or not they are related to each other. The hypothetical data on sex and type of offense will be used again to illustrate the construction and uses of cross-tabulation.

Constructing a Cross-Tabulation

The first step in constructing a cross-tabulation is to create a two-dimensional data grid, placing the values of the sex variable across the top of the grid and the values of the type-of-offense variable down the side (see Table 8.1). We have now created a table, called a *contingency table,* that has two separate *columns* (corresponding to the two values of the sex variable) and three separate *rows* (corresponding to the three values of the type-of-offense variable). The spaces in the table defined by the intersections of the columns and rows are called **cells.** Note that we could have placed the type-of-offense variable across the top and the sex variable down the side, thereby creating a table with three columns and two rows. In this case, too, the order in which the males and females are listed could have been reversed, and the order of the types of offense could

TABLE 8.1	Type of Offense by Sex of Offender	

| | Sex of Offender | |
Type of Offense	Male	Female
Petty Theft	cell 1	cell 2
Drug Possession	cell 3	cell 4
Assault	cell 5	cell 6

have been changed. The choice among these options is essentially arbitrary, because the variables with which we are dealing are measured at the nominal level. For a variable measured at the ordinal, interval, or ratio level, the values should be placed either in ascending or descending order on the grid.

The next step is to place the data into the grid space by going back to the original data sheets or to the computer where the information has been stored and searching for the various combinations of the two variables represented by Horsetail Switch convicts. If individual A is a male convicted of petty theft, he would be counted in the cell of the table corresponding to the intersection of the male column and the petty theft row. For this table, that means the individual is counted in the upper left-hand cell—cell 1. If the next person is a female convicted of assault, we find the female column and the assault row, or cell 6. If each person in the population of offenders was included, the table would look like Table 8.2. The numbers that appear in each of the cells are called **cell frequencies.** Here, they indicate the number of persons in our population who possess the corresponding combinations of values of the two variables. Note that the two columns of the table correspond to the two frequency distributions presented in Figure 8.1.

We can now add the cell frequencies that appear in each of the rows and in each of the columns to get the results shown in Table 8.3. The row sums 8, 8, and 10 are called *row marginal frequencies;* the column sums 13 and 13 are called *column marginal frequencies.* The number 26 in the lower right-hand corner of the table is the total number of cases included. This total (often referred to as n, as in $n = 26$) can be computed for any table by summing either the row or the column marginal frequencies. Because these two sums must be equal, comparing them provides a simple (though not fail-safe) check on the accuracy of our table construction procedures and calculations. If the marginal row and column sums are different, a mistake has been made in one or more of the cell entries or in the additions of those figures. Furthermore, if the table total (n) is not equal to the total number of cases studied, some cases were either left out or counted more than once in the process of generating the cross-tabulation. Of course, any mistakes must be corrected.

We are now in a position to observe other connections between frequency distributions and tables. The row marginal frequencies constitute a frequency distribution of the types-of-offense variable whereas the column marginal frequencies are a frequency distribution of the sex variable. Hence, a

TABLE 8.2   **Type of Offense by Sex of Offender**

Type of Offense	Sex of Offender	
	Male	Female
Petty Theft	2	6
Drug Possession	3	5
Assault	8	2

TABLE 8.3   **Type of Offense by Sex of Offender**

Type of Offense	Sex of Offender		Total
	Male	Female	
Petty Theft	2	6	8
Drug Possession	3	5	8
Assault	8	2	2
Total	13	13	$n = 26$

by-product of constructing a cross-tabulation of the sex and type-of-offense variables is the frequency distribution of each of the two variables. Again, this fact can be used to check the table, because the frequency distribution of each of the two variables must be the same as its respective marginal frequencies. If either is not, the process of cross-tabulation must be reexamined in order to correct the mistakes that have been made. Finally, the alert reader will have noted that the male and female columns of the table are the frequency distributions we constructed in Figure 8.1, this time expressed in numerical frequencies rather than as bars in a bar graph.

It should not be inferred from our discussion of the connections between frequency distributions and cross-tabulation, however, that marginal frequencies determine cell frequencies. Consider Table 8.4, whose marginal frequencies are specified, but whose cells are empty. Note that the marginal frequencies corresponding to a particular cell do impose some limits on that cell frequency. For example, the smaller of the two marginal frequencies corresponding to a given cell is the highest frequency that could appear in that cell. Still, many combinations of different frequencies could be entered in the cells of the table without changing the marginal frequencies. Therefore, knowing the frequency distribution of each of the two variables above does not tell us anything about the relationship between them.

The final step in the construction of a cross-tabulation is creating a title for the table, which should describe briefly but completely what the table includes.

TABLE 8.4	Type of Offense by Sex of Offender		
	Sex of Offender		
Type of Offense	*Male*	*Female*	*Total*
Petty Theft			8
Drug Possession			8
Assault			10
Total	13	13	$n = 26$

Generally, the title should contain at least the names of the variables used to construct the table. In most circumstances, especially when the text that accompanies the table is not very explicit, it is advisable to include a brief description of the persons (or cases) described in the table. For example, the tables illustrating this discussion are entitled "Type of Offense by Sex of Offender." To be somewhat more descriptive, a phrase such as "Horsetail Switch County Court, May 1–30, 1986" might have been added to the title. Good titles specify clearly and completely what the cross-tabulation represents. An incomplete, vague, or missing title can be seriously misleading, because the reader can only infer what the table concerns.

All cross-tabulations are constructed according to the basic principles we have just illustrated; however, a few complications that may be encountered need to be considered.

Collapsing Categories

Suppose we have a variable that we call "citizens' evaluation of police services." We have operationalized (measured) it on an ordinal scale of seven categories (values), beginning with (1) "police have provided excellent service" and ending with (7) "police have provided very poor service." We wish to examine the relationship of this variable to another variable (for instance, age) that we have operationalized with many more categories. In analyzing and presenting these data, we could construct a table having seven rows (for the seven values of the evaluation-of-police-services variable) and as many columns as we had ages in our study group. If the age variable ranges from 21 through 70 (having, therefore, fifty values) and there are seven values for the evaluation of services variable, a 50-by-7 table would be produced. It would have $50 \times 7 = 350$ cells, requiring a very large space for presentation. Making sense of the data might be very difficult, either because there are so many cells or because there might be numerous empty cells or cells containing very low frequencies, especially if we have relatively few subjects in our study.

Given these circumstances, the presentation of the data could be simplified by **collapsing categories.** By combining (collapsing) two or more of the original values of a given variable into a single new category, we can reduce the total number of cells in a table. For example, our evaluations variable could reasonably be treated as a three-category variable rather than a seven-category variable. The first two categories of our original scheme could be collapsed and include every person who scores either (1) or (2) (a "positive evaluation" score) on our scale. The next three categories of the original scheme might be collapsed to form a "neutral evaluation" category, and the remaining two categories could form a "negative evaluation" category. Now, the evaluation variable has three values rather than the original seven. Note that this is only one of several possible ways of collapsing categories for this variable.

The variable from which we can gain most by collapsing categories, however, is age. Again, the investigator must decide whether to collapse categories and, if so, into how many new values. The fifty values of the age variable could be reduced to two values; reducing it to one value—that is, putting everybody in the same age category—would, of course, be useless. We might create one new category of ages 21 through 45, and another of ages 46 through 70, or, we could create three new categories, or four, or five, or ten. If we decided on a three-category division of the evaluation variable and a five-category scheme for the age variable, we would then produce a 5-by-3 table that has $5 \times 3 = 15$ cells—a much more comprehensible table than one containing 350 cells.

What is at stake in deciding whether or not to collapse categories? Obviously, some possibly important detail is sacrificed if our variable is measured with a given number of possible values and the data are then analyzed and presented with fewer values. If, for example, there is a large difference between the evaluations of 35-year-olds and 38-year-olds, and we have lumped these two age groups into one new category, the difference will not show up in our analysis. One might also contend that some time and effort was wasted by measuring our variables in such detail if only a few general categories were to be used anyway. Although there is no point in measuring a variable with greater detail and precision than are justified by the purposes at hand, it is also true that—short of doing another study—the researcher will never have a greater level of detail available for analysis than that recorded originally. In analyzing the data, the researcher can always reduce the number of categories in the analysis, but it is never possible to increase the number of categories. Within reason, then, the original raw data might deliberately be collected in more detail than the researcher expects to use for the analysis. If, in analyzing the data, the researcher encounters unexpected or otherwise intriguing results, the more detailed data may come in handy as she pursues these leads.

How can you decide which categories to collapse? You can, of course, simply try several different ways of collapsing the data on a trial-and-error basis. However, this procedure is only acceptable as an exploratory strategy. It is especially important, when choosing to collapse categories, not to select for presentation only the results of those collapsing strategies that make the strongest case for the author's point of view without informing the reader of the exploratory nature of the analysis. As a general rule, the researcher should decide on a collapsing plan *before* analyzing the data and apply as much reason, common sense, and ethical judgment as possible throughout the process.

A number of factors might be considered in deciding which categories to collapse. First, you could locate seemingly natural divisions of a variable; for example, an age variable might be broken down into categories corresponding to infancy, childhood, adolescence, adulthood, and old age—if those divisions make sense with respect to the problem being investigated. Second, divisions could be based on the categories included in a theoretical proposition or hypothesis, such as "middle-class people are more likely to support the police than are upper-class or working-class people." If the social class variable were operationalized in terms of annual income, it would be reasonable to break these data into three categories corresponding to the three social classes mentioned in the hypothesis. Third, by examining the frequency distribution of the variable, the original categories could be combined so that a sufficiently large number of cases is represented in each category to permit meaningful analysis. Caution is in order here. Categories should not be collapsed in a way that violates the theoretical substance underlying the study, even though they may be expedient. Finally, in the absence of a better rationale, arbitrary collapsing decisions can be made. Many investigators, for example, divide the age range into five- or ten-year intervals (such as, 0–5, 6–10, 11–15 . . . , or 0–10, 11–20, 21–30 . . .) and proceed using those categories in their cross-tabulations.

Some or all of these considerations may be weighed in any decision to collapse categories in a particular way. You should remember, however, that the way data are collapsed may well influence the results that are produced. Consequently, collapsing should always be done honestly and in a way that is consistent with the variable categories implicitly or explicitly indicated by the research hypothesis.

Using Percentages in Cross-Tabulation

The cross-tabulations discussed so far have contained raw numbers (frequency counts) in the cells. In many cases it is easier to interpret the data if cell frequencies are converted to percentages; however, special complications may arise when converting to percentages.

The basic complication in using percentages in cross-tabulations becomes apparent if we attempt to answer the question: What base numbers shall we use in calculating the percentages? Consider the cross-tabulation in Table 8.5 of data concerning the variables "position on police force" and "job stress." Suppose we wanted to convert the cell frequencies in the table to percentages. The difficulty is that we could do so using three different base numbers, resulting in three different percentage figures for any given cell of the table.

First, we could express each of the cell frequencies as a percentage of the total number of cases (n) included in the table and produce Table 8.6. Percentages based on the total sample are useful to describe the proportion of cases falling into each of the categories of the table variables. Thus, Table 8.6 indicates that 43 percent of all of the subjects studied are patrol officers with low stress, 30 percent are sergeants with high stress, and so on. The sum of the cell percentages calculated in this way always equals 100 percent.

The two remaining possibilities for converting cell frequencies to percentages are to express them as percentages of the row or the column marginal

TABLE 8.5	Job Stress by Position on Police Force

	Job Stress		
Position on Police Force	*Low*	*High*	*Total*
Sergeant	30	60	90
Patrol Officer	86	24	110
Total	116	84	n = 200

TABLE 8.6	Job Stress by Position on Police Force

	Job Stress		
Position on Police Force	*Low*	*High*	*Total*
Sergeant	15%	30%	45%
Patrol Officer	43%	12%	55%
Total	58%	42%	100% *n* = 200

frequencies. The choice between these alternatives is based on which of the two variables we have defined as the independent, or causal, variable in the research hypothesis.

You will recall that an independent (causal) variable must precede a dependent variable in time. Our analysis, then, should address the question: Given a certain value of the independent variable, what happens to the dependent variable? To answer this question, the cell frequencies should be converted to percentages with each value of the independent variable treated separately. Then the percentage distribution of the dependent variable within any one category of the independent variable can be compared to the percentage distribution of the dependent variable within any other category of the independent variable. If the independent variable forms the columns of the table, the column marginal frequencies are used to convert cell frequencies to percentages. If the independent variable forms the rows of the table, the row marginal frequencies are used. This practice is referred to as **percentaging in the direction of the independent variable.**

Consider again Table 8.5. It seems reasonable to consider "position on the police force" the independent variable, because job stress clearly does not "cause" position. The appropriate strategy, therefore, is to use the row marginal frequencies (90 and 110) as the base numbers to convert the cell frequencies in each row to percentages, as in Table 8.7. Note that the sum of the percentages in each row (but not each column) equals 100 percent. This table permits us to compare positions on the police force in terms of the percentage of patrol officers

TABLE 8.7	Job Stress by Position on Police Force		
	Job Stress		
Position on Police Force	*Low*	*High*	*Total*
Sergeant	33%	67%	100% (*n* = 90)
Patrol Officer	78%	22%	100% (*n* = 110)

whose stress levels are in a particular range with the percentage of sergeants with stress in the same range. Thus, whereas 30/90 or 33 percent of the sergeants have low stress, 86/110 or 78 percent of the patrol officers have low stress, and so on. Note that, in reading the table, we compare categories in the direction opposite from the one we used in calculating the percentages. If the row marginal frequencies were used as the base for percentaging (as they were in our example), we compare figures in the same column. If the column marginal frequencies were used to calculate percentages, we compare figures in the same row. The table as a whole shows that sergeants tend to experience more stress than patrol officers. In short, the table depicts a concomitant variation between these two variables; that is, that stress level varies with position on the police force.

By observing that position on police force precedes stress in time and that the two variables do vary concomitantly, we have satisfied two of the three conditions for making causal inferences, as discussed in Chapter 3. The third condition, eliminating other causal factors, remains to be met. If the researcher has used an experimental design to generate the data, considerable control has been exercised over possible alternative causal variables by the structure of the research design. In other cases, the analyst may *assume,* on the basis of common sense and in the absence of other data or controls, that the relationship revealed by cross-tabulation may be genuine and not spurious. This is, as we have seen, a risky assumption at best. In still other cases, especially in survey research, the investigator can examine the effect of a third variable (referred to as a **control variable** or *test factor*) on the relationship between the two variables that were the original focus of the analysis. This additional analysis of the data may assist the researcher in eliminating alternative causal variables, thereby strengthening his argument that the relationship between variables is causal. This procedure is called **elaboration analysis.**

ELABORATION ANALYSIS

Consider once again the relationship we have observed between position on police force and stress. Suppose we are confronted by a skeptic who has examined Table 8.7 but contends that, because females tend to occupy positions of lower status in an organization or to experience less stress than males even when they hold identical positions, sex is the real cause of the stress differentials observed. How could we test the contribution of the sex variable to the apparent relationship between position on the police force and stress?[1]

By constructing two separate cross-tabulations, one for each value of the sex variable (male, female), we can consider all three variables at once. Suppose that Tables 8.8 and 8.9 were the result. These tables are called **first-order partial tables** because each represents a part of the original relationship and bears the following relationships to the original Table 8.5 (called a **zero-order table**):

1. The sum of the total number of cases in the two partial tables (130 + 70) equals 200, the total number of cases in the zero-order table.

2. Each of the cell frequencies in the zero-order table can be recovered by adding the two corresponding cell frequencies in the partial tables (for example, 28 + 58 = 86, and 46 + 14 = 60).

3. Similarly, the zero-order marginal frequencies can be obtained by adding the two corresponding marginal frequencies in the partial tables (for example, 60 + 30 = 90; 58 + 26 = 84).

These relationships occur whenever first-order partial tables are constructed from the same data used to construct a zero-order table. If the zero-order table cannot be reconstructed by combining the partial tables in this way, a mistake has occurred; the reasons for any discrepancies must be sought and the tables corrected before proceeding with the analysis.

TABLE 8.8   Job Stress by Position on Police Force

Position on Police Force	Job Stress		Total
	Low	High	
Sergeant	14	46	60
Patrol Officer	58	12	70
Total	72	58	$n = 130$

TABLE 8.9   Job Stress by Position on Police Force

Position on Police Force	Job Stress		Total
	Low	High	
Sergeant	16	14	30
Patrol Officer	28	12	40
Total	44	26	$n = 70$

Again, we can convert the cell frequencies to percentages to facilitate interpreting the data, using the row marginal frequencies as in Tables 8.10 and 8.11. In both tables, the proportion of patrol officers in the "low stress" category is greater than the proportion of sergeants in the same stress category, and the proportion of sergeants in the "high stress" category is greater than the proportion of patrol officers in the same category. Hence, the same general pattern or relationship between position on police force and stress level found in the zero-order table holds for each of the partial tables as well. In elaboration analysis, this result is called **replication.**

Our skeptic can take some consolation in the data, however, because the relationship between these two variables seems to be considerably stronger among males than among females. That is, when the differences in percentages for sergeants and patrol officers within a given stress category are compared in the two tables, these differences are larger for males than for females. For example, in the "low stress" category for males the difference is 83 − 23 = 60 percent, whereas for females in the same category, the difference is 70 − 53 = 17 percent. It appears that sex is a factor here as well.

The procedure we have just used to test the effect of the sex variable on the relationship between position on police force and stress can be repeated with all of the possible causal variables for which the researcher has data, in order to eliminate as many of them as possible. If the general relationship observed in the original zero-order cross-tabulation is observed in all the partial tables that are constructed, we can tentatively infer that the independent variable is at least one of the causal factors involved.

TABLE 8.10 Job Stress by Position on Police Force: Males

| | Job Stress | | |
Position on Police Force	Low	High	Total
Sergeant	23%	77%	100% ($n = 60$)
Patrol Officer	83%	17%	100% ($n = 70$)

TABLE 8.11 Job Stress by Position on Police Force: Females

| | Job Stress | | |
Position on Police Force	Low	High	Total
Sergeant	53%	47%	100% ($n = 30$)
Patrol Officer	70%	30%	100% ($n = 40$)

Explanation

Not all partial analyses result in the confirmation of the relationships observed in the zero-order table, however. In some cases, the relationship between the two zero-order variables will be substantially reduced, or even disappear, in *all* of the partial tables. Two accounts can be offered for this result in a partial analysis. The crucial factor that distinguishes between these two accounts is the time sequence of the variables. First, if the test factor precedes the independent variable, the zero-order relationship is called **spurious.** That is, what appears to be a causal relationship between the two original variables is a result of the causal relationship between a third variable (the test factor, which occurs before the independent variable) and each of the two original variables. This might be diagrammed as in Figure 8.2, where *x* is the assumed independent variable, *y* the assumed dependent variable, and *t* the third variable (test factor). We are justified in concluding that the original relationship is spurious if the test factor (*t*) either precedes or coincides with the independent variable and precedes the dependent variable in time. In such cases, the test factor is said to **explain** the apparent but spurious relationship between *x* and *y* in the zero-order table. (Note that this is a specialized use of the concept of explanation—not exactly equivalent to the way the term is typically used in science.)

Interpretation

The second circumstance in which the original relationship is substantially reduced or disappears in all of the partial analyses occurs when the test factor intervenes (comes between) the *x* variable and the *y* variable in time. In this case, the results can be interpreted to mean that a developmental sequence exists in the relationship among the three variables. This can be diagrammed as in Figure 8.3. When the test factor intervenes, the result is called an **interpretation**, and *t* is called an *intervening variable.*

Again, the determination of whether the analysis has resulted in an explanation or an interpretation is entirely dependent on the time sequence of the variables—the numbers or percentages in the corresponding cells of the tables

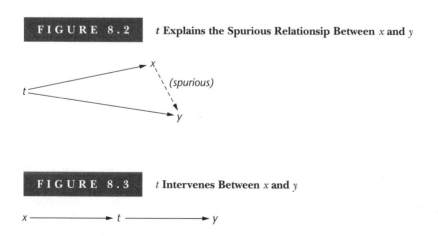

FIGURE 8.2   *t* **Explains the Spurious Relationsip Between** *x* **and** *y*

FIGURE 8.3   *t* **Intervenes Between** *x* **and** *y*

$x \longrightarrow t \longrightarrow y$

could be identical. Note further that in both explanation and interpretation, the test factor must be related to both of the original variables. To be sure that this latter condition has been met, we would have to construct two additional cross-tabulations to determine that there is a relationship between t and x and t and y.

Specification

It is also possible that when a test factor is introduced, the original relationship between the two variables may be substantially reduced or disappear in *some* but not all of the partial tables. When our analysis produces these results, we can specify those categories of the test factor within which the original relationship still holds and those in which it does not. This is called **specification,** for obvious reasons. When the original relationship holds only for some values of the test factor (control variable), or when its strength or even direction changes with different values of the control variable, the control variable is said to interact with the (original) independent variable. Such variable *interactions* are commonly found in criminal justice research, not only in elaboration analysis but in many types of statistical analysis, such as partial correlation to be discussed in Chapter 9.

Remember, we are justified in calling these results "specification" only if the test factor is *not* related to at least one of the original variables. If the test factor was related to both of the original variables, we would have an instance of either explanation or interpretation.

No Apparent Relationship in the Zero-Order Table

When the zero-order table shows no apparent relationship between two variables, a partial analysis may still reveal that a relationship between the original variables does exist within some or all of the categories of the test factor used to construct the partial tables. In cases of this type, the relationship between the two original variables within some categories of the test factor is the opposite of the relationship between the two original variables within other categories of the test factor. These opposing relationships tend to mask or cancel each other when combined in the zero-order table.[2]

We have summarized our discussion of elaboration analysis in Table 8.12, where x is an independent variable, y is a dependent variable, and t is a third, test variable.

Some Examples of Elaboration Analysis

Suppose that we had conducted a questionnaire survey of the relationship between ethnicity and support for the police. We have measured the nominal ethnicity variable by asking our respondents to indicate in which of the following ethnic groups they belong: Black; White; Hispanic; Asian; Native American; and other. Moreover, the ordinal support-for-the-police variable has been operationalized as a 5-point scale: (1) very supportive; (2) supportive; (3) neutral; (4) unsupportive; and (5) very unsupportive.

| TABLE 8.12 | Outcomes in Elaboration Analysis |

If in the zero order table	and	In the partial tables	and	The time sequence of the variables is	then	The tentative conclusion (inference) is
$x \rightarrow y$*		$x \nrightarrow y$ (in all partials)		x before y		Replication: x causes y
$x \rightarrow y$		$x \nrightarrow y$†		t before x before y		Explanation: x not a cause of y; t explains relationship between x and y
$x \rightarrow y$		$x \nrightarrow y$		x before t before y		Interpretation: If $t \rightarrow x$ and $t \rightarrow y$, x, t, and y form a causal chain; x causes t, t causes y; t interprets relationship between x and y
$x \rightarrow y$		$x \rightarrow y$ (in some but not all partials)		x before y; t occurs before y		Specification: If $t \rightarrow x$ or $t \rightarrow y$, t specifies causal relationship between x and y; x causes y only in some categories of t
$x \nrightarrow y$		$x \rightarrow y$ (in all partials but direction of relationship differs in different partials)		x before y; t occurs before y		Relationships in partials cancel each other

*for $\rightarrow$ read "is related to"
†for $\nrightarrow$ read "is not related to"

We hypothesize that ethnicity is the cause of support for the police; that is, ethnicity is our independent variable and support for the police is our dependent variable. As a first step to discovering whether a relationship exists between these two variables, we construct a cross-tabulation. Because there are so few respondents in some categories of both variables, we decide to collapse categories. We make our original six-category ethnicity variable a new three-category variable, taking Black and White as two of the categories and using "other" to combine the four categories of Hispanic, Asian, Native American, and other to create the third category. For the support variable, the original categories 1 and 2 are collapsed into one new category, categories 4 and 5 into a second new category, leaving the original category 3 the same in our new category system. Suppose that when we placed our data into the cross-tabulation, it looked like Table 8.13.

We can now convert the cell frequencies in the table to percentages. Because ethnicity is our presumed independent variable we use the column marginal frequencies for the conversion. Our table would look like Table 8.14 (with percents rounded to the nearest whole percent).

These data suggest that Blacks are predominantly unsupportive of the police whereas Whites are predominantly supportive. The others are about evenly divided in their level of support for the police. Hence, there appears to be a relationship between ethnicity and police support:

Ethnicity ⟶ Support for Police

Now suppose that we have also gathered data about whether our respondents have ever reported a crime to the police. We think that this might have a great deal to do with support for the police. Hence, we decide to perform an elaboration analysis. We divide our respondents into two categories (those who have and those who have not reported a crime to the police) and construct a cross-tabulation of our original two variables for each of these categories. Suppose the data looked like those in Table 8.15.

In this case the relationship we observed in the original zero-order table (Table 8.13) holds in both of the partial tables. Hence, reporting a crime to the police does not appear to affect the relationship between ethnicity and support (a *replication*). We are then still left with:

Ethnicity ⟶ Support for Police

But suppose the data appeared as in Table 8.16. In this case, the relationship between ethnicity and support for the police observed in the zero-order table (Table 8.14) disappears in the "reported crime" partial table. In the "never reported crime" partial, however, the zero-order relationship remains; in fact, it is even stronger in this partial than in the zero-order table. Assuming that the report-of-crime variable is related to one (but not both) of the zero-order table variables (although we haven't done so here, we would have to construct the two tables—report of crime by ethnicity and report of crime by support for police—to determine whether this condition holds), this example of elaboration analysis has resulted in a *specification*. That is, we can now specify in which category of the test variable the zero-order relationship is maintained (in this case, the "never reported crime" category).

Ethnicity ⟶ Support for Police
(among those who have never reported a crime)

Let us look at another example of elaboration analysis. Suppose we have studied 500 16- to 18-year-old juveniles and examined the relationship between their social class (the independent variable) and the number of self-admitted

| TABLE 8.13 | Support for the Police Ethnicity | | | |

Support for the Police Ethnicity

	Ethnicity			
Support for Police	Black	White	Other	Total
Supportive	100	400	250	750
Neutral	150	100	150	400
Unsupportive	400	200	250	850
Total	650	700	650	$n = 2,000$

TABLE 8.14   Percent Support for the Police by Ethnicity

	Ethnicity		
Support for Police	Black ($n = 650$)	White ($n = 700$)	Other ($n = 650$)
Supportive	15%	57%	38%
Neutral	23%	14%	23%
Unsupportive	62%	29%	38%
Total	100%	100%	99%*

*Totals not equal to 100% are due to rounding error.

TABLE 8.15   Percent Support for the Police by Ethnicity and Report of Crime

	Reported Crime				Never Reported Crime		
Support for Police	Black ($n = 325$)	White ($n = 350$)	Other ($n = 325$)		Black ($n = 325$)	White ($n = 350$)	Other ($n = 325$)
Supportive	16%	59%	38%		15%	56%	38%
Neutral	22%	14%	23%		24%	14%	23%
Unsupportive	62%	27%	38%		61%	30%	39%
Total	100%	100%	99%*		100%	100%	100%

* Totals not equal to 100% are due to rounding error.

delinquent acts in which they have engaged in the last year. We measured the social class variable in three categories (upper, middle, and lower) and the number of delinquent acts in three categories (less than two, three to five, and six or more). Suppose further that we have already constructed the zero-order table and discovered that there is indeed a relationship between these variables: the higher the social class, the lower the number of self-admitted

TABLE 8.16	Percent Support for the Police by Ethnicity and Report of Crime					
	Reported Crime			**Never Reported Crime**		
Support for Police	*Black* ($n = 290$)	*White* ($n = 270$)	*Other* ($n = 290$)	*Black* ($n = 360$)	*White* ($n = 430$)	*Other* ($n = 360$)
Supportive	31%	33%	34%	3%	72%	42%
Neutral	34%	33%	31%	14%	2%	17%
Unsupportive	34%	33%	34%	83%	26%	42%
Total	99%*	99%*	99%*	100%	100%	100%*

* Totals not equal to 100% are due to rounding error.

delinquent acts. We then introduce the test factor of ethnicity, measured in two categories (White and non-White) and obtain the results in Table 8.17.

In this case, the zero-order relationship disappears in both partial tables. Recall that when we get this result in an elaboration analysis, we have an instance of either *explanation* or *interpretation*. Which of these has occurred depends on the time sequence of the variables. If the test variable (in this case, ethnicity) occurs at the same time as or before the independent variable (social class) and before the dependent variable (number of delinquent acts), we have a spurious relationship in the zero-order table. It seems reasonable in our example to regard ethnicity as occurring simultaneously with the independent variable and prior to the dependent variable. That is, a person's ethnicity and social class are established at birth because a child's ethnicity and social class are determined by the ethnicity and social class of his parents, and both of these variables impact on the individual well before the delinquent acts being studied. Hence, assuming that our test factor (ethnicity) is also related both to the original independent variable (social class) and to the original dependent variable (number of delinquent acts), we may say that ethnicity is an *explanation* of the zero-order relationship. That is, the zero-order relationship is spurious.

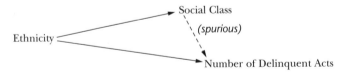

Now suppose that instead of ethnicity, we introduced junior high school attended (measured in two categories for the two junior high schools our subjects attended) as our test variable and obtained the same cell percentages as those in Table 8.17. In this case, we could reasonably argue that the school-attended variable occurs in time after the social class variable (our original independent variable), but before the number-of-delinquent-acts variable (our original dependent variable). The social class of juveniles is usually established at the time they are born; the delinquent acts in question are those committed

| TABLE 8.17 | Self-Admitted Delinquent Acts by Ethnicity and Social Class (in Percentages) | | | | | |

	White			Non-White		
Number of Delinquent Acts	Upper Class ($n = 42$)	Middle Class ($n = 108$)	Lower Class ($n = 100$)	Upper Class ($n = 25$)	Middle Class ($n = 95$)	Lower Class ($n = 130$)
Less than 2	35%	33%	34%	36%	34%	34%
3 to 5	33%	35%	33%	32%	33%	32%
6 or more	31%	31%	33%	32%	33%	34%
Total	99%*	99%*	100%	100%	100%	100%

* Totals not equal to 100% are due to rounding error.

by 16- to 18-year-olds in the year prior to the study, which means that, in most cases at least, they would have finished junior high school before they committed the delinquent acts in question. Hence, this result of our elaboration analysis is an instance of *interpretation*. The school-attended variable intervenes and interprets the relationship between social class and number of delinquent acts. The relationships among the three variables as suggested by our analyses might be diagrammed as follows:

Social Class ⟶ School Attended ⟶ Number of Delinquent Acts

As a last example of the possible results of elaboration analysis, suppose that a study we did produced zero-order Table 8.18. In this case, there is no apparent relationship between the type of defense attorney and trial outcome. We might nevertheless wish to explore this result through elaboration analysis. Suppose that we introduced sex of offender as a test factor and obtained the results shown in Table 8.19. This result is interesting because, although there was no relationship between the variables in our zero-order table (Table 8.18), there is a strong relationship in each of the partials. Note, however, that the relationships in the partials run in opposite directions. That is, males are more often found guilty when defended by a private attorney and innocent when defended by a public defender, whereas females are found guilty more often when defended by a public defender and innocent when defended by a private attorney. These two partial relationships cancel each other out, resulting in the absence of relationship in the zero-order table. No special name is given to this outcome in elaboration analysis.

Let us make one final observation about elaboration analysis. Which variable we begin with in our zero-order table is essentially arbitrary. That is, we could have begun our analysis with a zero-order relationship between ethnicity and reported crime and used our support-for-police variable as a test factor, or we could have begun with a zero-order table looking at the relationship between support for police and reported crime with ethnicity as our test factor. The point is that the researcher structures the analysis as he sees fit, being limited in his inferences only by the time sequence of the

TABLE 8.18	**Trial Outcome by Type of Defense Attorney (in Percentages)**

	Type of Attorney	
Trial Outcome	*Public Defender* ($n = 50$)	*Private Attorney* ($n = 50$)
Guilty	54%	56%
Innocent	46%	44%
Total	100%	100%

TABLE 8.19	**Trial Outcome by Type of Defense Attorney and Sex of Offender (in Percentages)**

	Sex of Offender			
	Male		*Female*	
Trial Outcome	*Public Defender* ($n = 24$)	*Private Attorney* ($n = 26$)	*Public Defender* ($n = 26$)	*Private Attorney* ($n = 24$)
Guilty	25%	81%	81%	33%
Innocent	75%	19%	19%	67%
Total	100%	100%	100%	100%

variables and whether the cross-tabulations actually show relationships among the variables.

The techniques of cross-tabulation and elaboration analysis may be used on variables assessed at any level of measurement (by collapsing categories in the case of interval or ratio level data, for example), but they are most appropriate when all the variables being studied are measured at the nominal level. More powerful statistical tools are available when variables are measured at the ordinal, interval, or ratio level. We turn to a discussion of two of the most widely used such statistical procedures—regression and correlation analysis—in Chapter 9.

REVIEW QUESTIONS

1. What is a contingency table?
2. What is the relationship between marginal frequencies in a contingency table and frequency distributions?
3. What does it mean to say that the categories of a variable may be collapsed? What should be kept in mind by the researcher when collapsing categories for purposes of analysis?

4. When converting cell frequencies to percentages, which marginal frequencies should be used?

5. What is elaboration analysis?

6. What is the difference between zero-order tables and first-order partial tables?

7. On what basis might we conclude that an elaboration analysis has produced an explanation? An interpretation? A specification? A replication?

EXERCISES

Use the following hypothetical data for the exercises below.

Subject	Ethnic Group	Convicted of a Crime?	Social Class	Score on Criminal Justice Test (% Correct)	IQ Score
1	non-White	no	middle	60%	101
2	White	no	lower	54	98
3	non-White	yes	lower	63	112
4	White	yes	lower	57	100
5	White	yes	middle	72	115
6	non-White	no	lower	70	130
7	White	yes	middle	59	99
8	non-White	no	middle	60	100
9	non-White	no	middle	68	126
10	non-White	yes	lower	64	118
11	White	no	middle	64	107
12	White	yes	middle	65	113
13	non-White	yes	middle	80	121
14	non-White	no	lower	55	99
15	non-White	no	middle	48	92
16	non-White	no	middle	68	119
17	White	yes	lower	61	101
18	non-White	no	middle	85	140
19	White	no	lower	92	132
20	non-White	no	middle	40	123

1. Construct a zero-order table relating ethnic group to conviction of a crime. Is there a relationship?

2. Construct first-order partial tables for the two variables in 1, using social class as the third variable. Is there a relationship between social class and ethnic group? Between social class and conviction record? How would you interpret the results of this elaboration analysis?

3. Collapse the IQ scores into three categories and construct a table for examining whether there is any relationship between social class and IQ. Is there a relationship?

NOTES

1. Elaboration analysis was introduced by Samuel Stouffer and formalized by Paul Lazarsfeld and his associates, especially Patricia Kendall.

2. For a more complete discussion of elaboration analysis, see Stephen Cole, *The Sociological Method* (Chicago: Markham, 1972), especially pp. 106–32; and Herbert Hyman, *Survey Design and Analysis* (New York: Free Press, 1954), pp. 275–327.

9

Descriptive Statistics: Measuring Relationships Between Two or More Variables Through Regression and Correlation Analysis

The basic ideas underlying regression and correlation analysis are similar, but they differ in the kinds of research question for which they are appropriate.[1] Regression analysis permits us to predict the values of a dependent variable (y) from the values of one or more independent variables (x). Correlation analysis measures the strength of the relationship between two or more variables. In a research project, correlation analysis is typically done first. If this analysis indicates a relatively strong linear (more about this term later) relationship between the variables, the researcher may then proceed to a regression analysis. The general idea of correlation is relatively simple. If the average income of a city's citizens goes up each year for ten years, for example, and the burglary rate goes down for the same time period, we say the two variables are correlated; that is, they change together, in this case moving in opposite directions. However, because the calculation of correlation statistics is easier to grasp once regression is understood, we shall begin our discussion with regression analysis.

First, however, to facilitate the discussion of both procedures, we need to introduce a new way of graphing data called the **scattergram.**

SCATTERGRAMS

Suppose that we have measured each individual in our study group on two continuous ratio variables. We shall call the independent variable Variable x and the dependent variable Variable y. We are interested in determining the strength of the relationship, if any, between these two variables. We might proceed by creating a graph with the values of Variable x arrayed along the horizontal axis and the values of Variable y arrayed along the vertical axis. We could then locate each individual in our study group on this graph by placing a dot where his scores on Variables x and y intersect (see Figure 9.1). The precise location of each dot in the graphic space is determined as follows. Suppose respondent A scored 4 on Variable x and 6 on Variable y. We would draw an imaginary line perpendicular to the horizontal axis at the point corresponding to a score of 4 on variable x and a line perpendicular to the vertical axis corresponding to a score of 6 on variable y. At the point where these two perpendicular lines intersect, we place a dot (see Figure 9.1). This dot is said to have coordinates written as (x,y)—in this case (4,6). If we plotted the scores on our graph for each individual in our study group, the result would be a graph scattered with dots representing the intersection of the scores on our two variables for the study group as a whole. This kind of graphic representation is called a *scattergram* or a *bivariate distribution*.

Suppose that when we finished this task our scattergram looked like the one in Figure 9.2. Note that the dots are scattered fairly evenly over the graph. Consider again a question we asked earlier in our discussion of relationships between independent and dependent variables: If we know the value of the independent variable, what can we say about the value of the dependent variable? The scattergram in Figure 9.2 would not permit us to say anything useful about the value of Variable y given a particular value of Variable x. Choose any value of Variable x and examine the corresponding values of Variable y arrayed directly above it. They are as likely to be low as they are to be medium or high. Hence, the scattergram represents a situation in which the two variables are unrelated.

Now, let us suppose that our scattergram looked like the one in Figure 9.3. (For the moment, ignore the straight slanting line in both Figures 9.3 and 9.4.) In this case, the dots fall into a definable pattern, running from the lower left-hand corner to the upper right-hand corner of the graphic space. Dots in the lower left-hand corner represent instances in which a low score on one variable was accompanied by a low score on the other variable; dots in the upper right-hand corner represent instances of a high score on one variable accompanied by a high score on the other variable. The pattern of dots (data) reflects a relationship between the two variables, in this case a *positive correlation* or relationship.

The scattergram in Figure 9.4 represents a *negative correlation* or relationship; that is, the pattern of dots (data) reflects instances of a low score on one variable accompanied by a high score on the other.

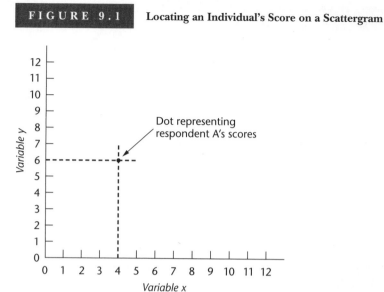

FIGURE 9.1   **Locating an Individual's Score on a Scattergram**

FIGURE 9.2   **A Scattergram Showing No Relationship Between Two Variables**

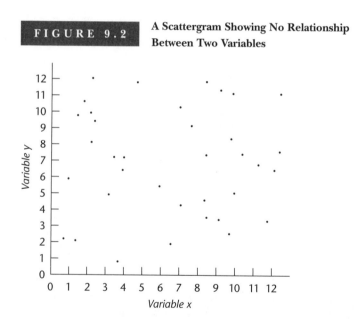

Linear and Nonlinear Relationships

Both positive and negative correlations of the kind we have just discussed are examples of a **linear relationship,** for the pattern of the dots can be approximately represented by a straight line that runs diagonally across the graph (see Figures 9.3 and 9.4).

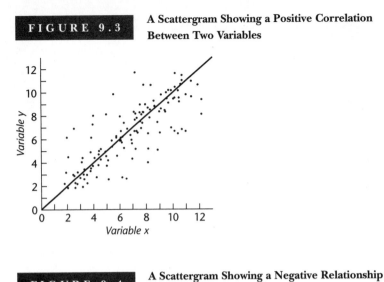

FIGURE 9.3

A Scattergram Showing a Positive Correlation Between Two Variables

FIGURE 9.4

A Scattergram Showing a Negative Relationship Between Two Variables

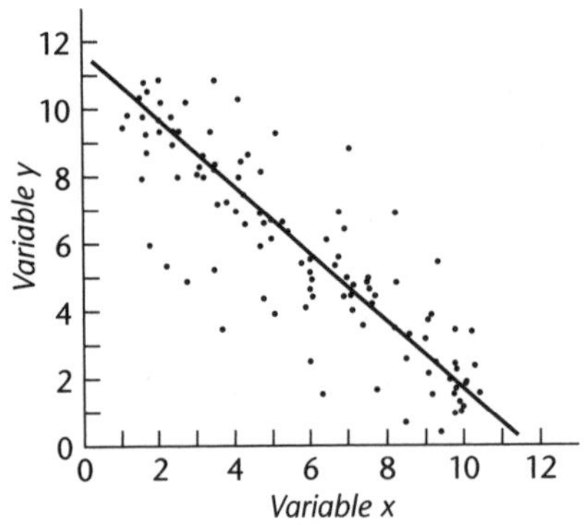

Of course, a scattergram can reveal a nonlinear relationship as well. Suppose our scattergram looked like one of those in Figure 9.5. In these, the dots (data points) clearly fall into a pattern, but not one well approximated by a straight line. A curved line does much better, reflecting what is called a **curvilinear relationship.** Although there are techniques for describing curvilinear data patterns, discussion of which may be found in advanced statistics texts, the procedures we will discuss below are appropriate only for linear relationships. We shall now turn to a discussion of regression analysis.

REGRESSION ANALYSIS

As we noted at the beginning of this section, regression analysis is aimed at predicting the values of a dependent variable (y) from the values of an independent variable (x). In order to make these predictions we shall use a straight line, called a regression line, to represent or approximate the pattern of dots in the

FIGURE 9.5	Scattergrams Showing Curvilinear Relationships Between Two Variables

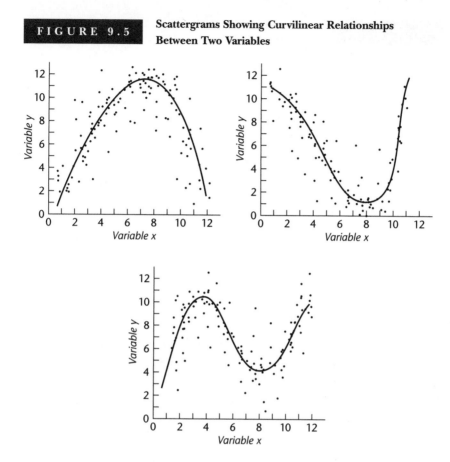

scattergram. We want a line that fits the pattern of dots well. If the dots form a pattern that slants up to the right (as in Figure 9.3, for example), our line must pass through the field of dots, slanting up to the right; if the dot pattern flows down to the right (as in Figure 9.4), our line must conform to this configuration. We can put this fit in more precise terms: The **regression line** for a scattergram (or bivariate distribution) is the line that minimizes the distance between it and the dots in the scattergram.

The alert reader may recognize that there are at least three ways of measuring this distance. It may be measured parallel to the x axis, parallel to the y axis, or perpendicular to the regression line. We shall return to the differences among these distance measures later. For now, assume that the distance is that parallel to the y axis as indicated in Figure 9.6.

Any straight line, including a regression line, in a graphic space like the ones we have been considering above can be converted into an algebraic formula (sometimes called a function) of the general form:

Formula 9.1

$y = a + bx$

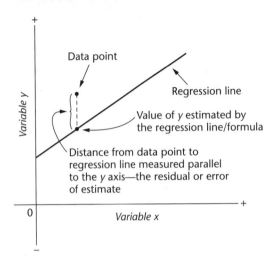

FIGURE 9.6 A Scattergram Showing Data Point, Regression Line, and Error of Estimate

For any particular regression line, *a* and *b* are constants (that is, they do not change) whereas *x* and *y* are variables. Note that *a* and *b* can have either positive or negative values and that *b* is referred to as the *regression coefficient*.

First let's consider *a*, often referred to as the **y intercept**. As this designation suggests, the constant *a* is determined by noting the value of *y* at the point where the regression line crosses the *y* axis, that is, the value of *y* when *x* is zero for a particular regression line. (We could also say that *a* is the *y* coordinate of the point on the regression line that has an *x* coordinate of zero.)

Now, what about *b*, which is referred to as the **slope** of the regression line? A slope can be defined as the number of units of change on the *y* axis (that is, in the *y* coordinate) when the *x* coordinate changes one unit. Both *a* and *b* can be either positive or negative. A positive *b*, for example, produces a regression line that travels up to the right in the graphic space, reflecting a positive association between the variables. A negative *b* reflects a negative association between the variables, and the regression line slants down to the right in the graphic space. Suppose that our scattergram looked like the one in Figure 9.7 and that we just eyeballed the pattern of dots, using a ruler to draw a straight line that appeared to be a good fit. In this case, $a = 0$ and $b = 2$, and the formula for this regression line would be: $y = 0 + 2x$. Note that when $x = 0$ and we solve the formula for y, $y = a = 0$, which is the *y* intercept of this regression line. The slope of the line (*b*) is positive and has the value 2. Hence, for every 1 unit we move up in value (that is, to the right) on the *x* axis, the *y* coordinate increases (goes up) two units. It follows that for every one unit of change on the *x* axis, there are two units of change on the *y* axis. For example, in Figure 9.7, if we move one unit on the *x* axis (say, from 2 to 3), the *y* coordinate changes two units, from 4 to 6. Note that the same ratio of change (one to two) holds no matter with which value of *x* we begin.

Suppose we have gathered data on two ratio level variables for each of the fifty largest cities (our units of analysis) in the United States: the per citizen

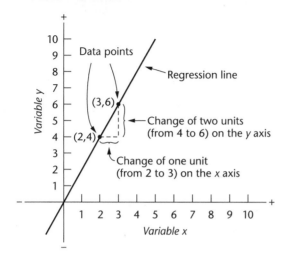

A Scattergram Showing the Elements for Interpreting the Slope of a Regression Line

$$\text{Slope} = b = \frac{\text{change in } y}{\text{change in } x} = \frac{2}{1} = 2$$

expenditure for police services, which for these purposes will be considered the independent variable (x), and crime rate, the dependent variable (y). Suppose, further, that the pattern of dots in the scattergram suggests that a negative and approximately linear relationship exists between the variables. That is, as per citizen expenditure goes up, the crime rate goes down. (Note that if the pattern of dots suggests no relationship or at least no linear relationship, there is little point in pursuing a regression analysis.) We decide to identify the formula for the regression line that best fits the data (that is, the straight line that minimizes the distances between it and the dots in the scattergram.) How do we determine the numerical value of the constants a and b in the linear function $y = a + bx$ for our scattergram?

We could do it by eyeballing or by trial and error, drawing a number of straight lines in the field of dots, measuring the distances between the dots and each of the lines, with a ruler, choosing the line that resulted in the lowest sum of differences. These procedures, however, leave us more or less guessing about the best-fitting regression line.

Once again, however, statisticians come to the rescue, employing what is called the *least (sum of) squares criterion*. The proof is complicated; for our purposes, we will simply note that, when x is designated as the independent variable, the slope (b) of the best-fitting regression line is given by:

Formula 9.2

$$b = \frac{\Sigma \, (x - \bar{x}) \, (y - \bar{y})}{\Sigma \, (x - \bar{x})^2}$$

Remembering that each data point has an x and a y coordinate, the numerator tells us to subtract the x coordinate for a particular data point from the mean of x, and the y coordinate for the same data point from the mean of y, and then multiply the result, to perform these calculations for every data point, and then sum these products. The formula for the y intercept (a) is:

Formula 9.3

$$a = \bar{y} - b\bar{x}$$

Having determined the values of the constants, a and b, we can enter them in Formula 9.1, which then becomes the formula (function) for the best-fitting regression line for our particular scattergram. For every value of x in our data, we can predict the corresponding y value by solving Formula 9.1 for y.

Suppose for our data set that we calculate $a = 175$ and $b = -2$. This result indicates that the y intercept for our regression line would be $y = 175$ when $x = 0$. The slope of the regression line would be -2, the minus sign indicating a negative relationship between the two variables, and the quantity 2 indicating that for every one unit of change on the x axis there will be two units of change on the y axis. The formula for our regression line would be:

$$y = 175 - 2x$$

Substituting a value for x (in our case, a particular per citizen expenditure amount) in this formula, we can solve the equation for y, thus arriving at a prediction or estimation of the crime rate associated with the expenditure.

Note that the predicted y values will only rarely fall exactly on the regression line. That is, our prediction of y, given a particular x value, will usually be in error to some extent. Hence, the ys predicted from our linear function are referred to as *estimates* of y. The difference between the actual and the predicted y coordinate of a data point in the scattergram is referred to as a **residual** or an **error of estimate** (see Figure 9.6).

In general, the smaller the sum of the residuals in our scattergram, the better the data fit the regression line. Put somewhat differently, the smaller the sum of the residuals, the more accurate our predictions of y from x will be.

So far in our discussion we have assumed that the residuals have been measured parallel to the y axis of the graph, reflecting the error in the y coordinate produced by our regression line prediction. This way of measuring the residuals is dictated by our designation of x as the independent variable. Formulas 9.2 and 9.3 (for the values of b and a) are based on this designation. The regression line formula that results is referred to as the function for the regression of y on x, symbolized as $y.x$.

Suppose that we designated y, instead of x, as the independent variable. In this case we would be measuring the residuals parallel to the x axis. The formula for b in the regression equation assuming this way of measuring the residuals would become:

Formula 9.4

$$b = \frac{\Sigma (x - \bar{x})(y - \bar{y})}{\Sigma (y - \bar{y})^2}$$

and the formula for a would be

Formula 9.5

$$a = \bar{x} - b\bar{y}$$

Compare Formula 9.2 with 9.4 and Formula 9.3 with 9.5. What similarities and differences do you find? It should be clear that, in most cases, when we designate *y* as the independent variable in the same scattergram and calculate the values of *b* and *a* by Formulas 9.4 and 9.5, they would be different from those arrived at by Formulas 9.2 and 9.3 based on *x* as the independent variable. Obviously, substituting the two different values for *b* and *a* into Formula 9.1 will result in different regression lines. The lines will have different slopes (*b*), and in the regression line for *x.y*, *a* will be the *x* intercept.

When using regression line formulas for prediction, two cautions must be noted. First, remember that the residual or error of estimate can be large. Second, it is dangerous to use a regression formula to predict much beyond the range of the values used to calculate the regression formula in the first place. Doing so essentially assumes the variable relationship remains linear over the entire range of variable values, and that, of course, may not be true. Consider the scattergrams in Figure 9.5. Suppose we calculated a regression line using values of *x* from 0 to 7 and values of *y* from 0 to 11 and then used the formula to predict the value of *y* for *x* = 12. How accurate would our predictions of *y* be if the actual relationship were as depicted in Figure 9.5 for values of *y* > 7?

CORRELATION ANALYSIS

These observations bring us to our discussion of correlation analysis. As we noted earlier, correlation analysis is primarily concerned with measuring the strength of the relationship between two variables. One way of thinking about the strength of a bivariate relationship is as a measure of the average distances between the dots and the corresponding best-fitting regression line. The smaller these distances, on average, the stronger or higher the correlation between the two variables. One of these measures, developed by Karl Pearson, is the correlation coefficient, symbolized by *r*.

Correlation coefficients indicate both the direction (positive or negative) and the degree of the relationship between two variables. They range from +1.0 to –1.0, the former (*r* = +1.0) being generated if all of the dots in a scattergram fall precisely on a diagonal line similar to the one in Figure 9.3, the latter (*r* = –1.0) being produced if all the dots fall precisely on a diagonal line similar to the one in Figure 9.4. The closer the dots fall to such diagonals, the higher the correlation coefficient generated by the data. The Pearson correlation coefficient can be used only with continuous data that have been measured at least at the interval level.

You will be spared the complicated procedures for deriving the formula used in calculating the descriptive statistic *r*. But we can think of *r* as a kind of average of the two slopes (*b*s) of the regression lines *x.y* and *y.x*. That is, *r* has the same value whether we consider *x* or *y* as the independent variable. We might think of r as based on measuring the residuals in the third way we noted earlier in our discussion—namely, perpendicular to the average of the two regression lines, $x.y$ and $y.x$.

One formula for calculating r that reflects its dependence on a combination of the two slopes (bs) of $x.y$ and $y.x$ is:

Formula 9.6

$$r = \sqrt{(b_{x.y}) \, (b_{y.x})}$$

Another formula algebraically equivalent to Formula 9.6, but based on sums of squares is:

Formula 9.7

$$r = \frac{\Sigma \, (x - \bar{x}) \, (y - \bar{y})}{\sqrt{\Sigma \, (x - \bar{x})^2 \, (y - \bar{y})^2}}$$

Let's examine one more formula for r expressed in terms of z-scores:

Formula 9.8

$$r = \frac{\Sigma \, (z_x) \, (z_y)}{n}$$

To use this formula, we would first convert the values of x and y into their standard score equivalents by Formula 7.4 in Chapter 7. Now recall that each dot in our scattergram can be designated by its coordinates (x,y). In this formula, z_x, is the standard or z-score equivalent of the x coordinate for a data point and z_y is the z-score equivalent of the dot's y coordinate. The numerator in this equation says that we should multiply the z-score coordinate values for each dot in our scattergram, sum these products, and then divide by n, the number of units of analysis in our study group. Note that, like the mean of a frequency distribution, the magnitude of this result can be influenced substantially by a few very large (or very small) coordinate values—often referred to (for obvious reasons) as *outliers* in a scattergram. If a scattergram includes outliers, as does the one in Figure 9.8, great caution must be exercised in interpreting quantitative results.

A comparison of r (the correlation coefficient) and b (the slope of a regression line) is instructive. Like regression functions, correlation coefficients have predictive value. If r is positive, say, $r = +0.85$, those who scored high on one variable also tended to score high on the other, and those who scored low on one variable also tended to score low on the other. A negative r indicates that those who scored high on one variable tended to score low on the other. However, if our correlation coefficient is close or equal to zero, knowing the value of one variable does not enable us to predict the value of the other.

As with b (the slope of a regression line), r can be positive or negative, indicating a positive or negative bivariate relationship. But Formula 9.8 tells us that r can be calculated from standard scores and is, therefore, itself a standardized statistic. It can assume values only from −1.0 to +1.0. In contrast, the b in a regression equation can, in principle, assume virtually any positive or negative value.

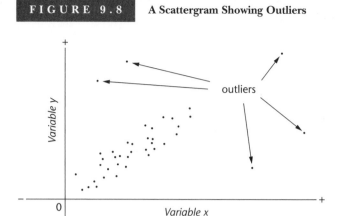

FIGURE 9.8   **A Scattergram Showing Outliers**

One other important difference between the regression coefficient (*b*) and the correlation coefficient (*r*) should be noted. First, in discussing the linear function $y = a + bx$, we noted that the regression line produced was the regression of *y* on *x*. If *y* were the independent variable, we would have another formula and, in almost all cases, a different regression line. Residuals would be measured parallel to the *x* rather than the *y* axis of the graph, and a different sum of residuals (or squares) would result. (Can you state the regression line formula, assuming *y* as the independent variable?) In contrast, *r* does not depend on the designation of an independent and dependent variable; it has the same value whichever variable we designate as independent.

Actually, the quantity r^2 (or $r \times r$), called the **coefficient of determination,** is somewhat easier to interpret. Recall our discussion in Chapter 7 of measures of dispersion of a frequency distribution. One of those measures was the variance (s^2), which is calculated by squaring another of the measures of dispersion, the standard deviation (*s*). Again, without going into the details of the underlying statistical rationale or the mathematical calculations, we can think of r^2 as a measure of the proportion of the variance in the dependent variable accounted for by the independent variable. Consider the two scattergrams in Figure 9.9, where the independent variables are on the horizontal axes and the dependent variables are on the vertical axes. We have raised a vertical dotted line above a given value of the independent variable in each scattergram and marked the range of values of the dependent variable that are associated with this value. This range can be taken as an indicator (a measure) of the amount of variance in the dependent variable accounted for by the independent variable. Note that in the scattergram in Figure 9.9, the range of scores on the dependent variable (from about 5 to 14) for the given value of the independent variable (6) is larger than the corresponding range (from about 8 to 11) in the lower scattergram. This can be interpreted to mean that the independent variable in the lower scattergram accounts for more of the variance in the

FIGURE 9.9

Two Scattergrams Showing Different Amounts of Variance in the Dependent Variable Accounted for by an Independent Variable

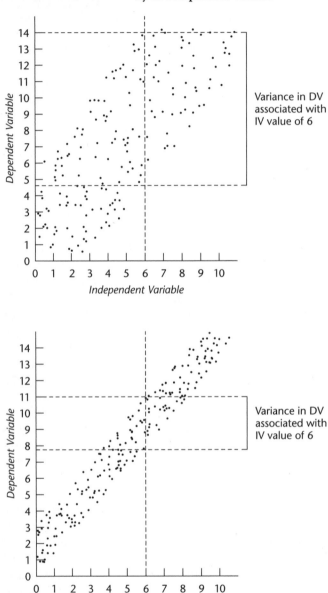

dependent variable. Note also that in both scattergrams, knowing the value of the independent variable does not permit one to predict perfectly what the value of the dependent variable will be. (Perfect prediction would result only if all of the dots fell on a straight line.) This can be interpreted to mean that some of the variance in the dependent variable remains unexplained by the independent variable. But we can say that the independent variable in the lower scattergram explains more of the dependent variable variance than does the independent variable in the upper scattergram.

Suppose the correlation coefficient (r) between crime rates and the proportion of the population who own handguns is +0.6, then $r^2 = 0.36$. In this case, variations in the proportion of handgun owners can be said to account for (or explain) 36 percent of the variations in crime rate. Of course, that means that 64 percent of the variation in crime rate remains unaccounted for. Remember that the word *explain* here refers only to **statistical explanation.** A causal explanation, as noted previously, requires an appropriate time sequence and the elimination of other potentially causal variables.

Multiple and Partial Correlation

Although we have discussed the correlational technique as a way of measuring the direction and degree of the relationships between two variables, the same basic idea can be extended to a measurement of the relationships between a dependent variable and two or more independent variables. One of the statistics used for quantifying these relationships is called the **multiple correlation coefficient,** usually symbolized by R. The corresponding R^2 is called the **coefficient of multiple determination,** and its interpretation is analogous to that of r^2. That is, R^2 is the proportion of variance in the dependent variable accounted for by the combined effects of however many independent variables are included in the calculations. Suppose, for example, that you are attempting to account for changes in the crime rate over time and assume that several variables contribute to these changes. If you can measure these variables at the interval or ratio level, you can use a multiple correlation analysis to determine the combined effects of all of your hypothesized independent variables. You could determine the combined contribution of, say, the proportion of the population owning handguns, the proportion of the population between the ages of 14 and 21, and the unemployment rate to the crime rate. As with r, R measures only *linear* relationships, so an R equal to or near zero means only that no linear relationship exists among the variables; however, nonlinear relationships may be present.

Another analytic strategy employing correlation coefficients is **partial correlation.** In partial correlation, the strategy is to hold the value of one independent variable constant and then examine the relationship between the remaining independent variables and the dependent variable. Perhaps, for example, we are interested in the independent variables "city population" and "rate of gun ownership" as they might relate to the dependent variable "homicide rate." We could first run a multiple correlation analysis to determine if population and gun ownership rate together were related to homicide. If there was a relationship, we could run a partial correlation analysis, say examining the relationship between gun ownership rate and homicide, holding population size constant. Note that this analysis is *not* equivalent to ignoring population size. Rather, it asks whether, in cities of about the same size (that's what "holding population size constant" means) there is a relationship between the rates of gun ownership and homicide rates. The basic ideas here are analogous (though not identical) to those underlying elaboration analysis with contingency tables (see Chapter 8). In the latter case, you will recall, we began with a zero-order, bivariate cross-tabulation. Each of the values of a third variable, which we called a control or test (t) variable, was then used to construct a partial table. By comparing the partial tables with each other and with the zero-order table, the test variable's influence, if any, on the original zero-order relationship could be assessed and implications for causal inference drawn. In partial correlation analysis, we examine t's influence on an original, zero-order, bivariate correlation coefficient. In the case of partial correlation analysis, however, we must assume that there is no interaction between t and our original independent variable.

The specific strategy involved in partial correlation analysis depends on the level at which t is measured. When t is nominal or ordinal, the study group is subdivided, creating a separate subgroup for each of the values of t. Separate rs are then calculated for each of these subgroups and compared with each other and with the zero-order r (r_{xy}). Interpreting the results of such an analysis follows essentially the same lines of argument we used in elaboration analysis. For example, assuming the time sequence of the variables was appropriate, if all of the partial rs were approximately zero, we would say the zero-order r was spurious; if the r for one of the partials was higher than the zero-order r, whereas the rs for the other partials were near zero, we would have a specification; and so on.

When t is measured at the interval or ratio level, we can calculate a single partial correlation coefficient that measures the impact of the third variable on the original r. The general formula for a partial correlation coefficient is:

Formula 9.9

$$r_{xy.t} = \frac{r_{xy} - (r_{xt})(r_{yt})}{\sqrt{(1 - r_{xt}^2)(1 - r_{yt}^2)}}$$

For $r_{xy.t}$, read the correlation between x and y with t held constant. The zero-order correlation coefficient between x and y is r_{xy}, the correlation coefficient between x and t is r_{xt}, the correlation coefficient between y and t is r_{yt}. In essence the formula gives us the correlation between the residuals of the regression of x on t and of y on t.

Interpreting $r_{xy.t}$ is essentially similar to the process discussed above. That is, if $r_{xy.t}$ is approximately equal to r_{xy}, we would say t has no influence on the relationship between x and y (a replication in elaboration analysis terms). If $r_{xy.t}$ is zero (or nearly so) we would say that r_{xy} is spurious.

Procedures and formulas for incorporating variables measured at the nominal or ordinal levels through the use of dummy variables and for analyzing the effects of two or more control variables simultaneously in correlation analysis are available in advanced statistics texts.

Because single, multiple, and partial correlation coefficients may have predictive value, a serious error in reasoning may occur in using them. That is, a researcher simply assumes that the existence of a correlation indicates causation. As we pointed out in Chapter 3, correlation (or concomitant variation) is a necessary but not sufficient condition for causation. High correlation coefficients alone do not permit us to make causal inferences.[2] In fact, in the social sciences, very high correlation coefficients (even multiple ones) arouse suspicion that they are spurious for one reason or another. The reader should keep this point in mind whenever correlation coefficients are presented as part of an analysis of data.

CORRELATION AND CROSS-TABULATION

Our earlier discussion of cross-tabulation focused on the importance of specific rows and columns and their comparison. When a cross-tabulation involves two variables measured at the ordinal level or above, however, it is often useful to examine the diagonals of a table to determine whether or not the two variables are correlated.

Diagonals

To gain a general understanding of the use of **diagonals** in reading a table, recall our earlier discussion of scattergrams and correlation. Figure 9.10 represents a scattergram with a data grid like the ones we used in constructing tables superimposed on it. Suppose we counted the dots included in each of the cells in the data grid, erased the dots, and entered the number of dots in the corresponding cells. We would then have a cross-tabulation of the two variables corresponding to the scattergram with which we began.

In converting the scattergram into a cross-tabulation, we have divided the range of the values (0 through 12) into four segments: 0.00–2.99, 3.00–5.99, 6.00–8.99, and 9.00–12.00. In the cross-tabulation, original scores ranging from 0.00 through 2.99 for each variable have been collapsed into a single new value, those from 3.00 through 5.99 form a second new category, and so on.

We can also approximate the pattern of the dots in some scattergrams by drawing a straight, solid line to represent the general pattern of the data. In this example, the line would pass from the lower left-hand cell of the table to the upper right-hand cell, and its path would take it through several other cells in the table as well. The cells through which the line passes constitute one diagonal of the table. Figure 9.11 shows that there are two diagonals in each table.

If the cell frequencies tend to be larger in the cells that lie on or near either one of the two diagonals than in those remote from it, we can conclude that a linear relationship exists between the two variables. (The reader should figure out which of the diagonals corresponds to a positive relationship and which to a negative relationship.) As in the case of correlation, the absence of a linear relationship (concentration of higher frequencies or percentages in the diagonals) does not necessarily mean that the variables are unrelated. If the cells we have connected with a dotted line in Figure 9.11 contained the higher frequencies, a nonlinear relationship between the variables would be indicated.

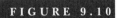

FIGURE 9.10 A Scattergram with Superimposed Data Grid

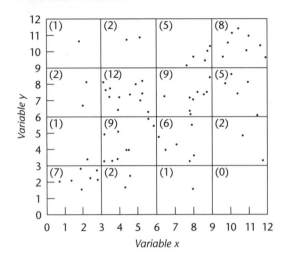

FIGURE 9.11 Linear and Nonlinear Relationships in Tables

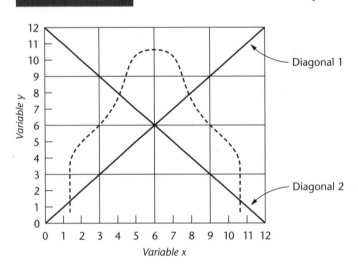

OTHER STATISTICAL MEASURES OF ASSOCIATION

Regression and correlation analyses assume interval or ratio measurements of at least two of the variables being correlated. There are other measures of association, some of which may be used with tables for variables measured at the nominal level, such as Lambda. Others can be used on variables measured at the ordinal level, such as the Spearman Rank Order Correlation Coefficient and Kendall's Tau. Like Pearson's r, they all rest upon certain assumptions about levels of measurement, size of the study group, and so forth. Any good statistical manual will provide you with a list of these assumptions and the appropriate uses of these measures of association.[3]

REVIEW QUESTIONS

1. What is a scattergram?

2. What is a regression line? What is the formula for a regression line?

3. What is the y intercept of a regression line?

4. What is the slope of a regression line?

5. What is a residual or error of estimate?

6. Compare and contrast regression and correlation analysis.

7. How do linear and curvilinear relationships differ?

8. Is there a relationship between the slope of a regression line (b) and the correlation coefficient (r)?

9. What does $r = +1.0$ mean? $r = -1.0$? $r = 0.0$? $r = +0.5$? $r = 0.2$?

EXERCISES

1. Using the data from the table at the end of Chapter 8, construct a scattergram of the "score on criminal justice test" and "IQ score" variables.

2. Draw an approximate regression line in the scattergram. Estimate the slope of the regression line and identify the y intercept. Write the formula for the regression line you have drawn.

3. In a scattergram space you create, draw regression lines with a slope of 0, +1, –1, +0.1, –10. Discuss the results. What does each of these regression lines tell us about the relationship between the variables?

NOTES

1. The correlation coefficient is often referred to as Pearson's r, after the late nineteenth- and early twentieth-century statistician, Karl Pearson, who developed this and related measures of association between and among variables. His work, in turn, is derived from that of Sir Francis Galton, who pioneered the study of correlation and regression analysis.

2. Richard Runyon and Audrey Haber, *Fundamentals of Behavioral Statistics*, 2nd ed. (Reading, MA: Addison-Wesley, 1971), p. 125.

3. See, for example, Herman J. Loether and Donald T. McTavish, *Descriptive Statistics for Sociologists* (Newton, MA: Allyn & Bacon, 1974); and Theodore Anderson and Morris Zeldich, Jr., *A Basic Course in Statistics* (New York: Holt, Rinehart & Winston, 1975).

CHAPTER

10

An Introduction to Inferential Statistics and Parameter Estimation

Suppose a researcher is interested in the distribution of some characteristic (that is, variable) concerning the police officers (or offenders or crimes committed) in a major U.S. city during a specified period of time. As we noted in our discussion of populations and samples in Chapter 4, the population being studied would consist of *all* of the officers (or offenders or crimes) in the particular city during the specified time period. The researcher's goal is to make descriptive statements about the entire set of persons, events, or other units included in the defined population. Collecting data on every unit might seem, therefore, to be the ideal research strategy.

For many reasons, however, it is often either impossible or impractical to study an entire population. In such circumstances, the best strategy is to select and study a sample and then use the data from the sample to learn something about the population as a whole. **Inferential statistics** are numerical tools that enable us to generalize from a sample to the population from which it was drawn with some specifiable degree of confidence that the generalizations are correct.[1]

Once a sample is selected and the data assembled, the distribution of any particular measured variable can be described by calculating a proportion, percentage, mean, standard deviation, or other measures of central tendency or dispersion discussed in Chapter 7. When these measures are calculated for distributions of sample data, they are called **sample statistics.** The corresponding measures for the population—that we do not know, but want to estimate by using sample statistics—are called **population parameters.**

If we could be certain that the sample accurately represented the population from which it was drawn, this task would be easy, for we would know that the values of the population parameters were the same as the values of the corresponding sample statistics. Unfortunately, when we take advantage of the convenience of sampling, we cannot avoid some uncertainty about the representatives of our sample. We might draw a sample whose statistics are exactly like the population parameters. But we might also get a sample whose statistics are very different from the population parameters. Furthermore, the degree of correspondence between statistics and **parameters** will vary from sample to sample drawn from the same population. In short, some samples will be more representative of the population than will others.

When there are differences between the sample statistics and the parameters of the population from which the sample was selected, we say that these differences are due to **sampling error.** The less representative the sample, the larger the sampling error, and the greater the difference between our sample statistics and the corresponding population parameters. Whenever we use a sample to represent a population, then, we run some risk of sampling error.

The researcher's uncertainty, created by the possibility of sampling error, is enhanced by another troublesome consideration: In most cases, we do not know and have no way of finding out exactly what the population parameters are. Therefore, it would appear that we have no way of knowing exactly how much, if any, sampling error has occurred. However, we can reduce these uncertainties and increase our confidence that samples can be used effectively if we do two things: (1) select our sample in the best way possible; and (2) use inferential statistics to make inferences about the population parameters from our sample statistics.

First, which methods of sampling are the best? A sample should be selected that has the best chance of being representative of the population, in order to minimize sampling error. As noted in Chapter 4, perhaps the most important sources of potential bias or error in a sample are the researcher's own conscious or unconscious biases during the sampling process itself. In our discussion of sampling techniques in Chapter 4 we pointed out that the best—that is, most representative—sample is most likely to be achieved through probability sampling, such as a simple random sample.

In a simple random sample, each unit in the population has the same chance (or probability) of being included in the sample, and each selection of a population unit is *independent* of the selection of every other unit from the population. To draw a random sample we must have a complete list of all elements in the population. Each element must be "tagged" with a unique number, and then the sample is drawn with the aid of a random numbers table. Remember that we use this carefully planned and controlled process to ensure that each element in the population has the same *probability* of being chosen for the sample. By drawing a sample in this way, we eliminate any conscious or unconscious biases of the researchers during the sample selection process. As a result, a random sample is much superior to a quota, accidental, purposive, or any other type of nonprobability sample where we have little or no control over the probability of an element being selected and where the conscious or unconscious biases of the researcher may be involved. In short, a probability sample is more likely to be representative of the population from which it is drawn than is any other type of sample. We can minimize the uncertainty in sampling by using a probability sampling technique.

An alert reader may very well agree with our argument so far, but point out that we have not yet solved the basic sampling issue. Probability samples may be better (that is, more representative of the population) than other types, but they too are subject to sampling error. The truth is that the possibility of sampling error cannot be eliminated, but by drawing a probability sample, some limits and, therefore, some control can be imposed over the sampling error uncertainties that remain through the use of inferential statistics.

It is beyond the scope of this text to consider in detail the mathematical theories upon which inferential statistics are based. In the sections of this chapter that follow, however, the general ideas involved will be introduced. Inferential statistics are based on a branch of mathematics called probability theory, and, although we did not mention it explicitly at the time, we used some elementary principles of probability theory to define a random sample. Because probability principles are built into the sampling process, probability-based inferential statistics can be used to estimate the amount of sampling error.

Before proceeding to a more technical discussion, let us introduce a rather simple example to describe what we are trying to accomplish through the use of inferential statistics. Suppose you spot a friend standing on the street corner outside the student union. Broke, as usual, you would like to buy a cup of coffee before returning to your study of research methods in criminology. Although you know that your friend does not like to lend money, you also know that she likes to gamble. Being a bit of a risk taker yourself, you decide that you might bet her the price of a cup of coffee that in 10 flips of her quarter, she will get no more than 4 heads. How would you determine your chances of winning the bet?

You recognize, of course, that if your friend accepts your bet and flips the coin 10 times, any number of heads, from zero to 10, might turn up. Furthermore, the outcome of the bet will be determined by the sum of the outcomes of 10 separate flips of the coin. Hence, your chances of winning the bet are tied in some way to the chances or odds of getting a head in a single flip of the coin. You are also aware that once your friend flips the coin 10 times, you will either win or lose the bet. Nevertheless, if you had some way of estimating the likelihood that your friend would turn up 4 heads or fewer in a sample of 10 tosses of the coin, you could estimate your chances of winning the bet.

DETERMINING PROBABILITIES
EMPIRICALLY AND MATHEMATICALLY

One way you might attempt to determine the likelihood that a given proportion of heads will turn up in 10 tosses of the quarter is to try it yourself. If your friend will let you borrow her quarter, you could flip it 10 times, noting the number of heads that came up. Suppose you found that the coin landed heads 8 times. Would you be willing to infer that you would get 8 heads in the next set of 10 tosses? Might you not observe 3 heads in the next set of 10 tosses, 6 in the next, and so on? In short, if you relied on the sample statistic (in this case, the number or proportion of heads) from any *single* sample of 10 coin tosses to estimate the corresponding parameter (in this case, the number or proportion of heads in all possible samples or sets of 10 flips of the coin), you would clearly be in danger of making an incorrect estimate because of sampling error.

Suppose, however, you took a large number of samples, each consisting of 10 tosses of the coin, and recorded the proportion of heads that turned up in each sample. To help you evaluate the data you have assembled regarding the proportion of heads in 10 tosses of a coin, you could construct a bar graph frequency distribution of your sample statistics. Table 10.1 shows our results when we took 100 samples consisting of 10 coin tosses each, whereas Figure 10.1 shows the bar graph distribution of our sample statistics.

TABLE 10.1	Record of Results from 100 Samples of 10 Coin Tosses Each*		
Proportion of heads obtained in 10 tosses of a coin		*Number of occurrences*	*Proportion of occurrences*
0.00		0	0.00
.10		0	0.00
.20	++++++	6	.06
.30	+++++++++++	11	.11
.40	+++++++++++++++++++	19	.19
.50	+++++++++++++++++++++++++++	27	.27
.60	++++++++++++++++++++++	22	.22
.70	++++++++++	10	.10
.80	+++++	5	.05
.90		0	0.00
1.00		0	0.00
		$n = 100$	Total = 1.00

*Note: Each (+) represents one sample of 10 tosses.

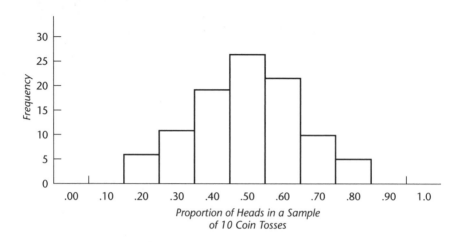

FIGURE 10.1

Bar Graph Frequency Distribution of Proportions of Heads in 100 Samples of 10 Tosses of the Coin

The distribution in Figure 10.1 can be used to estimate the probability that any given proportion of heads will occur in 10 tosses of a coin over the long run. Our distribution suggests, for example, that the most likely outcome, in proportion of heads, is .50 (occurring 27 percent of the time), followed closely by .60 (22 percent of the time), and .40 (19 percent of the time). Although outcomes of 0.0, .10, .90, and 1.00 are theoretically possible, they appear highly unlikely. In fact, these outcomes did not occur in any of our samples.

From the information provided by our distribution of sample statistics we could estimate the likelihood of getting more than 4 heads by observing that in 36 (6 + 11 + 19 = 36) of the samples we took, 4 or fewer heads turned up, whereas in the remaining 64 samples, more than 4 heads occurred. Hence, we might infer that, over the long run, you will win your bet 36 percent of the time and lose it 64 percent of the time. Those are not very good odds. Even though you might be lucky and win your bet this particular time, you had probably better offer to make a different kind of bet or plan on having that coffee another day.

Let us review what we have done in this example. We began with a bet concerning the proportion of heads that would turn up in 10 flips of a coin, noting that the bet would be won or lost in a single set of 10 flips and that a risk was involved in making the bet. We reasoned that if we could determine how often, in the long run, we could expect any given proportion of heads to turn up, we could use that knowledge to estimate our chances of winning the bet. Aware that sampling error might occur, we took a relatively large number of samples from the population consisting of all possible sets of 10 flips of a coin and examined the distribution of the sample statistic, proportion of heads, in these samples. From that distribution we estimated our chances of getting 4 or fewer heads.

Now suppose we change our perspective a bit about the distribution in Figure 10.1. Given an ordinary coin, we assume that each time we flip it honestly a head is just as likely to turn up as a tail. We might assume, therefore, that in any even number of flips, we should get exactly 50 percent heads and 50 percent tails. However, we also recognize that, in a given series of flips (say 10), we will not always get exactly 5 heads and 5 tails. We are aware that there is a chance factor involved. When we flip a coin 10 times and do not get exactly 5 heads and 5 tails, we assume that an error of some kind—in effect, an error due to chance—has occurred. Another way of looking at the distribution in Figure 10.1, then, is that it represents a distribution of errors due to chance, which occurred in our samples of 10 flips of the coin. This chance variation in our sample statistic is another way of defining the concept of sampling error, introduced at the beginning of this chapter. As we shall see later, the general idea of errors due to chance—sampling error—is extremely important in the use of inferential statistics.

Although the betting example illustrates what we are trying to accomplish through inferential statistics, it is impractical and unrealistic as a general procedure for determining the likelihood of particular outcomes. Usually, because of time and money limitations, we can only investigate one sample drawn from our population. Besides, if we had to take many samples to learn something about the distribution of our sample statistic, the usefulness of sampling as an alternative to studying the entire population would quickly diminish. We must be able to infer something about a population on the basis of data from a *single* sample. To do that we must determine the characteristics of the distribution for our sample statistic without actually taking a large number of samples.

SAMPLING DISTRIBUTIONS AND SAMPLING ERROR

Fortunately, a solution to this problem is provided through the application of certain mathematical procedures derived from probability theory. These procedures are commonly referred to as *inferential statistics,* because they are statistical ways of inferring some characteristics of a population from sample data.

Remember that we need a distribution of our sample statistic so that we can estimate *sampling error.* Instead of actually taking a large number of samples and deriving a distribution of sampling error empirically (as we did when we flipped our coin and created Figure 10.1), a hypothetical or theoretical distribution of a sample statistic can be derived mathematically. To do so, three specific theoretical (mathematical) steps must be taken. First, all of the mathematically possible outcomes (values) of the measurement of a variable pertaining to a particular unit of the population must be specified and a probability assigned to each (that's what we did when we said that the possible outcomes of flipping a coin were a head and a tail, and that a head was as likely as a tail). Second, all of the mathematically possible outcomes (values) of a series of such measurements must be specified (as we did in the left-hand column in Table 10.1). Third, probabilities must be assigned to each of the outcomes (values) specified in step 2 (we arrived at the figures in the right-hand column of Table 10.1 empirically, by actually flipping a coin; now we will create the right-hand column by mathematical calculation). The result of these procedures is a mathematically constructed distribution of the sample statistic. This theoretical or hypothetical distribution is called the **sampling distribution** for that particular sample statistic.

The sampling distribution serves the same purpose as the empirically derived distribution in Figure 10.1. That is, it permits us to make quantitative statements about the probabilities associated with getting a particular outcome in a single sample. (We used the distribution in Figure 10.1, you will remember, to tell us what the probability was of getting no more than 4 heads if we toss a coin 10 times.) The difference, again, is that our sampling distribution is created not empirically, but mathematically. Let us see now how we might construct a mathematically derived sampling distribution.

Suppose that we are interested in an event that has two possible outcomes, such as a decision made by an officer to arrest or not to arrest a juvenile stopped for questioning. Mathematically, this is equivalent to flipping a hypothetical coin—heads, let us say, represents a decision to arrest and tails represents a decision not to arrest. To make comparisons with what we have described in our betting example easier, we will use the hypothetical coin flip in the discussion that follows and call each single flip of the coin a *trial*. If we ignore the possibility that the coin may get lost or land on its edge, a trial has two possible outcomes: no head (that is, 1 tail), and 1 head.

We begin by assuming that the two possible outcomes of a single trial are equally probable. Expressed in probabilities, then, our initial theoretical assumption is that we expect to get no head 50 percent of the time (probability of no head $p_t = .50$) and one head 50 percent of the time (probability of one head $p_h = .50$). Note that the sum of the probabilities associated with the possible outcomes of this event is 1.00. This is always the case, no matter how many possible outcomes of an event there are, according to probability theory.

Now suppose we consider a series of trials consisting of a specified number of flips of the coin. We assume that for each trial in the series, $p_t = p_h = .50$. Here, too, we could identify all of the possible results, expressed in terms of the proportion of heads that could turn up in the series. The number of possible results would depend on the number of flips we assume to occur in the series; for example, there would be 11 possible results in a series of 10 trials (0, .10, .20, . . . 1.0), 101 possible results in 100 trials (0, .010, .020, . . . 1.0), 1,001 in 1,000 trials (0, .001, .002, .003, . . . 1.0), and so on.

Although the probabilities of the two possible outcomes in a single trial are equal, the probabilities associated with the possible results of a *series* of trials are not equal. That is, in a series of trials we would not always expect to get exactly .50 heads and .50 tails; we might get .40 heads in some, .80 heads in others. But if our initial assumptions about the equal probabilities of each of the possible outcomes in a single trial are correct, probability theory tells us something more about what we can expect. For example, we can expect to get .40 or .50 or .60 heads more often than we can expect to get .10, .20, or .90 heads. In fact, we can use a mathematical probability model known as the **binomial distribution** to determine the *exact* probability associated with each of the possible outcomes.

The Binomial Distribution

Suppose we want to know the exact probability of getting precisely 4 heads in 10 tosses of a coin. The calculation involves the following components:

$p(k)$	the probability of getting k heads
k	the number of heads specified (in our case, 4)
t	the number of trials or tosses (in our case, 10)
$t-k$	the number of tails (in our case, $10 - 4 = 6$)
p_t	the probability of getting a head in a single trial or toss of the coin (in our case $p = .50$)
P_h	the probability of getting a tail in a single trial or toss of the coin (remember that $p_t + p_h = 1.0$ and, therefore, that $1.0 - p_h = p_t$; in our case, then, $p_t = .50$)

The general binomial formula to be used in the calculation is:

Formula 10.1

$$p(k) = \frac{t!}{k!\,(t-k)!}\; p_t^{\,k} p_h^{\,t-k}$$

Note the similarity between the first term in Formula 10.1 and Formula 4.1 in Chapter 4. See the discussion of Formula 4.1 if you need to be reminded about how to interpret the factorial sign (!). To calculate the probability of getting exactly 4 heads in 10 trials we would proceed as follows:

$$p(4) = \frac{10(10{-}1)(10{-}2)(10{-}3)(10{-}4)(10{-}5)(10{-}6)(10{-}7)(10{-}8)(10{-}9)}{4(4{-}1)(4{-}2)(4{-}3)\;\;6(6{-}1)(6{-}2)(6{-}3)(6{-}4)(6{-}5)}\; .50^4\,.50^{10-4}$$

$$p(4) = \frac{10(9)(8)(7)(6)(5)(4)(3)(2)(1)}{4(3)(2)(1)\;\;6(5)(4)(3)(2)(1)}\; .50^4\,.50^6$$

$$p(4) = \frac{3628800}{17280}\,(.0625)\,(.015625)$$

$$p(4) = 210\,(.0625)\,(.015625)$$

$$p(4) = .205$$

Compare this result with the proportion of occurrences entry for .40 heads (the proportion 4 is of 10) in Table 10.1.

The binomial distribution can be used as a sampling distribution whenever we are investigating a series in which each trial has two possible outcomes. For example, it can be used as the sampling distribution for determining the chances of winning the coin toss bet, or for analyzing an officer's decision to arrest or not arrest a juvenile. The major difference is that our sampling distribution is mathematically derived on the basis of the assumption that the coin is unbiased—that is, that in each flip of the coin a head is theoretically just as likely to turn up as a tail. (A real coin, of course, may or may not be unbiased, or a

TABLE 10.2	Probability Sampling Distribution of Outcomes (in Proportion of Heads) for 10 Trials (Flips of Coin), from Binomial Distribution

Proportion of Heads	Probability (p)
.00	.001
.10	.010
.20	.044
.30	.117
.40	.205
.50	.246
.60	.205
.70	.117
.80	.044
.90	.010
1.00	.001
	Total 1.000

real coin flipper may or may not flip the coin honestly.) Table 10.2 shows the mathematical probabilities of obtaining various results in 10 tosses of a theoretical, unbiased coin, and Figure 10.2 is a bar graph distribution of the results in Table 10.2. Along the horizontal axis in this graph, we have placed all of the possible results (expressed as proportion of heads) in any single sample of 10 tosses of a coin—0, .10, .20, and so on—found in the left-hand column of Table 10.2; the vertical axis of the graph has been converted to proportions as well. That is, instead of representing the raw frequency with which a particular proportion of heads occurs, it indicates the proportion of times in a series of trials a particular proportion of heads is *likely* to turn up. The height of each bar in the graph is derived from the probabilities in the right-hand column in Table 10.2.

We can use this sampling distribution to determine the likelihood of obtaining any particular proportion of heads, providing we assume that tails are just as likely as heads in any single flip of the coin. Because (according to probability theory) the probability of obtaining any one of a *set* of possible results equals the sum of the probabilities associated with each of the results in the set, the probability of getting 4 heads or fewer—that is, the probability of winning our bet—can be determined by summing the probabilities associated with getting zero, 1, 2, 3, and 4 heads. The probability of winning our bet, then, is .001 + .010 + .044 + .117 + .205 = .377. Note how close this mathematically derived estimate is to the empirically derived estimate (.36) obtained by actually flipping a real coin 10 times on 100 occasions.

By this summation method, we can determine the probability of obtaining any specified range of results—say, of getting a proportion of .40 through .60 heads. Adding the respective probabilities associated with each of the results (from Table 10.2) would give us: .205 + .246 + .205 = .656. Thus, according to the binomial distribution, we have a .656 probability of getting 4, 5, or 6 heads, if the probability of a head is equal to the probability of a tail in a single trial.

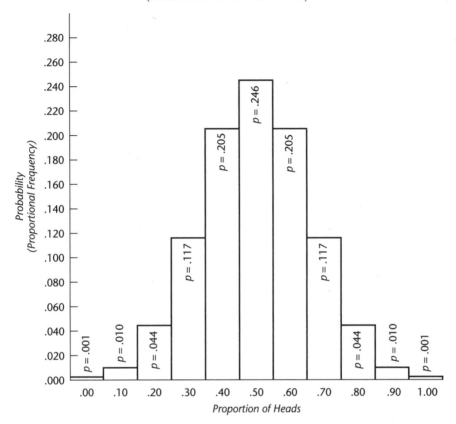

FIGURE 10. 2 Bar Graph Frequency Distribution of Probabilities
of Proportion of Heads in 100 Samples
of 10 Tosses of a Hypothetical, Unbiased Coin
(from the Binomial Distribution)

Now, look at the bar graph distribution in Figure 10.2 again. By converting this bar graph to a line graph, we would have the distribution in Figure
10.3. Note the shape of this distribution and compare it to the shape of the
normal curve in Figure 7.13. They are remarkably similar, aren't they? It
should not be difficult to imagine that, had we chosen to consider 1,000 samples of 10 tosses and then 10,000 samples of 10 tosses of our hypothetical coin,
we would get a distribution increasingly like the normal curve. For practical
purposes, we can say that if our sample size is large, say over 50, the binomial
distribution is essentially equivalent to the normal curve. Another way of saying this is that the normal curve is an approximation of the binomial sampling
distribution when the sample size is large.

Recall that we began our discussion of the binomial sampling distribution
by assuming that the probability of heads was equal to the probability of tails
in a single toss of our theoretical coin; that is, p_h (heads) = p_t (tails) = .50. Note
that the distribution of probabilities in Figure 10.3 has a mean proportion of
.50. Probability theory tells us that, if a head and a tail are equally probable in

FIGURE 10. 3 **Line Graph Frequency Distribution of Probabilities of Proportion of Heads in 100 Samples of 10 Tosses of a Hypothetical, Unbiased Coin (from the Binomial Distribution)**

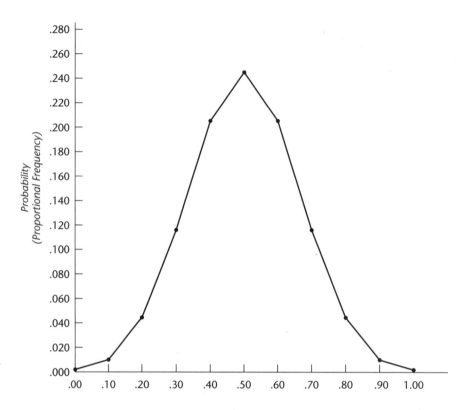

a single toss of the coin, the sampling distribution of proportion of heads in a series of tosses has a mean proportion of .50. If we were actually flipping a real, unbiased coin, .50 is the proportion of heads that we would expect to get in the long run if we flipped it many times, keeping track of the number (and proportion) of heads that turned up as we flipped. Note that .50 is also the mean proportion of heads we would expect to get if we took many actual samples consisting of 10 or 100 or 1,000 flips of the coin and averaged the results from all the samples we took. In the absence of other data, then, the best guess or estimate that we could make of the proportion of heads that would come up in any single trial or in any series of trials is this mean (.50).

One additional important point should be made about probability theory and the binomial sampling distribution. Although we will not provide the mathematical proof here, when probability principles are built into the sampling process (as in random sampling), the sampling technique itself provides an important part of the theoretical justification for using sampling distributions. By taking a random sample, for example, probability theory can tell us how our sample statistic (for example, proportion of heads) will "behave"—that is, how the proportion of heads will be distributed around the mean proportion of .50—in our sampling distribution. Any sampling distribution, whether it is normal, skewed, or some other shape, tells us how sample statistics will be distributed if we have used a probability sampling technique. As we shall see, knowing how a statistic from a random sample behaves—that is, knowing the shape of the sampling distribution—is extremely useful in making estimates of population parameters.

Having established that the binomial sampling distribution we have been considering can be approximated by the normal curve, we can take one further preliminary step. As we noted in Chapter 7, any normal curve can be converted to a standard normal curve, which has many important properties that can be used in our discussion of inferential statistics. It would be helpful to you to review the discussion of normal and standard normal curves and z-scores in Chapter 7 before reading further.

As previously discussed, the standard normal curve may be described as a unimodal curve, symmetrical about the mean, with a mean of zero and a standard deviation of 1. Recall, too, that areas under the curve can be expressed in standard units called z-scores.

In inferential statistics, a sampling distribution is considered a distribution of probabilities. Some sampling distributions, as we have noted, are normal distributions. Areas under a sampling distribution curve correspond to probabilities. Normal curve sampling distributions, then, can be converted to a standard normal curve of probabilities with a mean of zero and a standard deviation of 1. In order to distinguish it from the standard deviation of distributions based on actual data, the standard deviation of a theoretically derived normal sampling distribution is called its **standard error,** reminding us that a sampling distribution is, as we have seen, a distribution of sampling error.

We said at the beginning of the chapter that there were inevitable uncertainties about the representativeness of samples, and we described certain steps we could take to reduce those uncertainties. The first step was taking a probability sample. For illustrative purposes, we chose the random sampling technique because, in the absence of any other guide, it gave us our best chance of getting a representative sample. We noted that, in a random sample, elements in the population are equally likely to be included in the sample. The second step was to determine the sampling distribution of our sample statistic. The sampling distribution indicates the probabilities of securing a particular result (or range of results), given the probability assumptions we make in creating the sampling distribution. We noted that many probability sampling distributions have the shape of the normal curve, whose properties would be useful in making *estimates* of population parameters. In particular, these properties help specify (in probabilities) the amount of sampling error that may occur.

If we take probability samples and use inferential statistics, we have gone as far as we can in reducing the uncertainties associated with using samples to represent populations. We have not, of course, completely eliminated all uncertainties—it is, in fact, not possible to do so. Using inferential statistics on our sample data requires us to be content with *estimates* of population parameters and statements about the *probabilities* that these estimates are correct. But both the theory upon which inferential statistics are based and years of experience by researchers with these procedures testify to their usefulness.

SAMPLING DISTRIBUTIONS FOR OTHER SAMPLE STATISTICS

As noted, the binomial distribution is useful for creating a sampling distribution when there are two equally probable outcomes in a single trial. When the samples are large, it produces a normal sampling distribution, and we can use the properties of the normal curve to great advantage when those proportions are the sample statistics being used.

We can use this same general argument in constructing sampling distributions for many other, although not all, sample statistics. For example, it is easy to imagine that the distribution of the mean salaries calculated from many large samples of police officers on a large urban police force (such as Chicago's) would be normally distributed with a mean very near the actual mean salary for the entire population of officers. Samples where the mean salary would be at least close to the actual population mean would be more frequent than would samples whose mean salary was quite different from the population mean salary. In short, the sampling distribution for sample means is also a normal distribution. Furthermore, if we continued to sample Chicago's Police Department, the mean of the distribution of mean salaries from the various samples would come closer and closer to the actual population parameter, that is, the actual mean salary of all C.P.D. officers. But it is not necessary to actually draw a large number of samples to arrive at a sampling distribution of means for the C.P.D. Just as a mathematically derived binomial distribution can be used as a sampling distribution for proportions, a mathematically derived distribution of sample means can be generated and used as a sampling distribution for sample means.

In the case of means, the **central limit theorem** provides the basis for the mathematical derivation of the sampling distribution. According to this theorem, the sampling distribution of means for large samples will be a normal curve, with a mean equal to the mean of the scores for the population, and a standard error (that is, variance) equal to the population standard deviation divided by the square root of n, where n is the sample size.

For normal sampling distributions, when the mean of a sample statistic's sampling distribution is equivalent to its corresponding population parameter, the sample statistic is referred to as an *unbiased estimate* of the corresponding population parameter. As we have just seen, a sample mean is, in this sense, an unbiased estimator. (Note that just because a sample mean is an unbiased estimator, it may still differ from the actual population parameter, due to sampling error.) On the other hand, the mean of the sampling distribution of standard deviations (for large samples) is *not* equivalent to the population standard deviation; a sample standard deviation is therefore referred to as a *biased estimate* of the population standard deviation. When sample statistics are recognized as biased estimators, statisticians make adjustments in the calculation formulas to improve the estimate.

Not all sampling distributions are normal distributions, however; for example, the sampling distribution for standard deviations is skewed for small samples ($n \leq 100$). When the sampling distribution is not normal, it may be possible to determine the shape of the distribution through the application of other mathematical models. If that is not possible, the sampling distribution may be created by having a computer simulate the empirical method we used to construct the distribution in Figure 10.1. That is, the computer would simulate taking many samples from the same population, calculating the sample statistics in question for each sample, and then making a distribution of these sample statistics. Statisticians have used mathematical models or computer simulations to create sampling distributions for many sample statistics.

However it is derived, the sampling distribution is typically presented in the form of a table that gives the probabilities associated with the various values of the particular sample statistic being used. Regardless of the shape of the sampling distribution or the technique used to create it, however, the sampling distribution always serves the same basic purpose: It permits us to say how probable a particular result from a single sample is, given the initial assumptions used to create the sampling distribution.

A FEW WORDS
ABOUT NONPARAMETRIC STATISTICS

In discussions of inferential statistics and sampling distributions, two types of statistics—parametric and nonparametric—are usually differentiated. The type we have been concerned with primarily in this chapter is called **parametric inferential statistics.** Although there are disagreements among statisticians about the importance of the distinction between the two types of inferential statistics, for our purposes, we shall simply note the two differences between them that are commonly cited.

The first difference concerns the level of measurement of a variable that is appropriate for each type (for a review of levels of measurement, see Chapter 7). Parametric statistics assume the measurement of a variable at the interval or ratio level; **nonparametric inferential statistics** may be used with nominal or ordinal level data.

The second difference between parametric and nonparametric inferential statistics has to do with assumptions concerning the shape of the distribution of the values of the variable being studied. Parametric statistics are appropriate when the values are distributed normally in the population. Nonparametric statistics, on the other hand, are said to be "distribution free." That is, to use nonparametric inferential statistics, it is not necessary to assume anything about the shape of the distribution of the variable in the population.

Although parametric and nonparametric statistics may be distinguished in the ways we have discussed, there is one important similarity that should be mentioned. The sampling distributions for both types are based on the assumption that a probability (usually a random) sample has been chosen.

When a variable is measured at the nominal or ordinal level and when it seems inappropriate to assume that the variable is normally distributed in the population, nonparametric inferential statistics may be the best choice. Discussions of the most popular nonparametric statistics may be found in many inferential statistics texts.

We can now return to the issue with which we began this chapter: How can we use sample statistics to learn something about the parameters of the population from which the sample is drawn?

POINT AND INTERVAL ESTIMATION

Suppose we want to estimate a population parameter, say a population mean such as the mean IQ of police recruits. If we have taken a simple random sample, we could simply estimate that the mean IQ of the population is equal to the mean IQ of the recruits in our sample. In effect, we are making what is called a **point estimate** of the population parameter. It is called a point estimate because, although we recognize that the sample mean may vary from the population mean to some extent, only one value (or point) is used—namely, the numerical value of the sample mean—as our estimate. Point estimates have a desirable simplicity and specificity and are, in fact, our best single-value estimate of the population parameter. However, these attractive characteristics must be weighed against the fact that the probability of our sample mean being exactly the same as the population mean is relatively small. In short, the probability that the point estimate is in error to some extent is relatively high.

We could make a safer estimate of the population parameter if we used an **interval estimate** instead of a point estimate. That is, we could specify a range around the sample statistic and estimate that the population parameter falls within that range. Returning to our example of mean IQ scores, suppose we observe that the sample of recruits has a mean IQ of 120. Instead of saying that the estimate of the mean IQ in the population is 120 (a point estimate), we could add and subtract a fixed quantity (for example, 5 or 20) from the sample mean and say that it is somewhere between 115 and 125 or between 100 and 140 (interval estimates). Obviously, the wider the range we specify, the greater the likelihood that the specified interval will include the population mean. The increased confidence we gain by specifying a wide range, however, must be balanced against the decreased precision of our estimate.

Confidence Intervals and Confidence Limits

The interval around the sample statistics that we specify for the purpose of estimating the population parameter is called a **confidence interval.** The end points of the specified range are the **confidence limits** for the interval.

How do we establish a confidence interval and specify the confidence limits? Suppose, again, that we are interested in making an estimate of a population's mean IQ. Because we know that the sampling distribution of means is a normal probability distribution, we can use the special properties of normal curves and z-scores to create intervals of various sizes. By choosing a particular value of z, we can specify the probability that the interval we create includes the population mean.

To understand the process by which these intervals are created, we must introduce some additional mathematical symbols. Remember that we are using sample statistics to estimate population parameters. To distinguish between the mean IQ score for the population and the mean IQ score for our sample, we use the symbols $\overline{X}$ and $\overline{x}$. Likewise, S and s represent the standard deviation of IQ scores for the population and for our sample, respectively. $\sigma_{\overline{x}}$ refers to the standard error of the mean (that is, the standard deviation of the sampling distribution of means for a large number of random samples drawn from the same population), and $s_{\overline{x}}$ refers to an estimate of the standard error of the mean. As before, n is the number of police recruits in our sample.

Expressed in these mathematical terms, then, we want to make an interval estimate of $\overline{X}$, the mean IQ score of the population of police recruits that we have sampled. To do so, we will make use of the sample statistics $\overline{x}$, s, and n (which we can calculate from our sample data), as well as our general knowledge about sampling distributions for means, to make estimates of X, S, and $\sigma_{\overline{x}}$. These estimates will be used in conjunction with the standard normal curve (z-scores) to create the interval estimate of $\overline{X}$.

To establish the center point for the interval, the sample mean IQ score ($\overline{x}$) is used as the estimate for the population mean IQ score ($\overline{X}$). Next we need an estimate of the standard error of the mean ($\sigma_{\overline{x}}$). At first it might seem that the standard deviation of our sample statistic (s) could be used for this estimate. But think for a moment about the dispersion of scores in the two relevant distributions—the distribution of IQ scores in our sample of recruits and the distribution of the mean IQ scores from a large number of samples of a particular size (n) drawn from the same population. Suppose that the distribution of individual IQ scores looks like Figure 10.4.

The distribution of means from a large number of samples of size n drawn from the same population (that is, the sampling distribution) might look something like Figure 10.5. That is, the standard error of the mean ($\sigma_{\overline{x}}$) shown in Figure 10.5 would be considerably smaller than the standard deviation (s) of scores (Figure 10.4) in our sample. If we used the sample standard deviation to estimate the standard error of the mean, our estimate would be much too large.

All is not lost, however, because we have the central limit theorem. It tells us that there is a relationship between the standard error of the mean ($\sigma_{\overline{x}}$) and the standard deviation of the individual scores in the population (S) from which the sample was drawn. Without going into the details of its derivation, there is a constant relationship between these two quantities, which is represented by Formula 10.2.

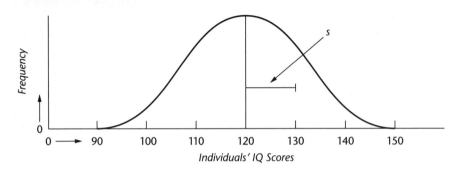

FIGURE 10.4

Distribution of Individuals' IQ Scores for a Sample of Size *n*, Showing the Standard Deviation (*s*)

Formula 10.2

$$\sigma_{\bar{x}} = \frac{S}{\sqrt{n}}$$

Here, $\sigma_{\bar{x}}$ is the standard error of the mean, S is the standard deviation of the individuals' IQ scores in the population, and n is the size of the sample. You may have noted that we still have not arrived at our goal of estimating the standard error of the mean. We do not know the value of S because we have observed only a sample statistic, not the entire population. We can, however, use our sample standard deviation (s) as an estimate of the standard deviation in the population (S).

Hence, we could use Formula 10.3 to estimate the standard error of the mean:

Formula 10.3

$$S_{\bar{x}} = \frac{s}{\sqrt{n}}$$

where $S_{\bar{x}}$ is our *estimate* of the standard error of the mean ($\sigma_{\bar{x}}$), s is the standard deviation of the individual scores of our sample statistic, and n is the size of our sample.

However as we noted just above, this would yield a biased estimate. Because the mean of the sampling distributions for standard deviations tends to be somewhat smaller than the corresponding population's standard deviation, the conventional means of improving the estimate is to subtract one from the sample size. Thus, to calculate the best estimate of the standard error of the mean, we use Formula 10.4.*

---

*Note that, in constructing the distribution in Figure 10.5, we have assumed for illustrative purposes that the mean of the sampling distribution has the same value as the sample mean (120)—an assumption that may, of course, be incorrect. In general, however, sampling distribution standard errors are much smaller than sample standard deviations.

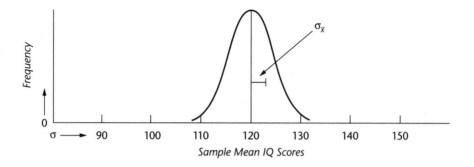

FIGURE 10.5

Distribution of Mean IQ Scores for a Large Number of Samples of Size _n_ (that is, a Sampling Distribution for Means), Showing the Standard Error ($\sigma_{\bar{x}}$).

Formula 10.4

$$S_{\bar{x}} = \frac{s}{\sqrt{n-1}}$$

It is useful at this point to review our progress. Our basic objective is to use a sample statistic (in this case, mean IQ, $\bar{x}$) to estimate the corresponding population parameter $(\overline{X})$. We know that some sampling error is likely whenever we sample, and that as a result, x probably will not have exactly the same value as X. We also know how the means of random samples of a fixed size (n), drawn from the same population, are distributed; that is, we know that the sampling distribution for means is a normal curve. We know, too, that there is a constant relationship between the standard error of the sampling distribution for means $(\sigma_{\bar{x}})$ and the standard deviation of the distribution of individual scores in the population (S), expressed in Formula 10.2. We know that the sampling distribution can be treated as a probability distribution; that is, that an area under the curve defined by specifying a range of values of the mean corresponds to the probability that a particular sample mean will fall within that range. We don't know the value of $\overline{X}$, but we can put together the statistics we calculate from our sample data with what we know about sampling distributions of means to make an interval estimate of the population mean. To do so, we make a number of estimates. We use x to estimate $\overline{X}$, and we use s and n to calculate $S_{\bar{x}}$, which, when factored into Formulas 10.3 and 10.4, gives us our estimate of $\sigma_{\bar{x}}$.

Having determined our estimate of the standard error of the mean, we can now turn to a discussion of the use of z-scores in creating confidence intervals for estimating population parameters from sample statistics. Remember that, in the absence of any other data, our best estimate of the population mean is the mean of our sample data. To improve our chances of making an accurate estimate of the mean IQ score for the population $(\overline{X})$, we want to create a range or interval around the sample mean $(\bar{x})$ within which we will estimate the population mean $(\overline{X})$ to fall. Furthermore, we want to state the probability that our population mean ($\overline{X}$) actually falls within the range we specify.

The general formula for constructing a confidence interval around our sample mean with a specified confidence level that the population mean falls within the interval is

Formula 10.5

$$cl = \overline{x} \pm z\, (S_{\overline{x}})$$

In Formula 10.5, cl stands for confidence limits, $\overline{x}$ is the sample mean, and $S_{\overline{x}}$ is the estimate of the standard error of the mean for samples of size n from Formula 10.4. The confidence interval is the range between $\overline{x} - z\,(S_{\overline{x}})$ and $\overline{x} + z\,(S_{\overline{x}})$. We calculate the values of $\overline{x}$ and $S_{\overline{x}}$ for our sample data. Then, by entering different values of z in this formula, we can construct confidence intervals of different sizes, with corresponding differences in our level of confidence that the range we have determined includes the population mean.

As we learned in Chapter 7, the proportion of area under the standard normal curve between $z = -1.96$ and $z = +1.96$ is .95 (see Figures 10.6 and 7.14). If we wanted to be 95 percent confident that the specified range will include the population mean we would enter a z value of 1.96 in Formula 10.5. If we wanted a 99 percent confidence interval, we would substitute 2.575 for z in Formula 10.5.

Returning to our example of police recruits, recall that our sample mean IQ ($\overline{x}$) is 120. Suppose our sample size (n) is 100, the standard deviation of IQ scores in our sample (s) is 16, and we decide to establish a 95 percent confidence interval. Our estimate of the standard error of the mean (from Formula 10.4) is given by:

$$S_{\overline{x}} = \frac{s}{\sqrt{n-1}} = \frac{16}{\sqrt{100-1}} = \frac{16}{\sqrt{99}} = \frac{16}{9.95} = 1.61$$

Our 95 percent probability or confidence limit formula would then give us

$$cl = 120 \pm 1.96\,(1.61).$$

The confidence limits would then be:

$$120 + 1.96(1.61) = 123.16$$

and

$$120 - 1.96(1.61) = 116.84$$

Hence, given our sample data, we can say that there is a .95 probability that the population mean IQ will be included in the interval between 116.84 and 123.16. By using the general formula and the table of z-scores in Appendix B, we can determine the confidence limits for any confidence level we wish, simply by substituting different values of z in Formula 10.5. The confidence interval that we establish constitutes our interval estimate of the population parameter (in this case, the mean IQ) in which we are interested.

FIGURE 10.6	**Using the Standard Normal Curve as a Probability Curve for Establishing Confidence Intervals**

95% of the area under the probability curve
is included in the interval $z = -1.96$ to $+1.96$

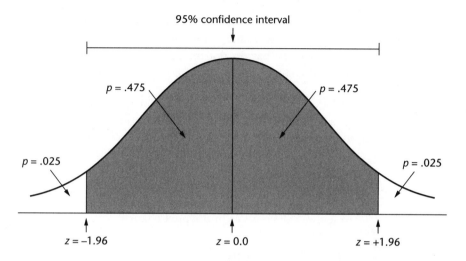

Note that in specifying an interval within which we estimate our mean to fall, we are, in effect, making an allowance for sampling error. The larger the interval we specify, the larger the sampling error for which we allow and the safer our estimate.

Note also that the formula we used to obtain our estimate of the standard error of the mean $(S_{\bar{x}})$ included the term, $\sqrt{n-1}$. Hence, sample size plays an important role in establishing confidence limits, but the size of the population is irrelevant in these calculations. This is true so long as we are dealing with relatively large samples of, say, at least 30 cases. Calculating confidence limits for small samples requires the use of additional correctional procedures in the formulas we have discussed. We will not discuss these procedures here. Nevertheless, an examination of Formulas 10.4 and 10.5 shows that as sample size (n) increases, the confidence interval associated with a particular confidence level (for example, 95 percent or 99 percent) gets smaller. This, in turn, means that as the sample size increases, our estimates of population parameters from sample statistics become more precise.

A few words of caution about inferring population parameters from sample statistics are in order. First, when you encounter a statistic, such as a crime rate, that purports to refer to the characteristics of a large population, you should ask yourself whether the data reported are actual population data or whether they are sample statistics used as point estimates of population parameters. It is permissible to make point estimates of population parameters, but it is important to indicate that this is what has been done.

Second, confidence limits should be interpreted with care. A confidence level of 95 percent, for example, means that if we took a large number of random samples and used each of the sample means to construct a confidence interval, approximately 95 percent of those confidence intervals would include the mean and approximately 5 percent would not. This suggests the usefulness of *replication*—repeating the study by drawing a different sample from the same population and calculating new confidence intervals at the same confidence level. The *two* confidence intervals can then be compared. The chances of getting two confidence intervals that do not include the population mean are much smaller than the chances that a *single* confidence interval does not include the mean.

Third, inferential statistics are based on probability theory principles that assume probability sampling, and enable us, therefore, to estimate sampling error. However, they do not enable us to assess the influence of other types of bias that may have entered into our research procedures, such as poor research design, careless operationalization of the variables, and so forth.

Finally, although some sampling distributions, such as those for proportions and means, are normal, some are not—for example, the distribution of chi square (χ^2), which we will consider in the next chapter.

REVIEW QUESTIONS

1. Compare and contrast population parameters and sample statistics.
2. What is sampling error?
3. What is a sampling distribution?
4. What are the principal differences between parametric and nonparametric inferential statistics?
5. Compare and contrast point and interval estimates of a population parameter.
6. Compare and contrast standard deviations and standard errors.
7. Why is the standard deviation of scores in a distribution larger than the standard error of the sampling distribution for the mean of those scores?
8. How and why can z-scores be used to create confidence intervals and establish confidence levels?

EXERCISES

1. Take your own 100 samples of 10 flips of a coin, recording the proportion of heads that occur in each sample of 10. (Be sure the coin is tossed so that it turns over several times in the air before you catch it.) Then construct a frequency distribution of sample results and compare it with Table 10.1 and Table 10.2. Construct a bar graph of your results and compare it with Figures 10.1 and 10.2. Are there differences? How would you account for these differences?

2. Suppose you have selected a random sample of forty persons from a population of 2,000 and measured their ages. Suppose further that the ages in your sample are normally distributed with a mean of 26 and a standard deviation of 2.5 years. Make a point estimate of the population mean. Calculate 50 percent, 95 percent, and 99 percent confidence intervals for estimates of the population mean. Write a paragraph interpreting the results.

3. Using the same sample statistics, calculate 50 percent, 95 percent, and 99 percent confidence intervals for a sample of size 200. Compare these with the results you obtained above. What do the differences in results tell you about the effects of sample size on interval estimates?

NOTE

1. The foundations of inferential statistics and probability distributions, such as the normal distribution, were developed in the eighteenth and nineteenth centuries by, among others, Abraham De Moivre, the Marquis de la Place, and Karl Friedrich Gauss. The work of the latter was so important that the normal distribution is sometimes referred to as "the Gaussian distribution." In its early development, the normal distribution was also referred to as the "great Law of Error" because it represented the variation (errors) in measurement of many different phenomena. For an interesting discussion of the origins and politics of the development and application of the descriptive and inferential statistics, see William Ray Arney, *Understanding Statistics in the Social Sciences* (New York: W. H. Freeman, 1990).

11

Inferential Statistics: Hypothesis Testing

TESTING HYPOTHESES

A hypothesis is a hunch or proposition that a researcher hopes to confirm or reject by assembling and analyzing relevant data. Whatever variable(s) the hypothesis may be about, it can usually be translated into an assertion about a population parameter or a relationship between population parameters. When we gather data on an entire population, we can confirm or reject our hypothesis by examining the data we have. Frequently, however, we must rely on sample data to test a hypothesis about a population; in this case, we can use what we learned in Chapter 10 about probability and sampling distributions to help us.

A hypothesis asserting that changes in the values of a particular independent variable will cause changes in the values of a dependent variable will be referred to here as a **research hypothesis.** We cannot test such a hypothesis directly, however, because any changes in the dependent variable that we observe in our sample data may have resulted from sampling error. Suppose, though, that we formulate an alternative hypothesis, referred to as a **null hypothesis,** asserting no changes in the dependent variable *except* those resulting from random (sampling) error. We can then construct a sampling distribution based on this assumption. This hypothetical distribution permits us to determine the probability that any given result will occur *if the null hypothesis is correct.* We can then test the research hypothesis indirectly by testing the null hypothesis directly. If our actual results have a very low probability if the null hypothesis is true, we have some empirical support for an alternative hypothesis—our research hypothesis. We must remember, though, that in rejecting the null hypothesis when our observed results have a low probability, we are still taking a risk. That is, even though the results that we obtain are unlikely to have occurred by chance under the null hypothesis, they still may have occurred by chance in this particular instance. Again, this possibility illustrates the importance of replication studies.

Type I and Type II Error

Actually, in making a decision to accept or reject a null hypothesis, we always risk making one of two possible types of error. The first, called a **Type I error,** occurs when we reject a null hypothesis that is, in fact, correct. The second, a **Type II error,** happens when we fail to reject a null hypothesis that should be rejected. Estimating the probability of making a Type II error is a complicated procedure beyond the scope of this text. Estimating the risk of making a Type I error, however, is considerably less difficult. In fact, this is what we do when we construct a sampling distribution, establish a significance level, and test the null hypothesis.

Suppose our research hypothesis is that children who watch a violent television program will be more violent in their play after the program than children who watch a nonviolent program. This research hypothesis might be translated into an assertion that the mean number of violent acts during play will be higher for children who watch a violent television program than for those who watch a nonviolent one. This is, in effect, an assertion about a population parameter: the mean number of violent acts of children in play. More particularly, it is an assertion about differences between means for two groups, one that had seen a violent program and another that had not. To assemble the relevant data, we select third-grade students in a school and draw two independent random samples of fifty students each from this population. One group is shown a violent television program, and the other group a nonviolent one. In a play period following the television program, the violent acts of each child are counted (of course, what constitutes violent behaviors has been determined in advance). We then calculate the mean number of violent acts for each group.

The null hypothesis in this case asserts that there will be no difference between the mean number of violent acts for these two groups; that is, in effect, the two groups are samples from the same population. To test the null hypothesis, we need the sampling distribution for the differences between two sample means, assuming that the samples were selected at random from the same population. The shape of this particular sampling distribution, called **Student's** t or simply t, varies with sample size. We shall consider the t test in more detail later in this chapter. For the present purposes, it will suffice simply to observe that if the sample is large (30 or more), $t = z$ and our sampling distribution is the standard normal (z-score) distribution (see Figure 7.14).

We could calculate z for the particular difference between the means we have observed. Then, referring to a sampling distribution of z in a z table (see

Appendix B), we could determine the probability of obtaining (by chance) a difference in mean number of violent acts as large as the one observed, if in fact the two sample means came from two different samples drawn at random from the same population.

Certain values of our sample statistic will permit us to reject the null hypothesis. Values that are highly improbable, assuming that the null hypothesis is true, are called **contradictory values.** These contradictory values constitute the **rejection region,** bounded by the *critical values* for the null hypothesis.

Significance Level

Which values of our sample statistics will lead us to reject the null hypothesis? The answer to this question depends on how much risk we are willing to take of rejecting a null hypothesis that is, in fact, true (that is, making a Type I error). Whatever risk we choose is called the **significance level** for our test of the null hypothesis. This level can be set at any value the researcher chooses in advance of the research, though the 5 percent and 1 percent levels are most commonly adopted. Establishing a significance level of .05 means that we run the risk of making a Type I error 5 times out of 100; a significance level of .01 reduces that risk to 1 in 100.

Suppose we select a .05 level of significance for the test of our hypothesis. We can now determine the *contradictory values* that comprise the rejection region on the sampling distribution curve for the null hypothesis. The critical values have been marked on the curve in Figure 11.1. Note that the critical regions begin at the point on the z axis where $z = +1.96$ and $z = -1.96$. These cutoff points, which establish the boundary lines between the rejection and acceptance regions, are called the critical values of the statistic. As you can see from the z table (Appendix B), 2.5 percent of the area under the right one-half of the curve lies beyond $z = +1.96$. Considering both halves of the curve, then, a total of 5 percent of the area under the curve lies outside $z = -1.96$ to $z = +1.96$.

Suppose that when we calculate z for the difference between means in our study, we get $z = 2.17$. Consulting the z table, we find that the probability of getting a difference between means of the magnitude we observed is .03 (that is, double the table value of .015, including both halves of the curve). Given that we chose a .05 level of significance, this result would permit us to reject the null hypothesis.

Remember that we are testing the null hypothesis (that is, that there is no statistically significant difference between the mean number of violent acts for our two samples of children). A probability of .03 means that only 3 times in 100 would a difference as large as the one observed occur if, in fact, there was no difference in the mean level. Another way of saying this is that we run a 3 percent risk of making a Type I error, that is, rejecting the null hypothesis when it is true. For a significance level of .05, we would reject the null hypothesis, leaving our research hypothesis as an alternative: Watching television violence is related to levels of violence in play. Note, however, that if we had set the significance level at .01, we could not reject the null hypothesis. Where we set the significance level depends upon what consequences may flow from

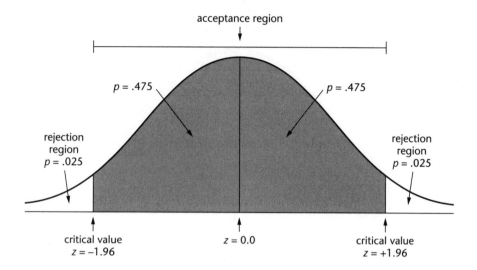

FIGURE 11.1   **Sampling Distribution for Differences Between Means from Two Large Random Samples Drawn from the Same Population, Treating *t* as a *z*-score, .05 Level of Significance—Two-Tailed Test.**

making a Type I or Type II error. What significance or confidence level would you set, for example, if the study concerned differences in death rates between two samples of patients, one of which was exposed to a controversial new drug?

One- and Two-Tailed Tests

The procedure just described is referred to as a **two-tailed test** of the null hypothesis, because areas in both the left- and right-hand tails of the sampling distribution were included in the rejection region (see Figure 11.1). In effect, by choosing a two-tailed test, we have declined to predict which of the two mean numbers of violent acts will be the larger one. Put another way, a two-tailed test is appropriate when the direction of the difference is not specified in our research hypothesis. (In such a case, our research hypothesis might be: The means of the two groups will be different.)

If, on the other hand, the research hypothesis does specify which mean will be larger (as ours does), we can use a **one-tailed test.** The advantage is that the percentage of area under the curve comprising the rejection region is now concentrated in only one tail of the sampling distribution. If, for example, we subtracted the mean for the control group (the group not exposed to the violent TV programs) from the mean for the experimental group (the group exposed to the violent TV programs), we would hypothesize that z would be positive. The critical value for a one-tailed test of the hypothesis at the .05 level of significance would be $z = 1.65$. (See Figure 11.2.) Hence, in this case, as compared with the critical values for a two-tailed test, smaller values of z (that is, smaller differences between the means) will permit the rejection of the null hypothesis; obviously, one-tailed tests are preferred whenever circumstances permit.

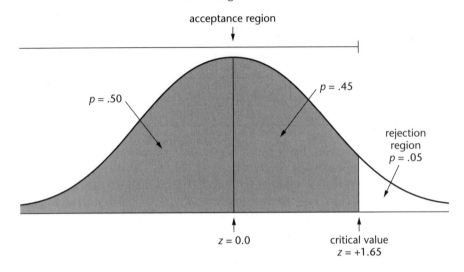

FIGURE 11.2 Sampling Distribution for Differences Between Means from Two Large Random Samples Drawn from the Same Population, Treating t as a z-score, .05 Level of Significance—One-Tailed Test

acceptance region

$p = .50$

$p = .45$

rejection region $p = .05$

$z = 0.0$

critical value $z = +1.65$

DIFFERENCE BETWEEN MEANS TEST (STUDENT'S t)

In the preceding section of this chapter, we noted that a t test for the difference between means could be used to help us decide whether exposure to violent TV programming affected violence in children's play.[1] This test is appropriate when the difference between two independent random sample means is to be tested for statistical significance. Obviously, because means are involved, the dependent variable must be measured at the interval or ratio level. The independent variable should be measured at the nominal or ordinal level; if it is measured at the interval or ratio level, more powerful techniques for assessing relationships between variables, such as correlation analysis, should be used. (You may wish to review the discussion of sampling distributions and standard error in Chapter 10 before continuing your reading here.)

As we saw in our discussion of parameter estimation and confidence intervals, to apply inferential statistics we need a sampling distribution, in this case for the difference between the means of two random samples drawn independently from the same population. We can get a general idea of the nature of this sampling distribution without going into all of the gory mathematical details. Suppose we draw two separate random samples of size n_1 and n_2, respectively, from a population, measure variable x for each element, and then calculate the mean of x for each of the samples ($\bar{x}_1$ and $\bar{x}_2$). (The subscripts 1 and 2 designate the first and second samples, respectively.) We could then subtract the second from the first mean ($\bar{x}_1 - \bar{x}_2$) and record the difference. Repeating this procedure many times and constructing a frequency distribution of the differences between the means would give us an empirically derived version of the sampling distribution we need.

Fortunately, statisticians have provided us with mathematically derived sampling distributions, called Student's *t* distributions, that we can use. We say distributions (plural) because there are different sampling distributions for different sample sizes when the samples are small. (Remember that when the samples are large [say, over 50], the *t* distribution closely approximates the normal distribution, and the values of *t* are essentially equivalent to those of *z*.)

As we also saw in our earlier discussion of confidence intervals, we need to know the mean and the standard error of our sampling distribution. Usually, all we have to work with in determining these characteristics of the sampling distribution are the data from our samples. In this case, though, a little thought should persuade you that in all such sampling distributions, the mean will be zero. You might think about it this way: If the two samples were, in fact, drawn from the same population and if there was no sampling error (that is, if the two samples were exactly representative of the population for variable *x*), $\bar{x}_1$ and $\bar{x}_2$ would have the same value (that is, $\bar{x}_1 = \bar{x}_2$) and the difference between $\bar{x}_1$ and $\bar{x}_2$ would be zero. Expressed in terms of a particular research situation, then, our null hypothesis is: $\bar{x}_1 - \bar{x}_2 = 0$.

Of course, as we have seen, whenever we sample we have to expect some sampling error. The question confronting us then becomes: How large can the difference between the sample means be before we should reject the null hypothesis and infer instead that the two samples were drawn from different populations? To answer this question we need to estimate the standard error (that is, σ, the square root of the variance, σ^2) of the sampling distribution.

Unlike for means, the standard errors for sampling distributions of differences between means vary with sample size. Hence, here, as in our earlier discussion of sampling distributions, we have to estimate the standard error for the appropriate sampling distribution using the information provided by our sample data. In this case, we have two samples and, therefore, two variances $(s_1^2$ and $s_2^2)$, which we can calculate from the respective samples.

Think again about our example of research on the effects of violent TV programming on violence in play. Here we had two samples: One watched a violent TV program, the other a nonviolent program. The amount of play violence after exposure to the TV programs was measured for each group. For each group we would calculate a mean number of violent acts and a variance, giving us two means and two variances to use for estimation purposes.

In most cases, for reasons that are beyond the scope of this text, the best estimate of the appropriate variance is achieved by combining the two sample variances to calculate what is called a **pooled sample variance,** which we can then use to estimate our sampling distribution's standard error. The formula for the pooled sample variance is:

Formula 11.1

$$S_p^{\,2} = \frac{(n_1 - 1)s_1^2 + (n_2 - 1)s_2^2}{(n_1 - 1) + (n_2 - 1)}$$

It can be demonstrated that Formula 11.1 is equivalent to the following one expressed in terms of the sum of squares:

Formula 11.2

$$S_p^{\,2} = \frac{\Sigma(x_1 - \bar{x}_1)^2 + \Sigma(x_2 - \bar{x}_2)^2}{(n_1 + n_2 - 2)}$$

Note the -2 in the denominator of Formula 11.2; this is a "correction" used to produce an unbiased estimate.

The pooled estimate of the standard error (the square root of the variance) for the sampling distribution of differences between two means is given by:

Formula 11.3

$$\sigma_{\bar{x}_1 - \bar{x}_2} = \sqrt{S_p^{\,2}\left(\frac{1}{n_1} + \frac{1}{n_2}\right)}$$

The formula for calculating t is:

Formula 11.4

$$t = \frac{\bar{x}_1 - \bar{x}_2}{\sqrt{S_p^{\,2}\left(\frac{1}{n_1} + \frac{1}{n_2}\right)}}$$

As noted above, for smaller samples, the sampling distribution of t is different for different sample sizes. Sample sizes are indicated by **degrees of freedom** (df).[2] The degrees of freedom for a given t statistic are arrived at by the following formula:

Formula 11.5

$$df = n_1 + n_2 - 2$$

Given a t table (see Appendix C), we can now determine the probability that a t we calculate occurred by chance if in fact the two samples are drawn from the same population. Once we decide on a significance level, we can consult the t table to determine whether we should accept or reject the null hypothesis.

To use the t test formulas presented above we must assume that we have two random samples drawn independently, a variable measured at the interval or ratio level (so that it makes sense to calculate means), approximately normal distributions of x, and approximately equal variances in the populations. Two samples are independent when selecting a unit for one sample has no effect on the probability of drawing any particular unit for the second sample. There are alternative formulas for t when the population variances are not equal and when the samples are not independently drawn (for example, when the study groups have been matched or the same group is measured before and after a "treatment" in an experimental design; see Chapter 3). Discussions of these procedures may be found in advanced statistics texts.

It is worth noting here, however, that when the sample sizes are about equal ($n_1 = n_2$), the formulas for t given here are applicable, even if the sample variances are divergent. Also, if the ns are large, Formula 11.4 can be used even if x is not normally distributed in the populations.

Finally, we can compare values of t and z for large ns, indicating, as we have noted previously, that the t distribution is approximately normal and that the values of t are approximately equivalent to z-scores. You can confirm this by comparing the values for df = infinity in the t table with the values of z in the z-score table (Appendix B). For example, find the row in the t table (Appendix C) corresponding to df = infinity (that is, the last row in the t table). Now find the column in this table corresponding to a level of significance of .025 for a one-tailed test and observe that the t value is 1.96. Now turn to the z score table (Appendix B). Find the entry in the table corresponding to a z value of 1.96. You will find the area beyond z to be .025.

Let us return briefly to the problem of differences in sample variances. As we noted, sampling error may produce differences in sample variances even if two random samples have been drawn from the same population. Actually, just as we can test for significant differences between sample means using the t test, we can test for significant differences between sample variances using another sampling distribution called the **F ratio**. The sampling distribution for the F ratio, typically referred to as the F distribution, is given in Appendix D.

Calculating F in this particular case is relatively straightforward. We simply determine which of the sample variances—s_1^2 or s_2^2—is the larger. Then we divide the larger sample variance by the smaller one. That is, we find the larger of:

Formula 11.6

$$F = \frac{s_1^2}{s_2^2} \text{ or } \frac{s_2^2}{s_1^2}$$

The F distribution also varies according to the size of both samples whose variances comprise the fraction used for calculating F. Hence, to read the critical value of F for the significance level we have chosen, we first find the F table corresponding to the selected significance level. (Note that there is a different table for different significance levels.) Then we locate the critical value of F in that table corresponding to the two ns involved. If the F we calculated is smaller than the critical value in the table, we can infer that the population variances do not differ, which means that we can use Formula 11.4 for calculating t, assuming, of course, that the samples have been drawn independently. If our F value is larger than the critical value, we can't assume equal variances, and an alternative t formula (available in more advanced texts) must be used.

We shall have occasion to consider the F ratio again (in slightly modified form) when we discuss analysis of variance in the next section of this chapter.

ANALYSIS OF VARIANCE (ONE WAY)

In certain research situations involving more than two independent random samples, testing for differences among means may be accomplished through a procedure called **analysis of variance**, or ANOVA.[3] In particular, as with the t test, ANOVA is appropriate when the independent variable is measured at the nominal or ordinal level and the dependent variable is interval or ratio. Also, as with the t test, the null hypothesis in ANOVA is that the means are equal (that is, that the real differences among the means is zero, and observed differences are due to sampling error). The sample statistic of concern in ANOVA is called the F statistic, and the applicable sampling distribution is the F distribution. As has been our practice, we shall attempt to convey only the general ideas underlying ANOVA.

First, let's return for a moment to our discussion of correlation, and in particular, r^2 (see Chapter 9). Recall that r^2 may be interpreted as the proportion of the variance in a dependent variable (y) explained (in the statistical, not the causal, sense) by variance in the independent variable (x). For example, if $r^2 = .36$, we said that 36 percent of the variance in y was explained by x. Of course, that leaves 64 percent of the variance in y "unexplained." (Put in terms of regression analysis, the slope of the regression line [b] reflects the explained variance; the residuals reflect the unexplained variance.) In effect, we partitioned the total variance of y into the sum of two parts: explained and unexplained variances.

The sampling distribution of the F statistic is a ratio of two variances, assuming the null hypothesis is correct (that is, that the three or more samples in our study were drawn randomly and independently from the same population). In particular, F is the ratio of explained to unexplained variance. In ANOVA, these two variances are referred to as the **between group variance** and the **within group variance,** respectively. The F ratio can be symbolically expressed as:

Formula 11.7

$$F = \frac{\text{between group (explained) variance}}{\text{within group (unexplained) variance}}$$

Now let's see what variances we're talking about in ANOVA. Suppose that the same written examination has been used as a part of the selection process for new police officers in four large cities. We wish to know whether the exam performances of the recruit pools in the four cities differ. To answer this question, we have taken a random sample of the exam scores over the last five years from each of the four cities. Suppose the scores in our samples were those in the four columns headed y in Table 11.1. Our research question can now be formulated as: Do the means of these four groups of exam scores differ significantly? Our null hypothesis is that they do not differ, which is the same thing as saying that the four samples were drawn from the same population, and any differences we observe among the four group mean scores are due to sampling error.

TABLE 11.1	**Exam Scores (y) for Police Recruits in Four Cities** **ANOVA-Related Calculations**

	City A		City B		City C		City D	
	y	y^2	y	y^2	y	y^2	y	y^2
	18	324	18	324	31	961	15	225
	16	256	25	625	39	1521	26	676
	30	900	22	484	17	289	19	361
	38	1444	37	1369	19	361	19	361
	22	484	40	1600	23	529	21	441
	35	1225	31	961	20	400	11	121
	19	361	40	1600	26	676	13	169
	25	625	34	1156	29	841	10	100
	33	1089	28	784	22	484	26	676
			40	1600	31	961	32	1024
			36	1296	21	441	28	784
			32	1024	26	676		

Σy	236		383		304		220	
							$\Sigma\Sigma y = 1143$	
n	9		12		12		11	
							$N = 44$	
$\bar{y}$	26.2		31.9		25.3		20.0	
Σy^2		6708		12823		8140		4938
							$\Sigma\Sigma y^2 = 32609$	
$(\Sigma y)^2$		55696		146689		92416		48400
$\dfrac{(\Sigma y)^2}{n}$		6188.4		12224.1		7701.3		4400.0

$$\text{GRAND MEAN} = \frac{\Sigma\Sigma y}{N} = \frac{1143}{44} = 25.98 \qquad\qquad \Sigma\frac{(\Sigma y)^2}{n} = 30513.8$$

What are the explained and unexplained variances for ANOVA, and how do we generate the sampling distribution for F under the null hypothesis? As in correlation analysis, we can think of the total variation in the dependent variable (y) as comprised of (that is, partitioned into) the sum of two other variances. To obtain a measure of the total variance, we begin by calculating the grand mean ($\bar{Y}$). The grand mean ($\bar{Y}$) is the sum of the individual scores from all four groups divided by the total number of scores for all four groups. (That is, we treat the individual scores from the four city groups as one group and calculate this group's mean score.) The total variance is then derived from the squared deviations of the scores from all four groups from the grand mean ($\bar{Y}$) using the formula for calculating the variance of a distribution with which you are already familiar (see Formula 7.2; squaring s gives the variance).

The two components into which this total variance is partitioned are derived as follows. First, within each city group, recruits' scores vary around that group's mean score. We calculate the variance for each city group separately and then add these four variances. The result is called the *within group variance*. Note that the magnitude of this variance is unrelated to whether or not the null hypothesis is true (that is, whether or not there are differences *between* the groups' means). As such, it is unexplained (random) variance. The second component (the remainder) of the total variance, called the *between group variance*, is the variance of the four mean scores (one for each of the four groups) from the grand mean (Y).

The between group variance includes sampling error as well as the effects, if any, of the independent variable. It includes sampling error in the sense that some differences among means are likely to occur by chance when, under the null hypothesis, independent random samples are drawn from the same population. Any effects of the independent variable (city, in our example) on the dependent variable (exam score) would increase the differences among the mean scores beyond those that would be expected from sampling error alone.

Recall that the between group variance is the numerator and the within group variance is the denominator in the F ratio. Hence, only when the variance in y that can be attributed to (explained by) the independent variable (that is, the between group variance) is larger than the within group (unexplained) variance will we have reason to argue that the means differ significantly. It's for this reason that F tables include only values for F equal to or greater than one. The question before us is: How much larger than one should it be before we conclude that the observed differences among the means for the dependent variable are unlikely to have occurred by chance?

Now, recall that the null hypothesis being tested is that the samples are drawn from the same population. To construct the sampling distribution for F under the null hypothesis, the grand mean (for all samples combined) is taken as an estimate of the population mean. The sample variances are treated as independent estimates of the population variance. It is also necessary to assume that the populations from which the samples are drawn are normally distributed for y and that their variances are equal. Given these estimates and assumptions, F has a known sampling distribution, the critical values for which are in Appendix D.

The numerators in the variance formulas for ANOVA are sums of squared deviations from the grand mean or from sample means, conventionally referred to as sums of squares or SS. The denominator for the between group variance is $k - 1$, where k is the total number of groups in the study (in our example, $k = 4$); for the within group variance, the denominator is $N - k$, where N is the total number of scores in all study groups (in our example, $N = 44$). The general formula for F then becomes:

Formula 11.8

$$F = \frac{\dfrac{\text{between sum of squared deviations}}{k - 1}}{\dfrac{\text{within sum of squared deviations}}{N - k}}$$

When we divide by $k-1$ and $N-k$, the results are referred to as *mean squares* (MS). We now have the two variances we need to calculate F.

In Table 11.1 we have recorded the scores from our four city samples in the four columns headed y and some of the calculations needed to complete the ANOVA for our study. Note that the formulas we use below make calculation easier. They are algebraically equivalent to their corresponding formulas expressed as squared deviations from the mean $[\Sigma(y-\bar{y})^2]$. Note, too, that the denominators $(N-1; N-k)$ are corrections to produce unbiased estimates. The double summation sign, as in $\Sigma\Sigma$, should be read: "sum the sums of." To calculate the total variance, conventionally referred to as the total sum of squares (TSS), we have:

Formula 11.9

$$TSS = \Sigma\Sigma y^2 - \frac{(\Sigma\Sigma y)^2}{N}$$

$$= 32609 - \frac{(1143)^2}{44}$$

$$= 32609 - 29692.0$$

$$= 2917$$

For the between sum of squares (BBS):

Formula 11.10

$$BSS = \Sigma \frac{(\Sigma y^2)}{n} - \frac{(\Sigma\Sigma y)^2}{N}$$

$$= 30513.8 - 29692.0$$

$$= 821.8$$

For the within sum of squares (WSS):

Formula 11.11

$$WSS = \Sigma\Sigma y^2 - \Sigma \frac{(\Sigma y)^2}{n}$$

$$= 32609 - 30513.8$$

$$= 2095.2$$

As a check on our calculations, note that the sum of the between sum of squares (821.8) and the within sum of squares (2095.2) equals the total sum of squares (2917).

The critical values of F for various significance levels are in Appendix D. Because the F distribution varies according to the denominators (referred to as degrees of freedom) of the two fractions in Formula 11.8, there is a separate table for each significance level. To use the F tables, we first choose a level of significance and its corresponding table. Then, to find the critical value of F, we find the entry in the table with the corresponding row and column degrees of freedom. (Note that dividing the sums of squares by the degrees of freedom is equivalent to creating an unbiased estimate.)

In general, if the F we calculated is smaller than the critical value in the table, we accept the null hypothesis that there are no significant differences among the means. If the F we calculated is larger than the critical value from the table, we may reject the null hypothesis, leaving us with our alternative or research hypothesis that the means do differ and, therefore, that the independent variable (city) does have some effect on the dependent variable (exam scores).

For example, in our study of exam scores, $k - 1 = 4 - 1 = 3$ and $N - k = 44 - 4 = 40$. Suppose we chose a significance level of .01. To find the critical value of F, we would locate the .01 F table, go to the column $k - 1 = 3$ and proceed down this column to the row corresponding to $N - k = 40$. The entry in the cell ($F = 4.31$) is the critical value of F for our study. Because in our study, $F = 5.23$, we can reject the null hypothesis.

A significant F tells us only that there is at least one significant difference between a pair of means. To determine which means differ significantly, we could run a t test for each of the logically possible pairs of means.

The results of an analysis of variance are presented in research reports in a variety of forms. A common one is illustrated in Table 11.2, using data from our study for illustrative purposes.

The analysis we have just completed is called a **one-way analysis of variance.** "One-way" refers to the fact that only one nominal level independent variable (in our example, city) has been used to categorize the values of an interval or ratio variable y. ANOVA is appropriate when random samples have been independently drawn, distributions of the variables in the populations are approximately normal, and population variances are approximately equal. The ANOVA procedures can be extended to situations where two or more nominal variables are used simultaneously. For example, we might have sampled by gender within each city, producing a "two-way" ANOVA. Although beyond our scope here, discussions of these procedures may be found in advanced statistics texts.

TABLE 11.2   ANOVA Summary

Source of Variation	Sums of Squares	Degrees of Freedom	Mean Squares	F
Between SS (treatment)	821.8	$k - 1 = 3$	273.9	5.23
Within SS (error)	2095.2	$N - k = 40$	52.4	$p < (.01)$
Total var.	2917.0	$N - 1 = 43$		

ASSESSING RELATIONSHIPS
BETWEEN VARIABLES IN TABLES

In Chapter 8, cross-tabulation was discussed as a technique for determining if two variables are related. A frequently used and easily understood statistic for assessing relationships between variables in tables is chi square.

Chi Square

Chi square (χ^2) is a statistic used *only with relatively large, random samples* to test for a relationship between two variables measured at the nominal level and cross-tabulated in a contingency table.[4] Through its calculation, we can determine if empirically obtained cell frequencies differ significantly from those we would have expected if no relationship existed between the variables. In short, chi square is a sample statistic that has a known sampling distribution, and, therefore, it can be used to test a null hypothesis. If the observed cell frequencies and the expected cell frequencies are identical, the chi square has a value of zero. The greater the difference between the observed and expected cell frequencies, the larger the value of chi square. By setting a significance level in advance, we can compare the value of the chi square we compute with the chi square distribution (Appendix E) and determine if the null hypothesis can be rejected.

Suppose we are interested in the effects of the sex of juvenile delinquents on court dispositions. Our null hypothesis states that there is no relationship between the sex of delinquents and court dispositions. We collect the sample data shown in Table 11.3.

Assuming, under the null hypothesis, that sex (the independent variable) and disposition (the dependent variable) were unrelated, we would expect that the proportional distribution of the study group on the dependent variable would be the same in each category of the independent variable. Because males comprise two-thirds of our sample $(100/150 = 2/3)$, two-thirds of the jailed delinquents and two-thirds of those released to parents should be males. Two-thirds of 114 (the number of delinquents jailed) is 76. Two-thirds of 36 is 24. Because we have a 2 × 2 table and we know the *marginal frequencies* do not change, we can subtract these figures from their respective column totals in our table of sample data to arrive at the *expected frequencies (E)* for each of the cells in the table. You can confirm that this results in the same proportional

---

TABLE 11.3   **Court Disposition by Sex (Observed Cell Frequencies)**

	Court Disposition		
Sex	*Jail Time*	*Released to Parents*	*Other*
Male	84	16	100
Female	30	20	50
Total	114	36	$n = 150$

distribution of the dependent variable in each category of the independent variable by percentaging Table 11.4 in the direction of the independent variable. The results are shown in Table 11.4. As a shortcut, you can determine the expected frequency for a particular cell by multiplying its row marginal frequency by its column marginal frequency and dividing by n. We can now compute chi square to see if the difference between the observed and the expected frequencies is statistically significant by using Formula 11.12.

Formula 11.12

$$\chi^2 = \Sigma \frac{(O-E)^2}{E}$$

where χ^2 is chi square, O is the observed frequency in a given cell of the observed data table, E is the expected frequency in the corresponding cell of the expected frequency table, and Σ represents the sum of the ratios calculated for the cells. Doing the calculation, we find that

$$\chi^2 = \frac{(8)^2}{76} + \frac{(8)^2}{24} + \frac{(8)^2}{38} + \frac{(8)^2}{12} = 10.5$$

After obtaining a chi square of 10.5, we must calculate the degrees of freedom (df) associated with this particular table because the sampling distribution of chi square is different for each different table size. For any particular table, we can calculate the degrees of freedom according to Formula 11.13:

Formula 11.13

$$df = (r-1)\,(c-1),$$

where r is the number of rows and c is the number of columns. In our example, the table has two rows and two columns, so degrees of freedom equal one. Using one degree of freedom, then, we can look up the value of chi square in the chi square table and find that a chi square of this size would have come about by chance less than 1 percent of the time. Thus, we can reject the null hypothesis. The table provides evidence that there is, indeed, some relationship between sex of delinquent and court disposition. Note that although chi square helps us determine whether or not a relationship exists between variables, it does *not* indicate how strong the relationship is. Chi square may be used with most any size table—2 x 3, 3 x 3, 3 x 4, 4 x 4, and so on. It assumes data collected from a random sample; contrary to the other tests we have considered, however, it is "distribution free"—that is, it may be used even if the variables are not normally distributed in the population. It also is most appropriate when both variables are measured at the nominal level. If even one is measured at the ordinal level or above, more powerful tests of association are available. The chi square formula given above should be used only with tabular data consisting of raw frequency counts (that is, not with percentages, rates, and so on). Furthermore, the magnitude of chi square is related to sample size. Large sample data are likely to yield statistically significant results, rendering the test less useful; results from small sample data, especially if any of the expected cell frequencies are less than 5, are also likely to be misleading.

| TABLE 11.4 | Court Disposition by Sex (Expected Cell Frequencies) |

	Court Disposition		
Sex	*Jail Time*	*Released to Parents*	*Other*
Male	76	24	100
Female	38	12	50
Total	114	36	$n = 150$

Modifications of the formula for calculating chi square for use in some of these and other circumstances are available in most advanced texts.

SIGNIFICANCE TESTS FOR THE CORRELATION COEFFICIENT

When both variables are measured at the interval or ratio level, the correlation coefficient can be used for hypothesis testing. The **correlation coefficient,** you will recall from Chapter 9, is a descriptive statistic that *measures the strength of association* between two variables. It may also be used to test hypotheses on random sample data, because the correlation coefficient (r) and the difference between correlation coefficients have known sampling distributions. Therefore, we can use the sampling distribution of r to determine the statistical significance of a sample r.

SOME FINAL CAUTIONS

Some words of caution about interpreting levels of significance and confidence intervals are in order. First, significance levels and confidence intervals tell us the *probability* of obtaining a particular result (difference in means) by chance when we draw different samples from a population. They do *not* tell us whether any *particular* sample statistic is the result of chance or nonchance factors.

Second, the differences between the random assignment of members of a study group to two research conditions (as we described in Chapter 3) and sampling from a larger population must be clearly understood. Random assignment is essentially a method of randomizing any differences that might exist between two or more subgroups of the total study group. When we randomly assign a group of subjects to different subgroups, we are actually taking two random samples, without replacement, of the population consisting of the total group of study participants. This group may or may not itself be a random sample of some other population; that is, the group we are sampling may have been selected at random from the population of all youngsters in a particular school, city, or state. Usually, however, participants are selected from these other populations using a purposive or some other nonprobability sampling technique. Random assignment *within* nonprobability samples can be used to measure the probability of differences between the randomly assigned groups in, for example, mean levels of violence observed. But, in such cases inferential statistics do not permit us to make estimates of parameters or test hypotheses pertaining to a larger population from which the subjects were selected using nonprobability sampling techniques. Unless the study group as a whole has been selected randomly, we have no way of knowing how typical it is of the larger population of which the members are a part. Randomly assigning members of the study group to two different study conditions does nothing to ensure their typicality as far as the population of all children or even children in a particular city or school is concerned. Unless we have selected a probability sample of some larger population, then, the population to which we may legitimately generalize our results is limited to the study group we selected and from within which we made random assignments.

Furthermore, it is extremely important to remember that inferential statistics don't give us any help in dealing with errors arising from sources in the research process other than probability sampling. Errors due to defective research designs; faulty sampling procedures; poorly operationalized variables; and sloppy field note taking, data recording, or data entry, for example, cannot be compensated for through the application of inferential statistics.

Finally, assessing the statistical significance of some result should not be confused with determining what we might call its **fundamental significance.** *Statistical significance* is a term that refers only to the implications of applying probability theory in the testing of hypotheses; *fundamental significance* refers to the practical or ethical importance or consequences of some research result in human life. Statistically significant results from an analysis of data say nothing at all about the fundamental significance of the topic being investigated or of the results obtained.

REVIEW QUESTIONS

1. What is hypothesis testing and how are inferential statistics used in hypothesis testing?
2. Compare and contrast research and null hypotheses.
3. Why do most inferential statistics permit testing only the null hypothesis directly?
4. What is a Type I error? How does it differ from a Type II error? Why are they important in inferential statistics?
5. What is a significance level and why is it important in inferential statistics? How is significance level related to Type I error? To Type II error? To the research and null hypothesis?
6. What are rejection regions and critical values and how are they related in a sampling distribution?
7. What is a *t* test? What assumptions are necessary for using it and for what research situations is it appropriate?

8. What is the relationship between the sampling distribution for t and the standard normal curve?

9. What is analysis of variance (ANOVA), on what assumptions is it based, and for what research situations is it appropriate?

10. Compare and contrast total variance, between group variance, and within group variance in analysis of variance. What are explained and unexplained variances? In what sense are they explained or unexplained?

11. What is the χ^2 statistic? When should it be used? How does it compare with correlation analysis?

EXERCISES

1. Formulate four research hypotheses and their corresponding null hypotheses.

2. For each of the four research/null hypotheses sets you constructed in exercise 1, write them in a way appropriate for a one-tailed test and then for a two-tailed test.

3. Suppose the significance levels you select for the four hypotheses you formulated in exercise 1 were .001, .01, .05, and .25, respectively. Assume that the appropriate sampling distribution for the test of your hypotheses is a normal curve. Draw the sampling distribution for each null hypothesis, identifying the rejection region for a one-tailed test of your hypothesis. Do the same for a two-tailed test.

4. Formulate three research hypotheses for which a t test would be appropriate. Discuss why it would be appropriate and how it would be applied in each case.

5. Below are calculated values for t and their corresponding dfs. At what level of significance would these data permit you to reject the null hypothesis for a one-tailed test? For a two-tailed test?

   $t = 2.481$, $df = 26$

   $t = 2.481$, $df = 3$

   $t = 1.265$, $df = 456$

   $t = 64.001$, $df = 1$

   $t = 3.321$, $df = 121$

   $t = 3.321$, $df = 2$

6. Discuss what you have learned about the different sampling distributions for t from completing exercise 5. (Hint: Discuss the relationships among significance level, t, and df by comparing and contrasting results when t is the same, but df differs, and so on.)

7. What would be the critical value for t for each of the following?

Sig. Level	df	test type
.05	3	one tail
.001	3	one tail
.05	12	two tails
.05	12	one tail
.10	100	one tail
.025	25	two tails
.025	25	one tail

8. Using the t table and the z table, show that, for large samples, $t = z$. Does this hold for both one- and two-tailed tests? Why or why not?

9. Formulate three research hypotheses for which ANOVA would be appropriate. Discuss why it would be appropriate and how it would be applied in each of these cases.

10. Discuss why in ANOVA the between group variance is said to be explained and the within group variance is said to be unexplained.

11. Below are six calculated values of F and the corresponding dfs. At what level would each be significant?

F value	$df\,1$	$df\,2$
2.55	5	29
2.55	40	10
1.00	infin	infin
99.00	1	2
12.00	60	4
12.00	4	60

12. Discuss what you have learned about the sampling distributions for F from completing exercise 11.

13. Calculate χ^2 for the following table:

Number of Days in Jail by Sex of Offender for First Offense, Theft over $150.00

	Number of Days in Jail		
Sex of Offender	*4 days or less*	*5 days or more*	
Male	32	148	180
Female	15	5	20
	47	153	200

How probable is the χ^2 you calculated? What does this result mean? Could a t test have been used to analyze these data? Why or why not?

NOTES

1. The "Student" in the name of this test and its corresponding sampling distributions is a pen name of the early twentieth-century mathematician, William S. Gosset.

2. As we'll see, degrees of freedom are calculated in different ways for different statistics. For a thorough discussion of degrees of freedom, see William Mendenhall, Lyman Ott, and Richard F. Larson, *Statistics: A Tool for the Social Sciences* (New York: Duxbury Press, 1974), p. 218.

3. Analysis of variance procedures were developed by the statistician R. A. Fisher.

4. Chi square analysis and the associated distributions were developed by Karl Pearson.

12

Common Errors
in Presenting and Interpreting
Research Findings

Most people have heard of loaded questions—questions that, because of the way they are asked, tend to elicit the response the asker favors. It is less well recognized, but no less important, that answers may be loaded as well.[1]

We have argued that researchers always conduct research in the context of their own values and collect data because either they or their employers recognize some issue as important. Because values affect the problem investigated (and perhaps also the conclusions or solutions proposed), it is always possible that others viewing the same problem may see it from a different, even opposite, value position. The researcher following the rules of the scientific perspective must, therefore, strive to gather and present data in as pure a form as possible; that is, with as little distortion or falsification based on personal values as possible. The researcher may—and in most instances should—provide the reader with his honest interpretations of the data, including any inferences he believes are justified. However, the researcher also has an obligation to keep the presentation of the data separate from the inferences and speculations he draws from them.

The reader, the consumer of research, should also be aware of the distinction between the data the researcher presents and the interpretations the researcher generates. This distinction is particularly important when data are presented in printed form because the reader is ordinarily not in a position to ask clarifying questions of the researcher. In this chapter, we want to indicate some of the principles and pitfalls of data presentation and analysis and suggest some ways to avoid deceiving and being deceived.

THE TRAPPINGS OF SCIENCE

Science is a highly valued activity in American society. There are, of course, the humorous and pathetic stereotypes of the scientist who cannot see the obvious and the sinister image of the mad scientist, but most people look upon science and scientists with great respect. Consequently, if one has something to sell— be it an underarm deodorant, a biochemical theory, or a program for reform of the truancy laws—the likelihood of having the product accepted is greatly increased if it can be linked to science. But the nature of the connection between science and the product may vary from extremely tenuous to very direct. Therefore, you should be both aware and critical of some of the aspects of this effort to have the prestige of science rub off on the product. We shall describe four commonly used means of connecting science with a product.

Scientific Costumes and Props

Many attempts to connect science with a product are based upon a reversal of the commonly known phenomenon of guilt by association. We might call it the attempt to establish credibility by association in which the presenter tries to give the product a scientific aura by associating it with some of the trappings of science. Where visual images are used—in newspapers, magazines, journals, television, motion pictures—the presenter may appear in a white lab coat in a setting that includes a collection of scientific instruments: microscopes, test tubes and beakers, computers, questionnaires, shelves full of books, and so forth.

Now, it is true that some scientists do wear lab coats, many depend upon well-equipped laboratories, and most have offices well stocked with books related to their work. Nonetheless, when the relevance of these props for the data and conclusions being presented is not obvious, the consumer should question whether the props are, in fact, related in any reasonable way to the message being presented. Is the man in the white lab coat who is talking about headaches someone who really knows about headaches? Does the drab-looking person with heavy rimmed glasses and elbow on the lie detector machine really know how to read and interpret a polygraph record and the pitfalls involved in its use?

Quoting or Relying on Authorities

Many individuals, including scientists, like to quote or otherwise rely on authorities to increase their own credibility and the credibility of their message. References to authorities, such as "Dr. X has found . . .," "Several physicians interviewed contend . . .," "A review of the psychological research on this topic indicates . . .," and "Professor Y believes . . .," are frequently found in the text of research reports. Research reports and theoretical articles are usually accompanied by extensive footnotes and bibliographies, which indicate to the reader the context of the research being presented and the source of the cited literature. Thus, if the researcher relies on authorities to support a particular argument, enough bibliographic information should be provided for the reader to decide whether such support exists. Careful consumers should demand such documentation and attempt to appraise the expertise of the cited authorities in relation to the issue under consideration. Since scientific training is specialized, one cannot expect a scientist trained in one field to have much knowledge about another. Most physicians are not experts on psychology, for example, and few political scientists are knowledgeable about the biochemistry of water pollution. When people see titles such as "Doctor" and "Professor" or abbreviations for degrees such as Ph.D., M.A., and J.D. after a researcher's name, they may be especially prone to accept the researcher's expertise in many fields, not just the one in which he was trained. When titles are used, the researcher should indicate the field or discipline specialty in which the title was earned.

Using Technical Vocabulary

Although everyday language is adequate for ordinary social communication, it often lacks the precision required for scientific purposes. Consequently, scientists have developed specialized, technical vocabularies, inventing new terms and assigning specialized meanings to ordinary ones. To work in a particular field, then, one must be familiar with its jargon, or specialized language (see Chapter 2). A presenter may try to give a scientific flavor to a presentation by suggesting or demonstrating familiarity with the jargon. For example, a reference to a PCV (pollution control valve in an automobile exhaust system) or dementia praecox (a medical term for a type of mental disorder) suggests that the presenter is an expert and knows all there is to know about the matter at hand. The use of disciplinary jargon can be roughly equivalent to name dropping. That is, the presenter may mention a few technical words—often in a deliberately offhand fashion—to give the impression of expertise or to suggest that scientific techniques have verified the quality of the product. Advertisers, scientists, lawyers, and social reformers alike sometimes do this. For example, a creme rinse is advertised as being "pH controlled," and a product for asthma sufferers is alleged to "relax tense bronchial muscles fast." Similarly, advocates select names for theories, reforms, or programs that may promise more than can be delivered—"Scared Straight," "holistic health," "officer-friendly," and "equitable justice" are examples. Laypersons as well as scientists must keep in mind that the use of a few technical words or catchy titles by themselves do not necessarily indicate either expertise or scientific support for claims.

The layperson often has little choice but to rely on a "translator" to put the theory and research of the discipline into more generally understood terms. Translation is, of course, a tricky business. Translators can overgeneralize the results of research, add inferences or interpretations not warranted by the data, or distort the inferences and interpretations of the original presenter. Consequently, although all of us will probably be forced to rely upon such translations to a greater extent in the future, we should be cautious in evaluating them. Does the translator have expertise in the area in which he is translating? Are other translations of the data available for comparison?

There is a second characteristic of the language used by scientists that is worth noting. One rarely finds a statement containing a personal pronoun, such as "*I* interviewed twenty-four subjects . . ." or "*We* think this information indicates . . .," in research reports. Researchers often consciously avoid using these pronouns in describing research and its results, preferring passive statements such as "Twenty-four subjects were interviewed . . ." and "The data indicate . . ." because they (or their editors) believe it is good article writing style or because it lends a detached, objective air to their scientific reports. The reader should note, however, that a researcher's use of the passive voice in reporting on research does not make either the research or the researcher more objective. Regardless of the writing style used to communicate the findings, the researcher is still a human being who may indeed fall victim to any or all of the pitfalls discussed in this book (and many others as well), even though he attempts to adhere to scientific perspectives and methods.

THE MANY USES AND MISUSES OF NUMBERS

Because numbers are directly associated with science, many people attach some degree of objectivity and precision to the study, evaluation, or other activity that produces such numbers. That is why presentations of the form "Two out of three doctors recommend . . .," "Fourteen percent of the respondents said . . ." and "Only 4.2 milligrams of tar . . .," are so popular. Compare the following pairs of sentences.

Joe has three brothers and two sisters.	Joe has only three brothers and two sisters.
The Defense Department estimates that about 50 percent of the young men who become 19 years old in 1973 will be drafted in 1974.	The Defense Department estimates that as few as 50 percent of the young men who become 19 years old in 1973 will be drafted in 1974! (Try substituting "as many as" in this sentence.)
The crude birthrate in country A is estimated to be 2.5 per 100.	The crude birthrate in country A is estimated to be as high as 2.5 per 100. (Try substituting "as low as" in this sentence.)
In this experiment, 15 percent of the male subjects manifested serious psychiatric symptoms, whereas 13 percent of the female subjects did so.	In this "experiment," 15 percent of the male subjects manifested serious psychiatric symptoms, *whereas only 13 percent of the female subjects did so!*

As these examples show, such presentations can be potentially misleading in several ways. First, words such as *just, only, as few as, as many as, as high as, as low as, more,* and *less* often have the effect—intentional or unintentional—of distorting the data being presented. Second, underlining, italicizing, capitalizing, or otherwise emphasizing certain words or phrases can also color the meaning. So can punctuations like exclamation points and question marks. Third, percentages and rates calculated on either small or very large base numbers may be extremely misleading: 1 out of 3 is 33 percent and 3,000 out of 3,000,000 is .001 percent; a change from 2 to 6 is a 200 percent increase and a change from 5,000 to 3,000 is a 40 percent decrease. We cannot really make sense of these percentages (or any other rates) without knowing what the base numbers are.

It has become fashionable, especially in mass media coverage of research results, to describe the findings in terms of increases or decreases in the risk of specified outcomes. It might be reported, for example, that failure to graduate from high school doubles the risk of being arrested as a young adult or that coming from a one-parent family triples the risk of a child being adjudicated delinquent. Such reports, although no doubt intended to assist the general public in understanding the data, nevertheless deserve close scrutiny. Why? Because vital, basic information is often left out of the reports. Here, too, we need to know some of the raw numbers to make good sense and/or good use of the information provided. For example, very small basic risks, say 1 in 500,000, can increase by ten times (to 10 in 500,000) and still not represent much of a risk, whereas initially high risks could increase by only a fraction and represent a very important change in vulnerability. And it is dangerous to generalize from one sample or population to another unless we know enough about them both to assure ourselves they are comparable. Also, unless the corresponding group statistic is 100 percent, it is never justified to infer an individual's characteristic from group data.

As a final note, the procedures for associating science with a particular product can be used singly or in combination, and although none of them is inherently misleading, each may be. In short, every effort should be made to keep the data separate from those aspects of their presentation that, though attractive, are irrelevant to the issue at hand. The consumer should ask the following questions to help separate the data from the props used in their presentation:

- What are the base "raw" numbers used in the calculations?

- So far as I can tell, are the calculations/results correct/reasonable?

- What value position is at stake in the presentation?

- Do the data presented support the conclusions offered?

- Are there alternative ways to interpret the data?

- How reliable and valid are the data?

- Is the presenter using any tricks to convince the audience of the truthfulness of the conclusions presented?

GRAPHS: THEIR USES AND MISUSES

Graphs are spatial representations of numerical data. They are among the most vivid means of communicating descriptive data to an audience. They come in many shapes and sizes and, if constructed with care and interpreted with caution, they communicate very well indeed. To the unwary, however, their striking visual characteristics may mask more than they reveal about the data upon which the graphic representation is based.

Bar Graphs

In addition to vertical bar graphs presented earlier, bar graphs can be horizontal. A *horizontal bar graph* is constructed by putting the frequency dimension of the graph on the horizontal axis and the response categories on the vertical axis, as in Figure 12.1.

Both horizontal and vertical bar graphs can also be segmental. A *segmented bar graph* uses the basic format of the bar graph but adds information by partitioning each bar into segments. Each segment represents a part of the whole, with the whole represented by the bar's total length. For example, a bar graph representing the amount of cocaine produced by five countries could have the bars divided into segments representing the proportion of cocaine consumed domestically and the proportion exported, as in Figure 12.2. Although each bar in this graph has only two segments, a bar can include as many segments as needed.

Pie Graphs

Pie graphs are constructed by drawing a circle, representing a whole, and dividing it into wedges, representing its component parts. The size of each wedge (measured in degrees) is proportional to the part of the whole (360°) that that particular segment represents. See Figure 12.3.

Pictographs

A *pictograph* uses symbols to represent data, usually in one of two ways. In one type of pictograph, a symbol of fixed size represents a specified number of objects, and several such symbols represent the total number. The number of law enforcement officers in three countries, for example, might be depicted with a graph as in Figure 12.4.

A second type of pictograph uses a single symbol and varies the size of the symbol to represent variations in the quantity of the objects represented. Thus, the number of dollars spent by two countries for law enforcement in a given year might be represented as in Figure 12.5.

Hazards in Interpreting Graphs

Because graphic presentations of data are powerful communicators, they may seriously mislead an observer who is not alert. What should the designer or the reader of a graph look for? First, the designer chooses the scale to which the

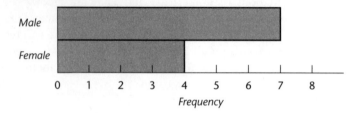

FIGURE 12.1   A Horizontal Bar Graph: Sex of Shoplifters

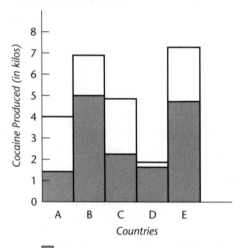

FIGURE 12.2   Cocaine Production and Disposition in Five Countries

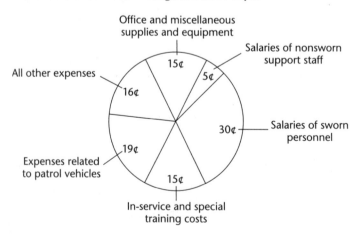

FIGURE 12.3   The Distribution of the Police Department Budget Dollar in City A

FIGURE 12. 4   **Law Enforcement Officers in Three Countries**

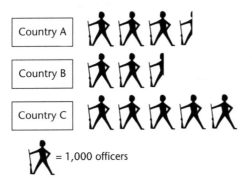

FIGURE 12. 5   **Number of Dollars Spent for Law Enforcement**

graph is drawn. The scale that is chosen affects the appearance of the graph and may affect how the graph is interpreted. Consider, for example, the bar graphs shown in Figure 12.6. Is it possible that all of these bar graphs are representations of the same data? The answer is yes. By changing the distance allocated to each frequency on the vertical axis and/or each category on the horizontal axis, very different visual impressions can be created. Changes in the radii of pie graphs can have the same effect. The scale can minimize or maximize the impression of differences. For this reason, the reader should watch for possible discrepancies between the visual impression created by the graph and the actual data. Such discrepancies cannot be detected, of course, unless one knows what the actual data are. Hence, the frequency dimension of bar graphs should be clearly marked, and the raw data for pie graphs and other spatial representations of data should be clearly indicated. Graphs for which no raw data are provided should be ignored, because it is impossible to interpret their meaning or importance.

Occasionally, one encounters a *broken bar graph* like the one in Figure 12.7(a). The separation of the bars demarked by wavy lines indicates that not all of the graph is shown Note that the frequency designations in Figure 12.7(a) jump from 3 to 40 over the gap and that all the variation occurs between 40 and 45. When the graph is sized down so that the break is not necessary, as in Figure 12.7(b), the differences among the bars become visually very small. Although a broken bar graph is preferable to one whose initial frequency mark is greater than zero, it is interesting to ask yourself why the distance for each unit on the

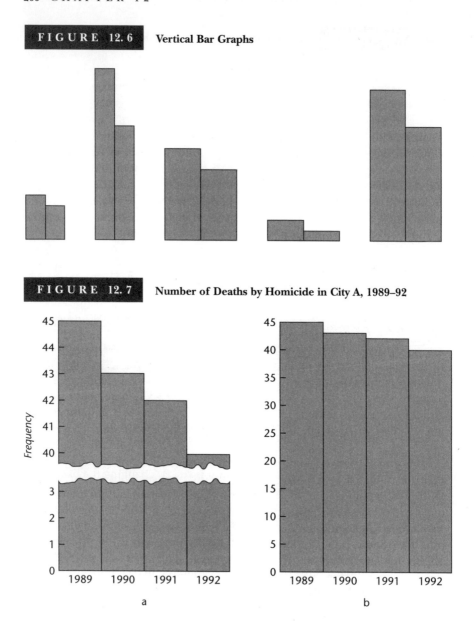

FIGURE 12. 6 Vertical Bar Graphs

FIGURE 12. 7 Number of Deaths by Homicide in City A, 1989–92

a

b

frequency dimension in graph (a) was not reduced so that the complete graph would fit into the space available. There may be good reasons for not doing so, but one should not automatically assume that there are.

Pictographs can present a related problem. Suppose you wanted to represent the change in handgun sales for a given state in the United States from one year to the next. Suppose, further, that handgun sales doubled, and you chose to represent this change in pictograph form, using a handgun silhouette for each year as a graphic symbol. You might represent the first year's production as in the left side of Figure 12.8, but now you need to indicate the next year's sales.

FIGURE 12.8   Handgun Sales in State A, 1991 and 1992

1991: 10,000 handguns sold   1992: 20,000 handguns sold

How do you proceed? You could double the height, or you could double the width of the gun. But either of these guns might look funny. To keep the gun proportional, you might choose to double both the height and the width to produce the gun shown on the right in Figure 12.8.

But what have you done in this case? Considering the vertical dimension of the guns alone, the pictograph is an accurate representation of the data, but pictures have two dimensions. The actual space encompassed by the second gun is four times that encompassed by the first, and the visual impact of the two guns reflects this quadrupling of space. Although this sort of mistake may seem unlikely, it occurs with surprising frequency and may be easily missed by a casual reader. One simple corrective for such situations is to analyze the raw numbers used to create the graph, and if these numbers are not available, the graph should be ignored.

CORRELATION AND CAUSATION

Perhaps it is worth repeating here that correlation does not necessarily indicate causation, even when the correlation coefficient has a high positive correlation, say $r = + .89$. For example, there is a high positive correlation between the amount of damage done in a fire and the number of fire trucks that respond to the fire alarm: The larger the number of trucks, the greater the damage. There is probably also a high positive correlation between the number of police officers on a scene and the severity of the offense—and between the number of lawyers and the severity or complexity of a crime. However, do any of these correlations represent causation?

One important consideration when examining assertions about the relationship between variables is the definition of the variables themselves. Significant correlations can easily be produced when the two allegedly different variables are really two different operationalizations (or measurements) of the same or nearly the same thing. Consider the potential correlation between theft rates and the monetary losses due to shoplifting, or between the size of law enforcement agencies' budgets and the number of officers on the payroll. In a sense, monetary losses due to shoplifting may be viewed as an indirect way of measuring the amount of one type of theft. However, a theft rate is also a measurement of the amount of theft. Hence, a correlation between these two variables is contaminated by the fact that theft rates include shoplifting as a part of the *definition* of theft and, therefore, of theft rates. It would be very surprising, indeed, if two different measurements of the same phenomenon did not produce a high correlation. To avoid misleading or being misled by others in such circumstances requires careful conceptual analysis and definitional precision. One should always be alert to the possibility of using different names for the same phenomenon, thereby producing a spurious correlation.

HYPOTHESIS TESTING AND PROBABILITIES

In their zeal to support conclusions, theories, or positions on public policy issues, scientists and people who use the findings of scientific research in their arguments may succumb to the often powerful temptation to make unjustified claims. The insatiable appetite of the news media for 15-second sound bites and of the Internet for instantaneous digital bits considerably exacerbates the situation. In the process, the nature of science as a human, and therefore inevitably error prone, endeavor may be overlooked; the principle of tentativeness discussed in Chapter 2 may be ignored; and probabilities are turned into certainties. When hypothesis testing and probabilities are involved, it is wise to keep in mind the following considerations.

First, in almost all cases, the hypothesis being tested statistically is the null hypothesis, and it is this hypothesis that is rejected, if the findings justify doing so. Of course, the researcher hopes to be able to reject the null hypothesis, so that support can be claimed for the alternative research hypothesis he or she has formulated. Remember, though, that such support is indirect (that is, the support comes from rejecting some other hypothesis rather than from directly affirming the research hypothesis). Furthermore, there may well be hypotheses or explanations in addition to the alternative or research hypothesis formulated by the researcher. It is a good practice to try formulating other alternative hypotheses and to look for or ask about levels of significance; doing so will remind us that there may be other ways to formulate the research question and that hypothesis testing involves the potential for a Type I error in inference. Of course, there are Type II errors with which to contend as well.

Unfortunately, though, levels of significance may easily be misused or misinterpreted, too. As we noted earlier, statistical significance should not be confused with *fundamental* or *practical significance*. Very small differences in frequencies and proportions, for example, can produce results that achieve a very high level of confidence or a very low significance level (that is, a very low probability of a Type I error) when the quantities being used for the statistical calculations are large. And no matter what the level of significance, it is always a probability—a very small probability perhaps, but a probability nevertheless. And that probability is never 100 percent confidence level or 0 percent significance level. There is no such thing as certainty in science. We can never be certain that a very low probability outcome didn't occur in our particular study.

Probabilities may be said to pertain to groups of persons, objects, or events or to individual constituents of these collectivities, but they always apply to what will happen in the long run. Furthermore, they apply to the **units of analysis** for which they were derived. It is a mistake to shift to a new unit of analysis without retaining the probabilistic language. For example, our research may indicate that persons under 17 years of age from families with annual incomes under $12,000 have a much higher probability of having an official juvenile court record than those in the same age group with family incomes greater than $30,000. These results might be summarized by saying that the two groups of juveniles are very different from each other or that they differ significantly. But we need to be alert to what is and what is not included in these summaries. What is almost always *not* meant is that every one of the individual members of one group are different from every one of the individual members of the other group. Peter, who was included in the study, is 16 and his family income is $10,000; José, also 16, has a family income of $35,000. What, if anything, can we say about Peter or José or comparisons between them on the basis of our overall results? Peter and/or José as particular individuals are now the units of analysis. We should not conclude that Peter has a juvenile record and José does not, even if the probability of a juvenile record for Peter's group is, say, .95 and for José's it is .15, because our findings apply to the groups as a whole and not to the individual units that make up the groups. In such a case, however, we could say that the probability of Peter having a record is .95—a statement that retains the probabilistic frame of the original statement. Inappropriately applying findings about groups expressed in terms of probabilities to individual cases is one version of what has been called *the fallacy of misplaced concreteness.* And, of course, applying findings to individuals or groups not included in the population(s) sampled is also a mistake. Research that includes only males or females should be identified as such, for example.

Then, too, the group of which Peter is a part may have a probability of having a juvenile record of .12, whereas the group from wealthier families has a .03 probability. That .12 may be interpreted by the researcher as a much higher probability and, in a sense, it may be. But we should also note that both .12 and .03 are low probabilities. We need to be alert to the larger context within which probabilities are derived and interpreted in order to make sense of the researcher's claim.

Furthermore, the difference between .12 and .03 may be significant at the .0001 level. When samples are large, small differences can be statistically significant. But that doesn't mean the results will help us very much if, for example, we want to identify children who should be exposed to a delinquency deterrence program. On the basis of such findings, it would be wiser either to forget the program or just expose everyone to it. The same conclusion might apply if, for example, the two probabilities in question were .87 and .93 and this difference was statistically significant.

Finally, hypothesis testing typically involves statistics whose sampling distributions are constructed on the basis of certain assumptions about the nature of the data and distributions of variable values. You should know what these assumptions are, whether in a particular case the assumptions are reasonable, and what effects violations of the assumptions might have on the statistic in question. Some statistical tests are more *robust* than others; violating their assumptions to some degree is less likely to provide misleading results/inferences.

REVIEW QUESTIONS

1. Why is it important to distinguish between data and the interpretation of the data?

2. Why is it important to present raw numbers along with graphic displays, percentage, and rates?

3. What are the advantages and disadvantages of graphic displays in presenting data?

4. Why is it important to distinguish between correlation and causation?

EXERCISES

1. Locate articles in magazines or newspapers you own (*not* those in a library), using each of the following:

   a. scientific costumes and/or props

   b. relying on authority

   c. technical vocabulary

   Write an analysis of the article, discussing the reasons why the author may have used these techniques and what, if any, relevance they have for the validity of the message being delivered.

2. What else would you want to know about the following statements before you might give them credence?

   a. Two out of three professors believe that students are much more motivated now than they were five years ago.

   b. The crime rate is decreasing; the rate of decline in the crime rate is increasing.

   c. Fifty percent of those interviewed said they would support a tax increase to raise salaries of judges.

   d. There has been a 100 percent increase in murders in Hitsville.

   e. Brand X has more medicine than Brand Y.

3. What is potentially misleading about the following graphics displays?

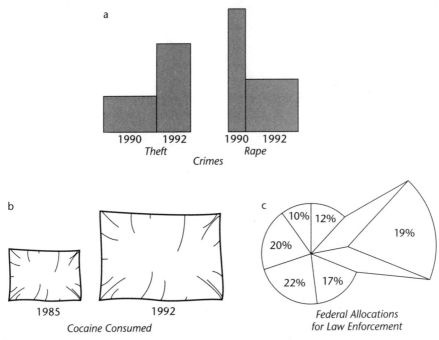

4. For some statistical humor go to *http://www.idea-bank.com/samples-statistics.html* and *http://eval1.crc.uiuc.edu/edpsy390/statjokes.html*

NOTE

1. For interesting discussions of the issues discussed in this chapter and other related issues in data analysis and presentation, see the classic text by Darrell Huff, *How to Lie with Statistics* (New York: W. W. Norton & Company, Inc., 1954) and the most recent discussion offered by Joel Best, *Damn Lies and Statistics: Untangling Numbers from the Media, Politicians and Activists* (Berkeley: University of California Press, 2001).

CHAPTER

13

Preparing and Reading Research Reports

Als noted in Chapter 1, most criminal justice practitioners and students are familiar with the preparation and reading of police investigative reports. To some extent, a research report or article resembles such reports. However, a good research report must contain several elements that may or may not appear in an investigative report. We discuss these elements in this chapter. They include the abstract, the introduction, a review of the literature, the statement of hypotheses or research questions, description of methodology, data analysis, conclusions, and bibliography.

There are several accepted ways of organizing research reports and arranging source and bibliographic citations; these can be found in recognized style manuals such as *The Chicago Manual of Style,* the Modern Language Association's (MLA) *Handbook for Writers of Research Papers,* the *Publication Manual of the American Psychological Association* (APA), and *English Simplified.* It should be remembered, though, that a research report for a professor or a chief administrative officer may require a format and citation style different from the specifications of a professional journal, and that different journals have their own styles. The structure and style of the report should conform to the requirements of the audience or publication for which it is prepared.

For the purposes of illustrating the typical components of a research report, we'll use excerpts from "Combating Crime in Public Housing: A Qualitative and Quantitative Longitudinal Analysis of the Chicago Housing

Authority's Anti-Drug Initiative," by Susan J. Popkin and co-authors.[1] We'll omit entirely portions of the article presenting and discussing statistical analyses more advanced than those we have considered in this text. Their research project is an example of third-party, evaluative (implementation and outcome) research using both qualitative and quantitative methods.

THE TITLE

A report's title should be succinct yet descriptive of the nature and purposes of the research project being reported on. The title of the article we're using here could be a bit more succinct. Compare the title above, for example, with a simplified version, such as "An Evaluation of the Chicago Housing Authority's Anti-Drug Initiative." Still, the title selected by the authors has the merit of indicating clearly the central research question being addressed as well as the methodological approaches used in their research project.

ACKNOWLEDGING SOURCES OF SUPPORT

Identifying where the financial support for research comes from is important for two reasons. First, it is certainly appropriate (and often mandated by funding agencies) to thank publicly those who made the research possible through financial assistance. It's also appropriate, of course, to thank publicly any others who provided significant nonfinancial support. Second, as we noted in our discussion of research types in Chapter 1, knowing who has financially underwritten the project is a first step in assessing the credibility of research results. The authors of this article acknowledge their support in a footnote as follows:

> This research was funded by National Institute of Justice Grants 93-IJ-CX-0037 and 95-IJ-CX-0011, and by Department of Housing and Urban Development Contract DU100C000018374, Task Order 6. The findings and conclusions presented here are those of the authors and do not necessarily reflect the positions of the two funding agencies.

THE ABSTRACT

An **abstract** is a brief summary (usually 200 words or less) of a research project placed at the beginning of the report. It enables a reader to quickly determine the relevance of the report for her own purposes. Abstracts usually contain a succinct statement of the research topic(s) covered in the report, a brief description of the methodology involved, and a summary of the findings or conclusions.

Although the abstract is found at the beginning of the research report, it cannot be written until the research has been completed, because a brief discussion of the outcome(s) of the research is included. The following is an abstract of the Popkins et al. research article:

The Chicago Housing Authority's (CHA) notorious high-rise developments are among the most dangerous public housing in America. In the early 1990s, the CHA launched an ambitious attack on crime, a comprehensive and collaborative crime prevention program known as the *Anti-Drug Initiative* (ADI). From 1994 to 1996 we tracked conditions in three of the CHA's high-rise developments, assessing the agency's success in implementing the ADI programs in each site as well as tracking other, related interventions. Using a combination of surveys and qualitative research methods, we examined the impact of these programs through the eyes of the residents and other key actors, looking at various outcome measures related to crime and disorder. Our findings indicate some positive results, but follow-up research conducted in 1996 documented the fragility of these changes and their vulnerability to gang influence.

THE INTRODUCTION

The introduction places the research problem in context. General historical and theoretical frameworks into which the current problem fits are discussed. Major theoretical trends and their principal proponents are mentioned. Finally, the areas in which the subject remains problematic are discussed, leading up to the current research, which addresses one or more of those areas. The introduction may be a distinct section of the research report, or it may be combined with the literature review.

Here are some excerpts from Popkins et al.'s introduction (we'll edit these excerpts and those that appear in subsequent sections pretty severely; our object is just to give you the flavor of the parts of a research report):

> The Chicago Housing Authority's (CHA) notorious high-rise developments are among the most dangerous public housing in America. . . . Almost two decades of management turmoil have exacerbated the disorder, leaving the gangs virtually unopposed. Because of the CHA's extreme management problems, the U.S. Department of Housing and Urban Development (HUD) took over the troubled agency in May 1995. . . .

An Urban War Zone

> CHA high-rises in the 1950s and 1960s were preferable to the slums they replaced, but within two decades crime, drug trafficking and substance abuse had become epidemic. Gangs dominated the social world of the developments, vying for control over individual buildings and open areas, recruiting young men and women, and operating a thriving drug business. . . . One resident of the Henry Horner Home described conditions in her development in 1996:
>
> > They (the gangs) shoot at each other every night. And sometimes it's like . . . whole weekends nobody can't come outside. Kids can't

come out and play, whatever. And it just follows the same pattern over and over and over again. Police come through, ride around for a minute; they always come after everything is over.

. . . Most residents were afraid to cooperate with the police because many felt that survival depended on "minding your own business" and looking the other way when crimes occurred. Most of the people responsible for the violence and drug trafficking were not strangers; they were the relatives, boyfriends, and neighbors of the leaseholders. . . . This resident of neighboring Rockwell Gardens spoke as follows in 1994:

> . . . You can't just tell on them boys like that. You go out there and bring the police to one of them boys. If they take him to jail, the rest of them boys is going to get you. That's just the way it is.

Combating Crime

. . . In 1988 newly appointed executive director Vincent Lane initiated Operation Clean Sweep, a massive law enforcement intervention that was gradually expanded over the next three years into a comprehensive and collaborative crime prevention program known as the *Anti-Drug Initiative* (ADI). From 1994 to 1996 the CHA launched its most ambitious attack on crime, spending approximately $80 million per year—more than half of its funds for major building repairs—on security and anti-drug activities in its developments.

During the three years of the CHA's most intensive efforts to contain crime, we tracked conditions in three high-rise developments: Rockwell Gardens, Henry Horner Homes, and Harold Ickes Homes. We assessed the agency's success in implementing the ADI programs in each site, as well as tracking other, related interventions. . . .

In this article, we present our findings on the impact of the ADI on residents' perceptions of crime and disorder in their developments. We review the relevant research, describing the CHA's efforts in the context of the current thinking on the most effective ways to address crime in public housing. We present a detailed description of the different anti-crime initiatives. Finally, we examine the impact of living with such extreme violence on residents' lives, and discuss the implications for research and policy.

THE LITERATURE REVIEW

The **literature review** is a comprehensive summary of published theory and research relevant to the study presented in the report. Depending on the subject matter and the writer's perspective, the literature review is presented in chronological, thematic, or chronological *and* thematic order.

In many research reports the introduction and literature review sections are separate, whereas in most criminal justice journals they are combined and left untitled. Excerpts from Popkin et al.'s literature review, which in this case is labeled as such, follow:

LITERATURE REVIEW

Policy makers and researchers have offered a variety of explanations for the prevalence of crime and disorder in public housing. . . .

In addition to physical isolation and poor design, in Chicago as elsewhere, housing authority policies often determined that these developments would be completely racially segregated (Massey and Denton 1993). . . .

Historically, federal housing policies also have contributed to the concentration of problems in public housing. . . .

Crime Prevention in Public Housing

Because the problems in distressed public housing are so severe, policy makers agree that controlling crime is a necessary first step to improving conditions (National Commission on Severely Distressed Public Housing 1992a, 1992b). In this section, we review the research on major crime prevention strategies that have been implemented in public housing and other poor communities, including environmental design, situational crime prevention, intensive law enforcement, and community crime prevention programs.

Environmental design. Much research effort has focused on the Crime Prevention Through Environmental Design (CPTED) approach, which grows out of Newman's (1972, 1996) work on defensible space. . . .

The moderate impacts found in evaluations of CPTED interventions may be due, in part, to the complexity of the problems involved. . . .

Situational crime prevention. "Situational crime prevention" measures generally involve attempts to reduce the opportunities for committing specific crimes in particular locations (Clark 1980; Clarke and Mayhew 1980). . . .

Law enforcement strategies. During the early 1980s, the focus of crime prevention efforts in housing developments shifted from changes in physical design to aggressive law enforcement tactics such as creating mini-precinct stations, intensifying police patrols, and conducting undercover investigations (Annan and Skogan 1992; Cuyahoga Metropolitan Housing Authority 1993; Greensboro Housing Authority 1993; Wilkins 1989). . . .

Community involvement. By the late 1980s, researchers, managers, and policy makers agreed that successful anti-crime efforts in public housing should involve collaboration among the police, the public housing authority (PHA), and residents (Weisel 1990). Because residents have the largest stake in keeping developments safe, their active participation in crime prevention through organized programs or other initiatives came to be considered essential. . . .

The failure of community crime prevention programs to substantially reduce crime and disorder is often attributed to residents' inability or unwillingness to participate. Yet, because many of these communities lack the economic or psychological resources to mount organized anti-crime efforts, this view may be tantamount in some respects to "blaming the victim" (Buerger 1994; Helpern 1995). . . .

Comprehensive programs. Successful anti-crime programs typically contain elements of all the strategies discussed above, including aggressive law enforcement, security enhancements, tenants' participation, and social services. Most also include improvements in housing authority management. . . .

Keyes (1992) studied anti-crime efforts in privately subsidized public housing developments in Boston, New York, and San Francisco. He found that the most effective management approaches to combating crime involved careful screening of tenants and reliance on in-house security forces (as opposed to private security guards). He also reported that local police cooperation and organized tenant patrols were important in the aftermath of initial police sweeps or raids. Finally, he found that the most successful housing authorities worked closely with social service agencies to address residents' needs. . . .

Such a comprehensive approach is now a major direction of HUD's policies for addressing the problems of severely distressed public housing. . . .

The literature review should include references to classic works in the area as well as professional journals, books, periodicals, newspapers, papers presented at professional meetings, doctoral dissertations, court cases, Web sites, and other sources. The more thorough the review, the less likely that the work will be open to criticism on the grounds that others have conducted the same or similar research in the past (unless one is replicating a study), or that important areas that others have pointed out have been overlooked. In addition, the researcher may find the literature helpful in developing measurement techniques, locating relevant samples, deciding what type of an analysis should be conducted, and avoiding pitfalls along the way.

Initiating the Literature Review

One of the questions most frequently asked by students is, How do I begin my literature review? Although there are a variety of possibilities, a first and unfortunately often neglected approach involves asking your criminal justice professor or someone with relevant expertise for any related bibliographic material. This step may well save you considerable time and effort by preventing you from reinventing the wheel as far as your project is concerned.

Second, the literature search may begin with a subject search on the Web in the college library. Third, the various indices to criminal justice material contained in the journals and periodicals index in the college library or on the Web may be of great value (for example, the *Criminal Justice Periodical Index*, *Psychological Abstracts*, and *Reader's Guide to Literature in the Social Sciences*). These sources generally contain material by subject and author's name and are updated annually. Some of the journals most often used by criminal justice researchers are the following: *Criminology, Journal of Criminal Justice, Police Studies, Crime and Delinquency, Journal of Police Science and Administration, Justice Quarterly,* and *Social Problems*.

Fourth, computer searches by topical area are available through most libraries, which can provide a list of books, periodicals, and audiovisual and other materials available as well as their locations. Although some libraries offer interlibrary loans to allow you to secure materials from other libraries, you should determine how long it will take to procure a particular source and whether you will need a special library authorization.

Fifth, articles appearing in newspapers and magazines based upon government reports or recent research may provide leads to further sources of information. Note that using information contained in general circulation newspapers or magazines is risky. Reporters who file these articles may have little understanding of the complexities of research design or data analysis, and often they are not receptive to the carefully qualified statements good scientists make in communicating their results. Articles may also be edited or shortened in such a way as to seriously distort the actual research results. By using the government documents section of the library, searching the Web, or writing to the authors of the reports cited, however, you may be able to find the source document(s) for the article. Among the more career specialized magazines or professional journals used in criminal justice research are *Police Chief, Police,* and *Corrections*. Although magazines like these are written by and intended for criminal justice professionals, it's worth noting that they may have their own biases. And not all criminal justice professionals understand much about research. Among the most useful government documents are *Crime in the United States* and newsletters of government agencies involved in criminal justice research.

Once the first sources have been identified, the process of locating and reviewing additional literature is under way. By examining the endnotes, footnotes, and bibliographies contained in your sources, you can begin to identify and review the same literature that others interested in your research problem have utilized.

Completing the Literature Review

Another question frequently asked by students preparing a research report is, How many sources do I need? The answer to this question depends upon the type of research report being written, but, in general, you will be through with the literature review when you find the same names and the same articles and books appearing repeatedly in your search. After examining these works thoroughly, you will reach a saturation point, at which time you will be familiar with the classics in your research area and the most recent updates of those classics. At this point further search for literature will only delay the beginning of your report. If, however, new materials become available as you are working on your research project, these also should be reviewed and incorporated into the literature review. The point at which the literature review comes to an end, then, is arbitrary, because you could go on searching for additional literature indefinitely.

Referencing

References, an essential aspect of the research report, are required in the following situations:

- Quoting directly from the work of another
- Paraphrasing closely the work of another
- Presenting statistics or data that are not common knowledge
- Referring the reader to a source that will clarify a point that the current report does not elaborate, but that is necessary to a complete understanding of it

Failure to give others credit in these situations constitutes *plagiarism* (see Chapter 2), or claiming others' work as one's own, a serious violation of research ethics.

References may be presented in a variety of styles and locations in the report; whatever style you select should be used consistently throughout the report. One style uses "footnotes," so called because they appear at the foot or bottom of the page on which the item being referenced is mentioned. Another style places the references after the conclusion of the report in "endnotes." In either style, you would number each point of reference sequentially, beginning with the number 1, at the appropriate location in the text (often at the end of a quotation or a sentence). Then, either at the bottom of the same page (for footnotes) or at the end of the report (for endnotes), you would repeat the number(s) you placed in the text. Following the corresponding number, you would cite the publication or other source being referenced. In the case of books, the information usually includes the author's name, the book's title, the place published, the name of the publisher, and the date of publication. Where appropriate (for example, when citing a quotation), the specific page on which the reference material is to be found in the source document is added. To cite a journal article, the author's name is followed by the title of the article, the name of the journal in which the article appeared, the volume and/or issue number and its date of publication, and the pages occupied by the article in the journal. If specific pages are to be cited, they usually appear last in a journal citation. For example, a reference to this book might be:

1. Jack D. Fitzgerald and Steven M. Cox, *Research Methods and Statistics in Criminal Justice: An Introduction,* 3rd ed. (Belmont, CA: Wadsworth, 2002), p. 266.

A reference to an article might be:

> 2.　William Jones, "Crime in Gotham City," *Criminology,* Vol. 5, No. 4 (June 1999): 312–325.

If you referred to our book again as the second reference, you might simply write "Ibid." (to indicate the work cited immediately above) and give the page number(s). If you cited the work of another author as reference three, then cited our book again in reference four, you might give our last names (Fitzgerald and Cox), the words *op. cit.* (to indicate that you were referring to a work previously cited), and the page number(s).

Sometimes, rather than source references, foot- or endnotes are brief narratives that clarify, qualify, or otherwise comment on the referenced materials in the text. In this case, references to published sources might be cited as in the APA style discussed below. Sometimes, too, both source references and supplementary narratives are included among the notes that accompany an article.

Perhaps the most widely accepted referencing styles in criminal justice studies follow the general pattern advocated by the American Psychological Association. In this style, the points of reference in the text are marked not by numbers, but by parentheses containing the authors' last names and date of publication. If, for example, you wished to refer to this book in your research report, you might do so by reporting the desired material and then referring to the book as follows: (Fitzgerald & Cox, 2002). If we had published more than one book in 2002, you would refer to the first book cited as (Fitzgerald & Cox, 2002a), the second book as (Fitzgerald & Cox, 2002b), and so on. At the end of the article, all the works cited in the text are listed alphabetically by author's last name, the year of publication, followed by the book or journal article title. As with footnotes and endnotes, the conventions for dealing with books and journal articles differ somewhat. Illustrations of different kinds of citations using APA style follow.

For a Book

Braithwaite, J. (1989). *Crime, shaming, and reintegration.* New York: Cambridge University Press.

For a Journal Article

Worden, A. P. (1993). The attitudes of women and men in policing: Testing conventional and contemporary wisdom. *Criminology,* 31, 203–241.

For an Article in a Book

Jackson, P. I. (1992). Minority group threat, social context, and policing. In A. E. Liska (Ed.), *Social threat and social control* (pp. 89–102). Albany: SUNY Press.

The Internet has become an increasingly popular source for statistical data as well as research reports among criminal justice students, practitioners, and researchers. Citation and bibliographic styles for the Internet and other e-sources are evolving. We'll make some suggestions here; others may be found in the most recent editions of the style manuals mentioned at the beginning of this chapter and at several Web sites (see the Web exercise at the end of this chapter).

When conventionally published books or journals are also made available online, the citation might begin with any of the formats discussed above for such materials and then conclude with a notation such as: "(book [or journal] online), available at *http://. . .* (that is, the Internet address or path; *be specific*; cite the address or path of the particular page(s) from which information was drawn, not just a home page or its equivalent), accessed month/day/year (that is, the date the researcher took information from the site)." Appropriate modifications could be made in the above for materials available exclusively online, including articles and databases as well as information on CD-ROM. As usual, consult your instructors or editors to determine their e-source citation preferences.

Although the information available on the Internet is growing very rapidly, and its importance for those interested in criminal justice is bound to burgeon as well, we urge caution in using this resource for two related reasons. First, information on the Internet is more ephemeral and fungible than that in printed books or journals. Items may be posted today and gone tomorrow. If it is gone, it is gone forever unless it has been archived in some form; even if it has been archived, accessing it may be extremely difficult. Furthermore, the content of a Web page (or pages) may be altered substantially without notice. (If the date of the most recent update of Web site information is provided, it should be included in the citation.) Second, and in part for the reasons just cited, you should be skeptical about Web content, just as you should with printed or spoken materials. Perhaps even more skepticism is justified for the Internet because much of the content is self-published.

Although the opportunity for creativity (or at least freedom from ordinary institutional constraints) is a significant advantage, self-published material usually escapes the professional editorial and peer review required for publication in many conventionally printed books and journals; this serves an important "community of scholars" function in scientific work. Web content may be peer reviewed too, but unless you are explicitly informed that it has been, you should assume it has not. In any event, you should verify information from other sources (including printed documents and other e-sources) whenever possible and investigate thoroughly the credibility of sites before relying upon their information.

We can now return to our discussion of the major components of a research report. In most reports, the literature review is followed by a presentation of various aspects of the research process, including the major research questions or hypotheses to be examined and the methodology(ies) used.

In our example, the literature review is followed by a description of the various components of the CHA's anti-drug initiative, the program being evaluated in the research. This section is, in turn, followed by a discussion of the methodologies the authors used in carrying out their research.

METHODS

The fourth section of a research report, the methods or research procedures section, describes the procedures employed to collect the data presented later in the report in such detail that any reader wishing to replicate the research project would be able to do so. All the methods used to accumulate information about the research topic are described, including archival research, physical evidence, various types of observation, interviews, and questionnaires. Sampling techniques used to select respondents for an interview or questionnaire survey are described. For example, the number of respondents included in the sample would be indicated, along with the sampling technique by which they were chosen for inclusion, whether a simple random sample, cluster sample, or other type of probability sample, or a purposive or other type of nonprobability sample. The setting in which the research occurred (for example, the size of the community and, perhaps, the mood or attitude of the community associated with research events) is described. Details of the specific research techniques utilized and the rationale for these techniques, such as the development of a questionnaire through any pretest procedures, would be discussed. A copy of the questionnaire or interview schedule and cover letter employed are usually provided (often in an appendix) in books but not in journal articles.

The methods section also contains a discussion of the type of data analysis to be conducted. Specifically, it states how the hypotheses will be tested or the research question(s) addressed. Some excerpts from the Popkin et al. article follows.

METHODS

Study Sites

The evaluation focused on the impact of the ADI in three CHA high-rise developments: Rockwell Gardens, Henry Horner, and Harold Ickes Homes. Horner and Ickes have been included in a preliminary evaluation (Popkin et al. 1993; Popkin et al. 1995) and were selected because of their diversity as to crime rate, level of social organization, and implementation of ADI program components. . . .

Table 13.1 lists the site characteristics, including development size, building type, and level of crime and social cohesion. Three buildings in each of the three developments were chosen for the study sample.

Data Collection

The ADI comprises a complex set of programs implemented over an eight-year period from 1988 to 1996. During the period of program evaluation, the CHA frequently changed its crime-prevention strategies. Therefore, to fully evaluate the program's effectiveness and its impact on levels of crime and social disorder, we collected several different types of data. These allowed us to assess the program and the effects of residents' lives from multiple perspectives:

Resident surveys. We conducted four waves of resident surveys approximately six months apart—May 1994, January 1995, May 1995, and December 1995. . . . Our interviewing staff consisted of current and former CHA residents who were trained to work as interviewers. We conducted most of the interviews between 9 a.m. and 3 p.m., Monday through Friday; because of safety concerns, interviews generally were not held in the evenings or on weekends (see Gwiasda, Taluc, and Popkin 1997).

We completed a total of 396 interviews in May 1994, for an overall response rate of 61 percent. In Wave 2 we increased our number of completed surveys to 547, a 75 percent response rate, and maintained that level of cooperation for Waves 3 and 4.

The survey respondents were representative of the CHA's resident population; . . .

The survey included a series of outcome measures designed to capture the impact of various components of the ADI. The key variables included the perceived severity of violence and other crime problems; the perceived severity of specific disorder problems; levels of fear of crime; victimization experience; and residents' sense of empowerment. Residents were also asked about various components of the ADI (guards, tenant patrols, sweeps, maintenance, and social services); special attention was given to their awareness, participation, and evaluation of these programs and activities.

TABLE 13. 1   **Site Characteristics**

Rockwell Gardens

    1,313 units; approximately 45% vacant; all high-rise

    Extremely high-crime; multiple gangs

    Socially isolated; moderate community organization; private management and Nation of Islam-affiliated guards from 1994 to 1996

Henry Horner Homes

    1,777 units; approximately 40% vacant; predominantly high-rise

    Extemely high-crime; multiple gangs

    Socially isolated; low community organization; redevelopment initiated in August 1995

Harold Ickes Homes

    803 units; approximately 5% vacant

    Moderately high-crime; one gang controlled drug trade

    Located adjacent to business district, institutions; high community organization

We constructed indices from the items measuring residents' perceptions of the severity of problems with physical disorder, social disorder, and violent crime both inside and outside the buildings; these indices allowed us to test for changes over time. . . .

In-depth resident interviews. To supplement the findings from the resident surveys, we conducted in-depth interviews with a small sample of well-informed residents from all three sites. Each respondent was asked general questions about some or all of the following topics: crime and maintenance problems in the selected buildings; awareness of and opinions on various ADI components including tenant patrols, CADRE centers, sweeps, and security guards; resident empowerment, including residents' ability to work together to control crime; victimization experiences; and experiences in reporting crime to police or guards.

. . . In the first round we completed 77 interviews divided almost evenly between the three sites. For the subsequent rounds of interviews, we selected approximately 32 of these respondents, who were particularly articulate and well informed, to serve as our "key informants."* The purpose of the follow-up interviews was to inquire about changes in CHA's ADI procedures and policies, such as the security guards, tenant patrols, social services, and crime. . . .

Staff interview. In addition to the resident interviews, we conducted periodic interviews with site staff members and interviewed all key ADI program staff members at least once. We also interviewed other key actors outside the CHA, including the chief of the Chicago Police CHA unit and attorneys representing tenants in the lawsuits over the constitutionality of the ADI. . . .

Ethnographic observations. The project ethnographer observed the study sites over a 15-month period. His goal was to speak with a broader range of residents than we reached through the surveys and key informant interviews, particularly the young men who lived in the developments. . . . He kept field notes on his observations and interviews, analyzed these notes for salient issues and themes, and prepared an ethnographic report on each development.

Analysis Strategy

Survey data. Analyzing change between survey waves was quite complex because of the change in the composition of the survey sample over time. Researchers typically assess change by making comparisons between independent samples (i.e., respondents at wave 1 are completely different from respondents at wave 2) or by testing for change

---

*At the end of the first round of interviews, the interviewer was asked to answer a few questions about the quality of the information obtained from the respondent. That information was used as the basis for selecting our key informants. We attempted to reinterview four residents per building but because of difficulties in locating some respondents, the actual number of key informants from each building ranged from three to five.

within correlated samples (i.e., the same respondents are surveyed at both waves). The present study is a combination of these two types of samples; therefore it cannot be analyzed easily with conventional statistical techniques.

. . .

Qualitative data. The resident interviews were tape-recorded and transcribed. On the basis of reviews of the interview transcripts, we developed a codebook that identified key themes and issues discussed in the interviews, and coded each interview. To ensure consistency and reliability, a team of two coders coded all the interview transcripts. Any questions about the way to code certain segments were discussed and resolved. A third member of the team reviewed the coding as she entered the material.

The coded interviews were entered into the Ethnograph (Qualis Research Associates 1998), a qualitative database program, for analysis. The Ethnograph allows researchers to sort a large database of qualitative interviews by the codes they have developed. . . .

Finally, we performed a content analysis of the two major Chicago newspapers, the *Tribune* and the *Sun-Times*, to track major events that had affected the CHA over time. . . . The in-depth interview data, staff interview data, ethnographies, and information from the content analysis were integrated with the survey data to allow for comparisons and to enrich our understanding of change over time.

PRESENTATION AND ANALYSIS OF DATA

In this section of the report, the collected data are described in tables, graphs, and narrative form. The presentation may include raw numbers, percentages, and proportions as well as statistical summary measures (for example, measures of central tendency and dispersion). The results of any statistical tests are given; important "findings" revealed in tables and graphs are noted and discussed. However, statements concerning the reasons for the various results and the conclusions drawn from the data should be reserved for the following section. That is, the presentation and discussion of data should be kept separate from interpretations of the meaning of the data. A look at the discussion of the findings from the Popkins et al. article will help clarify the distinction between data analysis and conclusions based upon such analysis.

FINDINGS

It appears that the components of the ADI were implemented to different degrees in each of the three sites. In general the program was implemented most successfully in Ickes and least successfully in Horner. In this section we summarize residents' perceptions of the impact of the ADI interventions on various outcome measures related to crime and disorder. We also examine the program's impact on reported victimization and fear of crime.

Physical Disorder

As described above, in each survey wave we asked residents about their perceptions of the severity of problems with broken light bulbs, graffiti, and trash and junk in the halls and on the development grounds. In May 1994, residents from all three developments reported serious problems with physical disorder. Our fieldwork indicated that the Ickes Homes had a more powerful resident council, which was able to demand better janitorial service; in addition, at the time, the development was experiencing few problems with gang conflict. As expected, the proportion of residents reporting problems there was consistently lower than in the other developments. . . . These results are illustrated in Figure 13.1. . . .

The reduction in physical disorder in Rockwell was the most significant change we documented in this development. As one key informant noted:

> It's better. They just don't have enough residents. We got . . . almost like a half-empty building, but it's cleaner, it stay cleaner . . . The janitors, they come, clean it, mop it down, sweep it, re-bulb it, re-light it up if the bulbs is out.
>
> . . .

Social Disorder

Virtually all of the ADI interventions were intended to reduce problems with drug sales and use. In each resident survey, we asked respondents about the severity of problems with social disorder inside and outside their buildings, including groups of people hanging out; *young people controlling the building*,[†] drug sales, and drug use. We use the term "young people controlling the building" as a proxy for gang dominance: . . .

In May 1994, residents from all of the developments reported serious problems with drug use and sales; in Rockwell and Horner, a majority also reported major problems with loiterers and people "controlling" the buildings. . . .

In Rockwell, several of the ADI interventions designed to reduce social disorder, including the security guards, tenant patrols, and CADRE center, were relatively unsuccessful. Despite the problems with implementation, however, the proportion of respondents reporting major problems with social disorder both inside and outside decreased from about 75 percent in May 1994 to about 50 percent in December 1995 (see Figure 13.1). The situation in Rockwell was complicated by the fact

---

[†]Because the interviews were generally conducted in the hallway, we used the phrase *young people controlling the building* to avoid the need to ask respondents directly about gang activity. Our pretesting of the instrument and the indepth interviews showed that respondents interpreted the question as we intended.

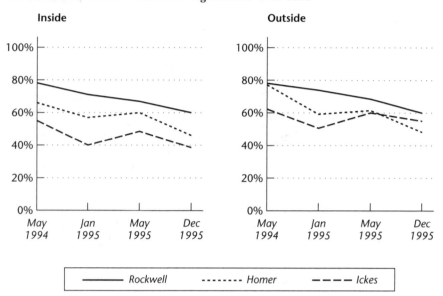

FIGURE 13.1

Physical Disorder: Percentages Reporting This as a "Big Problem" over Time

that subanalyses showed that respondents from a resident-managed building reported much greater improvements than those from the other two sample buildings. Further, even though residents perceived some improvements during this period, Rockwell experienced serious problems with drug trafficking, substance abuse, and (particularly) gang members controlling entryways;

> Yeah, I'd say (drug dealing) is less outside of the building, 'cause it's all really just inside the building right in that little lobby. . . . The drug dealers are in the lobby, so I guess the users are everywhere else. They come from everywhere, I guess.

. . .

These excerpts should provide a general idea of what is involved in data presentation and discussion. Note how the authors combine quantitative (numerical and graphic) and qualitative (interview excerpts and content analysis of newspapers) research methods to create a persuasive argument. If tests for statistical significance are employed, or if means, modes, and medians are used to describe the data, they are also discussed in this section of the report. Notice that conclusions based upon the data presented have not been discussed. These interpretive and evaluative comments should be reserved for the conclusion section of the report. The analysis contained in this section should allow the reader to examine and comprehend the data presented and to draw his own conclusions, which can then be compared with those presented in the concluding section of the report.

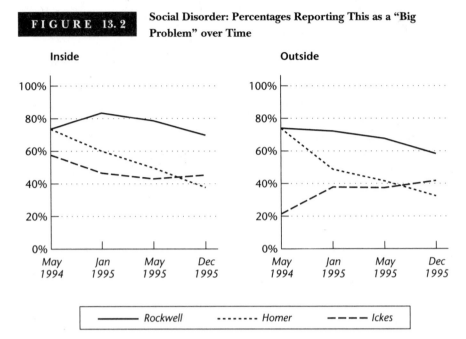

FIGURE 13.2 Social Disorder: Percentages Reporting This as a "Big Problem" over Time

THE CONCLUSION

In the conclusions and recommendations section of the research report, the data presented in the preceding section are interpreted, conclusions are drawn, and attempts are made to relate the data collected in this study to prior research and to the theoretical framework serving as a guide to the current research. Although there is often a strong temptation to draw broader conclusions about the relationships among the variables involved, the conclusions in this section should be limited to the data presented in this research report and not based upon preconceived notions concerning these relationships. In the Popkin et al. article, conclusions are drawn in the final two sections: one that discusses some follow-up data and one that discusses future research and policy implications. The benefits of combining qualitative and quantitative methods are evident.

CHANGES AFTER DECEMBER 1995

If this project had ended with the last round of surveys in December 1995, we probably would have ended this article in a cautiously optimistic note. Our findings suggested that, even in the face of tremendous odds, the CHA's efforts produced notable and statistically significant reductions in crime and disorder, particularly in Rockwell Gardens. . . . Even with the somewhat better conditions, [however] none of these developments could be regarded as "good" places to live; Rockwell and Horner remained quite dangerous. Further, qualitative research and subanalyses indicated that much of the improvement we documented in both Rockwell and Horner was limited to a single building in each development.

Follow-Up Research in 1996

Subsequent research documented just how fragile many of these changes were, and how vulnerable to changes in gang turf conflicts. We continued to conduct in-depth interviews and ethnographic observations through the summer of 1996. In addition, as part of a survey of a larger sample of CHA residents conducted for HUD, we held another round of surveys in our three sample developments (Popkin el al. 1998).[††]This follow-up research revealed that some of the biggest improvements we had documented between May 1994 and December 1995 had disappeared rapidly. . . .

Reasons for Deteriorating Conditions

Our qualitative research suggested some reasons for the dramatic deterioration of conditions in Ickes and the continuing problems in Horner and Rockwell. Two factors appear to be most important: a new outbreak of gang turf battles in CHA developments, and changes in housing authority policy. The outbreak of gang violence was precipitated by a major crackdown on gang leaders, as well as by the redevelopment of several CHA properties. . . .

IMPLICATIONS FOR RESEARCH AND POLICY

These findings suggest that addressing the problems of severely distressed public housing is a daunting task. Gangs dominated the social world of CHA's developments, influencing the level of drug trafficking and violence more strongly than either the police or the housing authority management. The CHA experienced some successes with its ADI, but most of these occurred in Ickes, where the problems were less extreme. . . .

Our findings also indicate the importance of care in implementing any anti-crime efforts. On paper at least, between 1994 and 1996, the CHA operated a model program that was both comprehensive and collaborative. The program eventually incorporated the strategies thought to be most effective in reducing crime, including both situational crime prevention and community policing. Often, however, these efforts were not implemented well; even when they were managed properly, ineffective follow-up and rapid changes in strategy undermined their effects. . . .

Further, the ADI interventions were intended to exclude "outsiders." Yet many of the people causing problems—selling drugs, using drugs, vandalizing buildings, and committing violent crimes—were not outsiders

---

[††]In this survey we included all of the nine sample buildings and used the same methodology as in our earlier research. The sample size for the 1996 survey was 396 (the decrease was due to the decline in population in Horner); the response rate was 71 percent.

but neighbors, relatives, partners, and friends of the witnesses or victims of these crimes. . . .

In the end, the demolition of the worst developments may be the only realistic strategy for the CHA; it certainly receives much political support. At least in the short run, however, our follow-up research indicates that this strategy is actually worsening conditions in CHA housing by disrupting key gang territories and creating escalating tension and insecurity. Further, it is not clear whether demolition will ultimately improve the lives of current residents. . . .

In the conclusion, the extent to which the accumulated data from all our sources supported or failed to support our hypotheses would be discussed, and any known reasons for such support or lack of support would be noted. Any serious problems with the research project and areas requiring further research might also be mentioned. The end product of this section of the report should be a summary of the results of the study, their importance in the development of the theories, and, where appropriate, a critique of the procedures employed.

THE BIBLIOGRAPHY
OR LIST OF REFERENCES

At the end of the research report is a list of the sources and resources employed in compiling the report. It is neither necessary nor desirable for the researcher to list every book, article, or paper examined in the preparation of the report. Instead, the **bibliography** or reference list should be organized alphabetically by author and include only those materials the researcher actually drew upon in writing the report, including those from which references, concepts, statistics, or quotations have been taken. This list will enable the reader to examine the same sources used by the researcher and will indicate the extent to which the literature was useful to the researcher. A standard bibliographical or reference list format is used, as found in the style manual of choice.

Popkin et al. include a list of references. We'll include only the first few to indicate the style the journal in which the article was published prefers (a slightly modified version of the APA style discussed earlier).

REFERENCES

Annan, S.O. and W.F. Skogan. 1992. *Drugs and Public Housing: Toward an Effective Police Response.* Washington, DC: Police Foundation.

Bourgois, P. 1995. *In Search of Respect: Selling Crack in El Barrio.* Cambridge, UK: Cambridge University Press.

Bowly, D. 1978. *The Poorhouse: Subsidized Housing in Chicago, 1895-1976.* Carbondale: Southern Illinois University Press.

Boydstun, J. 1975. *The San Diego Field Interrogation Experiment.* Washington, DC: Police Foundation.

Buerger, M.E. 1994. "A Tale of Two Targets: Limitations of Community Anticrime Actions." *Crime and Delinquency* 40:422–36.

Bursik, R.J. and H.G. Grasmick. 1993. *Neighborhoods and Crime: The Dimensions of Effective Community Control.* New York: Lexington Books.

Chicago Housing Authority. 1991. *The Public Housing Drug Elimination Program:* A Request to the U.S. Department of Housing and Urban Development.

Clarke, R.V. 1980. "Situational Crime Prevention: Theory and Practice." *British Journal of Criminology* 20:136–47.

———. ed, 1992. *Situational Crime Prevention: Successful Case Studies.* New York: Harrow and Heston.

———. 1995. "Situational Crime Prevention." Pp. 91–150 in *Building a Safer Society: Strategic Approaches to Crime Prevention,* edited by M. Tonry and D.P. Farrington. Chicago: University of Chicago Press.

Clarke, R.V. and P.H. Mayhew. 1980. *Designing Out Crime.* London: Her Majesty's Stationery Office.

Conklin, J.F. 1975. *The Impact of Crime.* New York: Macmillan.

Cuyahoga (Ohio) Metropolitan Housing Authority. 1993. "Police Division Overview." Presented at the Council of Large Public Housing Authority Conference on Public Housing Security, Washington, DC.

APPENDICES

Important but lengthy documents that enhance the report can be included in appendices. Such documents and their locations are referred to in the main body of the report, and the reader may decide whether it is worth his or her time to read them. For example, the researcher may indicate in the methodology section of the report that a copy of the questionnaire may be found in Appendix A.

A FINAL NOTE ON RESEARCH REPORTS

Although we have discussed each section of the research report individually, it should be apparent that a thorough consideration of all sections must be accomplished before the report is written or the research carried out. Although the abstract comes at the beginning of the report, it cannot be written until the research is completed. Similarly, the material contained in the introduction and literature review requires consideration of the methods to be employed and the type of analysis to be undertaken. Although the research report can be written a section at a time, it must be conceived in the mind of the researcher as a more or less well-integrated whole.

REVIEW QUESTIONS

1. What purposes do the abstract and references of an article serve?

2. How and why should a researcher review previous research? How should he or she select which previous research to review?

3. Why should a researcher describe the methodology and methods used to collect data?

4. Why should a researcher be skeptical of Internet information?

EXERCISES

1. Find an article in a criminal justice research journal that does not have an abstract and write one for the article.

2. Suppose you were preparing a research report on a study you had done examining the relationship between length of sentence and recidivism. Using library resources locate at least three examples of previous research on this topic and write a literature review using the studies you have located.

3. Construct a properly formatted bibliographic listing of the three sources you found in completing exercise 2.

4. Identify three different criminal justice journals in your library and compare the formats of an article in each one, including the outline reflected in the major sections of each article and referencing styles.

5. Review the additional recommendations for e-source citation styles found at *http://english.ttu.edu/kairos/1.2/inbox/mla_archive.html* and *http://www.columbia.edu/cu/cup/cgos/idx_basic.html*.

NOTE

1. Susan J. Popkin, Victoria E. Gwiasda, Dennis P. Rosenbaum, Jean M. Amendolia, Wendell A. Johnson, and Lynn M. Olson, "Combating Crime in Public Housing: A Qualitative and Quantitative Longitudinal Analysis of the Chicago Housing Authority's Anti-Drug Initiative," *Justice Quarterly* 16 (September 1999): 519–557. © Academy of Criminal Justice Sciences. Excerpts reprinted with permission.

14

Computers in Criminal Justice Research

In 1946, the first digital computer was built at the University of Pennsylvania. It filled a large room (1,500 sq. ft.), weighed 30 tons, and cost more than a half million dollars. Although it relied on 18,500 vacuum tubes and could not run more than seven or eight minutes without a tube failure, it helped revolutionize the world. IBM installed its first computer in 1948 and its first major business model in 1951. With the development of transistors and solid state circuitry in the 1960s, the revolution has continued. The astonishingly rapid growth of the Internet, including the World Wide Web, especially in the last five years, has itself transformed computing and e-source utilization once again.

In the past decade, the use of computers in all fields of work has increased tremendously, and criminal justice is no exception. It is now possible to access data stored in another computer thousands of miles away using conventional telephone lines, to analyze data and generate statistical reports using packaged programs, and to print research reports using a word-processing program. All of these tasks can be accomplished using a computer and accessories that can be purchased for less than $2,000. Computers, then, are economically feasible for most criminal justice agencies, and more and more agencies are purchasing, leasing, or sharing time on computers. In addition, virtually all academic and research institutions have sophisticated research-oriented computer systems. The range of possibilities for computer use in criminal justice research is boundless. Those who are not familiar with the basics of computers are going to be at a serious disadvantage in the coming years.

COMPONENTS OF THE COMPUTER

Mainframe computer systems that have a very large storage capacity are capable of supporting many users at one time, whereas microcomputer systems have a much smaller memory capacity and support only one or a few users. In between are a variety of possibilities in terms of size and complexity. Things are changing so rapidly in computer technology, however, that many of today's desktop PCs are capable of handling more data in more sophisticated ways than could the larger mainframes only a few years ago.

All computer systems contain the same basic components: a central processing unit (including memory, input/output circuitry, and support circuitry), data storage device(s), input devices (keyboards and/or answer sheet readers), and output devices (CRT screens and/or printers).

The central processing unit controls the operation of the computer and the flow of information within the computer. Complex switching circuits allow it to perform or execute a large variety of instructions at a high speed. To perform a particular function, the computer follows a list of instructions called a *program.* Programs may be written in a wide variety of *programming languages* (for example, Fortran, Pascal, COBOL, or BASIC), but the computer must translate these to its own unique *machine language* before it can follow the instructions. The program is put into the memory of the computer so that the computer can easily find the next instruction to follow. Additional segments of memory are reserved for storage and manipulation of data supplied by the user. There are two basic types of internal memory, read/write **random access memory (RAM)** and **read-only memory (ROM).** Programs may be contained in ROM if they need not be altered, but other programs and all data must utilize the read/write capability of RAM. The support circuitry consists of additional circuits that are required for the central processing unit to function, whereas the input/output circuitry enables the central processing unit to communicate with other components (peripherals) of the computer system.

Data storage devices permit some or all of the contents of the memory section to be written on a magnetic medium and stored for future access. In this way, programs and data can be retained while memory space is cleared for other programs or data. When the stored information is needed later, it can be read back into the computer's memory. The simplest data storage devices use magnetic tape and function like a standard tape recorder. Only entire programs and data sets may be stored and retrieved with these devices. Disk storage devices use a similar magnetic medium on either a hard or floppy disk and may be designed to permit easier access to portions of programs or data sets.

Input devices permit the human operator to enter commands or data. The most common input devices are *keyboards,* similar in appearance and function to typewriter keyboards. Also in use are **optical readers,** which can read bar codes or pencil marks on special forms such as those used in standardized examinations, and **scanners,** which can transfer words or images from printed documents to digital storage devices (floppy disk, compact disc, or tape), making distribution to many proximate or remote locations easy and inexpensive and greatly facilitating document editing.

Output devices permit the computer to communicate to the human operator. The printer translates the output of the computer into characters typed onto paper, or hard copy. Some printers produce hard copy that resembles a typewritten page and are termed *letter quality.* Other printers form characters using a dot matrix pattern and are usually capable of very high speeds. When hard copy is not required, data can be displayed on a *CRT,* a cathode ray tube, that resembles a television screen.

PREPARING DATA
FOR COMPUTER ANALYSIS

If you are preparing data for computer analysis, the first step, as we indicated in Chapter 5, is *coding* the information on each questionnaire, interview recording sheet, observational log, or whatever other device has been used to gather the data. (To facilitate the coding process, researchers often use the precoding technique discussed briefly in Chapter 5.) Ordinarily, each unit of analysis (questionnaire, individual respondent, or event) the researcher is studying is assigned a unique identification number. This number is written on the original questionnaire, event or interview record, and so on, so that the researcher is able to return to the original data source to verify the accuracy of the data entered into the computer. For each unit of analysis, a **data array** of numbers is entered onto tape or disk so that the computer can read the information. A portion of the array for a particular respondent on the sample questionnaire reprinted in Chapter 5 might look like the one below.

The ID number and the data for each variable (for example, age and sex) are assigned to a particular location (field) in the array. For every respondent, the ID number is recorded as the first three numbers, age is recorded as the fourth and fifth numbers, the code for sex as the sixth number in the array, and so on.

The process we have just described involves transferring data from the place where it was initially recorded (such as on the questionnaires or from field observation notes) to another recording device that the computer can read. Of course, whenever we are transferring information from one place to another and changing its form (such as, from check marks on the questionnaire to a number code standing for a yes or no answer to the corresponding question), errors may occur. Errors can be minimized if competent, well-trained people enter the data. Even then, however, it is important to *verify* the accuracy of the transfer process.

There are several ways to accomplish this. Perhaps the simplest one to illustrate is duplicate data entry. Essentially, after the data have been entered, they are entered again. A special entry verification program alerts the data entry person when the entries do not match. The data enterer can then check the data from its original source again and punch the appropriate keys, as if he or she were entering them for the first time. When an entry by the operator does not match the corresponding entry, the machine buzzes to signal the discrepancy. The data enterer can then check the original data source to determine which entry is incorrect and make any necessary changes in the "master" record that will be used in the analysis. Essentially the same process may be used for verifying data on any data storage media.

There is another strategy for detecting errors in the raw data entry process. It is more crude than the item by item verification just described, but it is nevertheless useful. The first step in this procedure is to have the computer print out the data arrays for all respondents so that the fields corresponding to each variable for each respondent are listed one under the other. The field for each variable can then be identified, and one can read down the list or column(s) for each variable field, checking for incorrect or inappropriate code numbers. For example, one could locate the sixth number in the first array on the list (the number corresponding to the codes for the sex variable) and read down that column. The only numbers that should appear in this column are 1 (male), 2 (female), and 9 (no information). If any other number appears in that column, an error has been made and should be corrected. Of course, the computer can be programmed to perform this check as well. These and other procedures for verifying the accuracy of the data entry process are often called *data cleaning*. Clean (that is, accurately entered) data are, of course, essential for accurate data analysis.

Because the relevant codes for each variable are located in the same place (field) in the array for each respondent, the researcher can specify which variable or variables are to be counted, cross-tabulated, or otherwise manipulated by specifying the location of the information in the array. The computer can then count and print out the number of 1s and 2s entered where sex has been coded for all of the respondents, indicating how many males and females have been included. Similarly, the computer can count and print out the number of males (code 1 in the sex field) who answered yes on question 1 (code 1 in the answer to the question 1 field), the number of females who answered yes to question 1, the number of males who answered no, and so on, producing a cross-tabulation of these two variables The computer can also calculate descriptive and inferential statistics, create bar or line graphs, scattergrams, regression lines and planes, and so on. All of these calculations can be done with great accuracy, and in a matter of a few seconds or minutes, depending on the operating speed of the computer and the number of arrays the computer has to read to perform the calculations. Performing these operations by hand would be much less accurate and much more time consuming. The capacity to process great quantities of data accurately in a very short period of time is a principal advantage of computers in research.

A major resource of academic and research institutions is the availability of large capacity computers and sophisticated data analysis programs. There are several prepackaged programs available for use, including SPSS^x (Statistical Package for the Social Sciences) and SAS (Statistical Analysis System), that are designed for "batch" (time-delayed) processing. Data and commands are entered via keyboard with these systems. SPSS^x is a similar package that allows the user to perform data analysis online, entering data and commands via a terminal. In either case, the data are processed according to the instructions contained in the program, and the results are made available to the researcher in the form of a detailed readout or printout. These programs are particularly attractive because they provide output in the form of tables and graphs that are clearly labeled, as well as a wide variety of statistics. If a prepackaged program is unavailable or inappropriate for the analysis desired, the researcher may use any of a number of programming languages to write his or her own program. However, the variety and sophistication of available programs seldom makes this necessary.

One final note about computer data analysis. Just as data entry is an important potential source of error, so also is programming. Although packaged programs are generally reliable, in our experience, it is not unusual for self-written programs to contain significant errors or for researchers to enter incorrect instructions for locating and/or manipulating data and/or calculating statistics. Often programming and calculating errors will be obvious when the output or results are examined, but sometimes they are not. It's a good idea to double check the programming instructions you give the computer. It's also a good idea to run the data on two different programs or data analysis packages and compare the results.

CURRENT COMPUTER APPLICATIONS IN CRIMINAL JUSTICE

The wide use of computers in criminal justice has made available a wealth of research information. While there is great variation among agencies and new systems are constantly being introduced, the following computer applications are common.

In law enforcement, local agencies routinely computerize information on criminal complaints and are able to retrieve individual complaint records by incident number, location, type, and name. In addition, reports can be generated from these files showing overall patterns and trends, including those required for state and federal Uniform Crime Reports (UCR). Local systems may also support *computer-aided dispatch (CAD)*, logging calls automatically, verifying addresses, indicating nearest intersection, and even identifying closest available police or ambulance units. These systems often can generate reports on number of calls, types, time and place distributions, response time, and time to clear responding units.

Telephone and wireless linkups to computers at state and federal enforcement agencies such as the National Crime Information Center and the Secretary of State's office permit local agencies to run a variety of checks on information such as vehicle tags, operators' permits, stolen vehicles, stolen/recovered property, and criminal histories. However, these state and federal files/memory banks generally are limited in terms of access for research, and few summary reports are routinely generated. On the other hand, the files maintained by the FBI and many state enforcement agencies on UCR and IBR data (including reported crimes, arrests, and manpower/ employment information) are designed to support research objectives, and frequent reports are generated and distributed.

In court administration, computer systems maintain court dockets and manage the serving of legal notices. Other systems maintain records for court supervision and probation activities. Although none of these systems is primarily designed to support research, an authorized researcher can often pull together information from their files for valuable reports.

In many correctional institutions, computerized files are maintained on all inmates, parolees, or persons under mandatory supervised release. Terminals linked by telephone to other state or federal agencies permit access to criminal histories nationwide and notification of other agencies in the event of escapes or parole or supervised-release violations. Again, although these systems were not designed primarily for researchers, they can yield some reports of great value. A number of criminal justice agencies also maintain computer files on personnel, vehicles, equipment, budgets, expenditures, and so on, that may be useful to an authorized researcher.

The growing use of computers in academic and research institutions also offers a number of new opportunities for the criminal justice researcher. Many major libraries have computerized their card catalogues, permitting on-line searches by title, author, or call number and limited searches by subject. The development of national bibliographic databases also makes it possible to conduct elaborate subject searches (on a time-delayed basis) through most major libraries. In addition, most law libraries now provide access to computerized case-law systems, such as LEXIS or WestLaw, that permit searches by citation or subject.

Further, many databases are now available to academic and research institutions through the Criminal Justice Archive and Information Network. Data concerning crime, victimization, the criminal justice system, and juvenile delinquency are maintained specifically for use by the criminal justice system researcher.

Many criminal justice agencies, including city or county police departments, have data analysts on staff and computer equipment capable of complex analysis. Among the more common uses are applied research projects (for example, identifying crime or traffic accident hot spots) that assist managers in deploying personnel and alert government agencies to take appropriate action.

Researchers may also use computer simulations to examine complex relationships among variables. The investigator provides real or dummy data for several variables and mathematical formulas for the relationships among them. The computer is then instructed to change the values of one or more of the variables and work out the corresponding changes in the other variables as determined by the formulas. Of course, unless the data are real and the mathematical formulas used have been empirically verified in actual research, these simulations are little more than computer-aided exercises of the researcher's imagination.

LIMITATIONS OF COMPUTERS

The basic advantages of the computer in research are the speed and accuracy with which it performs routine, repetitive operations that would take the researcher hours or days to perform otherwise. In addition, computers make it possible to communicate and share data with others across the nation and around the world in a very short time. As a result, the rapid growth of computers in criminal justice agencies has created wonderful opportunities for the criminal justice researcher. However, some limitations should be noted.

One major difficulty is that many of the systems are incompatible with one another, and, therefore, information cannot simply be exchanged or transferred from one computer to another. Hardware (the actual machines) and software (the programs) have been designed to allow such exchanges, but they are sometimes very troublesome, and errors in transmission and translation are not uncommon. A local police agency may automatically generate its UCR statistics, but data may have to be reentered manually at both the state and federal levels. Even programs within the same computer may be unable to communicate with one another (or use each other's data). Systems designed only to store records often do not include the software for analysis that researchers need. Suppose a researcher needs to know whether defendants making bail are more likely to be found not guilty than those without bail. He may have to search an automated docket system for a sample of cases, manually record relevant information, and reenter the data on another computer system in order to perform the desired statistical analysis.

Just as with numbers and statistics, a basic danger in computer use is that the researcher may come to think of the data as unquestionable. A researcher must constantly be alert to the fact that there is nothing magical about data generated by computers. The value of the data is dependent upon the skills of the researcher as he or she gathers, analyzes, and interprets them in terms of a theoretical framework. Whether the output is a simple frequency distribution or complex inferential statistics, the printout should be carefully examined for errors and interpreted cautiously. The researcher must be sure that the computer performed the proper operations on the data and must realize that a great deal of information contained on the printout may not be relevant to the research at hand, especially if "canned" statistical analyses programs that automatically generate a variety of statistical measurements and tests have been used.

Most importantly, the data contained on the printout will be no better than the data entered: "Garbage in, garbage out" is a familiar saying to those who work with computers. If the wrong questions were asked on the questionnaire, if the questions were ambiguous, if the variables were poorly defined, if the sample was improperly selected, if the wrong instructions were given to the computer, or if errors were made in coding or entering the data, the output will be tainted by these errors or weaknesses. Computer output requires the researcher's engagement for proper interpretation. Computers are extremely useful tools, but they are just that—tools. They can only do what they are told to do and cannot compensate for weaknesses in research design or execution.

THE INTERNET AND SCIENTIFIC RESEARCH

Use of the Internet to locate resources for scientific research has increased dramatically in the last five years. The Internet is a collection of computer networks that allows virtually instantaneous global communication among computers. The *World Wide Web* (*www.* or *Web*) is the graphically based, hyper-linked collection of information sites on the Internet.[1] By typing in a URL (Uniform Resource Locator), you can connect your computer with another computer that you hope contains the information you are seeking. Then, by typing in a word or series of words, you can locate, and often retrieve, resources in which the key words appear. If you do not know of a URL that might contain the information you require, you can use a search engine (such as *www.google.com, www.yahoo.com,* or *www.altavista.com.*) to search through Web indices to find Web sites that you think might contain the information you are seeking.

Although we certainly encourage the use of any resource that expands the available horizons, some cautions are in order. The Internet, despite its advantages of speed and accessibility, is no substitute for thorough scholarly research. A good deal of the information presented on the Internet is unsubstantiated, biased, and just plain inaccurate. As we noted in Chapter 13, the source of any information obtained from the Internet should be clearly noted, and only those sources that qualify as reputable should be used as references for research. Among these sources are a variety of online journals and abstracts that provide legitimate information and/or references to such information. There are also a number of Web sites providing excellent starting points for research. Among these are the following:

http://www.ojp.usdoj.gov/nij   *National Institute of Justice*

http://www.ojp.usdoj.gov/BJA   *Bureau of Justice Assistance*

http//www.ncjrs.org   *National Criminal Justice Reference Service*

http//www.ojjdp.ncjrs.org   *Office of Juvenile Justice and Delinquency Prevention*

http//www.ojp.usdoj.gov/bjs   *Bureau of Justice Statistics*

http//www.fbi.gov   *FBI home page*

http//www.lectlaw.com   *The 'Lectric Law Library*

http//www.corrections.com   *The Corrections Connection*

For detailed lists of Web sites and a more comprehensive discussion of the use of the Internet for criminal justice research, see Cecil Greek[2] or Robert Harris.[3]

REVIEW QUESTIONS

1. Why should researchers become familiar with computers?

2. What are the major advantages and the major limitations of computers in criminal justice research? In criminal justice bureaucracies?

3. How is the coding of data related to storage and analysis of data by computer?

4. What is "data cleaning" and why is it important?

5. What are some of the current applications of computers in criminal justice?

EXERCISES

1. Using the example of a questionnaire from Chapter 5, construct a code book and a corresponding data array for at least ten of the variables included in the questionnaire.

2. Go to the computer center at your college or university and identify the statistical analysis programs that are available and what descriptive and inferential statistics these programs provide.

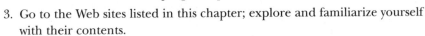 3. Go to the Web sites listed in this chapter; explore and familiarize yourself with their contents.

NOTES

1. Robert Harris, *WebQuester: A Guidebook to the Web* (Guilford, CN: Dushkin/McGraw-Hill, 1999).

2. Cecil Greek, *The Definitive Guide to Criminal Justice and Criminology on the World Wide Web* (Upper Saddle River, NJ: Prentice-Hall, 1999).

3. Harris. (See Note 1 above.)

15

Conclusions

In this text, we have characterized science as a process that strives to arrive at *statements of fact*. This formulation clearly indicates the role of language and symbolic perspectives in science and the results obtained through its methodology and its methods. Descriptive statements and hypotheses assert what we think to be fact; descriptions and hypotheses supported through the application of the scientific perspective and scientific method can be interpreted as statements of fact. A set of logically related statements, at least some of which have been tested and supported empirically, is a theory. If we remind ourselves from time to time that science deals with supposed statements of fact, formulated and tested by all too fallible humans who have chosen to become researchers, we will be able to keep an appropriately critical attitude toward the processes and products of science.

The entire scientific enterprise is filled with selectivity and choice. At the outset, researchers decide that the scientific perspective, rather than some other perspective, is appropriate to the investigation of some kinds of questions. Researchers further select, or permit others to select for them, what topics or issues deserve study. Once these general matters are determined, someone must identify the appropriate units of analysis and what particular hypotheses will be tested, which style of research is appropriate, which research design will be used, which variables are relevant, how to define the concepts and variables operationally, and which research methods and techniques to use. Problems of sampling; choosing a method of observation; preparing a laboratory, questionnaire, interview, or observation schedule; and entering the field must be resolved. A method for recording, organizing, and coding the assembled data must be devised, and the type of analysis and form of data presentation must be chosen. Finally, the results of the analysis must be interpreted and a judgment made about whether the data are consistent with the original hypothesis. Where appropriate, an assessment must be made of whether a causal inference is justified. At each of the stages in the research process, the researcher makes decisions that activate only part of the full range of possibilities. Each choice carries with it both advantages and disadvantages, and each focuses on some aspects of the problem and ignores others.

If choice is an inevitable component of scientific activity, that choice brings researchers many obligations to themselves, their audiences, and their subjects. As for their obligations to themselves, the investigator should first be aware of the many decisions he or she is making; awareness of making choices is the first step in rational and objective research. The researcher should assess the implications of these choices, including both their beneficial and detrimental consequences, and indicate these to the audience in the research report. Reporting the reasoning that led to particular choices helps those evaluating the study, especially when the consumers of the research are not professionals in the researcher's field.

Second, the researcher should be cautious in interpreting the results he or she obtains. A researcher who understands the philosophical and practical complexities of scientific study will understand why scientific conclusions are tentative.

Third, researchers should provide as complete a description of the research process as possible to allow other researchers to appraise the research intelligently and critically and to replicate the study if they desire. Without a detailed description, the usefulness of the study and the validity of its results cannot be adequately assessed.

Fourth, when statistical analysis is called for, the good researcher will weigh the advantages and disadvantages of different sampling procedures, select appropriate summary statistics for describing distributions of single variables (depending on their levels of measurement), and choose attractive but not misleading graphical displays of data. If relationships among variables are being described, the strengths and limitations of measures of association such as correlation and cross-tabulation will be considered. If hypotheses are to be subjected to tests for statistical significance, the degree to which the data conform to the assumptions underlying the selected sampling distribution will be carefully assessed. The data entry and computer analysis process will be thoroughly checked for errors and the statistical results will be interpreted with caution. Statistics, after all, are not ends in themselves; rather they are tools that help researchers make judgments about data. Statistical significance should never be confused with substantive importance.

An explanation of the nature, purposes, procedures, and results should be disseminated at least in summary form to the participants being studied. Even if a researcher thought it necessary to give subjects only partial information, or to give them false information, once the research is completed, the subjects should have the opportunity to obtain complete and correct information about the research and, where appropriate, to comment on or to correct the research report.

Finally, the ethics of the research process should be carefully considered. Where physical, social, or psychological danger to subjects is a clear possibility, the researcher must take special care to inform the subjects of the risks involved before beginning the research. Researchers also must protect the anonymity and confidentiality of subjects. Most organizations of professional social scientists (such as the Academy of Criminal Justice Science, the American Society of Criminology, the American Sociological Association, the American Psychological Association, and the American Political Science Association) and many agencies and organizations that provide funds for research (for example, the National Institutes of Health) publish and enforce a statement of ethical principles for conducting research with human subjects. Local institutional review boards provide ethics code monitoring in many situations. As in most professions, however, the primary responsibility for abiding by these ethical principles rests with the individual professional conducting the research, and that responsibility should be taken seriously.

The audience, or consumers, of scientific research owe themselves something in this process as well. First, they must invest time and effort to ensure that they understand the process that produced the results presented. Second, the audience should retain a healthy skepticism about research and researchers, and like researchers, regard reported data and conclusions drawn from them as tentative. Third, the consumer should demand a complete, accurate, and understandable account of the research. This should include possible alternative explanations for the results obtained, an assessment of the strengths and weaknesses of the study reported, and an evaluation of the extent to which the results correspond to the results of other studies of the same or similar phenomena.

Obviously, all researchers are thoroughly human, possessing the same capacities and subject to the same limitations as other people. Although researchers often construct elaborate instruments to assist them in the observational process, ultimately their own sensory perceptions are limited. Like all humans, researchers learn to speak and write a specialized language. Although language makes communication possible, the symbols used form, select, and organize experiences along particular lines, making some aspects of experiences salient while deemphasizing or obscuring others. By narrowing our focus of attention and interest, however, we can too easily forget that specialization in criminal justice, no less than specialization in other disciplines, can produce a highly selective view of the world.

Like other people, researchers occasionally experience lapses of memory, make errors of observation and reasoning, and fail to recognize the significant or obvious, in spite of precautions taken to avoid such mistakes. Because researchers have invested a great deal of time, money, and effort in their careers, and take pride in what they do, they are inclined to emphasize their successes and hide their failures, to enjoy the prestige that comes with work favorably received by peers, and to respond defensively and sometimes irrationally to criticisms of their work. Researchers also are influenced by personal preferences and prejudices, desires and dislikes, values and vulnerabilities, and their work is at least to some extent a reflection of these personal proclivities, despite their efforts to achieve objectivity.

Because most people work for someone else, in order to keep their jobs and earn a living, they must at least occasionally please their employers, and that, in turn, often means sacrificing some personal values and behaving in ways that conflict with their own interests or the principles of science. Those who do in-house and hired-hand scientific research are often caught in moral and practical dilemmas regarding research design, analysis, presentation, and interpretation of the data collected. Data can be fabricated, or assembled, presented, or interpreted in ways that deliberately distort their meaning as easily as they can be compiled in ways that are thorough, honest, and straightforward. Statistics can be used to illuminate or to mask important aspects of the evidence. Researchers are no more or less honest, no more or less subject to temptations to act in their own self-interest or that of their employers, than anyone else.

Still, science—as a perspective and as an activity—does differ in some important ways from some of the other perspectives by which people try to learn about themselves and the world they live in. Science as a means of justifying knowledge operates according to a set of explicitly stated rules, rules that emphasize the importance of precise statements of research questions and hypotheses to be investigated, precise definitions of the concepts or variables to be studied, the careful construction of research design, the strict adherence to the rules of logic, the cautious interpretation of research results, and constant reference to empirical (observable) data as a test of the investigator's interpretations or hypotheses. The application of these rules is most evident in the researcher's most powerful procedure, the experiment, a deliberate exercise in thorough planning, applied logic, controlled observation, and careful analysis.

Seldom are ideal conditions available for scientific research, and researchers must, in practice, compromise in varying degrees with the principles of science. Nonetheless, the scientific perspective and method provide—to the extent that they can be employed—a powerful technique for generating knowledge.

We have discussed the basic scientific perspective and some of the basic methodologies and methods of science as applied to the study of human behavior in this text. We have tried to put the reader in a position to appraise intelligently and critically at least some of the examples of research he or she may encounter, whether in textbooks, professional journals, or the mass media. We have discussed the pitfalls of scientific research, including the critiques of science offered by critical theorists, feminists, and postmodernists, at some length because we believe that this aspect of science is too frequently underemphasized. It is our conviction that students should understand and appreciate the basic strengths of the scientific perspective, as well as its shortcomings.

Consistent with our orientation throughout this book, we should point out that all we have said here is based on perspectives. Like the researcher, we have selected some topics for discussion and excluded others. We have stressed some aspects of the research process and given only brief consideration to others. Each of us has done research, read the research of others, and encountered many of the problems discussed in the foregoing chapters. Each of us has taught research methods. Each of us believes that scientific methodology, properly understood and carefully applied, can make a significant contribution to our efforts to understand human behavior and that, for those questions for which the scientific approach is appropriate, it offers the greatest chance of producing valid and useful results. Happy researching!

A

Table of Random Numbers

HOW TO USE THE TABLE OF RANDOM NUMBERS

The numbers in Table A.1 (see p. 308) have been randomly generated by computer. The researcher can use them to help in drawing a random sample from a population. First, however, each element in the population from which the sample is to be drawn must be assigned a unique number. This is usually done by numbering the elements in the population consecutively. If there were 286 elements in the population, for example, they would be numbered 001, 002, 003, . . . 286. Here is one procedure for using Table A.1 to select a random sample:

1. Determine a starting point in the table by closing your eyes and placing the point of your pencil somewhere in the table.

2. Using the starting point you have selected, begin reading the numbers in the table either across the rows or down the columns. If your population consisted of 99 or fewer elements, read the numbers in two-digit units; for 999 or fewer elements in the population, read the numbers in three-digit units, and so forth. If a table number does not correspond to a number assigned to one of the elements in the population (for example, 323 for our population of 286) or is the same as a

number already read from the table, skip that number and read the next. (Note that skipping a number already drawn is equivalent to sampling without replacement.) Continue until you have selected as many unique, valid numbers as there are elements in your desired sample.

3. The population elements that comprise the random sample are those whose numbers correspond to the numbers read from the table.

TABLE A.1   **Random Numbers**

11805	26316	36130	72714	27162
53798	66223	30061	13563	54828
14027	08593	86968	95905	52891
28607	99101	22303	50520	95572
38547	13770	52858	84369	33254
63317	65118	03482	57702	23757
27398	19570	61450	41899	19261
68622	98554	07116	75341	96538
01648	75908	53730	48420	98608
57619	82490	74605	78133	67807
84213	83004	00250	73800	28970
26441	77854	25573	46711	96741
68696	44733	05941	08194	84841
21762	55986	67660	07426	91523
32494	06751	02201	52567	89055
57490	55146	73035	56771	31495
91697	68418	12788	99723	34857
25747	37272	14363	32062	72895
31560	70952	74042	16372	55152
38200	43864	46432	64863	67563
25236	92827	61430	72439	81076
43783	26124	70269	21758	04868
69379	59828	76701	09757	40419
44336	68973	01784	09980	35675
56793	68672	51732	50831	16348
05572	15869	65918	93576	57505
91221	22556	20495	48881	92896
93289	57606	44655	52074	43890
36826	78857	42367	61222	91588
82311	20013	79016	42047	74945
05418	00962	01510	25556	48577
17093	63850	42949	92775	83637
17228	41093	14655	31509	84864
58404	74622	02194	10688	79856
26755	55576	28115	55501	37025
99277	41277	65281	31048	31185
05372	16764	25265	57526	64707

TABLE A.1	Continued			
10275	27829	78222	30479	55728
38277	95115	98996	79178	58105
81728	69680	06509	56831	51192
50352	66593	69338	07960	99411
92625	07337	30948	09456	19121
58247	04001	00599	33094	70302
42028	59691	83109	51317	86211
90181	06951	41082	01135	61973
95880	25087	94319	10450	82572
93210	34949	15575	34560	04589
52513	37099	48804	61642	20111
12315	36592	04971	00556	65335
01413	25163	21487	47119	99682
17934	77862	49489	73593	39933
17043	22264	34097	14201	49308
35371	98701	09595	47201	15108
31358	34890	25959	03526	49036
26791	26979	85278	40612	48973
82311	60301	48100	14313	22570
35208	90923	14046	40646	93067
81401	21608	01768	56646	18168
64730	22009	84419	32738	47953
03805	35936	15364	19143	57613
38849	54269	53821	47811	44106
73996	42503	62356	12631	50452
30758	89897	94253	71272	26652
08222	76753	04336	75918	45037
38611	05163	63154	18262	22888
22960	78799	32227	29195	06750
93725	91389	10851	91575	97765
18079	38119	78745	88786	12134
56204	06838	07600	34684	35518
36092	00478	36260	16910	25925
04231	14492	92580	31507	62353
22941	27077	93599	85948	67835
23085	99884	65049	02944	09276
75295	58425	25160	94823	46768
23915	75472	81485	10381	12465
95476	87922	06504	40536	11267
94929	01637	08543	77226	15286
17797	09714	19817	52154	01887
26171	86969	94344	41203	75834
22095	55143	42808	85581	37355

Source: Reprinted by permission of The Rand Corporation from The Rand Corporation, *A Million Random Digits with 100,000 Normal Deviates* (Santa Monica, CA: Rand, 1955), p. 59.

B

Areas Under
the Normal Curve

HOW TO USE THE TABLE OF AREAS
UNDER THE NORMAL CURVE

The standard normal curve upon which the values in this table are based has a mean of 0.0 and a standard deviation of 1.0. The total area under the standard normal curve and the corresponding probability are 1.0000.

The variable in question must be normally distributed. Before using this table, you must convert the raw scores to z-scores. Remember that a normal curve is symmetrical about the mean (that is, 0.5000 of the area lies on either side of the mean), and that z-scores can be positive or negative. Positive z-scores fall above (to the right of) the mean, and negative z-scores fall below (to the left of) the mean. Figure B.1 shows the relationship between the values in the table and the areas (and corresponding probabilities) under the standard normal curve.

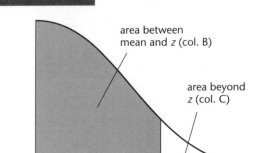

FIGURE B.1   **Areas Under One-Half the Normal Curve**

TABLE B.1   **Areas Under the Normal Curve**

A	B Area Between Mean and	C Area Beyond	A	B Area Between Mean and	C Area Beyond
z	z	z	z	z	z
0.00	.0000	.5000	0.25	.0987	.4013
0.01	.0040	.4960	0.26	.1026	.3974
0.02	.0080	.4920	0.27	.1064	.3936
0.03	.0120	.4880	0.28	.1103	.3897
0.04	.0160	.4840	0.29	.1141	.3859
0.05	.0199	.4801	0.30	.1179	.3821
0.06	.0239	.4761	0.31	.1217	.3783
0.07	.0279	.4721	0.32	.1255	.3745
0.08	.0319	.4681	0.33	.1293	.3707
0.09	.0359	.4641	0.34	.1331	.3669
0.10	.0398	.4602	0.35	.1368	.3632
0.11	.0438	.4562	0.36	.1406	.3594
0.12	.0478	.4522	0.37	.1443	.3550
0.13	.0517	.4483	0.38	.1480	.3520
0.14	.0557	.4443	0.39	.1517	.3483
0.15	.0596	.4404	0.40	.1554	.3446
0.16	.0636	.4364	0.41	.1591	.3409
0.17	.0675	.4325	0.42	.1628	.3372
0.18	.0714	.4286	0.43	.1664	.3336
0.19	.0753	.4247	0.44	.1700	.3300
0.20	.0793	.4207	0.45	.1736	.3264
0.21	.0832	.4168	0.46	.1772	.3228
0.22	.0871	.4129	0.47	.1808	.3192
0.23	.0910	.4090	0.48	.1844	.3156
0.24	.0948	.4052	0.49	.1879	.3121

TABLE B.1　Continued

A	B Area Between Mean and	C Area Beyond	A	B Area Between Mean and	C Area Beyond
z	z	z	z	z	z
0.50	.1915	.3085	0.90	.3159	.1841
0.51	.1950	.3050	0.91	.3186	.1814
0.52	.1985	.3015	0.92	.3212	.1788
0.53	.2019	.2981	0.93	.3238	.1762
0.54	.2054	.2946	0.94	.3264	.1736
0.55	.2088	.2912	0.95	.3289	.1711
0.56	.2123	.2877	0.96	.3315	.1685
0.57	.2157	.2843	0.97	.3340	.1660
0.58	.2190	.2810	0.98	.3365	.1635
0.59	.2224	.2776	0.99	.3389	.1611
0.60	.2257	.2743	1.00	.3413	.1587
0.61	.2291	.2709	1.01	.3438	.1562
0.62	.2324	.2676	1.02	.3461	.1539
0.63	.2357	.2643	1.03	.3485	.1515
0.64	.2389	.2611	1.04	.3508	.1492
0.65	.2422	.2578	1.05	.3531	.1469
0.66	.2454	.2546	1.06	.3554	.1446
0.67	.2486	.2514	1.07	.3577	.1423
0.68	.2517	.2483	1.08	.3599	.1401
0.69	.2549	.2451	1.09	.3621	.1379
0.70	.2580	.2420	1.10	.3643	.1357
0.71	.2611	.2389	1.11	.3665	.1335
0.72	.2642	.2358	1.12	.3686	.1314
0.73	.2673	.2327	1.13	.3708	.1292
0.74	.2704	.2296	1.14	.3729	.1271
0.75	.2734	.2266	1.15	.3749	.1251
0.76	.2764	.2236	1.16	.3770	.1230
0.77	.2794	.2206	1.17	.3790	.1210
0.78	.2823	.2177	1.18	.3810	.1190
0.79	.2852	.2148	1.19	.3830	.1170
0.80	.2881	.2119	1.20	.3849	.1151
0.81	.2910	.2090	1.21	.3869	.1131
0.82	.2939	.2061	1.22	.3888	.1112
0.83	.2967	.2033	1.23	.3907	.1093
0.84	.2995	.2005	1.24	.3925	.1075
0.85	.3023	.1977	1.25	.3944	.1056
0.86	.3051	.1949	1.26	.3962	.1038
0.87	.3078	.1922	1.27	.3980	.1020
0.88	.3106	.1894	1.28	.3997	.1003
0.89	.3133	.1867	1.29	.4015	.0985

| TABLE B.1 | | | Continued | | |

A	B	C	A	B	C
	Area Between Mean and	Area Beyond		Area Between Mean and	Area Beyond
z	z	z	z	z	z
1.30	.4032	.0968	1.70	.4554	.0446
1.31	.4049	.0951	1.71	.4564	.0436
1.32	.4066	.0934	1.72	.4573	.0427
1.33	.4082	.0918	1.73	.4582	.0418
1.34	.4099	.0901	1.74	.4591	.0409
1.35	.4115	.0885	1.75	.4599	.0401
1.36	.4131	.0869	1.76	.4608	.0392
1.37	.4147	.0853	1.77	.4616	.0384
1.38	.4162	.0838	1.78	.4625	.0375
1.39	.4177	.0823	1.79	.4633	.0367
1.40	.4192	.0808	1.80	.4641	.0359
1.41	.4207	.0793	1.81	.4649	.0351
1.42	.4222	.0778	1.82	.4656	.0344
1.43	.4236	.0764	1.83	.4664	.0336
1.44	.4251	.0749	1.84	.4671	.0329
1.45	.4265	.0735	1.85	.4678	.0322
1.46	.4279	.0721	1.86	.4686	.0314
1.47	.4292	.0708	1.87	.4693	.0307
1.48	.4306	.0694	1.88	.4699	.0301
1.49	.4319	.0681	1.89	.4706	.0294
1.50	.4332	.0668	1.90	.4713	.0287
1.51	.4345	.0655	1.91	.4719	.0281
1.52	.4357	.0643	1.92	.4726	.0274
1.53	.4370	.0630	1.93	.4732	.0268
1.54	.4382	.0618	1.94	.4738	.0262
1.55	.4394	.0606	1.95	.4744	.0256
1.56	.4406	.0594	1.96	.4750	.0250
1.57	.4418	.0582	1.97	.4756	.0244
1.58	.4429	.0571	1.98	.4761	.0239
1.59	.4441	.0559	1.99	.4767	.0233
1.60	.4452	.0548	2.00	.4772	.0228
1.61	.4463	.0537	2.01	.4778	.0222
1.62	.4474	.0526	2.02	.4783	.0217
1.63	.4484	.0516	2.03	.4788	.0212
1.64	.4495	.0505	2.04	.4793	.0207
1.65	.4505	.0495	2.05	.4798	.0202
1.66	.4515	.0485	2.06	.4803	.0197
1.67	.4525	.0475	2.07	.4808	.0192
1.68	.4535	.0465	2.08	.4812	.0188
1.69	.4545	.0455	2.09	.4817	.0183

TABLE B.1 Continued

A	B Area Between Mean and	C Area Beyond	A	B Area Between Mean and	C Area Beyond
z	z	z	z	z	z
2.10	.4821	.0179	2.50	.4938	.0062
2.11	.4826	.0174	2.51	.4940	.0060
2.12	.4830	.0170	2.52	.4941	.0059
2.13	.4834	.0166	2.53	.4943	.0057
2.14	.4838	.0162	2.54	.4945	.0055
2.15	.4842	.0158	2.55	.4946	.0054
2.16	.4846	.0154	2.56	.4948	.0052
2.17	.4850	.0150	2.57	.4949	.0051
2.18	.4854	.0146	2.58	.4951	.0049
2.19	.4857	.0143	2.59	.4952	.0048
2.20	.4861	.0139	2.60	.4953	.0047
2.21	.4864	.0136	2.61	.4955	.0045
2.22	.4868	.0132	2.62	.4956	.0044
2.23	.4871	.0129	2.63	.4957	.0043
2.24	.4875	.0125	2.64	.4959	.0041
2.25	.4878	.0122	2.65	.4960	.0040
2.26	.4881	.0119	2.66	.4961	.0039
2.27	.4884	.0116	2.67	.4962	.0038
2.28	.4887	.0113	2.68	.4963	.0037
2.29	.4890	.0110	2.69	.4964	.0036
2.30	.4893	.0107	2.70	.4965	.0035
2.31	.4896	.0104	2.71	.4966	.0034
2.32	.4898	.0102	2.72	.4966	.0033
2.33	.4901	.0099	2.73	.4968	.0032
2.34	.4904	.0096	2.74	.4969	.0031
2.35	.4906	.0094	2.75	.4970	.0030
2.36	.4909	.0091	2.76	.4971	.0029
2.37	.4911	.0089	2.77	.4972	.0028
2.38	.4913	.0087	2.78	.4973	.0027
2.39	.4916	.0084	2.79	.4974	.0026
2.40	.4918	.0082	2.80	.4974	.0026
2.41	.4920	.0080	2.81	.4975	.0025
2.42	.4922	.0078	2.82	.4976	.0024
2.43	.4925	.0075	2.83	.4977	.0023
2.44	.4927	.0073	2.84	.4977	.0023
2.45	.4929	.0071	2.85	.4978	.0022
2.46	.4931	.0069	2.86	.4979	.0021
2.47	.4932	.0068	2.87	.4979	.0021
2.48	.4934	.0066	2.88	.4980	.0020
2.49	.4936	.0064	2.89	.4981	.0019

TABLE B.1 **Continued**

A	B Area Between Mean and	C Area Beyond	A	B Area Between Mean and	C Area Beyond
z	z	z	z	z	z
2.90	.4981	.0019	3.13	.4991	.0009
2.91	.4982	.0018	3.14	.4992	.0008
2.92	.4982	.0018	3.15	.4992	.0008
2.93	.4983	.0017	3.16	.4992	.0008
2.94	.4984	.0016	3.17	.4992	.0008
2.95	.4984	.0016	3.18	.4993	.0007
2.96	.4985	.0015	3.19	.4993	.0007
2.97	.4985	.0015	3.20	.4993	.0007
2.98	.4986	.0014	3.21	.4993	.0007
2.99	.4986	.0014	3.22	.4994	.0006
3.00	.4987	.0013	3.23	.4994	.0006
3.01	.4987	.0013	3.24	.4994	.0006
3.02	.4987	.0013	3.25	.4994	.0006
3.03	.4988	.0012	3.30	.4995	.0005
3.04	.4988	.0012	3.35	.4996	.0004
3.05	.4989	.0011	3.40	.4997	.0003
3.06	.4989	.0011	3.45	.4997	.0003
3.07	.4989	.0011	3.50	.4998	.0002
3.08	.4990	.0010	3.60	.4998	.0002
3.09	.4990	.0010	3.70	.4999	.0001
3.10	.4990	.0010	3.80	.4999	.0001
3.11	.4991	.0009	3.90	.49995	.00005
3.12	.4991	.0009	4.00	.49997	.00003

Source: Richard Runyon and Audrey Haber, *Fundamentals of Behavioral Statistics,* 2nd ed. Table A (pp. 289–291). © 1971 Addison Wesley Longman Ltd. Reprinted by permission of Addison Wesley Longman.

C

Student's *t* Distributions Table

HOW TO USE THE STUDENT'S *t* DISTRIBUTIONS TABLE

First, determine whether a one-tailed or a two-tailed test is appropriate—that is, whether you will be using the column headings in the first or the second row of the table (see p. 317). Next, select the level of significance for your test from the row you have selected; the column of the table you will be using has now been determined. Finally, calculate *df* for your data and locate its value (or nearest value) in the left-hand column, thereby determining the row of the table you will be using. The quantity in the cell of the table at the intersection of the row and the column you have identified is the critical value of *t* for your test. If you have calculated a *t* whose value is equal to or larger than the quantity in this cell, the difference between means is statistically significant at the level you have chosen.

TABLE C.1	Student's *t* Distributions

	Level of Significance for One-Tailed Test					
	.10	.05	.025	.01	.005	.0005
	Level of Significance for Two-Tailed Test					
	.20	.10	.05	.02	.01	.001
df						
1	3.078	6.314	12.706	31.821	63.657	636.619
2	1.886	2.920	4.303	6.965	9.925	31.598
3	1.638	2.353	3.182	4.541	5.841	12.941
4	1.533	2.132	2.776	3.747	4.604	8.610
5	1.476	2.015	2.571	3.365	4.032	6.859
6	1.440	1.943	2.447	3.143	3.707	5.959
7	1.415	1.895	2.365	2.998	3.499	5.405
8	1.397	1.860	2.306	2.896	3.355	5.041
9	1.383	1.833	2.262	2.821	3.250	4.781
10	1.372	1.812	2.228	2.764	3.169	4.587
11	1.363	1.796	2.201	2.718	3.106	4.437
12	1.356	1.782	2.179	2.681	3.055	4.318
13	1.350	1.771	2.160	2.650	3.012	4.221
14	1.345	1.761	2.145	2.624	2.977	4.140
15	1.341	1.753	2.131	2.602	2.947	4.073
16	1.337	1.746	2.120	2.583	2.921	4.015
17	1.333	1.740	2.110	2.567	2.898	3.965
18	1.330	1.734	2.101	2.552	2.878	3.922
19	1.328	1.729	2.093	2.539	2.861	3.883
20	1.325	1.725	2.086	2.528	2.845	3.850
21	1.323	1.721	2.080	2.518	2.831	3.819
22	1.321	1.717	2.074	2.508	2.819	3.792
23	1.319	1.714	2.069	2.500	2.807	3.767
24	1.318	1.711	2.064	2.492	2.797	3.745
25	1.316	1.708	2.060	2.485	2.787	3.725
26	1.315	1.706	2.056	2.479	2.779	3.707
27	1.314	1.703	2.052	2.473	2.771	3.690
28	1.313	1.701	2.048	2.467	2.763	3.674
29	1.311	1.699	2.045	2.462	2.756	3.659
30	1.310	1.697	2.042	2.457	2.750	3.646
40	1.303	1.684	2.021	2.423	2.704	3.551
60	1.296	1.671	2.000	2.390	2.660	3.460
120	1.289	1.658	1.980	2.358	2.617	3.373
∞	1.282	1.645	1.960	2.326	2.576	3.291

Source: Adapted from Table III of R. A. Fisher and F. Yates, *Statistical Tables for Biological, Agricultural and Medical Research*, 1948 edition. Reprinted by permission of Addison Wesley Longman Ltd.

D

F Distribution Tables

HOW TO USE THE F DISTRIBUTION TABLES

The table (see p. 319) is divided into two separate sections, each consisting of two pages. The first section gives critical values of F for the .05 level of significance; the second section gives critical values of F for the .01 level of significance. First, decide the appropriate level of significance for your test—that is, whether you will be using the first two pages or the last two pages of the table. The first row of each table lists various values for df_1, the degrees of freedom associated with the categories or groups of the independent variable. Calculate the value of df_1 ($df_1 = k - 1$) for your data and locate it in the first row of the section of the table you have selected. Next, calculate df_2 ($df_2 = n - k$) for your data and locate it in the left-most column. The quantity in the cell corresponding to the intersection of the row and column you have identified is the critical value of F for your test. If the F you have calculated for your data is equal to or greater than this quantity, your results are statistically significant at the level you have chosen.

TABLE D.1				Distribution of *F*; *P* = 0.05				
df_1	1	2	3	4	5	6	8	10
df_2								
1	161.4	199.5	215.7	224.6	230.2	234.0	238.9	241.9
2	18.51	19.00	19.16	19.25	19.30	19.33	19.37	19.40
3	10.13	9.55	9.28	9.12	9.01	8.94	8.85	8.79
4	7.71	6.94	6.59	6.39	6.26	6.16	6.04	5.96
5	6.61	5.79	5.41	5.19	5.05	4.95	4.82	4.74
6	5.99	5.14	4.76	4.53	4.39	4.28	4.15	4.06
7	5.59	4.74	4.35	4.12	3.97	3.87	3.73	3.64
8	5.32	4.46	4.07	3.84	3.69	3.58	3.44	3.35
9	5.12	4.26	3.86	3.63	3.48	3.37	3.23	3.14
10	4.96	4.10	3.71	3.48	3.33	3.22	3.07	2.98
11	4.84	3.98	3.59	3.36	3.20	3.09	2.95	2.85
12	4.75	3.89	3.49	3.26	3.11	3.00	2.85	2.75
13	4.67	3.81	3.41	3.18	3.03	2.92	2.77	2.67
14	4.60	3.74	3.34	3.11	2.96	2.85	2.70	2.60
15	4.54	3.68	3.29	3.06	2.90	2.79	2.64	2.54
16	4.49	3.63	3.24	3.01	2.85	2.74	2.59	2.49
17	4.45	3.59	3.20	2.96	2.81	2.70	2.55	2.45
18	4.41	3.55	3.16	2.93	2.77	2.66	2.51	2.41
19	4.38	3.52	3.13	2.90	2.74	2.63	2.48	2.38
20	4.35	3.49	3.10	2.87	2.71	2.60	2.45	2.35
21	4.32	3.47	3.07	2.84	2.68	2.57	2.42	2.32
22	4.30	3.44	3.05	2.82	2.66	2.55	2.40	2.30
23	4.28	3.42	3.03	2.80	2.64	2.53	2.37	2.27
24	4.26	3.40	3.01	2.78	2.62	2.51	2.36	2.25
25	4.24	3.39	2.99	2.76	2.60	2.49	2.34	2.24
26	4.23	3.37	2.98	2.74	2.59	2.47	2.32	2.22
27	4.21	3.35	2.96	2.73	2.57	2.46	2.31	2.20
28	4.20	3.34	2.95	2.71	2.56	2.45	2.29	2.19
29	4.18	3.33	2.93	2.70	2.55	2.43	2.28	2.18
30	4.17	3.32	2.92	2.69	2.53	2.42	2.27	2.16
40	4.08	3.23	2.84	2.61	2.45	2.34	2.18	2.08
60	4.00	3.15	2.76	2.53	2.37	2.25	2.10	1.99
80	3.96	3.11	2.72	2.48	2.33	2.21	2.05	1.95
120	3.92	3.07	2.68	2.45	2.29	2.17	2.02	1.91
∞	3.84	3.00	2.60	2.37	2.21	2.10	1.94	1.83

TABLE D.1 Distribution of F; $P = 0.05$, Continued

df_1	12	15	20	30	40	60	120	∞
df_2								
1	243.9	245.9	248.0	250.1	251.1	252.2	253.3	254.3
2	19.41	19.43	19.45	19.46	19.47	19.48	19.49	19.50
3	8.74	8.70	8.66	8.62	8.59	8.57	8.55	8.53
4	5.91	5.86	5.80	5.75	5.72	5.69	5.66	5.63
5	4.68	4.62	4.56	4.50	4.46	4.43	4.40	4.36
6	4.00	3.94	3.87	3.81	3.77	3.74	3.70	3.67
7	3.57	3.51	3.44	3.38	3.34	3.30	3.27	3.23
8	3.28	3.22	3.15	3.08	3.04	3.01	2.97	2.93
9	3.07	3.01	2.94	2.86	2.83	2.79	2.75	2.71
10	2.91	2.85	2.77	2.70	2.66	2.62	2.58	2.54
11	2.79	2.72	2.65	2.57	2.53	2.49	2.45	2.40
12	2.69	2.62	2.54	2.47	2.43	2.38	2.34	2.30
13	2.60	2.53	2.46	2.38	2.34	2.30	2.25	2.21
14	2.53	2.46	2.39	2.31	2.27	2.22	2.18	2.13
15	2.48	2.40	2.33	2.25	2.20	2.16	2.11	2.07
16	2.42	2.35	2.28	2.19	2.15	2.11	2.06	2.01
17	2.38	2.31	2.23	2.15	2.10	2.06	2.01	1.96
18	2.34	2.27	2.19	2.11	2.06	2.02	1.97	1.92
19	2.31	2.23	2.16	2.07	2.03	1.98	1.93	1.88
20	2.28	2.20	2.12	2.04	1.99	1.95	1.90	1.84
21	2.25	2.18	2.10	2.01	1.96	1.92	1.87	1.81
22	2.23	2.15	2.07	1.98	1.94	1.89	1.84	1.78
23	2.20	2.13	2.05	1.96	1.91	1.86	1.81	1.76
24	2.18	2.11	2.03	1.94	1.89	1.84	1.79	1.73
25	2.16	2.09	2.01	1.92	1.87	1.82	1.77	1.71
26	2.15	2.07	1.99	1.90	1.85	1.80	1.75	1.69
27	2.13	2.06	1.97	1.88	1.84	1.79	1.73	1.67
28	2.12	2.04	1.96	1.87	1.82	1.77	1.71	1.65
29	2.10	2.03	1.94	1.85	1.81	1.75	1.70	1.64
30	2.09	2.01	1.93	1.84	1.79	1.74	1.68	1.62
40	2.00	1.92	1.84	1.74	1.69	1.64	1.58	1.51
60	1.92	1.84	1.75	1.65	1.59	1.53	1.47	1.39
80	1.88	1.80	1.70	1.60	1.54	1.49	1.41	1.32
120	1.83	1.75	1.66	1.55	1.50	1.43	1.35	1.25
∞	1.75	1.67	1.57	1.46	1.39	1.32	1.22	1.00

| TABLE D.1 | | Distribution of F; $P = 0.01$ | | | | | | |

df_1	1	2	3	4	5	6	8	10
df_2								
1	4052	4999.5	5403	5625	5764	5859	5982	6056
2	98.50	99.00	99.17	99.25	99.30	99.33	99.37	99.40
3	34.12	30.82	29.46	28.71	28.24	27.91	27.49	27.23
4	21.20	18.00	16.69	15.98	15.52	15.21	14.80	14.55
5	16.26	13.27	12.06	11.39	10.97	10.67	10.29	10.05
6	13.75	10.92	9.78	9.15	8.75	8.47	8.10	7.87
7	12.25	9.55	8.45	7.85	7.46	7.19	6.84	6.62
8	11.26	8.65	7.59	7.01	6.63	6.37	6.03	5.81
9	10.56	8.02	6.99	6.42	6.06	5.80	5.47	5.26
10	10.04	7.56	6.55	5.99	5.64	5.39	5.06	4.85
11	9.65	7.21	6.22	5.67	5.32	5.07	4.74	4.54
12	9.33	6.93	5.95	5.41	5.06	4.82	4.50	4.30
13	9.07	6.70	5.74	5.21	4.86	4.62	4.30	4.10
14	8.86	6.51	5.56	5.04	4.69	4.46	4.14	3.94
15	8.68	6.36	5.42	4.89	4.56	4.32	4.00	3.80
16	8.53	6.23	5.29	4.77	4.44	4.20	3.89	3.69
17	8.40	6.11	5.18	4.67	4.34	4.10	3.79	3.59
18	8.29	6.01	5.09	4.58	4.25	4.01	3.71	3.51
19	8.18	5.93	5.01	4.50	4.17	3.94	3.63	3.43
20	8.10	5.85	4.94	4.43	4.10	3.87	3.56	3.37
21	8.02	5.78	4.87	4.37	4.04	3.81	3.51	3.31
22	7.95	5.72	4.82	4.31	3.99	3.76	3.45	3.26
23	7.88	5.66	4.76	4.26	3.94	3.71	3.41	3.21
24	7.82	5.61	4.72	4.22	3.90	3.67	3.36	3.17
25	7.77	5.57	4.68	4.18	3.85	3.63	3.32	3.13
26	7.72	5.53	4.64	4.14	3.82	3.59	3.29	3.09
27	7.68	5.49	4.60	4.11	3.78	3.56	3.26	3.06
28	7.64	5.45	4.57	4.07	3.75	3.53	3.23	3.03
29	7.60	5.42	4.54	4.04	3.73	3.50	3.20	3.00
30	7.56	5.39	4.51	4.02	3.70	3.47	3.17	2.98
40	7.31	5.18	4.31	3.83	3.51	3.29	2.99	2.80
60	7.08	4.98	4.13	3.65	3.34	3.12	2.82	2.63
80	6.96	4.88	4.04	3.56	3.25	3.04	2.74	2.55
120	6.85	4.79	3.95	3.48	3.17	2.96	2.66	2.47
∞	6.63	4.61	3.78	3.32	3.02	2.80	2.51	2.32

TABLE D.1		Distribution of F; $P = 0.01$, Continued					

df_1	12	15	20	30	40	60	120	∞
df_2								
1	6106	6157	6209	6261	6287	6313	6339	6366
2	99.42	99.43	99.45	99.47	99.47	99.48	99.49	99.50
3	27.05	26.87	26.69	26.50	26.41	26.32	26.22	26.13
4	14.37	14.20	14.02	13.84	13.75	13.65	13.56	13.46
5	9.89	9.72	9.55	9.38	9.29	9.20	9.11	9.02
6	7.72	7.56	7.40	7.23	7.14	7.06	6.97	6.88
7	6.47	6.31	6.16	5.99	5.91	5.82	5.74	5.65
8	5.67	5.52	5.36	5.20	5.12	5.03	4.95	4.86
9	5.11	4.96	4.81	4.65	4.57	4.48	4.40	4.31
10	4.71	4.56	4.41	4.25	4.17	4.08	4.00	3.91
11	4.40	4.25	4.10	3.94	3.86	3.78	3.69	3.60
12	4.16	4.01	3.86	3.70	3.62	3.54	3.45	3.36
13	3.96	3.82	3.66	3.51	3.43	3.34	3.25	3.17
14	3.80	3.66	3.51	3.35	3.27	3.18	3.09	3.00
15	3.67	3.52	3.37	3.21	3.13	3.05	2.96	2.87
16	3.55	3.41	3.26	3.10	3.02	2.93	2.84	2.75
17	3.46	3.31	3.16	3.00	2.92	2.83	2.75	2.65
18	3.37	3.23	3.08	2.92	2.84	2.75	2.66	2.57
19	3.30	3.15	3.00	2.84	2.76	2.67	2.58	2.49
20	3.23	3.09	2.94	2.78	2.69	2.61	2.52	2.42
21	3.17	3.03	2.88	2.72	2.64	2.55	2.46	2.36
22	3.12	2.98	2.83	2.67	2.58	2.50	2.40	2.31
23	3.07	2.93	2.78	2.62	2.54	2.45	2.35	2.26
24	3.03	2.89	2.74	2.58	2.49	2.40	2.31	2.21
25	2.99	2.85	2.70	2.54	2.45	2.36	2.27	2.17
26	2.96	2.81	2.66	2.50	2.42	2.33	2.23	2.13
27	2.93	2.78	2.63	2.47	2.38	2.29	2.20	2.10
28	2.90	2.75	2.60	2.44	2.35	2.26	2.17	2.06
29	2.87	2.73	2.57	2.41	2.33	2.23	2.14	2.03
30	2.84	2.70	2.55	2.39	2.30	2.21	2.11	2.01
40	2.66	2.52	2.37	2.20	2.11	2.02	1.92	1.80
60	2.50	2.35	2.20	2.03	1.94	1.84	1.73	1.60
80	2.41	2.28	2.11	1.94	1.84	1.75	1.63	1.49
120	2.34	2.19	2.03	1.86	1.76	1.66	1.53	1.38
∞	2.18	2.04	1.88	1.70	1.59	1.47	1.32	1.00

Source: Adapted from Table V of R. A. Fisher and F. Yates, *Statistical Tables for Biological, Agricultural and Medical Research*, 1948 edition. Reprinted by permission of Addison Wesley Longman Ltd.

E

Chi Square Table

HOW TO USE THE CHI SQUARE TABLE

To use this table (see p. 324), first compute the value of chi square by using the formula for calculating chi square given in the text. Next, compute the degrees of freedom (df) by following the instructions given in the text. Now, to find the probability of obtaining a chi square equal to the one you have computed locate your table's number of degrees of freedom in the column headed df on the left-hand side of the table. Then read across the row of the table corresponding to this df value until you come to a value in the table equal to or larger than the chi square value you have calculated. If the value in the table is equal to the value you have calculated, the probability is determined by noting the probability indicated above the column in which the value appears. If the chi square value you have calculated falls between the values in adjacent columns in the table, the probability of the calculated chi square value is less than the probability that appears above the left column and greater than the probability that appears above the right column of the table.

TABLE E·1   Chi Square Table

df	.99	.98	.95	.90	.80	.70	.50	.30	.20	.10	.05	.02	.01	.001
							Probability							
1	.0³157	.0³628	.00393	.0158	.0642	.148	.455	1.074	1.642	2.706	3.841	5.412	6.635	10.827
2	.0201	.0404	.103	.211	.446	.713	1.386	2.408	3.219	4.605	5.991	7.824	9.210	13.815
3	.115	.185	.352	.584	1.005	1.424	2.366	3.665	4.642	6.251	7.815	9.837	11.341	16.268
4	.297	.429	.711	1.064	1.649	2.195	3.357	4.878	5.989	7.779	9.488	11.668	13.277	18.465
5	.554	.752	1.145	1.610	2.343	3.000	4.351	6.064	7.289	9.236	11.070	13.388	15.086	20.517
6	.872	1.134	1.635	2.204	3.070	3.828	5.348	7.231	8.558	10.645	12.592	15.033	16.812	22.457
7	1.239	1.564	2.167	2.833	3.822	4.671	6.346	8.383	9.803	12.017	14.067	16.622	18.475	24.322
8	1.646	2.032	2.733	3.490	4.594	5.527	7.344	9.524	11.030	13.362	15.507	18.168	20.090	26.125
9	2.088	2.532	3.325	4.168	5.380	6.393	8.343	10.656	12.242	14.684	16.919	19.679	21.666	27.877
10	2.558	3.059	3.940	4.865	6.179	7.267	9.342	11.781	13.442	15.987	18.307	21.161	23.209	29.588
11	3.053	3.609	4.575	5.578	6.989	8.148	10.341	12.899	14.631	17.275	19.675	22.618	24.725	31.264
12	3.571	4.178	5.226	6.304	7.807	9.034	11.340	14.011	15.812	18.549	21.026	24.054	26.217	32.909
13	4.107	4.765	5.892	7.042	8.634	9.926	12.340	15.119	16.985	19.812	22.362	25.472	27.688	34.528
14	4.660	5.368	6.571	7.790	9.467	10.821	13.339	16.222	18.151	21.064	23.685	26.873	29.141	36.123
15	5.229	5.985	7.261	8.547	10.307	11.721	14.339	17.322	19.311	22.307	24.996	28.259	30.578	37.697
16	5.812	6.614	7.962	9.312	11.152	12.624	15.338	18.418	20.465	23.542	26.296	29.633	32.000	39.252
17	6.408	7.255	8.672	10.085	12.002	13.531	16.338	19.511	21.615	24.769	27.587	30.995	33.409	40.790
18	7.015	7.906	9.390	10.865	12.857	14.440	17.338	20.601	22.760	25.989	28.869	32.346	34.805	42.312
19	7.633	8.567	10.117	11.651	13.716	15.352	18.338	21.689	23.900	27.204	30.144	33.687	36.191	43.820
20	8.260	9.237	10.851	12.443	14.578	16.266	19.337	22.775	25.038	28.412	31.410	35.020	37.566	45.315

TABLE E.1 Continued

Probability

df	.99	.98	.95	.90	.80	.70	.50	.30	.20	.10	.05	.02	.01	.001
21	8.897	9.915	11.591	13.240	15.445	17.182	20.337	23.858	26.171	29.615	32.671	36.343	39.932	46.797
22	9.542	10.600	12.338	14.041	16.314	18.101	21.337	24.939	27.301	30.813	33.924	37.659	40.289	48.268
23	10.196	11.293	13.091	14.848	17.187	19.021	22.337	26.018	28.429	32.007	35.172	38.968	41.638	39.728
24	10.856	11.992	13.848	15.659	18.062	19.943	23.337	27.096	29.553	33.196	36.415	40.270	42.980	51.179
25	11.524	12.697	14.611	16.473	18.940	20.867	24.337	28.172	30.675	34.382	37.652	41.566	44.314	52.620
26	12.198	13.409	15.379	17.292	19.820	21.792	25.336	29.246	31.795	35.563	38.885	42.856	45.642	54.052
27	12.879	14.125	16.151	18.114	20.703	22.719	26.336	30.319	32.912	36.741	40.113	44.140	46.963	55.476
28	13.565	14.847	16.928	18.939	21.588	23.647	27.336	31.391	34.027	37.916	41.337	45.419	48.278	56.893
29	14.256	15.574	17.708	19.768	22.475	24.577	28.336	32.461	35.139	39.087	42.557	46.693	49.588	58.302
30	14.953	16.306	18.493	20.599	23.364	25.508	29.336	33.530	36.250	40.256	43.773	47.962	50.892	59.703

Source: Adapted from Table IV of R. A. Fisher and F. Yates, *Statistical Tables for Biological, Agricultural and Medical Research*, 1948 edition. Reprinted by permission of Addison Wesley Longman Ltd.

Excerpts from the Code of Ethics of the Academy of Criminal Justice Sciences

I. PREAMBLE

Criminal Justice is a scientific discipline and those who teach, research, study, administer or practice in this discipline subscribe to the general tenets of science and scholarship. They also recognize that the discovery, creation, transmission and accumulation of knowledge in any scientific discipline involves ethical considerations at every level.

The Code of Ethics of the Academy of Criminal Justice Sciences (ACJS) sets forth (1) General Principles and (2) Ethical Standards that underlie members of the Academy's professional responsibilities and conduct, along with the (3) Policies and Procedures for enforcing those principles and standards. Membership in the Academy of Criminal Justice Sciences commits individual members to adhere to the ACJS Code of Ethics in determining ethical behavior in the context of their everyday professional activities. Activities that are purely personal and not related to criminal justice as a scientific discipline are not subject to this Code of Ethics.

The General Principles contained in this Code express the values and ideals of the Academy of Criminal Justice Sciences for ethical behavior in the context of the professional activities of individual members of the Academy. The general principles should be considered by members in arriving at an ethical course of action in specific situations, and they may be considered by the Ethics

Committee and the Executive Board of the ACJS in determining whether ethical violations have occurred and whether sanctions should be applied.

The Ethical Standards set forth enforceable rules for the behavior of individual members of the Academy in specific situations. Most of the ethical standards are written broadly, to provide applications in varied roles and varied contexts. The Ethical Standards are not exhaustive—conduct that is not included in the Ethical Standards is not necessarily ethical or unethical. The Ethical Standards should always be interpreted in the context of the General Principles.

Violations of the Code of Ethics may lead to sanctions associated with individual membership in the Academy of Criminal Justice Sciences, including restrictions on or termination of that membership.

II. GENERAL PRINCIPLES

In their professional activities, members of the Academy are committed to enhancing the general well-being of society and of the individuals and groups within it. Members of the Academy are especially careful to avoid incompetent, unethical or unscrupulous use of criminal justice knowledge. They recognize the great potential for harm that is associated with the study of criminal justice, and they do not knowingly place the well-being of themselves or other people in jeopardy in their professional work.

Members of the Academy respect the rights, dignity and worth of all people. The worth of people gives them the right to demand that information about them remain confidential. In their work, members of the Academy are particularly careful to respect the rights, dignity and worth of criminal justice personnel, crime victims and those accused or convicted of committing crimes, as well as of students and research subjects. They do not discriminate on the basis of age, gender, race, ethnicity, national origin, religion, sexual orientation, health condition or domestic status. They are sensitive to individual, cultural and role differences among peoples. They acknowledge the rights of other people and groups to hold values, attitudes and opinions that are different from their own.

Members of the Academy are honest and open in their professional dealings with others. They are committed to the free and open access to knowledge, to public discourse of findings, and to the sharing of the sources of those findings whenever possible. They do not knowingly make false, misleading or deceptive statements in their professional roles. In particular, they do not knowingly present false, misleading or deceptive accounts of their own or other people's professional work for any reason.

Members of the Academy strive to maintain high levels of competence in their work. They recognize the limits of their expertise and undertake only those tasks for which they are qualified by education, training and experience.

In some situations, the above general principles may seem to come into conflict with each other, in the sense that different principles may seem to call for different courses of action. In addition, members of the Academy might be members of other organizations with their own code of ethics, which at times might dictate different courses of action. The following Ethical Standards attempt to clarify the present thinking of the Academy of Criminal Justice Sciences regarding ethical courses of action in some of those situations. However, to some extent, each individual member of the Academy should evaluate the ethical requirements of a specific situation, decide on an ethical course of action for that situation, and take responsibility for those actions.

III. ETHICAL STANDARDS

. . .

B. Members of the Academy as Researchers

Objectivity and Integrity in the Conduct of Criminal Justice Research.

1. Members of the Academy should adhere to the highest possible technical standards in their research.

2. Since individual members of the Academy vary in their research modes, skills, and experience, they should acknowledge the limitations that may affect the validity of their findings.

3. In presenting their work, members of the Academy are obliged to fully report their findings. They should not misrepresent the findings of their research or omit significant data. Any and all omitted data should be noted and the reason(s) for exclusion stated clearly as part of the methodology. Details of their theories, methods, and research designs that might bear upon interpretations of research findings should be reported.

4. Members of the Academy should fully report all sources of financial support and other sponsorship of the research.

5. Members of the Academy should not make commitments to respondents, individuals, groups or organizations unless there is full intention and ability to honor them.

6. Consistent with the spirit of full disclosure of method and analysis, members of the Academy, after they have completed their own analyses, should cooperate in efforts to make raw data and pertinent documentation available to other social scientists, at reasonable costs, except in cases where confidentiality, the client's rights of proprietary information and privacy, or the claims of a field worker to the privacy of personal notes necessarily would be violated. The timeliness of this cooperation is especially critical.

7. Members of the Academy should provide adequate information, documentation, and citations concerning scales and other measures used in their research.

8. Members of the Academy should not accept grants, contracts or research assignments that appear likely to violate the principles enunciated in this Code, and should disassociate themselves from research when they discover a violation and are unable to correct it.

9. When financial support for a project has been accepted, members of the Academy should make every reasonable effort to complete the proposed work on schedule.

10. When a member of the Academy is involved in a project with others, including students, there should be mutually accepted explicit agreements at the outset with respect to division of work, compensation, access to data, rights of authorship, and other rights and responsibilities. These agreements should not be exploitative or arrived at through any form of coercion or intimidation. Such agreements may need to be modified as the project evolves and such modifications should be clearly stated among all participants. Students should normally be the principle author of any work that is derived directly from their thesis or dissertation.

11. Members of the Academy have the right to disseminate research findings, except those likely to cause harm to clients, collaborators and participants, those which violate formal or implied promises of confidentially, or those which are proprietary under a formal or informal agreement.

Disclosure and Respect of the Rights of Research Populations by Members of the Academy

12. Members of the Academy should not misuse their positions as professionals for fraudulent purposes or as a pretext for gathering information for any individual, group, organization or government.

13. Human subjects have the right to full disclosures of the purposes of the research as early as it is appropriate to the research process, and they have the right to an opportunity to have their questions answered about the purpose and usage of the research. Members should inform research participants about aspects of the research that might affect their willingness to participate, such as physical risks, discomfort, and/or unpleasant emotional experiences.

14. Subjects of research are entitled to rights of personal confidentiality unless they are waived.

15. Information about subjects obtained from records that are open to public scrutiny cannot be protected by guarantees of privacy or confidentiality.

16. The process of conducting criminal justice research must not expose respondents to more than minimal risk of personal harm, and members of the Academy should make every effort to ensure the safety and security of respondents and project staff. Informed consent should be

obtained when the risks of research are greater than the risks of everyday life.

17. Members of the Academy would take culturally appropriate steps to secure informed consent and to avoid invasion of privacy. In addition, special actions will be necessary where the individuals studied are illiterate, under correctional supervision, minors, have low social status, are under judicial supervision, have diminished capacity, are unfamiliar with social research or otherwise occupy a position of unequal power with the researcher.

18. Members of the Academy should seek to anticipate potential threats to confidentiality. Techniques such as the removal of direct identifiers, the use of randomized responses, and other statistical solutions to problems of privacy should be used where appropriate. Care should be taken to ensure secure storage, maintenance, and/or destruction of sensitive records.

19. Confidential information provided by research participants should be treated as such by members of the Academy, even when this information enjoys no legal protection or privilege and legal force is applied. The obligation to respect confidentiality also applies to members of research organizations (interviewers, coders, clerical staff, etc.) who have access to the information. It is the responsibility of administrators and chief investigators to instruct staff members on this point and to make every effort to insure that access to confidential information is restricted.

20. While generally adhering to the norm of acknowledging the contributions of all collaborators, members of the Academy should be sensitive to harm that may arise from disclosure and respect a collaborator's need for anonymity.

21. All research should meet the human subjects requirements imposed by educational institutions and funding sources. Study design and information gathering techniques should conform to regulations protecting the rights of human subjects, regardless of funding.

22. Members of the Academy should comply with appropriate federal and institutional requirements pertaining to the conduct of their research. These requirements might include, but are not necessarily limited to, obtaining proper review and approval for research that involves human subjects and accommodating recommendations made by responsible committees concerning research subjects, materials, and procedures.

C.   Members of the Academy in the Publication and Review Process

Questions of Authorship and Acknowledgment for Members of the Academy

1. Members of the Academy should acknowledge persons who contribute to their research and their copyrighted publications. Claims and ordering of authorship and acknowledgments should accurately reflect the contributions of all participants in the research and writing

process, including students, except in those cases where such ordering or acknowledgment is determined by an official protocol.

2. Data and material taken verbatim from another person's published or unpublished written work should be explicitly identified and referenced to its author. Citations to original ideas and data developed in the work of others, even if not quoted verbatim, should be acknowledged.

. . .

Members of the Academy in the Review Process

8. Members of the Academy should decline requests for reviews of the work of others where strong conflicts of interest are involved. Such conflicts may occur when a person is asked to review work by teachers, friends, or colleagues for whom he or she feels an overriding sense of personal obligation, competition, or enmity. Members of the Academy should also decline requests for reviews when such requests cannot be fulfilled on time, or when they feel unqualified to review the work.

9. Materials sent for review should be read conscientiously, carefully, and confidentially. Evaluations should be justified and explained clearly. Reviews of manuscripts should avoid personal attacks upon the author(s).

10. Members of the Academy who are asked to review manuscripts and books they have previously reviewed should inform the editor requesting review of this situation.

. . .

E. Members of the Academy as Experts

1. In situations in which members of the Academy are requested to render a professional judgment, they should accurately and fairly represent their areas of expertise, qualifications, and authority.

2. In their role as practitioners, researchers, teachers, and administrators, members of the Academy have an important social responsibility because their recommendations, decisions, and actions may alter the lives of others. They should be aware of the situations and pressures that might lead to the misuse of their influence and authority. Members of the Academy should take steps to ensure that these situations do not produce deleterious results for clients, research participants, colleagues, students and employees.

F. Members of the Academy as Practitioners

1. Practitioners who are members of other professional organizations are expected to adhere to those organizations' codes of ethics. This code is not meant to supersede the codes of other professional organizations, but rather it is intended to compliment those codes. However,

when members who are practitioners act as academics (e.g., teaching, conducting research), they are bound by this code of ethics while acting in their capacity as academics.

. . . .

H.   Adherence to the Code of Ethics

1. Members of the Academy have an obligation to be familiar with the Code of Ethics, and its application to members of the Academy. Lack of awareness or misunderstanding of an ethical standard is not a defense to a charge of unethical conduct.

2. When members of the Academy are uncertain whether a particular situation or course of action would violate the Code of Ethics, they should consult other members of the Academy knowledgeable about ethical issues, the Ethics Committee of the ACJS, or with other organizational entities such as institutional review boards.

3. Members of the Academy should not discriminate against a person on the basis of his or her having made an ethics complaint.

4. Members of the Academy should not discriminate against a person based upon his or her having been the subject of an ethics complaint. This, however, does not preclude taking action against an individual based upon the outcome of an ethics complaint.

5. When members of the Academy have substantial reason to believe that there may have been an ethics violation by a member of the ACJS, they should attempt to resolve the issue by bringing it to the attention of that individual if an informal resolution appears appropriate or possible. Additionally they may seek advice about whether or how to proceed based on this belief, assuming that such activity does not violate any confidentiality rights. Such action might include referral to the ACJS Ethics Committee.

6. ACJS members are obliged to cooperate in ethics violation investigations, proceedings, and resulting requirements of the ACJS. In doing so, they should make reasonable efforts to resolve any issues of confidentiality. Failure to cooperate is an ethics violation, and may result in a separate ethics investigation.

7. Members of the Academy do not file or encourage the filing of ethics complaints that are frivolous and are intended to harm the alleged violator rather than protect the integrity of the discipline and the public.

IV.   POLICIES AND PROCEDURES

The Ethics Committee (EC) appointed by the Executive Board of the Academy of Criminal Justice Sciences (ACJS) will act in a timely and equitable manner and shall have responsibility for:

- providing guidance on ethics issues,
- promoting ethical conduct among Members of the Academy,
- interpreting and publicizing this Code,
- receiving inquiries about violations of the Code,
- investigating complaints concerning the ethical conduct of members of the Academy of Criminal Justice Sciences in an equitable manner,
- mediating disputes to assist the parties in resolving their grievances,
- holding hearings on charges of misconduct, and
- recommending courses of action to the Executive Board of the Academy of Criminal Justice Sciences.

. . .

Committee Mandate

1. At any time, not necessarily in the context of the investigation of a particular case, the EC may advise the Executive Board of the ACJS of its views on general ethics questions, which the Executive Board may elect to publish in appropriate publications of the Academy.

2. The EC shall receive complaints of violations of the Code of Ethics and endeavor to resolve them by mediation, and proceed to a hearing if mediation is unsuccessful or a decision not to mediate is made. If, after a hearing, the EC determines that an ethical violation occurred, it should notify the parties and prepare a report for Executive Board, which may or may not recommend one or more of the following actions:

   a. Apply no sanctions,

   b. Private reprimand,

   c. Public reprimand,

   d. Denial of membership privileges for a specified period of time (e.g., participation in meetings, editorial boards, etc.) which becomes public record, or

   e. Termination of membership, which becomes public record.

This code takes effect on March 21, 2000*

---

*This code and these procedures were developed using the American Sociological Association's Code of Ethics, with its permission. Last modified: June 12, 2000.

GLOSSARY

abstract A brief summary of the issues addressed, methodologies and methods employed, hypotheses tested, and results obtained from a research project.

accidental sample A nonprobability sample composed of individuals who happen to come into contact with the researcher.

accretion evidence Evidence produced by the accumulation or deposit of materials.

after-only design A research strategy for assessing the effect of a particular event or change (independent variable) after it has occurred, with no prior observation of the dependent variable.

analysis of variance A statistical test of differences between three or more means and variances when the independent variable is nominal or ordinal.

anonymity An ethical principle requiring that the identity of research participants not be revealed.

applied research Research addressing specific, concrete questions or pragmatic problems.

appropriate sequence in time In a causal argument, the requirement that the causal (independent) variable precede the effect (dependent) variable in time.

average deviation The arithmetic average of the differences between a distribution's mean score and each of the individual scores in the distribution.

basic research Research addressing general and fundamental questions about the nature of phenomena.

before-after design A research strategy in which the researcher observes/measures the dependent variable before the occurrence of the independent variable and then observes/measures the dependent variable again after the occurrence of the independent variable.

before-after-with-control design A research strategy in which the dependent variable is observed/measured in both an experimental and control group prior to the occurrence of the independent variable in the experimental group. The independent variable is observed/measured again in both groups after the independent variable's occurrence in the experimental group.

between group variance In analysis of variance, that portion of the total variation in the dependent variable explained by the independent variable.

biased estimate An estimate of a population parameter when the mean of the sampling distribution for the corresponding sample statistic is not equivalent to the population parameter.

bibliography A listing of the sources and references used in a research report, usually located at the end of the report.

binomial distribution A mathematically derived distribution of probabilities useful as a sampling distribution for determining the probability of outcomes of a series of events, each event having two equally probable outcomes.

causal chain A sequence of three or more variables, each causally related to the one that follows.

causal relationship A relationship between variables satisfying the three criteria for a causal inference.

cell A location in a table representing the intersection of one value of one variable and one value of the other variable used to construct the table.

cell frequency The number appearing in the cell of a table, representing the number of elements in the sample or population that possess the values of the two variables that intersect in the cell.

central limit theorem A mathematical theorem used in constructing some sampling distributions.

chi square A statistic used to determine the probability of getting the observed cell frequencies in a cross-tabulation, given the null hypothesis that there is no relationship between the variables.

cluster sampling Dividing a population into a number of approximately equal-sized collections of units using a theoretically neutral criterion and then selecting some of these collections for inclusion in a sample.

coefficient of determination (r^2) A measure of the strength of the relationship between two variables; the amount of the variance in the values of one variable statistically predictable from the values of another variable.

coefficient of multiple determination (R^2) A measure of the strength of the relationship between one dependent variable and two or more independent variables taken together; the amount of variance in one variable statistically predictable from the values of two or more other variables taken together.

cohort design   The study of a (typically large) group of research subjects sharing some general, theoretically neutral, characteristic over an extended period of time.

collapsing categories   Combining two or more values of a variable, thus creating a smaller number of variable values to facilitate data analysis and presentation.

complete observer   A field researcher whose subjects are unaware they are being observed and who does not take part in the subjects' activities.

computer program   Instructions that determine which mathematical or other operations will be performed by the computer and in which order they will be performed.

concepts   Symbolic, short-hand ways of representing selected aspects of objects or events.

concomitant variation   A relationship between two or more variables; one of the three prerequisites of a causal inference.

conditional proposition   A proposition that takes the general form "If x, then y."

confidence interval   The range of values between the confidence limits for an estimated population parameter calculated from sample statistics using inferential statistics, with a specified probability that the population parameter falls within the range.

confidence limits   The smallest and largest values of the estimate of a population parameter calculated from sample statistics using inferential statistics, with a specified probability that the population parameter falls between these values.

confidentiality   An ethical principle requiring that information subjects provide to researchers not be revealed.

consensual statement   Statements referring to phenomena that are external to the communicator and available to others' senses, requiring little or no elaboration to convey their meaning.

consensual validation   Agreement among members of a community about the meaning of words and other symbols, most often achieved about consensual statements.

construct validity   The extent to which the derivation of a concept or measuring device is logically coherent and logically related to other concepts or measures in the same realm of inquiry.

content analysis   Systematic examination of the characteristics of selected "texts," including photographs, police reports, song lyrics, newspaper stories, television broadcasts, and so on.

continuous variables   Variables that can assume an infinite number of values.

contradictory values   The values of a statistic that result in the rejection of a null hypothesis.

control condition   The element in an experimental research design wherein the treatment (the independent variable) is withheld.

control group   In the classic experimental design, a group of subjects *not* exposed to the hypothesized independent variable.

control variable   In elaboration analysis, a third variable whose possible effects on a zero order relationship are tested in partial tables.

correction for continuity An adjustment in some statistical formulas when variables are discrete rather than continuous.

correlation Synonym for *concomitant variation*.

correlation coefficient (**r**) A measure of the strength of the relationship between two variables; varies between +1 and –1.

critical region Synonym for *rejection region*.

critical theory Explanations of the ideology and behavior of individuals and the shape of social structures emphasizing inequalities in wealth and power and how those inequalities are established, maintained, and changed.

cross-sectional design A research strategy in which a larger group is divided into subgroups and each of the subgroups is observed at a given point in time.

cross-tabulation A device for determining whether two variables are related, consisting of cells, cell frequencies, and marginal frequencies; conjoint frequency distributions.

curvilinear relationship A relationship between variables such that the values change with respect to each other but not in a linear fashion; for example, as the values of one variable go up, the values of the other variable at first go up and then go down.

data The recorded observations and measurements researchers gather, analyze, and synthesize searching for meaningful patterns.

data array A series of data and/or codes representing original data gathered on an element of a sample or population and arranged in a predetermined sequence in predetermined locations on a computer-readable storage device (hard drive, magnetic tape, floppy disk, and so on).

deconstructionism A perspective emphasizing that all human products, including science and scientific research, are best viewed as created texts that should be taken apart with the objective of identifying hidden values, political agenda, and other forms of bias and distortion.

deductive logic Argument from generalizations to particular observations/ conclusions.

degrees of freedom A way of specifying the appropriate sampling distribution.

dependent variable A variable believed by the researcher to be an effect of an independent (causal) variable.

descriptive research Research in which the goal of the researcher is to identify and communicate important properties or characteristics of a particular category of objects or events.

descriptive statistics Statistics that summarize the distribution of a variable or a relationship between variables.

determinism The belief that every event is preceded by one or more events that cause it to occur.

diagonals In a cross-tabulation, the cells that lie on or near a line drawn from the upper left to the lower right cells or from the upper right to the lower left cells.

discrete variables Variables that can assume only a finite number of whole unit values.

disguised observer An observer who misrepresents himself to his subjects and observes them while participating as a group member.

disproportionate sampling A sampling strategy in which all elements have known, but different, probabilities of being included in the sample.

document research A type of research based on systematic analysis of existing sources of information (documents).

elaboration analysis A strategy for analyzing a relationship between two variables by introducing a third, control variable and creating partial tables; helps determine if the apparent (zero-order) relationship is causal or spurious and, if causal, the nature of the relationships among the three variables.

empiricism The practice of seeking answers to questions through direct observation.

erosion evidence A form of evidence used in nonreactive research; evidence based on use or wear.

error of estimate Synonym for *residual error.*

ethical neutrality A principle of science requiring that moral and ethical beliefs not be allowed to influence data gathering or analyses.

evaluation research Studies focusing on the implementation, coherence, effectiveness, or efficiency of policies or programs.

evaluative statements Statements that convey values, choices, or preferences.

exhaustive categories A set of categories that includes all possible answers to the question posed.

experiment A research project bound by the perspective and rules of science, conducted according to a research design, in which the researcher has at least partial control over the environment and some of the variables regarded as independent or causal.

experimental condition A condition that involves the researcher measuring the experimental group on the dependent variable.

experimental design A research strategy that allows the researcher to attempt to eliminate possible causes for changes in the dependent variable, other than the proposed independent variable(s).

experimental group The group in an experimental design in which the independent variable occurs or is introduced by the researcher.

experimental treatment Synonym for *independent* or *presumed causal variable.*

explanation In elaboration analysis, the result when the relationship between the two zero-order table variables disappears in all of the first-order partial tables, the control variable is related to both zero-order variables, and the control variable occurs before the independent variable; the zero-order relationship is spurious. (See also *causal relationship.*)

explained variance Synonym for *between group variance.*

explanatory research Research projects in which the researcher attempts to go beyond description to determine why a phenomenon has occurred.

exploratory research Preliminary, informal investigation to learn more about a phenomenon of interest or a research setting before designing and initiating a more formal study.

external validity The applicability of research results to persons or events other than those actually included in the study; generalizability of research findings.

F *ratio* A ratio of sample variances used in statistical tests of hypotheses, especially analysis of variance.

face validity The extent to which a concept or measuring device appears to represent or measure what a researcher claims it does.

false negative An incorrect prediction that some specified outcome would not occur.

false positive An incorrect prediction that some specified outcome would occur.

feedback relationship A relationship among variables such that each variable is connected to at least several other variables; for example, a change in variable *a* will produce a change in some or all other variables, and these changes may, in turn, produce another change in *a*.

feminist perspective A perspective emphasizing the pervasive influence of sex and gender in human behavior (including scientists' behavior) and social structures (including science).

field research Research relying primarily on participant observation strategies in natural settings.

first-order partial tables In elaboration analysis, tables created by introducing a third control variable in the analysis of the relationship between two other variables; one partial table is created for each value of the control variable.

fixed-alternative questions Questions that require the respondent to choose an answer from a predetermined list of choices.

formal interview A structured, standardized interview with a fixed-alternative question content and structure.

formative research Synonym for *process research.*

frequency distribution An arrangement of data indicating the number of times each value of a particular variable has been observed.

fundamental significance The importance of some finding in the real world, which is sometimes in contrast with statistical significance.

Hawthorne effect Changes in subjects' behavior produced by their knowledge that they are being observed and/or their desire to please the observer.

hired-hand research Research carried on by an outside organization/group that is independent of, but paid by, the organization/group under study.

histogram Synonym for *line graph.*

history A threat to the internal validity of research results arising from changes in the external environment (social, political, or economic change, for example) of the research project.

hypothesis A statement about what effects or results certain causes or actions might produce, often in the form of if *x*, then *y*.

impact research   Studies of the effectiveness of programs and services in accomplishing stated objectives.

independent variable   A variable believed by the researcher to be a cause of a dependent variable.

inductive logic   Argument that moves from a number of particular and separate observations to generalizations/conclusions.

inferential statistics   Statistics that enable us to generalize from a sample to the population from which it was drawn with some specifiable degree of confidence that the generalizations are correct.

informal interviews   Unstructured interviews, often using open-ended questions.

informed consent   Voluntary agreement to participate in a research project after having been informed of any hazards or dangers that may be present.

in-house research   Research conducted by a staff member of the organization/group being studied.

institutional review boards (IRBs)   Local groups empowered to review research proposals to ensure research subjects' rights are protected.

interaction   When a relationship between two variables is different in strength or direction for different values of a second independent variable.

internal validity   The degree to which the three criteria for causal inference have been satisfied in a particular research design.

Internet   A network of computers, a major component of which is the World Wide Web.

interpretation   In elaboration analysis, the result when the relationship between the two zero-order table variables disappears in all of the first-order partial tables, the control variable is related to both zero-order variables, and the control variable is an intervening variable.

interpretive/inferential statement   Statements about people's states of mind, emotions, intentions, motivations, and so on.

interval estimate   A range of values around a sample statistic (for example, the mean value of a particular variable) used to estimate the value of the corresponding population parameter.

interval level measurement   A measurement scale without an arbitrary zero point but equal distances (intervals) between any two adjacent units.

interval variable   A variable that can be categorized and ordered and for which the quantity of variation between values can be specified.

intervening variable   A variable that occurs in time between the independent and dependent variable, creating a causal chain of variables.

language   The set of symbols and their relationships that enables humans to communicate and that shapes thoughts and perceptions.

level of analysis   The different types of phenomena in terms of which research questions are asked and explanations of phenomena are sought, including, for example, biological, psychological, and sociological variables.

Likert scales   Measurement scales that allow us to measure the degree to which respondents hold certain attitudes.

linear relationship   A relationship between variables such that the values of the two variables tend to change together; that is, as the values of one variable go up, the values of the other go up, as in a positive correlation, or down, as in a negative correlation. When plotted on a graph, the relationship is represented by a straight line that runs diagonally up or down across the graph.

literature review   A comprehensive summary of relevant theories and/or research related to the study being described in a research report.

longitudinal design   A research strategy in which the same group of subjects is observed on two or more occasions over a period of time.

marginal frequency   The sum of a row or a column in a cross-tabulation.

matching   A technique for ensuring that subjects in control and experimental groups are as similar as possible on variables believed by the researcher to be relevant in a particular study.

maturation   Changes (physical and/or experiential) that occur in a group of subjects as the result of passage of time.

mean   The arithmetic average of the scores that make up a distribution.

measures of association   Statistical measures of the degree and direction of a relationship among variables.

median   The score in a distribution of scores above which and below which half of the scores are found; the middle score.

methodology   The general plan formulated for achieving the ultimate goals of the researcher in a scientific investigation.

methods   The specific tactics or techniques selected for use in a research project.

mode   The most frequently occurring score in a distribution of scores.

multimodal distribution   A distribution of scores with more than one mode.

multiple causation   Several conditions causally related to a single other condition, with each contributing separately or in combination to the determination of that condition.

multiple correlation coefficient **(R)**   A measure of the strength of the relationship between one variable and two or more other variables taken together; varies between +1 and −1.

multiple group trend design   A research design in which similar, but different groups of subjects are observed at different points in time.

multistage sampling   A probability sampling procedure in which cluster sampling techniques are used in successive stages or combined with random sampling techniques.

mutually exclusive categories   Categories established so that there is one and only one response category appropriate for each respondent.

nominal level measurement   A level of measurement in which variables can be placed in mutually exclusive, exhaustive categories, but cannot be ordered further.

nonconsensual statements   Statements referring to phenomena not readily observable by others and requiring considerable elaboration to convey their meaning.

nonparametric inferential statistics Inferential statistics that do not assume a normal distribution of variable values in a population; that is, they are distribution free.

nonprobability sampling A sampling technique in which the probability of any element being included in the sample cannot be determined.

nonreactive research A data collection technique that removes biases introduced by the research process itself by eliminating the subjects' knowledge that they are being studied.

normal distribution A unimodal, symmetrical distribution with characteristics useful in a variety of statistical calculations.

null hypothesis The hypothesis that there is no relationship between two variables; used to generate sampling distributions for testing hypotheses in inferential statistics.

objectivity A goal of scientists achievable only in degrees and requiring that they set aside as best they can their personal values and prejudices during data gathering and analysis.

one-tailed test Hypothesis testing where the rejection region is located in only one of the tails of the sampling distribution.

one-way analysis of variance A test for differences among means involving only one independent variable measured at the nominal or ordinal level.

open-ended question A question for which no response categories are provided.

operational definition The specification of exactly how the researcher will categorize and/or measure variables.

optical reader A machine that reads bar codes or pencil marks on special forms.

ordinal level measurement A level of measurement in which it is possible not only to categorize but to rank elements in a population according to the degree to which a certain attribute is present.

outcome research Synonym for *impact research*.

panel design A research design in which the same group of subjects is observed or measured at two or more points over time.

parameter The value of a measure of central tendency or dispersion for the distribution of the values of a variable for a population.

parametric inferential statistics Inferential statistics that assume a normal distribution of variable values in a population.

parsimony A principle of science requiring that among numerous equally strong explanations of a particular phenomenon, the simplest is preferred.

partial correlation analysis Study of the effect of one independent variable, holding one or more other independent variables constant.

participant observation Data collection through immersion to greater or lesser degrees in the activities being studied.

percentaging in the direction of the independent variable Using the marginal frequencies corresponding to the values of the independent variable to convert cell frequencies to corresponding percentages in cross-tabulations.

perspectival subjectivity The inevitable distortions in human observations or interpretations arising from the necessity of using a perspective in order to observe or know.

perspective A worldview that selects and organizes our sensory experiences.

plagiarism Claiming others' ideas, work, or words as one's own; failing to give credit to others for their words, work, or ideas used in one's own publications.

point estimation A sample statistic used as a single-value estimate of the corresponding population parameter.

pooled sample variance In the *t* test, a quantity used in estimating the standard error of the sampling distribution.

population The entire group of subjects, objects, or events from which a particular sample is drawn.

population parameter A numerical description of a characteristic of the distribution of a variable in a population. (See *parameter.*)

positivistic empiricism (positivism) A philosophy emphasizing the reliability of the senses and the possibility of objective observation and analysis in determining universal scientific truth.

postmodernism A perspective denying the possibility of objective observation and analysis as well as the existence of universal scientific truth, emphasizing instead local, multiple, value-laden realities and truths.

precision Refers to the number of subcategories of a concept (values of a variable) available for observation or measurement.

prediction research Research designed to develop reliable instruments for forecasting specified outcomes (for example, parole success).

predictive validity The extent to which predictions derived from a concept or measuring device are accurate and/or consistent with other independently validated concepts or measures.

preexperimental designs After-only and before-after research designs.

probability The likelihood of an event or series of events occurring, usually expressed as a decimal (for example, .05, .001).

probability sampling A sampling technique in which the probability of each particular element of the population being included in the sample is specified before the sample is drawn.

process research Studies of the ongoing operations of groups or organizations.

proportionate sampling A sampling strategy in which the random sample drawn from each stratum of a population is adjusted so that the proportion of elements in the sample is equal to the proportion of the whole population contained in that stratum.

publication Reporting to others the procedures and results of research so that they may critique it, replicate it, and/or apply it.

purposive sample   A nonprobability sampling strategy based on the assumption that the researcher has enough skill to select subjects who ought to be included in the sample; also referred to as typical-case sampling.

qualitative research   Research emphasizing open-ended information-gathering strategies, sustained face-to-face contact between researchers and their subjects, and narrative rather than quantitative research reports.

quantiles   The general term used to refer to quartiles, deciles, and percentiles.

quantitative research   Research emphasizing numerical measurement of variables and statistical analysis.

quasi-experimental procedures   Research projects in which the researcher has less than ideal control of the study environment and/or the independent variables (for example, field experiments).

quota sample   A nonprobability sampling procedure in which the researcher attempts to ensure that various elements of the population will be included in the sample.

random-access memory   Data or program storage areas in a computer whose contents can be altered through the keyboard of the computer and that can be accessed at any specified location.

random assignment   The process of assigning subjects to the different groups in an experimental research design according to the principles of probability sampling.

random numbers   Numbers generated by a computer programmed so that each number from 0 to 9 is equally likely to be printed next.

random sample   A sample drawn from a population in such a way that each element in the population has an equal chance of being selected for the sample.

range   The lowest and the highest scores in a distribution.

rate   The expression of the frequency of an event in relation to a fixed unit of measurement, often time or population (for example, "per 1000").

ratio level measurement   A level of measurement with the properties of nominal, ordinal, and interval measurement and, in addition, an absolute zero point.

read-only memory   Data or program storage areas in a computer that can only be read from; that is, its contents cannot be altered through the keyboard of the computer.

regression line   A straight line that best represents the dots (data) in a scattergram; technically, it is the line that minimizes the distance between it and the dots in the scattergram, the distances measured parallel to the y axis.

regression toward the mean   A threat to the internal validity of research results, especially when a relatively large proportion of the subjects selected for study are characterized by extreme (high or low) values or scores on variables being studied.

rejection region   The range(s) of statistical test values (for example of t or F) of a sampling distribution (and the corresponding areas under the curve) within which the null hypothesis is rejected.

replication (a) The repetition of a study previously done; or (b) in elaboration analysis, the result when the relationship between the two zero-order table variables remains the same in all of the first-order partial tables.

research hypothesis The hypothesis that two variables are related; it is tested indirectly by testing the null hypothesis using inferential statistics.

residual The difference between the predicted value of a variable and the actual, observed value.

response rate The number of completed questionnaires/interviews returned divided by the total number of questionnaires/interviews distributed.

sample A subset of elements drawn from a population and used to represent the population.

sample statistics The value of a measure of central tendency or dispersion for the distribution of the values of a variable for a sample.

sampling distribution An empirically or mathematically derived distribution of sample statistics, usually assuming a large number of random samples drawn from the same population.

sampling error The differences between the values of sample statistics and the values of the corresponding population parameters. These differences may arise from many factors (for example, a researcher's bias, chance); inferential statistics make it possible to estimate only the sampling error arising from probability sampling procedures.

sampling frame A list of the elements in a population from which a sample is drawn.

scanner Devices that transfer words or images from printed documents to digital storage devices.

scattergram A graphic device for determining whether or not two variables are related, consisting of two axes at right angles on which the values of the two variables are arrayed; a dot is located at the intersection of values of the two variables for each element in the sample or population.

science A systematic search for the most accurate and complete description and/or explanation of events, relying on the principles of empiricism, objectivity, relativism, skepticism, ethical neutrality, parsimony, at least a modified determinism publication and replication as guides.

secondary analysis A research technique in which researchers reanalyze for their own purposes data previously gathered by others.

selection bias A threat to the internal and/or external validity of research results when those chosen for study are not representative of the population from which they were selected.

significance level The probability set by the researcher that determines whether the researcher will accept or reject a null hypothesis; the probability of making a type I error.

skepticism A principle of science requiring that researchers search for disconfirming evidence and continue to question their conclusions and knowledge.

skewed distribution A distribution with scores bunched toward one tail or the other; an asymmetrical distribution.

slope In regression analysis, the slant of the regression line, representing the amount of change in the dependent variable for every unit of change in the independent variable.

snowball sampling A procedure for selecting research subjects in which subjects recommend others like themselves for inclusion in the study.

Solomon four-group design An addition of two research groups to the classic experimental design, permitting measurement of certain variables in the research process (for example, the effects of the premeasurement of the dependent variable).

species-based subjectivity The inevitable distortion of human observations and interpretations arising from the physiological limitations of the senses and the preprogrammed ways sensory information is organized by the mind.

specification In elaboration analysis, the result when the relationship between the two zero-order variables disappears in *some* but not all of the first-order partials and the control variable is *not* related to at least one of the zero-order table variables.

split-half reliability The extent to which a randomly selected half of the items in a multiple-item measure of a particular variable yields the same result as the remaining half of the items.

spurious relationship An apparent but false (not causal) relationship between two variables; the appearance of a relationship is produced by a causal relationship between each of the two variables and a third variable that precedes both of the original two variables in time, as in explanation in elaboration analysis.

standard deviation The square root of the average of the squared deviations from the mean.

standard error The standard deviation of a sampling distribution.

standard normal curve A normal curve with a mean of 0 and a standard deviation of 1.0.

standard score A score computed from a given raw score by subtracting the sample mean from the given raw score and dividing by the sample standard deviation.

statistical explanation The amount of variance in one variable predictable from the variance in the other variable(s); refers only to correlations, which are not necessarily causal relationships.

stratified random sample A probability sampling technique that assumes that relevant information about the variables that may effect responses is available, enabling the researcher to divide the population into categories (strata) ensuring that each element falls into one and only one of the established categories.

Student's t A statistic used to determine the probability that mean values of the same variable calculated from data for two different randomly selected groups are two samples from the same population.

subjectivity Distortion or bias in observations or interpretations arising from a variety of sources, including the researcher's values, perspectives, and so on.

subject mortality The loss of subjects from a research group during the study (for example, subjects refusing to continue, disappearing, and so on).

summative research   Synonym for *impact research.*

systematic sampling   A sampling technique in which the researcher selects every *k*th element from a population list for inclusion in the sample.

tentativeness   A principle of science requiring scientists not to consider their results or conclusions as universal, absolute truths.

test-retest reliability   The extent to which repeated applications of the same measuring device to the same unit of analysis yields the same result.

theory   A more or less integrated set of propositions and/or hypotheses that purport to explain phenomena and that guide research.

third-party research   Research conducted by an independent outsider.

triangulation   Collecting different types of data from different sources with respect to a single research question; used to increase researchers' confidence in their findings and to bring discrepancies in data to light.

t-test   Synonym for *Student's* t.

true negative   A correct prediction that some specified outcome would not occur.

true positive   A correct prediction that some specified outcome would occur.

two-tailed test   Hypothesis testing where rejection regions are located in both tails of the sampling distribution.

Type I error   Rejecting a true null hypothesis.

Type II error   Accepting a false null hypothesis.

typical case sample   Synonym for *purposive sample.*

unbiased estimate   An estimate of a population parameter when the mean of the sampling distribution for the corresponding sample statistic is equivalent to the population parameter.

unexplained variance   Synonym for *within group variance.*

unimodal distribution   A distribution with only one mode.

units of analysis   The particular persons, objects, entities, or processes being studied; the elements of a sample or population being studied.

validity   The extent to which a categorization/measurement reflects a characteristic or property of the real, empirical world.

variable   A category (concept) that may be divided into two or more subcategories or measured values.

variance   A statistic computed by squaring the difference or deviation from the mean of each score in a distribution, summing these squared deviations, and dividing the sum by the total number of scores in the distribution.

verification of theory   Providing empirical support for a theory.

verstehen   A research method relying on empathy or interpretive understanding of subjects' behavior, referring to the person's beliefs, motives, and so on.

verstehen subjectivity   Interpreting or explaining behavior by referring to a person's internal psychological states, intentions, values, choices, and so on.

volitional subjectivity   The distortion or bias in human observations or interpretations arising from the necessity of choosing among alternatives in order to act.

within group variance   In analysis of variance, that part of the total variation in the dependent variable unexplained by the independent variable.

y intercept   In regression analysis, the point where the regression line crosses the y axis; the value of y when x is zero.

zero-order table   In elaboration analysis, the table showing the original relationship between two variables; this relationship will be analyzed through the introduction of one or more control variables and the creation of partial tables.

INDEX